STRATEGIES FOR SOCIAL CHANGE

Social Movements, Protest, and Contention

Series Editor   Bert Klandermans, Free University, Amsterdam

Associate Editors   Ron R. Aminzade, University of Minnesota
David S. Meyer, University of California, Irvine
Verta A. Taylor, University of California, Santa Barbara

For more books in the series, see pages 319–20.

STRATEGIES FOR SOCIAL CHANGE

Gregory M. Maney, Rachel V. Kutz-Flamenbaum,
Deana A. Rohlinger, and Jeff Goodwin, editors

Social Movements, Protest, and Contention
Volume 37

 University of Minnesota Press
Minneapolis • London

Portions of chapter 7 previously appeared in Nancy Whittier, *The Politics of Child Sexual Abuse: Emotion, Social Movements, and the State,* published by Oxford University Press, 2009.

Portions of chapter 12 previously appeared in Sharon Erickson Nepstad and Stellan Vinthagen, "Strategic Changes and Cultural Adaptations: Explaining Differential Outcomes in the International Plowshares Movement," *International Journal of Peace Studies* 13, no. 1 (2008): 15–42.

Published by the University of Minnesota Press
111 Third Avenue South, Suite 290
Minneapolis, MN 55401-2520
http://www.upress.umn.edu

Library of Congress Cataloging-in-Publication Data

Strategies for social change / Gregory M. Maney . . . [et al.], editors.
(Social movements, protest, and contention ; 37)
Includes bibliographical references and index.
ISBN 978-0-8166-7289-9 (hc : alk. paper)
ISBN 978-0-8166-7290-5 (pb : alk. paper)
1. Social change. 2. Social movements. 3. Social participation. I. Maney, Gregory M.
HM831.S7697 2012
303.4—dc23
2011044235

Printed in the United States of America on acid-free paper

The University of Minnesota is an equal-opportunity educator and employer.

19 18 17 16 15 14 13 12   10 9 8 7 6 5 4 3 2 1

This book is dedicated to each of you
making another world possible.

Contents

III. Formation and Development of Strategy

IV. Strategy and the Consequences of Movements

Preface

This volume began with the planning of the 2007 American Sociological Association (ASA) Collective Behavior and Social Movement (CBSM) section workshop on Movement Cultures, Strategies, and Outcomes. Along with the rest of a workshop organizing committee, which included Andy Andrews, John Krinsky, Ellen Reese, and Dingxin Zhao, we sought to make room for the breadth of research interests within the section while also taking advantage of recent developments within our field and the discipline as a whole.

One major objective was to use the workshop to advance our understanding of social movement strategy. Theoretically, early discussion did not address the relationship between culture and strategy. Culture can be a source of strategy, a goal of mobilization, an obstacle to social change, or an opportunity for social change. The implications of recent scholarship on not only cultural but also structural aspects of social movements for strategy have yet to be fully considered. Indeed, strategy opens up new avenues of dialogue and potential synthesis between structuralist and culturalist theories that have often been at odds with one another. At the same time, the trade-offs inherent in any strategic decision highlight the role of agency in mobilization and contention, a role that has often been neglected in both structuralist and culturalist theories.

Perhaps because of the relative lack of attention to agency, activists typically find little insight from academic theory and research on social movements. Yet strategy and its relationship to social change provide an important point of convergence where the theoretical and methodological tools of the discipline can be harnessed around questions of ongoing significance for practitioners. The topic of the conference complemented and extended the theme of the national ASA conference that immediately followed. At its heart, strategy involves, as the annual meeting theme statement asserts, making "the connections between everyday life and large social forces." The workshop-organizing committee believed that sociologists should take the lead in producing action-oriented research that facilitates collective empowerment.

This volume includes only a small part of the remarkable work produced for the workshop at Hofstra University. We thank the many scholars and activists whose ideas and research helped to shape the chapters in this volume. A big part of strategy is envisioning a sequence of actions and reactions that will result in the achievement of desired objectives. In this context, we offer our deep appreciation to everyone who shared generously their visions, time, and resources to make the workshop and this book possible, including the American Sociological Association's Fund for the Advancement of the Discipline, members of the CBSM Section Council, the CBSM chair at the time of the workshop, Rhys Williams, and the administrators, faculty, students, and staff at Hofstra University. Last but not least, we thank Amaka Okechukwu for producing a detailed yet accessible index in very short order.

The creation and deployment of strategy is a place where scholars can do much to help activists and where activists have much to teach scholars. We hope this volume contributes toward such mutually empowering partnerships.

An Introduction to Strategies for Social Change

Gregory M. Maney, Kenneth T. Andrews,
Rachel V. Kutz-Flamenbaum, Deana A. Rohlinger,
and Jeff Goodwin

Strategy in Action: An Example

The teleconference was scheduled for 1:00 in the afternoon. To the surprise of many, most of those invited to participate dialed in on time. Jokes about fashionable lateness among activists glossed over the realities of underfunded organizations and overworked individuals. The unusual punctuality reflected a deep sense of urgency, anger, and dismay. County legislators had just introduced a bill that threatened the goals of coalition participants. Similar legislation enacted elsewhere had produced disastrous consequences, inflicting tremendous pain and needless suffering on the most vulnerable and disadvantaged segments of society.

The conversation sometimes bordered on the chaotic, with twenty to thirty people on the phone at the same time. A side conversation broke out in a different language from the primary one used during the call. Some on the road had to pause to focus on their driving. Some participated more than others. Some opinions seemed to carry more weight than others; some were discussed at length; others were met with stony silence.

Despite these distractions and differences, the conference call soon came to focus on developing a plan of action. In broad strokes, participants identified opponents and allies. Some expressed discomfort when it was suggested that the business community should be mobilized to oppose the bill. Although their influence over legislators was not denied, it was felt that business owners did not have the interests at heart of those who would be most negatively affected by the bill's passage. This discomfort was offset by a proposal to mobilize clergy who would highlight social justice principles.

It was agreed eventually to hold a simultaneous picket and press conference in front of the legislative building. The event would feature both clergy and business people. The message would be two-pronged: the proposed legislation was morally wrong, and it would negatively affect the economy. The bifurcated nature of the message, in part, reflected a disagreement between coalition members as to whether public support could best be generated through appeals to the pocketbook or to moral principles.

The facilitator then asked whether anyone knew of sympathetic clergy and business people willing to participate in the event. A brainstorming session drew several new voices into the conversation, with people volunteering their personal connections within the community. Excitement grew as the list of names swelled. Typically, when a name was mentioned, others would pipe in, "Oh yes, she's an excellent speaker and really knowledgeable on the issue."

The discussion proceeded to focus on legislators. One of the coalition members who did not participate in the call had developed a power map illustrating who was firmly supportive of the legislation, who was firmly opposed, and who remained undecided. On the basis of this map, the discussion centered on undecided legislators. The facilitator asked for volunteers to help organize pressure on specific politicians. Call participants unveiled their various connections to the legislators. One had children in the same school. Someone else had worked extensively with one legislator on a bill a few years earlier. General characteristics were discussed in detail as well. The geographic location of their constituencies, voting records on other issues, former occupations, alma maters, religious affiliations, and ethnic identities were all raised in an effort to determine who should lobby whom.

One participant suggested a sit-in or takeover at the office of a legislator who was a perennial thorn in the side of the coalition. Everyone laughed when the initiator suggested that participants dress up as American Revolutionary War heroes, as the legislator in question had a rather royal-sounding name. While expressing a shared desire to turn up the heat, some noted how increased penalties and jail time for recent instances of similar actions would make it difficult to convince enough people to participate. Heightened surveillance and arrests by authorities had thinned participation in even legal demonstrations, particularly among those belonging to marginalized and vulnerable groups. Others argued that the portrayal of the opposition as extremists generated sympathy for the coalition and its cause. Engaging in actions that the media could portray as extreme would take away this source of sympathy. At this point, a few key participants had to exit the call to pick up their children. The teleconference quickly ended.

The picket and the press conference received extensive, positive media coverage. However, in their strategizing, the coalition failed to anticipate the actions of a highly organized set of grassroots opponents. During the hearing before the legislative vote, members of a residents' association and the chapter of a local union arrived early and managed to pack the gallery. No one participating in the teleconference had anticipated this possibility. Those testifying in opposition to the bill were heckled loudly. One of those who testified in favor promised convincingly to personally visit every day for the rest of their lives the office of any legislator who voted against the bill. Despite the success of the coalition in blocking similar pieces of legislation in the past, the bill narrowly passed. By emphasizing fairness in their media messaging and by mobilizing some local organizations that were previously silent on the issue, the coalition's opponents managed to score a decisive victory.

Soon after the defeat, the coalition set up a meeting to discuss what had gone wrong. The postmortem meeting evaluated what had worked, what didn't, lessons learned, and next steps. Avenues of legal recourse and upcoming elections were discussed as opportunities to reverse the setback. The need to anticipate and preempt opposition tactics was underscored. It was widely recognized that a grassroots plan of action was needed to win the hearts and minds of those undecided on the issue and to translate sympathy into action. Participants laughed as they brainstormed about pithy slogans that would appeal to different constituencies. A sense of determined defiance began to emerge as lessons were divined for the ongoing struggle for social justice.

A Review of the Sociology of Strategy

One of the editors actively participated in the strategic process just described. We suspect that elements of that meeting are as familiar to many of you reading this as they are to us. Similar scenarios are taking place all the time across the United States and in many other societies. The time and effort that so many put into these meetings suggests a firm belief among participants that ordinary people can make history despite the often powerful forces that are likely to oppose them. These meetings are all about developing and implementing strategy. They are about making difficult choices. For many activists, strategy is both the compass and the map. Without a clear and viable strategy, their dreams of reaching a better destination will never be fulfilled.

Strategies for social change should hold a deep fascination for sociologists. Emotions, identity, ideology, power, social inequalities, technology, mobilization structures, and dynamics—all matter in the development and implementation of strategies. In the 1970s, sociologists studying social movements did, in fact, devote significant attention to questions of strategy. William

Gamson's groundbreaking *The Strategy of Social Protest* (1975) generated broad debate about whether social movements could enhance their likelihood of success through their strategic choices. As part of the broader development of Resource Mobilization and Political Process theories, scholars argued forcefully for a view of those involved in movements as strategic actors rather than irrational, frustrated, maladapted individuals. Protest was politics by other means (Oberschall 1973; Freeman 1975; Schwartz 1976; Jenkins and Perrow 1977; Tilly 1978).

Frances Fox Piven and Richard Cloward's *Poor People's Movements* (1977) furthered debate about the strategy of disruption, contending that movements derived power from insurgency and that building mass membership organizations undermined a movement's collective power. Their critics countered that bottom-up organizations were crucial to generating and sustaining popular mobilization (Morris 1984; Rupp and Taylor 1987). Challenging the core claims of Gamson as well as Piven and Cloward, Jack Goldstone (1980) argued that movements were a consequence rather than a cause of broader political changes.

With the heady days of 1968 receding into the background, social movement researchers largely moved away from the topic of strategy.[1] This early discussion provides an important foundation for contemporary scholars, but it only scratches the surface of questions about strategy. Some issues remain unresolved, while other important issues have not been broached.

Methodologically, the dialogue offers little insight regarding how to establish the existence of strategy. For example, how do we know whether the organization and forms of contention are the outcomes of deliberation and planning? Research on strategy remains susceptible to ad hoc, ex post facto rationalizations by activists and scholars. Rather than simply being the product of individual-level decisions of leaders, strategy may be better thought of as something collectively formed through (often heated) discussion. The approach used by Gamson is ill suited to capturing this formative process.

Empirically, Gamson's finding that centralized organizations are most effective in securing political change appears inconsistent with recent victories scored by the global justice movement—a movement that relies heavily on the Internet to mobilize decentralized networks of activists sharing broadly similar concerns (Bennett 2005; della Porta 2005). Furthermore, the early consensus that violent disruption is most effective in bringing about social change has come under heavy challenge within the field of social movements and within the field of peace, war, and social conflict (e.g., Tilly 2003; Schock 2005; Sharp 2005).

Theoretically, the early discussion did not address the relationship between culture and strategy. More recent scholarship suggests that cultural factors influence the organization, goals, forms, targets, and claims of contention (Snow et al. 1986; Snow and Benford 1988, 1992; Benford and Hunt 1992; Benford and Snow 2000; Goodwin, Jasper, and Polletta 2000). Moreover, culture can be the subject of strategy, a goal of mobilization, an obstacle to social change, or an opportunity for social change (Bernstein 1997; Jasper 1997; Woehrle, Coy, and Maney 2008).

The implications of recent scholarship on not only cultural but also structural aspects of social movements for strategy have yet to be fully considered. Indeed, strategy opens up new avenues of dialogue and potential synthesis between structuralist and culturalist theories that have often been at odds with one another (Goodwin and Jasper 1999; McAdam, Tarrow, and Tilly 2001). Focusing on strategy casts new light on questions about agency in social movements that remain underdeveloped (Jasper 2004). Political opportunities must be perceived and people must be convinced to take advantage of them (Gamson and Meyer 1996; Kurzman 1996; Alimi 2007). At the same time, the cultural turn in social movement theory runs the risk of assuming that actors can simply will or spin a movement to success in the face of cultural and structural obstacles. Recent efforts toward theoretical synthesis provide one important basis for a nuanced understanding of strategy (e.g., Meyer, Whittier, and Robnett 2002).

Early theories of strategy also did not conceptualize the interactions between challengers, countermovements, and authorities. Scholars have called for more dynamic approaches to social movements through an examination of sequences of contention (McAdam, Tarrow, and Tilly 2001). Here, formal modeling and game-theoretical approaches provide an important starting point (Schelling 1960; Lichbach 1987; Axelrod 1997; Oliver and Myers 2002). From the vantage point of contemporary movement theory, however, these approaches are limiting through their individualistic and cognitive assumptions about strategic choice. Additional insights could be gleaned from relatively untapped sources in the field, including neoinstitutional analysis and other forms of organization theory (Davis et al. 2005).

In addition, a growing number of scholars in the field have called for increasing attention to research that is of greater relevance to social movements (Bevington and Dixon 2003; Flacks 2003). Activists typically find little insight from academic theory and research on social movements. Yet strategy provides an important point of convergence where the theoretical and methodological tools of the discipline can be harnessed around questions of ongoing significance for practitioners. After all, movement actors invest a great deal of energy, passion, and insight into developing and implementing strategies of social change. Authorities and opponents also devote endless hours to considerations about whether, and if so, how, to engage the claims and actions of social movements. Such discussions are often generated in response to the sudden rise of movements, the seeming intransigence of power holders, desires to mobilize a broader public, and increasing repression of protesters.

Because of neglect of the subject since the 1970s, scholars have failed to study many of the exciting strategic debates among activists that animate today's movements. For example, important discussions are taking place regarding when big protests matter and whether the event form is always the best way to gain influence and build a strong movement. These debates may well have contributed to the recent surge of massive, internationally coordinated protests against war and for immigrant rights and global justice.

For all of these reasons, a book addressing social movement strategy is long overdue. Strategy itself can serve as a lynchpin between structure, culture, and agency as well as between affective, expressive, normative, and instrumental dimensions of collective action. Focused engagement on the subject of strategy, therefore, has the potential to build on and connect several strands of recent work in the field and to move scholarship and activism in fruitful new directions.

Fortunately, much has happened in the field over the last twenty-five years that we believe proves useful in deepening our understanding of strategy. As this book's contents reveal, scholars have now identified several additional structural and cultural factors influencing strategies and their outcomes. We have moved beyond strict assumptions of rationality to acknowledge the important roles of emotions, ideologies, and identities for those making difficult decisions whose social consequences are often mixed and far from obvious. We now recognize a greater variety of social changes desired by activists and a greater variety of paths toward achieving these changes.

Making History: Theorizing and Researching Social Movement Strategy

This book represents an attempt to generate knowledge about the ways that people passionately and purposefully act together in the hopes of achieving changes to what we believe and to how we act. In particular, we address seven important questions regarding social movement strategy that have yet to be satisfactorily answered: (1) How do we define strategy? (2) Can we differentiate between strategies? (3) How do we measure strategy? (4) How is strategy developed? (5) Does context constrain strategic choices? (6) Do strategies in action create social change? (7) Is the sociology of strategy relevant to activists? We now address each of these questions in turn.

How Do We Define Strategy?

As Meyer and Staggenborg note in chapter 1, sociologists lack "even a consensual definition of social movement strategy." Our review of the literature reveals four main differences in emphasis. First, although most scholars define strategy as involving one or more actions in pursuit of one or more goals, there is considerable difference in emphasis regarding what goals are pursued, why they are pursued, and how they are pursued. Some researchers focus on internal movement building (e.g., Minkoff 1999; Taylor 2007); others focus on external transformations (e.g., Snow 1979; McCammon et al. 2008). Even scholars emphasizing external transformations vary in their emphasis on structural change versus cultural change (see Polletta 1997).

This difference often reflects contrasting assumptions regarding why activists are pursuing certain goals. Although rational choice theorists have tended to emphasize material interest, other scholars have recognized affective, expressive, and normative bases for goal formation (Ferree 1992; Goodwin, Jasper, and Polletta 2000; Goodwin and Jasper 2003). Even when agreeing on what goals are being pursued and why they are being pursued, scholars have varied in their assumptions regarding how goals are pursued through strategy. Some scholars assume strategies involve the coercion of targeted actors (e.g., Gamson 1975; Piven and Cloward 1977). Others, however, have emphasized personal transformation, persuasion, cooperation, and negotiation as strategic processes (e.g., Snow 1979; Bernstein 1997; Smithey and Kurtz 2003; de Alwis 2009).

Second, scholars have defined strategy as being formulated and implemented at different levels of social aggregation. Strategy has been studied at the individual level (e.g., Fine 2006; Chaney 2007), the organizational level (e.g., Minkoff 1999; Ganz 2000; Saunders 2009), the coalition level (e.g., Eimer 1999; Maney 2001; Smith 2008; Van Dyke and McCammon 2010), and the movement level (e.g., Meyer and Staggenborg 2008; Walker, Martin, and McCarthy 2008; Bernstein and de la Cruz 2009).

Third, definitions of strategy have not only differed in terms of the level of analysis emphasized, but also in terms of time. Some have presented strategy as a discrete short-term action that focuses on a tactic within a specific limited context (e.g., Barker and Lavalette 2002; Jasper 2004). Others, however, present strategy as a series of actions that encompass a longer-term campaign or even series of campaigns involving multiple events and tactics (e.g., Minkoff 1999; King and Cornwall 2005; McCammon et al. 2008).

In an effort to bridge these distinctions, we define strategy as a plan of collective action intended to accomplish goals within a particular context.

Strategy therefore entails defining, interpreting, communicating, and implementing a plan of collective action that is believed to be a promising way to achieve a desired alternative future in light of circumstances. The types of goals that could be pursued are bounded only by the assumptions and imaginations of those formulating them. Similarly, how activists construct the circumstances around them can vary widely. Components of social context include but certainly are not limited to history, geographic scope and scale linkages, institutional norms, repertoires of contention, ideologies, identities, discourses, emotions, networks, resources, organizational structures, conflict and alliance systems, opportunities, threats, and dilemmas. The range of choices that can form a plan of action is similarly wide. They include choices regarding demands and positions, frames and audiences, identity and presentation of self, emotional dynamics, organizational forms and processes, recruitment, resource acquisition, skills utilization, message dissemination, arenas, allies, targets, and tactics of collective action.

As such, we see strategy as an inherently symbolic, relational, interactive, and multilevel process. Strategy is both influenced by and influences people's emotions (see chapter 2), discourses (chapter 3), personal and collective identities (chapter 7), ideologies (chapter 8), and relationships to others (chapter 1). As Francesca Polletta puts it in chapter 3, not only can culture be strategic, but what counts as strategic is also cultural. Rational choice–based understandings of strategy are inaccurate in their characterization of what people want to achieve, why they want to achieve it, what they know about the world around them, and their expectations regarding how change will take place. Although emphases differ, each contribution to this book at least implicitly acknowledges interactions across levels where influences at one level affect interactions at another. Chapter 1 explicitly addresses the subject.

Can We Differentiate between Strategies?

To the extent that this book generates consensus within the field regarding how to define strategy, it also assists in differentiating between strategies. The contributors believe it is useful to look for variations within each of the three interrelated components of our definition of strategy: goals, contexts, and plans of action.

Collectively, the chapters in this book frequently make distinctions between goals, contexts, and plans of action based on the level of social aggregation (micro, meso, or macro), institution (civil society, economy, education system, family, media polity, religion), geographic scope (local, regional, national, transnational), duration (short term, medium term, long term), cultural characteristics (attitudes, beliefs, discourses, emotions, frames, ideologies, identities, norms, objects, repertoires of contention, rituals, symbols and symbolic repertoires, traditions, tropes, values), and structural characteristics (alliance and conflict systems, capacities, degrees of centralization, decision-making processes, divisions of labor, dynamics, organizational fields, degrees of formality, communication and mobilization infrastructures, heterogeneity or homogeneity, leadership roles, networks, opportunities, and threats, power relations, resources). For instance, as components of strategy, goals can vary by level of social aggregation (personal change, small group change, organizational change, institutional change), institutional focus (changing media coverage, changing government policies), relationship to time (short-term, medium-term, and long-term goals), and type of change sought (changes in beliefs, distribution of opportunities and resources, division of labor, decision-making processes, authority). Defining strategy in ways that permit categorical differentiation facilitates empirical analysis.

How Do We Measure Strategy?

Each of the different choices between goals, interpretations of context, and plans of action is observable and therefore enables us to demarcate strategies (see chapter 1). Nonetheless, it is far from obvious how we create valid and reliable measures of strategy. The dialogue on strategy in the 1970s offers little insight regarding how to establish the existence of strategy.

This book offers several insights in this regard. First, it is important to actually measure strategy and not to simply assume that contention reflects efforts to achieve a set of clearly articulated goals through carefully designed plans of action (see chapter 2). Sometimes activists have not developed strategies (e.g., chapter 4). Although ad hoc, ex post facto assumptions of strategy lead to less resource- and time-intensive data collection, they could overstate the presence of intentionality in action.

Second, because of the symbolic, interpretive, and communicative nature of strategy, research methods such as archival searches, field observations, and activist–scholar research partnerships are well suited for measuring strategy (see chapters 4, 5, 6, 8, and 12). Through these backstage methods, the researcher arrives at a deeper understanding of the understandings of goals, contexts, and plans of action of those formulating and implementing strategy.

Third, in keeping with our view of strategy as a relational process, we encourage researchers to explore not only variations in strategy within movements, but also the strategies of other movements, targets, and opponents (see chapters 1 and 8). These strategies form an important part of the context in which activists develop plans of action in pursuit of their goals.

As such, interpretations of the strategies of other players may play key roles in the formation of strategy.

Fourth, as an interactive process, strategy may change over time (see chapters 1, 4, 5, 6, and 8). As part of an iterative cycle of praxis, activists may reflect on whether their plan of action had the intended effects. Divergences between expectations and outcomes can lead to the alteration of goals, reinterpretation of contexts, and revision of plans of action. Accordingly, longitudinal research on strategy is highly useful. Once strategies are understood through qualitative methods, quantitative methods such as network, sequence, and time-series regression analyses can capture the dynamic interplay of challengers, countermovements, and authorities. Through triangulated research designs, we can see both the modification and outcomes of strategies applied in contention.

Fifth, in keeping with our understanding of strategy as a multilevel process, researchers should be aware of not only the possibility of a lack of strategy in action, but also the possibility of multiple strategies residing within the same institution, target, opponent, movement, coalition, and even organization (see chapters 1, 2, 8, and 12). Large numbers of individuals and organizations making the same demands, targeting the same actors, and using the same forms of contention suggest a single or at least prevailing movement strategy. Yet individuals within the same organization, let alone multiple organizations, participating in the same movement frequently differ in their goals or hold contrary opinions regarding how to achieve the same goals. Measuring differences in strategy helps us to understand dynamics both within and across levels of analysis.

How is Strategy Developed?

Additional methodologically rigorous empirical research on strategy can help us to better establish how activists develop strategies. Collectively, the chapters in this book suggest that the following are frequently part of the process: (1) clarifying goals and formulating demands; (2) constructing constraints, threats, and opportunities; (3) envisioning sequences of actions and reactions; (4) resolving choice points; (5) developing emotional dynamics; (6) considering models of action; (7) agreeing (or disagreeing) on roles; and (8) revisiting and assessing the effectiveness of strategic choices once implemented.

Clarifying Goals and Formulating Demands

Scholars have sometimes missed the many clashes among goals, as well as the conflicts between individual and group goals (however, see Benford 1993; Coles 1999; Caruso 2004; Downey and Rohlinger 2008). Sometimes, individuals defect from team goals (see chapter 2). Other times, they pursue personal goals and group goals at the same time. We need to further examine facilitative processes that engender consensus or conflict regarding goals and demands (see chapters 4, 6, 8, and 12).

Constructing Constraints, Opportunities, and Threats

In forming strategies, activists define the circumstances around them and interpret their implications for the relationship between possible courses of action and their objectives (see chapter 1). Typically activists not only try to identify obstacles in their paths (i.e., constraints), but also paths of least resistance and greatest vulnerability, if not the enthusiastic receptivity of those capable of bringing about the desired changes (i.e., opportunities). The possibility or reality of developments that are regarded as endangering fundamental goals (i.e., threats) can also anchor the construction of context. In the process, activists try to achieve a good, if not perfect, fit between their plan of action and the broader context (see chapters 10 and 12).

Envisioning Sequences of Actions and Reactions

We reject the assumption of rational choice theory that players have perfect information about the future. We also reject models that assume that, as players, activists focus only on short-term goals. These rejections make strategy all the more relevant in that actors must collectively develop visions of uncertain futures (see chapter 8). They must anticipate what the reactions of targets, opponents, the media, and other parties will be to their actions (see chapters 4 and 10).

Resolving Choice Points

Choice points are moments or situations when compound or simple players face alternatives, when they could do something different from what they in fact do (see chapter 2). It is in the face of dilemmas—situations where activists recognize that any choice they make has a cost—that the process of strategy formation becomes its most creative and inspiring.

Developing Emotional Dynamics

Forming strategy is not only a purposeful process, but also a passionate one. In expressing and processing emotions, activists come to choose words, images, and actions designed to trigger certain emotions in others. In particular, the process involves a dynamic that Jasper refers to as an emotional battery, whereby there is an interaction between negative and positive emotions (see chapter 2).

Considering Models of Action

Scholars have emphasized the diffusion of strategy (e.g., McAdam and Rucht 1993; Doherty 1999; Oliver and Myers 2002; King and Cornwall 2005). The chapter by Nepstad and Vinthagen stresses that attributions of similarity are not necessary for diffusion. Moreover, they suggest that models are rarely adopted without modification to make them fit better with the particular context in which activists are working. Similarly, chapters 4, 5, 10, and 12 highlight the way that strategy is shaped in response to specific perceived contexts and within specific campaigns.

Agreeing (or Disagreeing) on Roles

Different players bring different attitudes, identities, knowledge, resources, skills, and connections to the table. Strategy formation often involves deciding how best to utilize these differences in the pursuit of shared objectives (see chapter 5). Organizations may develop a tactical division of labor so that new organizations can distinguish themselves from existing ones and avoid competition for membership and funding (see chapters 1 and 9). This relationship is rarely without tension, as leaders of more moderate groups may resent ceding media attention while leaders of more radical groups resent the allies who bargain on their behalf. Nonetheless, movement organizations will often cooperate, developing distinct but compatible task specializations that allow them to combine resources to achieve common goals.

Revisiting and Assessing Effectiveness

Strategy is formed through collective definition, interpretation, communication, and interaction often involving multiple players and arenas. As a process, strategy unfolds over time and therefore may change. Perceptions that plans of action have not met expectations can lead to the modification of strategies (see chapter 1). By affecting the mix of players, changes in coalitions (i.e., exits and additions) can encourage changes in strategy (see chapter 2). Interactions with targets and opponents and the diffusion of alternative strategies can also encourage changes in strategy by shifting goals (see chapter 8).

Changes in strategy that are perceived as more effectively promoting objectives are likely to become entrenched over time (see chapter 1). Moreover, actors may not perceive changes in context or interpret these changes as being consistent with their existing strategies (see chapter 3). Organizations with particularly strong ideologies are unlikely to revise their strategies, particularly during the early stages of contention and when the tactics used are quasi-institutionalized and flexible (see chapters 8 and 10). Complicating matters further, the tropes used by activists in their discourses to bring about changes in strategy can, over time, make further change more difficult (see chapter 3). All of this suggests that activists may or may not revisit and assess strategy.

Does Context Constrain Strategic Choices?

Our definition of strategy links a plan of action to context. One might reasonably inquire about the relationship between the two. Our book offers a spirited debate over the degree to which strategy is constrained by context. In chapter 1, David S. Meyer and Suzanne Staggenborg argue that a sociology of strategy should focus on factors limiting or constraining the choices that activists can make: "Studies of strategic decision making should consider these structural constraints and the ways in which activist choices can alter them over time. A meaningful understanding of activist agency only comes from a realistic assessment of what is possible." In contrast, James Jasper argues in chapter 2 that a sociology of strategy should be focused on the choices that activists make:

> The main problem with the current idea of constraints is that they tend to dichotomize strategic choices into those that are possible and those that are not. This follows from the root metaphor of a structure: you can walk through a door but not a wall; a window of opportunity is either open or closed. But this is a misleading view of strategic options, which generally fall along continua: from less costly to more, from less risky to more, and from lower potential payoffs to greater ones.

In chapter 4, Charlotte Ryan, Karen Jeffreys, and Linda Blozie present these separate approaches as a dilemma. On the one hand, the approach taken by Meyer and Staggenborg runs the risk of overdetermined models where activists either do not have choices or would be incredibly stupid not to make one choice. On the other hand, Jasper's approach runs the risk of undetermined models where activists' decisions become capricious as every choice carries its own benefits and costs.

The editors believe that the sociology of strategy must, to quote Ryan, Jeffreys, and Blozie, "dance on a tightrope between over- and underdetermination." Activists do not strategize in a vacuum. The likely success or failure of their strategy will hinge on its fit with the circumstances to which it is applied. Whether and how activists interpret their circumstances is a product of the symbolic cultures of which they are a part. Yet rarely do activists face a situation where they have no choice regarding their goals, demands, tactics, targets, and arenas. The concept of constraints is perhaps even too deterministic in that activists can choose bad strategies—and often do. Culture can encourage certain interpretations of context, but activists can play with discourses or invoke conflicting norms to advocate for certain strategies (see chapter 3).

What all of this suggests to us is that contextual factors influence strategy by encouraging certain choices while discouraging others. Activists still have to decide which messages and forces to embrace and which to reject. Moreover, the decisions that activists make, in turn, can both directly and indirectly encourage and discourage subsequent choices. For instance, Polletta argues in chapter 3 that the trope of metonymy can be a symbolic tool of agency that, if successfully applied, also becomes a cultural influence over strategy. Accordingly, one of our central themes is that the rigid, and at times exclusive, distinctions between structure, culture, and agency are erroneous and can get in the way of our understanding strategic action and decisions within social movements.

Do Strategies in Action Create Social Change?

Over the last two decades, sociologists have grappled with the question of how to assess the outcomes of social movements (e.g., Amenta, Halfmann, and Young 1999; Earl 2000; Maney 2001; Ganz 2000; Andrews 2004; Edwards and McCarthy 2004). Scholars have encountered difficulties in sustaining assertions that movements matter, let alone that movements matter in ways that their participants intended.

Establishing a relationship between strategy and outcomes requires definitions and measures of strategies and outcomes. In addition to offering definitions and measures of strategy, this book offer several different definitions and measures of success, including the following: sustained mobilization and movement longevity (chapters 10 and 12); observable changes in authorities' positions or policies (chapters 10 and 12); observable changes in public opinion (chapter 2); changes in public practices (chapter 7); observable changes in resource distribution (chapter 10); observable changes in media standing and media capacity (chapter 4); consultation of movement representatives by authorities (chapter 7); the creation of deliberative bodies by authorities to address issues raised by the movement (chapter 10); and inclusion of movement representatives on these deliberative bodies (chapter 4). Together, these measures highlight the range and degrees of success that activists can achieve through their strategies.

Nonetheless, the question remains, how do we know that these social changes are a product of the strategies being pursued? It is a difficult question to answer given the presence of many competing variables. Nonetheless, some of the chapters in this book provide examples of useful methods that begin to control for alternative explanations. Chapter 11 by Tina Fetner and Carrie Sanders as well as chapter 12 by Sharon Erickson Nepstad and Stellan Vinthagen analyze two cases selected on the basis of key similarities and key differences. Fetner and Sanders selected two cases of the Christian right. By eliminating differences in strategy, the authors were able to highlight contextual differences that contributed to different outcomes in the two cases. Like Fetner and Sanders, Nepstad and Vinthagen selected two cases of Plowshares movements developing during the same time period in societies with comparable structural conditions. The difference between the cases was the degree of success in sustaining participation. By controlling for structural conditions, the authors were able to focus on a difference that contributed to divergent outcomes: the decision-making processes of both movements.

While comparing cases of landless movements using nonviolent methods, Kurt Schock (chapter 10) strengthens his claims by also examining cases of other movements using violent methods in comparable political regimes. The success of both cases where nonviolent methods were used couple with the failure of all reported cases where violent methods were used strengthen confidence in his conclusions regarding the fit between nonviolent methods and high-capacity democratic regimes.

In chapter 4, Ryan, Jeffreys, and Blozie take a longitudinal approach to assessing the efficacy of strategy. The authors constructed case studies of successful media campaigns using meeting minutes, press releases, and news coverage to identify all participants and establish a time line. The resulting collaborative history traced the outcomes media planning and communication practices, and measured these against news outcomes over time.

If we accept that these methods are rigorous, what have their applications suggested is the relationship between social movement strategy and social change? Social movements sometimes fail to achieve the goals of their participants. Strategies that generate power for movements may be insufficient to overcome opposition by even more powerful forces. As Jasper notes in chapter 2, the social inequalities that movements struggle to remedy often result in no good strategic choices, only least bad ones.

Nonetheless, our book reveals instances where carefully developed strategies clearly contributed to social changes such as expanded civil rights for an ethnic minority group (chapter 8), increased land redistribution (chapter 12), and provided greater social acceptance, understanding, and support for those surviving abuse (chapters 4 and 7). Collectively, these findings suggest that people can, in certain circumstances, realize their visions of another world by acting together.

On the one hand, our book affirms and nuances insights from recent scholarship on movement strategies and outcomes. For strategies to be successful, at least in the short term, they must be well suited to the particular political, cultural, and geographic context The chapters in part IV all support the political mediation model whereby movement outcomes depend on the ability of movements to take advantage of various opportunities to advance their claims (Amenta, Caren, and Olasky 2005; Amenta, Halfmann, and Young 1999).

On the other hand, our book challenges several conventional academic wisdoms regarding which types of strategies work best.

Identity Politics Can Be Effective Strategy

In contrast to many scholars (with notable exceptions such as Bernstein 1997), chapter 7 by Nancy Whittier shows the cultural transformative potential of identity politics. The author finds that the strategy of coming out effectively redefined the personal and collective identities of survivors as well as changed discourses on childhood sexual abuse found in the media and the general public.

Decision-Making Processes Can Matter More than Organizational Forms

Gamson (1975) posits that a centralized organization increases a movement's chance of success and survival, while Piven and Cloward (1977) argue that decentralized movements are more likely to sustain an effective radical edge. Chapter 12 by Nepstad and Vinthagen diverges from both these works in maintaining that the process of establishing the infrastructure and its perceived purpose may be more important than its particular form. In chapter 9, Belinda Robnett and Jessica Ayo Alabi conclude that leaders may find it beneficial to make key decisions beforehand—such as the type of movement organization and decision-making process that will be used—to avoid tensions that can restrict their ability to mobilize.

Unruly but Nonviolent Works Best

In contrast to the prevailing misreading of Gamson (1975) that violent methods are most successful, Schock (chapter 10) shows that movements using nonviolent, unruly tactics are far more likely to be effective than movements using violence in contexts with relatively high-capacity democratic regimes and cultures familiar with and receptive toward ideologies of nonviolent resistance.

But Unruly Only Up to a Point

In contrast to the findings of both Gamson (1975) and Piven and Cloward (1977), Nepstad and Vinthagen (chapter 12) find that the British Trident Plowshares movement's shift from highly disruptive tactics (i.e., sabotaging weaponry) to less disruptive methods of protest (i.e., blockades) did not undermine its ability to sustain action or influence public opinion. In fact, this tactical adaptation aided the movement by lowering the cost of participation, thereby facilitating recruitment. In short, more disruptive tactics that require greater sacrifice may not automatically lead to greater activist commitment or movement longevity.

Inside versus Outside: Effective Strategy, Not a Dilemma

Whereas as many studies have noted tensions between players using institutional and extrainstitutional tactics, Aunio (chapter 5) reports that a coalition deliberately divided its members into these roles. The bifurcated strategy helped to broaden support for the movement. Schock (chapter 10) similarly finds that movements in high-capacity democratic regimes (even those among more marginalized populations) benefit from a mixture of institutional and extrainstitutional tactics.

Embracing Paradoxes: Corporate-Style Structures Can Help Promote Progressive Change

Most researchers assume that because corporate forms of organization are based on the pursuit of profit, they would do little to assist movements. As reported in chapter 9, however, Robnett and Ayo Alabi find that social movement organizations adopting certain characteristics of corporate organizations gain several advantages, including reduced reliance on external funding, more tactical flexibility, and a greater ability to focus on public messaging instead of organizational maintenance.

Mobilization Structures Matter

The macrolevel and external focus of the political mediation model has glossed over earlier, mesolevel insights provided by resource mobilization theory. In chapter 11, Fetner and Sanders report that although religiosity and political systems differ between Canada and the United States, the greater success of the Christian right in the United States is also attributable to considerably stronger institutional infrastructures. Ryan, Jeffreys, and Blozie (chapter 4) similarly emphasize the importance of a strong infrastructure to effective publicity efforts by a coalition against domestic violence. Actions that fail to directly involve the grassroots of a movement are likely to fail. This is even the case when it comes to generating publicity for a movement. Social marketing and media advocacy are two publicity strategies often heralded in the academic literature, but the authors find these strategies less likely to succeed because they fail to draw on and build on the base of the movement. They find that participatory communication designed to maximize member participation is more effective in successfully disseminating movement messages. At the same time, Jackie Smith (chapter 6) notes the challenges of developing inclusive mobilization structures in the context of segregation and social inequalities.

Charge Those Emotional Batteries

Emotional dimensions of strategy play an important role in their outcomes. Aunio's study (chapter 5) confirms the advantages of Jasper's emotional battery (see chapter 2). Given the prevailing doom and gloom around global warming, climate activists found that actions with positive, humorous spins were well received by the mass media and their targets.

In addition to these valuable challenges to truisms in the field, this volume also highlights an area in need of further research. Ryan, Jeffreys, and Blozie (chapter 4) find that an inclusive and equitable decision-making process facilitated grassroots participation in forming and distributing the message of a coalition against domestic violence. This finding supports Ganz's (2000) study of the United Farm Workers of America whereby a similar decision-making process enhanced the strategic capacity of the organization.

Two other studies in our book, however, raise cautionary flags. Nepstad and Vinthagen (chapter 12) find that relatively closed, brief, and firm decision-making processes about organizational form and tactics by leaders of the British Plowshares movement resulted in a more effective adaptation of the U.S. movement's strategy than the open, inclusive, and elongated decision-making process engaged in by Swedish organizers. In chapter 8, Gregory Maney similarly finds that attempts to have open, equitable, and inclusive decision-making processes contributed to ongoing differences over strategy that manifested themselves in factionalism and tactical divergences. Whereas the literature has presented horizontal, nonhierarchical connective structures as factors that help to sustain movements by facilitating cooperation, the findings of both these chapters suggest that by bringing together a diverse array of actors, these structures could have the opposite effect. For movements with heterogeneous memberships, capacities to implement effective strategies are diminished rather than enhanced by the formation of broad-based coalitions with inclusive decision-making processes. On the basis of these findings, we conclude that more research is needed on how processes of strategy formation and development affect movement outcomes.

Is the Sociology of Strategy Relevant to Activists?

The sociological literature on social movements often posits theories of motivation that are entirely independent of how activists account for themselves. Consequently, scholarship often does not accurately reflect the purposes and passions of activists; nor does it benefit from the lessons learned by activists in the course of trying to make (and, at times, succeeding at making) history.

Moreover, as Jasper discusses in chapter 2, the structural orientation of most sociological theorizing on strategy has resulted in insufficient attention being paid to the choices that activists can and must make in the pursuit of their objectives. Activists have often been told to wait—for more resources, for an opportunity, for a threat, for a focusing moment or event. Yet by definition, activists do not want to wait for history to happen. They want to make history through their actions. They want theories that help them to make good decisions with favorable outcomes.

Not surprisingly, many activists have looked to models of decision making offered by economists and political scientists—models that many sociologists find to be oversimplified at best and legitimating of systems of oppression at worst. By studying the choices made by activists, our research becomes more relevant to activists. Strategy is the key not only to understanding the dynamism of collective action, but also to remaining relevant to those movements we purport to understand and explain.

As Smith points out in chapter 6, making our research accessible and useful to activists is an important component of public sociology. By identifying creative and efficacious strategic processes and choices well suited to particular contexts, we help ordinary people make extraordinary changes that give voice to the marginalized, meet human needs, and protect the environment. For less experienced activists or the rank and file, illuminating the relational elements of decisions and putting strategic decisions in their historical, political, and cultural contexts make strategic decision making and planning more transparent to newcomers and outsiders and therefore facilitate innovation and movement expansion. In taking the time to explain the history and process, questionable assumptions may often be uncovered and new possibilities considered. Such research also demystifies activism. Grandiose stories of movements often make it difficult for ordinary people to imagine how to effect change. By showing the challenges, successes, and failures of activists, it becomes clear that creating strategies is something that real people do (and something that often has a steep learning curve).

Yet the culture and constraints of our discipline discourage public sociology. In chapter 5, Aunio notes the irony that while many of us became social movement scholars because of our participation in movements, the norms and exigencies of our academic lives often remove us from being directly engaged with movements. Given this irony, Smith (chapter 6) calls on us to strategize about transforming our field, departments, and universities in ways supportive of public sociology.

As noted in chapters 4 and 6, sustained collaboration between scholars and activists is the exception rather than the rule. Forging long-term relationships is not without its challenges for both players. Competing commitments, indecipherable academic jargon, and a frequent lack of systematic record keeping by activists are but a few of the challenges. Yet the second section of our book provides three examples of these relationships and their mutual benefits. For instance, Ryan, Jeffreys, and Blozie as well as Smith emphasize the importance of selecting partners with the time, resources, collectivities, and commitment necessary to engage in a project that would take several years to unfold. In recognition of the power and resource disparities that often exist between university and community players, the authors also underscore the importance of activists being equal partners in all phases of the research project, from research design and literature review to data collection and analysis. The benefits that accrue from such a relationship reflect its interdependent nature. Both partners achieve more of their objectives than either would accomplish alone.

There may be a concern that engaged scholarship is bad scholarship in that researchers lose their objectivity. As all the authors in part II demonstrate in their chapters, grounding our research more in the real, as Jasper calls on us to do, not only makes our research more useful to activists, but also deepens our understanding of movement strategy. Scholars honestly want to help movements, yet we often find ourselves behind the curve because what we are studying is not happening now, but rather has already happened. Collaborations with activists not only help scholars to understand changes in real time, but also enable us to create theoretical models that reflect contemporary dynamics. As a symbolic, relational, and interactive process, strategy cannot be deduced a priori. Instead, it has to be induced through up-close empirical research. In chapter 5, Aunio details how participatory research helped her to understand the lifeworld of coalition participants as well as how this knowledge deepened her understanding of how the coalition dealt with change, the roles that participants designed for themselves, and the consequences of these definitions for their relationships and actions together. In chapter 6, Smith writes about how her participation in a local coalition of activists highlighted both obstacles and opportunities to translating strategies developed in global and regional forums into local practices.

The activist–scholar team of Ryan, Jeffreys, and Blozie demonstrate that forming long-term partnerships with activists provides an opportunity to evaluate the predictive power of theory through its application in practice (see chapter 4). Through a rigorous process of iterative cycles of planning, action, and reflection, we can develop sociological theories of action that exceed the predictive power of theories advanced by other social science disciplines precisely because our theories more accurately capture the interplay of agency and context. In the process, we empower activists. For instance, the authors note that organizers found that the activist–scholar team had anticipated every reporter's questions, giving them a strategic advantage in framing debates. Other organizers soon learned of the team's strategy and successfully implemented it to improve media coverage of their issues.

When not making a priori assumptions regarding motivations, scholars often assume that what activists say they are doing is what they are really doing, rather than recognizing the strategic planning that happens behind the scenes. For example, Aunio (chapter 5) points out how scholars often reify the differences between insiders and outsiders, while activists often knowingly construct these differences for strategic purposes. By becoming engaged with the people we study and in the movements we study through participatory observation and/or research projects where activists are equal partners with scholars, scholars gain a more accurate understanding of the processes and outcomes of activists' decision making.

When taken together, the chapters that follow affirm Karl Marx's insight that people make history, but not in circumstances of their own choosing. Although influenced by their environment, the strategies that actors develop are by no means predetermined. They often reflect vivid imagination and inspired creativity in conditions of imperfect information, heightened uncertainty, and cultural ambiguity. Whether the spark of strategic action ignites into a wildfire of social change usually depends on a mixture of perceived and actual circumstances. Revolutionaries influenced by Marx, such as Rosa Luxemburg, recognized that the structural contradictions of capitalism would not produce social change in the absence of mass awareness of these contradictions. Sometimes the widespread belief in an opportunity for change is all that is needed to bring it about, even in the absence of fortuitous circumstances. Nonetheless, as the Prague Spring and the Tiananmen Square protests remind us, the harsh realities of power and inequality can dash the hopes of the most inspired, committed, and influential activists.

Overview

Each section of this book endeavors to answer key questions about strategizing by social movement activists. The first grapples with the key conceptual issues regarding social movement strategy. How should we define and operationalize strategy? What are recurring dilemmas and emotions that arise in the process of strategizing? How is strategy related to other factors internal and external to social movements? What are the main structural and cultural forces shaping strategy? Collectively, the authors of chapters in this section answer these questions by envisioning strategy as purposeful and passionate choices regarding demands, arenas, and tactics. The chapter by Meyer and Staggenborg emphasizes how resources, mobilization structures, political opportunities, and the dynamics of contention influence these decisions. Jasper's chapter highlights the microlevel mechanisms through which activists creatively make decisions. Polletta's chapter uses repertoires of contention, institutional norms, and the trope of metonymy as tools for analyzing the multiple levels and ways that culture shapes movement strategy.

The second section discusses not only the potential benefits of social movement theory for activists' strategies, but also the advantages of movement-relevant and collaborative research for theory building. The authors in this section engaged in grounded research within movements. Ryan, Jeffreys, and Blozie's chapter examines the multifaceted benefits of activist–scholar collaboration and provides a model that may be useful for other scholars to reproduce as they seek to generate opportunities for establishing connections between activists and scholars. Aunio's chapter on the Climate Action Network looks at the relationship between insiders and outsiders and uncovers some of the intentional strategic decision making that structures such designations. Smith's chapter reflects on her research on transnational activism to explore the relationship between scholars and activists.

The third section examines specific empirical cases of interactive processes through which strategies are developed and adapted over time. Whittier's chapter examines how victims of child abuse developed and used the notion of coming out to claim individual experience, to build a collective identity, and to push for social change. Maney's chapter looks at the consequences of ideologically based differences in strategy for coalition dynamics and tactics in the Northern Ireland civil rights movement. Robnett and Ayo Alabi's chapter examines a newly emergent type of social movement organization within the hip-hop movement—what they call corporate SMOs—

based on philanthropic leaders who place a greater emphasis on marketing than on organizational maintenance.

The fourth and final section of the book explores the trajectories of strategies as well as their consequences for social movements. Broadly, the chapters in this section examine the effectiveness of different kinds of strategies and the characteristics of the political and social context that make strategies more or less effective. Schock's chapter illuminates the power of nonviolent strategies. Schock highlights nonviolent strategies that social movement groups can effectively use to mobilize people and challenge repressive governments. Fetner and Sander's chapter underscores the importance of political and social contexts to successful strategies. The authors find that the religious Christian movement in Canada has been relatively unsuccessful because activists have adopted (but not adapted) the strategies of American religious activists. Nepstad and Vinthagen compare the strategic choices of peace activists in order to understand why the British Plowshares organization prospered in Britain but struggled and collapsed in Sweden.

In our conclusion, we go into greater detail about the lessons offered collectively by the chapters in this volume. The conclusion builds further on the research presented in this book and presents challenges for scholars to account for in future research. By moving social movement theory and research in new directions, we hope not only to make history in our discipline, but also to assist activists in making history outside the ivory tower.

Notes

We thank Lyndi Hewitt for her insightful comments.

1. Recent exceptions include but are not limited to Andrews (2004); Edwards and McCarthy (2004); Jasper (2004); McCammon, Hewitt, and Smith (2004); Amenta, Olasky, and Caren (2005); Amenta (2006); and McCammon et al. (2008).

References

Alimi, Eitan Y. 2007. "The Dialectic of Opportunities and Threats and Temporality of Contention." *International Political Science Review* 28, no. 1:101–23.

Amenta, Edwin. 2006. *When Movements Matter: The Townsend Plan and the Rise of Social Security.* Princeton, N.J.: Princeton University Press.

Amenta, Edwin, Drew Halfmann, and Michael P. Young. 1999. "The Strategies and Contexts of Social Protest: Political Mediation and the Impact of the Townsend Movement in California." *Mobilization* 4:1–23.

Amenta, Edwin, Neal Caren, and Sheera Joy Olasky. 2005. "Age for Leisure? Political Mediation and the Impact of the Pension Movement on U.S. Old-Age Policy." *American Sociological Review* 70:516–38.

Andrews, Kenneth T. 2004. *Freedom Is a Constant Struggle: The Mississippi Civil Rights Movement and Its Legacy.* Chicago: University of Chicago Press.

Axelrod, Robert. 1997. *The Complexity of Cooperation: Agent-Based Models of Competition and Collaboration.* Princeton, N.J.: Princeton University Press.

Barker, Colin, and Michael Lavalette. 2002. "Strategizing and the Sense of Context: Reflections on the First Two Weeks of the Liverpool Docks Lockout, September–October 1995." In *Social Movements: Identity, Culture, and the State,* edited by David S. Meyer, Nancy Whittier, and Belinda Robnett, 140–56. New York: Oxford University Press.

Benford, Robert D. 1993. "Frame Disputes within the Nuclear Disarmament Movement." *Social Forces* 71:677–701.

Benford, Robert D., and Scott A. Hunt. 1992. "Dramaturgy and Social Movements: The Social Construction and Communication of Power." *Sociological Inquiry* 62:36–55.

Benford, Robert D., and David A. Snow. 2000. "Framing Processes and Social Movements: An Overview and Assessment." *Annual Review of Sociology* 26:611–39.

Bennett, W. Lance. 2005. "Social Movements beyond Borders: Understanding Two Eras of Transnational Activism." In *Transnational Protest and Global Activism,* edited by Donatella della Porta and Sidney Tarrow, 203–26. New York: Rowman & Littlefield.

Bernstein, Mary. 1997. "Celebration and Suppression: The Strategic Uses of Identity by the Lesbian and Gay Movement." *American Journal of Sociology* 103:531–65.

Bernstein, Mary, and Marcie de la Cruz. 2009. "'What are you?': Explaining Identity as a Goal of the Multiracial Hapa Movement." *Social Problems* 56:722–45.

Bevington, Douglas, and Chris Dixon. 2003. "An Emerging Direction in Social Movement Scholarship: Movement-Relevant Theory." Working manuscript. Santa Cruz: University of California.

Caruso, Giuseppe. 2004. "Conflict Management and Hegemonic Practices in the World Social Forum." *International Social Science Journal* 56:577–89.

Chaney, Paul. 2007. "Strategic Women, Elite Advocacy and Insider Strategies: The Women's Movement and Constitutional Reform in Wales." *Research in Social Movements, Conflicts and Change* 27:155–85.

Coles, Roberta. 1999. "Odd Folk and Ordinary People: Collective Identity Disparities between Peace Groups in the Persian Gulf Crisis." *Sociological Spectrum* 19:325–57.

Davis, Gerald F., Doug McAdam, W. Richard Scott, and Mayer N. Zald. 2005. *Social Movements and Organization Theory.* New York: Cambridge University Press.

de Alwis, Malathi. 2009. "Interrogating the 'Political': Feminist Peace Activism in Sri Lanka." *Feminist Review* 91:81–93.

della Porta, Donatella. 2005. "Multiple Belongings, Tolerant Identities, and the Construction of 'Another Politics': Between the European Social Forum and the Local Social Fora." In *Transnational Protest and Global Activism,* edited by Donatella della Porta and Sidney Tarrow, 175–202. New York: Rowman & Littlefield.

Doherty, Brian. 1999. "Manufactured Vulnerability: Eco-activist Tactics in Britain." *Mobilization* 4:75–89.

Downey, Dennis J., and Deana A. Rohlinger. 2008. "Linking Strategic Choice with Macro-organizational Dynamics: Strategy and Social Movement Articulation." *Research in Social Movements, Conflicts and Change* 28:3–38.

Earl, Jennifer. 2000. "Methods, Movements and Outcomes: Methodological Difficulties in the Study of Extra-movement Outcomes." *Research in Social Movements, Conflicts and Change* 22:3–25.

Edwards, Bob, and John D. McCarthy. 2004. "Strategy Matters: The Contingent Value of Social Capital in the Survival of Local Social Movement Organizations." *Social Forces* 83:621–51.

Eimer, Stuart. 1999. "From 'Business Unionism' to 'Social Movement Unionism': The Case of the AFL-CIO Milwaukee County Labor Council." *Labor Studies Journal* 24:63–81.

Ferree, Myra Marx. 1992. "The Political Context of Rationality: Rational Choice Theory and Resource Mobilization." In *Frontiers in Social Movement Theory,* edited by Aldon D. Morris and Carol McClung Mueller, 29–52. New Haven, Conn.: Yale University Press.

Fine, Gary Alan. 2006. "Notorious Support: The America First Committee and the Personalization of Policy." *Mobilization* 11:405–26.

Flacks, Richard. 2003. "Knowledge for What? Thoughts on the State of Social Movement Studies." In *Rethinking Social Movements: Structure, Meaning, and Emotion,* edited by Jeff Goodwin and James M. Jasper, 135–53. Lanham, Md.: Rowman & Littlefield.

Freeman, Jo. 1975. *The Politics of Women's Liberation.* New York: David McKay.

Gamson, William A. 1975. *The Strategy of Social Protest.* Homewood, Ill.: Dorsey Press.

Gamson, William A., and David S. Meyer. 1996. "Framing Political Opportunity." In *Comparative Perspectives on Social Movements: Political Opportunities, Mobilizing Structures, and Cultural Framings,* edited by Doug McAdam, John D. McCarthy, and Mayer N. Zald, 275–90. Cambridge: Cambridge University Press.

Ganz, Marshall. 2000. "Resources and Resourcefulness: Strategic Capacity in the Unionization of California Agriculture, 1959–1966." *American Journal of Sociology* 105:1003–62.

Goldstone, Jack. 1980. "The Weakness of Organization: A New Look at Gramson's *The Strategy of Social Protest.*" *American Journal of Sociology* 85:1017–42.

Goodwin, Jeff, and James. M. Jasper. 1999. "Caught in a Winding, Snarling Vine: The Structural Bias of Political Process Theory." *Sociological Forum* 14:27–54.

———, eds. 2003. *Rethinking Social Movements: Structure, Meaning, and Emotion.* Lanham, Md.: Rowman & Littlefield.

Goodwin, Jeff, James M. Jasper, and Francesca Polletta. 2000. "The Return of the Repressed: The Fall and Rise of Emotions in Social Movement Theory." *Mobilization* 5:65–84.

Jasper, James M. 1997. *The Art of Moral Protest: Culture, Biography, and Creativity in Social Movements.* Chicago: University of Chicago Press.

———. 2004. "A Strategic Approach to Collective Action: Looking for Agency in Social Movement Choices." *Mobilization* 9:1–16.

Jenkins, J. Craig, and Charles Perrow. 1977. "Insurgency of the Powerless: Farm Worker Movements (1946–1972)." *American Sociological Review* 42:249–68.

King, Brayden G., and Marie Cornwall. 2005. "Specialists and Generalists: Learning Strategies in the Woman Suffrage Movement, 1866–1918." *Research in Social Movements, Conflicts and Change* 26:3–34.

Kurzman, Charles. 1996. "Structural Opportunity and Perceived Opportunity in Social-Movement Theory: The Iranian Revolution of 1979." *American Sociological Review* 61:153–70.

Lichbach, Mark Irving. 1987. "Deterrence or Escalation? The Puzzle of Aggregate Studies of Repression and Dissent." *Journal of Conflict Resolution* 31:266–97.

Maney, Gregory M. 2001 "Rival Transnational Networks and Indigenous Rights: The San Blas Kuna in Panama and the Yanomami in Brazil." *Research in Social Movements, Conflicts and Change* 23:103–44.

McAdam, Doug, and Dieter Rucht. 1993. "The Cross-National Diffusion of Movement Ideas." *Annals of the American Academy of Social and Political Science* 528:56–74.

McAdam, Doug, Sidney Tarrow, and Charles Tilly. 2001. *Dynamics of Contention.* Cambridge: Cambridge University Press.

McCammon, Holly J., Soma Chaudhuri, Lyndi Hewitt, Courtney Sanders Muse, Harmony D. Newman, Carrie Lee Smith, and Teresa M. Terrell. 2008. "Becoming Full Citizens: The U.S. Women's Jury Rights Campaigns, the Pace of Reform, and Strategic Adaptation." *American Journal of Sociology* 113, no. 4: 1104–47.

McCammon, Holly J., Lyndi Hewitt, and Sandy Smith. 2004. "'No weapon save argument': Strategic Frame Amplification in the U.S. Woman Suffrage Movements." *Sociological Quarterly* 45:529–56.

Meyer, David S., and Suzanne Staggenborg. 2008. "Opposing Movement Strategies in U.S. Abortion Politics." *Research in Social Movements, Conflicts and Change* 28:207–38.

Meyer, David S., Nancy Whittier, and Belinda Robnett. 2002. *Social Movements: Identity, Culture, and the State.* New York: Oxford University Press.

Minkoff, Debra C. 1999. "Bending with the Wind: Strategic Change and Adaptation by Women's and Racial Minority Organizations." *American Journal of Sociology* 104:1666–703.

Morris, Aldon. 1984. *The Origins of the Civil Rights Movement: Black Communities Organizing for Change.* New York: Free Press.

Oberschall, Anthony. 1973. *Social Conflict and Social Movements.* Englewood Cliffs, N.J.: Prentice-Hall.

Oliver, Pamela E., and Daniel J. Myers. 2002. "Formal Models in Studying Collective Action and Social Movements." In *Methods of Research in Social Movements,* edited by Bert Klandermans and Suzanne Staggenborg, 32–61. Minneapolis: University of Minnesota Press.

Piven, Frances Fox, and Richard Cloward. 1977. *Poor People's Movements.* New York: Pantheon Books.

Polletta, Francesca. 1997. "Culture and Its Discontents: Recent Theorizing on the Cultural Dimensions of Protest." *Sociological Inquiry* 67, no. 4:431–50.

Rupp, Leila J., and Verta Taylor. 1987. *Survival in the Doldrums: The American Women's Rights Movement, 1945 to the 1960s.* New York: Oxford University Press.

Saunders, Clare. 2009. "It's Not Just Structural: Social Movements Are Not Homogenous Responses to Structural Features, but Networks Shaped by Organisational Strategies and Status." *Sociological Research Online* 14, no. 1. doi:10.5153/sro.1856.

Schelling, Thomas C. 1960. *The Strategy of Conflict.* Cambridge, Mass.: Harvard University Press.

Schock, Kurt. 2005. *Unarmed Insurrections: People Power Movements in Nondemocracies.* Minneapolis: University of Minnesota Press.

Schwartz, Michael. 1976. *Radical Protest and Social Structure.* Chicago: University of Chicago Press.

Sharp, Gene. 2005. *Waging Nonviolent Struggle: 20th Century Practice and 21st Century Potential.* Boston: Extending Horizons Books.

Smith, Jackie. 2008. *Social Movements for Global Democracy.* Baltimore: Johns Hopkins University Press.

Smithey, Lee A., and Lester R. Kurtz. 2003. "Parading Persuasion: Nonviolent Collective Action as Discourse in Northern Ireland." *Research in Social Movements, Conflicts and Change* 24:319–59.

Snow, David A. 1979. "A Dramaturgical Analysis of Movement Accommodation: Building Idiosyncrasy Credit as a Movement Mobilization Strategy." *Symbolic Interaction* 2:23–44.

Snow, David A., and Robert D. Benford. 1988. "Ideology, Frame Resonance and

Participant Mobilization." In *International Social Movement Research,* volume 1, edited by Bert Klandermans, Hanspeter Kriesi, and Sidney Tarrow, 197–217. Greenwich, Conn.: JAI.

———. 1992. "Master Frames and Cycles of Protest." In *Frontiers in Social Movement Theory,* edited by Aldon D. Morris and Carol McClung Mueller, 133–55. New Haven, Conn.: Yale University Press.

Snow, David A., Jr., E. Burke Rochford, Steven K. Worden, and Robert D. Benford. 1986. "Frame Alignment Processes, Micromobilization, and Movement Participation." *American Sociological Review* 51:464–81.

Taylor, Judith. 2007. "Organizational Elaboration as Social Movement Tactic: A Case Study of Strategic Leadership in the First U.S. School-Sponsored Program for Gay and Lesbian Youth." *Social Movement Studies* 6:311–26.

Tilly, Charles. 1978. *From Mobilization to Revolution.* Englewood Cliffs, N.J.: Prentice-Hall.

———. 2003. *The Politics of Collective Violence.* Cambridge: Cambridge University Press.

Van Dyke, Nella, and Holly J. McCammon, eds. 2010. *Strategic Alliances: Coalition Building and Social Movements.* Minneapolis: University of Minnesota Press.

Walker, Edward T., Andrew W. Martin, and John D. McCarthy. 2008. "Confronting the State, the Corporation, and the Academy: The Influence of Institutional Targets on Social Movement Repertoires." *American Journal of Sociology* 114:35–76.

Woehrle, Lynne M., Patrick G. Coy, and Gregory M. Maney. 2008. *Contesting Patriotism: Culture, Power, and Strategy in the Peace Movement.* Lanham, Md.: Rowman & Littlefield.

I
Conceptual Foundations and Agendas

1

Thinking about Strategy

David S. Meyer and Suzanne Staggenborg

On June 24, 2007, a homemade bomb failed to explode near the home of Dr. Arthur Rosenbaum, a research ophthalmologist at UCLA. The Animal Liberation Brigade claimed credit for the bomb, issuing a communiqué on an animal rights website. According to the Brigade, "130am on the twenty forth of june: 1 gallon of fuel was placed and set a light under the right front corner of Arthur Rosenbaums large white shiney BMW He and his wife . . . are the target of rebellion for the vile and evil things he does to primates at UCLA" (http://www.animalliberationpressoffice.org/communiques/2007-06-27_rosenbaum.htm). The bomb alerted scientists to dangers they might face if they used certain animals in experiments, and it signaled to animal rights sympathizers that aggressive action was possible. The FBI's counter-terrorism division in Los Angeles also responded. According to Larry Gordon, writing for the July 25, 2007, *Los Angeles Times,* it offered a reward of $110,000 for information leading to the arrests and convictions of those responsible for the attack.

On the same day that the FBI announced its reward, July 25, 2007, the *New York Times* published an analysis of the recent influence of the animal rights movement—in its food and dining section rather than in its news coverage. According to *Times* writer Kim Severson, the influence of the movement reflected the "maturation and sophistication" of animal activists (F1). Over the past twenty-five years, activists have moved from guerilla media campaigns outside fast food restaurants and "rescues" of farm animals bred for consumption to "more subtle tactics, like holding stock in major food corporations, organizing nimble political campaigns and lobbying lawmakers . . .

'Instead of telling it like it is, we're learning to present things in a more moderate way,'" explained one-time animal rescuer Gene Baur. "Would I love everyone to be vegan? Yes. But we want to be respectful and non-judgmental" (F1). This goal presents a counterpoint to the employment of violence against property—and potential persons.

These recent reports on animal rights efforts underscore several elements of social movement strategy. First, strategy includes decisions about tactics, claims, targets, and alliances, and these decisions are interrelated. Firebombers do not schedule meetings with scientists. Second, the intervention of state authorities changes the available options for everyone. Counterterrorist investigations of those who practice violent tactics can exacerbate schisms within the animal rights movement. Third, movements are not unitary actors. Even as some activists are marching toward an institutional accommodation with one-time enemies, others continue to attack these same people. Fourth, strategic decisions are debatable, and activists debate them often. Whereas some activists see the cultivation of demand for cage-free eggs, for example, as a leading edge for broader education about how animals are treated, others view it as a sell-out that compromises the movement.

These general points are not, of course, limited to the contemporary campaigns around animal rights and welfare. Social movement strategy sits at the intersection of structure and agency, as activists seek to respond to changing political and cultural circumstances and maximize their impact. Yet the existing literature on social movements lacks even a consensual definition of social movement strategy, and it is extremely difficult to assess the selection and outcomes of different strategies over either the short or long term. Here, we offer the beginnings of a theoretical framework for understanding and evaluating social movement strategy, providing an operational conception of social movement strategy. We emphasize the constraints that activists face in making strategic decisions. We argue that strategic decisions are shaped by interactions among fields of actors, and that strategic options and outcomes are constrained and influenced by a web of relations formed over time.

For activists, strategy refers to choices about claims, issues, allies, frames, identity and presentation of self, resources, and tactics. They act as though these choices matter, and we generally assume that they do, but the accumulation of activist knowledge is inevitably ad hoc. Although it is heuristically attractive to treat each decision about an issue, tactic, or alliance as discrete, the choices of the past heavily constrain present possibilities. Activists pick not from a catalog of infinite possibilities, but from a more limited repertoire of contention (Tilly 1978), one constrained by the general social norms of claims making, then further constrained by each group's resources, goals, and identity. To have a meaningful conception of agency, we need to know what choices are actually possible. We need to ask how the repertoire of contention is limited, how and why different groups select various tactics, and what the consequences of their choices are. Both proximate and long-term outcomes are affected by the strategic decisions of activists as well as by the responses of allies, bystanders, authorities, and opponents. This constrains the choices of the future.

We aim to provide a manageable way of conceptualizing strategy and thinking about influences on strategic choices and outcomes. Our approach identifies several major elements of strategic decision making: the *demands* or claims made by collective actors; the *arenas* or venues of collective action; and the *tactics* or forms of collective action. All of these choices imply the selection of particular *targets* of collective action. We clarify different levels of strategic action and influences on strategy, ranging from the *large-scale* cultural and political to movement *community* and *organizational* level dynamics. We identify key questions about the selection and impact of strategy and we offer an operational way of thinking about strategic choices, comprising the visible expression of decisions about claims, venues, and tactics. By thinking about strategy as multiple decisions by multiple actors, and by using different levels of analysis, we argue that it is possible to trace the range of factors affecting the expression of strategic choices and their consequences.

We recognize that activists make strategic decisions mindful of multiple and distinct audiences, including various authorities, movement opponents, organized allies and potential allies, supporters with varying degrees of commitments, and potential supporters and opponents. Importantly, decisions that appeal to (or provoke) one audience are likely to produce the reverse response from other audiences. Activists effectively choose their allies and opponents, and each decision constrains the next round of decisions. We can think about strategic choices as exercises a group takes in positioning itself in relationship to potential allies and opponents. Metaphorically, each decision moves an actor across a field filled with a range of other actors, both institutional and extrainstitutional, that are also making choices at the same time. For example, an animal rights group may take an absolutist stand on meat eating that secures the loyalty and commitment of its supporters while simultaneously distancing the group from policy makers and a potential influence on policy. Groups quickly become entangled in a web of relationships that limits subsequent options.

We begin with an expanded discussion of our conceptual approach before examining different levels of influences on strategic choices and outcomes.

Conceptualizing Strategy

Despite the obvious importance of strategy, the literature on social movements suffers from a deficit of systematic theoretical and empirical work on the topic. Indeed, Gamson's classic *Strategy of Social Protest* (1990) did not directly examine strategic choices, focusing instead on organizational characteristics, and Gamson purposefully neglected changes in opportunities over time. There are, to be sure, many case studies that examine particular strategic choices or capacities (e.g., Barkan 1979; Bernstein 1997; Ganz 2000) and various theoretical offerings of definitions and approaches (e.g., Turner 1970; Freeman 1979; Rucht 1990; Ganz 2004; Jasper 2004; Taylor and Van Dyke 2004). Collectively, however, we have been slow to develop a larger synthetic understanding of these choices. For example, researchers have identified various strategic dilemmas (e.g., Jasper 2004) but have not yet developed an understanding of how such dilemmas are interrelated and how their solutions are constrained.

Strategy encompasses a series of decisions regarding demands, arenas, and tactics of collective action. Movement activists make these decisions in interaction with supporters and opponents in the movement's multiorganizational field (Curtis and Zurcher 1973; Klandermans 1992) as they survey their resources, goals, and available opportunities. In doing so, activists attempt to maximize their influence while balancing sometimes conflicting interests and pressures (Meyer 2007). Matching strategy to opportunities enhances policy impact (Amenta, Caren, and Olasky 2005). Importantly, however, influence is multidimensional, playing out over both long and short time frames and affecting the responses of authorities and the potential to mobilize resources in the future.

To understand how strategic choices are made, we point to a series of interactions within a movement and between movement actors and targets, opponents, and potential allies. Activists learn various strategies, assess their opportunities, and position themselves for new rounds of collective action in distinct contexts and as a consequence of their relationships with actors inside and outside the movement. This iterative process depends on the reactions of others engaging the same sets of issues and constituencies, which can alter the next round of opportunities and constraints.

Collective action demands, arenas, and tactics are three key elements of strategy. Each involves the selection of targets, decisions about timing, and various types of relationships and strategic dilemmas.[1] These choices are naturally related, and each decision opens up some strategic possibilities while foreclosing others. Once activists are drawn into particular venues, they learn to formulate demands and devise tactics appropriate to them. Activists who prefer particular tactics and demands are also likely to be attracted to venues where they could work. Oliver and Marwell (1992, 256) point out that strategy involves a combination of "specific goals, production technologies, and mobilization technologies" that are "chosen together, as packages." Constraints on one of these elements create constraints on the others. Depending on how they mobilize supporters, groups limit the arenas in which they can act collectively.

Demands

One of the basic choices movement actors face is what demands or claims they will put forward—claiming particular rights, calling for injustices to be redressed, arguing for specific policy reforms or social changes. Virtually all social movement organizations (SMOs) have multiple concerns, and they must decide what to emphasize at any given time. Activists want to choose the piece of their concerns that best serves their mobilizing and policy goals, allowing for substantive progress on matters of policy while maintaining their supporters' attention. These decisions about issue frontiers (Gornick and Meyer 1998) usually change over time. Thus, the same environmental group may battle nuclear power in the 1970s, toxic waste in the 1980s, and global climate change in the contemporary era.

In making demands, movement actors appeal for the attention of a variety of actors in a multiorganizational field: supporters called on to mobilize in response to threats or opportunities; potential allies asked to support movement claims; mass media encouraged to cover movement issues and events; opponents challenged by the demands; and authorities or other targets pressed to respond. Activists must choose not only what issues to pursue, but how to describe or frame what they are doing. Issues can be presented as discrete concerns or as part of much larger ones, and as more or less threatening to authorities and other elites (Ash 1972). These choices are shaped by expectations about the responses of targets and bystanders as well as by their actual responses. The history of past claims making and experience with targets and other actors is thus critical to subsequent demands.

Movements face trade-offs in choosing among broad demands to attract widespread support, radical or particular claims to please narrow constituencies, or moderate claims to cultivate support from authorities. Relationships with one set of actors, such as elite allies, can threaten those with another group such as grassroots constituents. To understand changing movement demands, we need to assess interactions with other actors in the multiorganizational field and how these relationships, as well as the positions of movement actors, shift over time.

Arenas

Movement actors need to select arenas or venues in which to press their claims. Major arenas include legislatures, courts, electoral politics, mass media, and the public. Each venue provides access to different targets and audiences, and each requires different skills and styles of rhetoric and action. To pursue a strategy based on litigation, for example, one needs legal expertise to write briefs and make arguments in terms of the law (Meyer and Boutcher 2007); engaging in electoral campaigns places a higher value on the mobilization of people and money. Activists assess their opportunities and competencies in various arenas and the impact that activities in the arenas will have on supporters and opponents. As Ganz (2004, 185–86) notes, the "possession of domain-relevant skills" allows for creative strategies and problem solving within particular settings.

Focus on one arena may lead to the neglect of others, as action in some arenas requires significant resources and dedicated skills. The resources and skills required for noninstitutionalized arenas are different than those needed for work in institutional settings. Within established venues, different institutions move at distinctly different paces, and activists occupied in one arena may allow opportunities in alternative arenas to pass unexploited. Moreover, advantages and expertise developed in one venue do not necessarily translate into viable resources in other venues. For instance, organizations such as Greenpeace, which develop extensive expertise for targeting the mass media, may as a result be less capable of building grassroots support. Similarly, organizations that develop extensive lobbying skills may sacrifice the ability to act in public arenas.

In selecting venues of interaction, movements also select targets and levels of action. The federal system in the United States, for example, provides multiple layers of government that could conceivably respond to movement demands on many issues. In general, higher levels of government offer more substantial responses, but also additional obstacles, including better organized and more powerful opposition. Some movements engage in upward or downward scale shift from local to national or international arenas, depending on their alliances and perceptions of opportunities (see Tarrow 2005), building on small victories to make larger claims.

Tactics

Activists also select tactics, which are the specific means of implementing strategy, the forms of collective action taken by movement actors. Movements need to find tactics such as demonstrations and lawsuits with which to press claims directed at targets in various arenas. Taylor and Van Dyke (2004) argue that tactics are *intentional* efforts to create change, which involve *contestation* with targets and the development of *collective identity* within challenging groups. Collective action tactics include *direct-action tactics,* which bypass established channels of action, and *institutionalized tactics,* which use well-established procedures and channels for action. Both direct-action and institutionalized tactics may serve mobilization goals as well as more instrumental political purposes. Recognition of the mobilization functions of many tactics is necessary to an understanding of the tactical choices of movement organizations.

Choosing tactics primarily intended to mobilize supporters rather than to effect concrete changes is one dilemma, potentially exacerbating tensions within movements over "whether to play to inside or outside audiences" (Jasper 2004, 10). If insufficient attention is paid to internal mobilization, movements may forfeit the internal resources needed for some tactics. If too much attention is paid to mobilization, movement organizations may neglect effective means of influencing external targets. Another important tactical choice has to do with the selection of more disruptive or more orderly tactics. Gamson (1990, 88) found that groups that used violent tactics were likely to gain new advantages because their targets were vulnerable. He also found that other, nonviolent types of disruptive activities, such as strikes and boycotts, were likely to produce successes, thus challenging the idea that the most orderly protestors will succeed, at least in circumstances where they enjoy public support.

Constraints on Strategic Choices

Activists make decisions about demands, arenas, and tactics, but they do not make those decisions independently or anew. Each decision is embedded in numerous historical constraints. We can examine influences on strategic choices and their effects at different levels of interaction: (1) the political and cultural environment, where movement actors encounter political and cultural opportunities and interact with their targets, opponents, bystanders, mass media, and potential allies; (2) the movement community, where various organizations and individuals within the movement interact; and (3) the movement organization, where leaders and members of the organization interact. These different levels of interaction are connected insofar as influences at one level affect interactions at another. Histories of interactions and strategic choices and their outcomes influence subsequent strategies by actors in the multiorganizational field. Although it is tempting analytically to view each decision as distinct and discrete, the legacies of the past, including the development of specialized expertise, distinct resources, and a web of relationships with supporters and authorities, constrain subsequent decisions. Analytically, we can view constraints in layers, commencing with large-scale environmental influences, and including movement-level and organization-level constraints.

Environmental Influences and Outcomes

Movement actors formulate strategies in the context of a larger environment consisting of numerous potentially relevant actors and elements, such as laws and court rulings, repression and support from government actors and other authorities, potential allies, opponents, mass media, public opinion, cultural norms and discourse, master frames, and repertoires of collective action. Some environmental elements, such as laws, may be products of previous rounds of collective action, which limit or expand subsequent strategic choices. Some aspects of the environment, such as freedom of assembly in democratic states, are features that are taken for granted, while others, such as the actions of allies and opponents, are closely watched opportunities and obstacles. Elements of the environment affect the positioning of collective actors and the ways in which movement actors interact with other actors in particular arenas. Researchers have raised a number of important questions regarding the influences of environmental structures and relationships on movement strategies.

Political opportunities include both relatively stable structural elements of the movement environment and more volatile features (Gamson and Meyer 1996). The structural characteristics of states affect the general availability and attractiveness of different venues and tactics (Kitschelt 1986; Kriesi et al. 1995). Relative tolerance of more moderate forms of claims making is likely to lure activists into established arenas and more routine politics and away from more confrontational tactics (Meyer and Tarrow 1998). In political systems that provide more points of access, collective actors are likely to choose assimilative over confrontational strategies, and movements can make procedural gains. Various features of political systems, such as the number of political parties and the independence of the legislature and judiciary from the executive, affect choices of strategy and their likely outcomes. Depending on the nature of such political structures, movement actors gain access to different types of resources and occupy different positions vis-à-vis interest groups and authorities.

Movements change strategies over time in response to shifts in the more volatile aspects of political opportunity. As political alignments change and new governments come to power, movements may enjoy greater resources and new positions of access, resulting in new strategic options and outcomes.

Alternatively, increased threats or decreased responsiveness from authorities make institutional strategies appear inadequate. The cultural context of movement activism also influences strategic choices. Brand (1990) argues that framing strategies vary with broad shifts in the cultural climate such as the changes he discerns from the "complacency" and "privatistic values" of the 1950s to the idealism and optimism of the 1960s. Such climatic shifts affect many movement claimants, producing characteristic styles of claims making. Cross-nationally, differences in political culture result in differing movement strategies. For example, Engel (2001) argues that differences in the strategies of gay and lesbian movements in the United States and Britain resulted from responses to differing cultural opportunities. Whereas the American movement used a civil rights frame, this frame was out of place in Britain, where activists framed arguments in terms of conscience and the acceptability of homosexuality as a private, rather than public, behavior. Activists are influenced by political culture when they create frames, and they seek to frame their claims in terms that resonate with their audiences.

Thus, collective actors are limited by structural features of their environments, by political and cultural contexts, and by their own perceptions of what is likely to be most effective. Political structures and opportunities influence arenas of conflict by creating routes of influence and setting limits on access to resources, allies, and authorities. Cultural assumptions and master frames influence movement selection of particular collective action frames. Depending on their assessments of opportunities and perceptions of what is possible, movement activists make different claims, act in different venues, and use different tactics.

Movement strategists make initial strategic decisions on the basis of perceptions about the likely responses of authorities as well as other potential allies and opponents in the field. They then adjust as they interact with their targets and make judgments about their prospects in different arenas. At the same time, authorities and other targets of collective action have their own perceptions of movement activists (Skrentny 2006), and they in turn adjust their own tactics in response to challenging movements. McAdam's (1983) analysis of tactical interaction in the civil rights movement, for example, shows how authorities learn to manage disruptive opposition, and movements continually devise new tactics in response. A movement's ability to invent tactics and its opponents' ability to adapt to the innovations affect the growth and effectiveness of the movement.

Movements and countermovements also forge their strategies in interaction with one another (Meyer and Staggenborg 1996). When an opposing movement shows signs of success in a particular arena, the original movement is usually forced to respond. A movement will not necessarily adopt the same tactics as the countermovement, but organizers within it will look for viable ways to counter its opponent. Thus, elements of the abortion rights movement filed lawsuits against Operation Rescue's efforts to shut down women's health clinics through force. Important outcomes such as major legislation or court rulings are particularly likely to trigger strategic responses from the opposing movement. If an outcome forecloses action in one venue, the opposing movement is likely to shift to another arena. Moreover, countermovements respond not only to a particular law or court ruling, but also to prior movement–countermovement interactions and the whole history of movement strategy within communities (Andrews 2002). In response to opponents, activists are similarly influenced by the history of interaction as they make strategic calculations, and can be more or less flexible (or opportunistic) in responding to events, policies, and positions their opponents generate.

Opposing movements compete to construct frames that will gain media attention, appeal to the public, and mobilize supporters. In general, mass media forums have far greater reach and more diverse audiences than internal movement organs, and SMOs depend on mass media to project themselves and their concerns to broader publics. Mass media outlets also have their own concerns about audience and newsworthiness that make it hard for activist groups to present themselves without distortion. Nonetheless, by understanding how particular outlets make decisions about content, learning news routines and cultivating journalistic contacts, groups can increase their coverage and perhaps even change the way in which their demands are framed (Rohlinger 2006). Groups that make favorable coverage a goal wisely play to mass media by adopting tactics that provide attractive images and copy and by cultivating relationships with journalists and television producers. Such strategies help movements to gain standing and position themselves as important players in the policy-making process (Gamson and Wolfsfeld 1993).

Activists also make strategic choices in interaction with bystander publics, potential allies, and their own supporters (Turner 1970). Often, tensions arise from attempts to target strategies at multiple groups because what works in one context can backfire in another. Strategic actors may find themselves enmeshed in a web of relationships that limits innovation. Tactics that generate mass media attention can also alienate potential supporters and close doors in mainstream political institutions. In particular, groups face the challenge of pitching to authorities and movement constituencies simultaneously, with the former valuing moderation and the latter clarity.

To some extent, choices about strategy are a product of targeted audiences and resources. Groups assess goals, resources, and targets, then try to plan accordingly. Barkan (1979) argues that groups with a low potential for disruption combined with low internal resources and skills are most likely to select strategies that will attract public support, while groups with high disruptive potential and internal resources need not be concerned with their public images. In some instances, movements employ strategies with no realistic chance of policy success not because activists are irrational, but because their efforts are aimed at mobilizing support rather than other outcomes. For example, Smith (1999) explains how the Canadian gay and lesbian movement used lawsuits to raise consciousness among constituents and the public in the period *before* the adoption of the Charter of Rights and Freedoms turned legal tactics into weapons for policy change. Activists used tactics aimed at mobilization in the hope of generating future opportunities. Critical events, including those created by movements, produce significant changes in the movement environment, affecting subsequent rounds of movement strategy (Staggenborg 1993).

Thus, various actors and structural features in a movement's environment affect strategic choices and outcomes. Moreover, the results of each round of collective action affect the range of strategic choices in the future. Movements that use strategies to build constituencies later have new possibilities because of newly mobilized resources, but they may also be constrained by their constitutents' expectations.

Interorganizational and Movement Community Influences

Allies and potential allies within a social movement community also constrain strategic choices. This community consists of networks of actors who support and advance the goals of a movement, including political organizations, cultural groups, institutional allies, and service and advocacy organizations, as well as individual constituents who are not necessarily part of any movement-associated organization. Movement communities of compatible social movements are connected to one another through overlapping members and leaders, resulting in shared culture, organizational structures, and tactical repertoires (Meyer and Whittier 1994; Staggenborg 1998). Both formal organizational ties and less formal norms and beliefs affect strategic choices by influencing resources and ideologies. An organization's putative allies exercise a latent veto over some potential claims and tactics.

Movement communities are united by informal communications networks, friendship and support networks, overlaps in memberships of organizations, movement of paid staff among organizations, central gathering places, and formal coalitions or umbrella organizations. Affective ties within movement communities help to create collective identity and submerged networks that sustain communities and allow for long-term strategies (Taylor and Rupp 2002; Roth 2005). In some movement communities, coordinating groups or leadership teams capable of uniting heterogeneous groups within and across movements play a key role in developing demands and tactics. Gerhards and Rucht (1992) describe the work of "mesomoblization actors" in carrying out strategic campaigns involving multi-movement coalitions. These actors are "groups and organizations that coordinate and integrate micromobilization groups" that activate and inform individual sympathizers and members of the public (558). Mesomobilization actors help create organizational structures capable of mobilizing diverse groups, and they integrate groups ideologically by extending master frames to encompass the concerns of numerous constituents. Such alliances make some kinds of actions possible but restrict other sorts of innovation that cannot be accommodated ideologically or organizationally.

Organizations also forge formal agreements to work on particular campaigns. Coalition work affects strategic options by increasing available resources and (sometimes) creating bonds of trust among cooperating groups. By pooling their resources, groups acting together can afford more expensive strategies than those acting alone, and resources saved by coalition work on one type of tactic can be used on others (Staggenborg 1986). Cooperating organizations can coordinate strategic specialization to enhance a movement's profile. A history of successful coalition work on a campaign, such as a large national demonstration, generates bonds of trust that carry over to subsequent coalition efforts. At the same time, a successful coalition effort can obscure other efforts and even the identity of cooperating groups, leading to a "least common denominator" politics and constricting possible claims and tactics (Meyer and Corrigall-Brown 2005). Similarly, tensions in coalitions and failed campaigns constrain subsequent strategic efforts.

Ongoing relationships among activists and with allies and supporters may enhance resources and provide exposure to new values and ideas regarding arenas, tactics, and demands, and help to diffuse tactical repertoires and collective identities. However, if conflicts develop within domestic or international networks, strategic cooperation and influence is unlikely (Maney 2000). Scale shifts are most likely when local and national or international activists are connected to one another, resulting in new arenas, targets, claims, and identities (Keck and Sikkink 1998; Tarrow 2005). Movement organizations are likely to adopt some of the demands and tactics of other groups and allies with which they interact, while more isolated groups may lack the stimulus to expand their strategic repertoire (Rootes 2006). Connections among organizations also affect the likelihood that movements will select strategies that exploit changes in politics or culture (Banaszak 1996). Moreover, the history of relationships among activists in different locations or different movements influences strategic choices (Armstrong and Crage 2006).

As movements expand, organizations may develop a tactical division of labor so that new organizations can distinguish themselves from existing ones and avoid competition for membership and funding (Gerlach and Hine 1970). Organizations adopting moderate tactics may experience support and success as a result of the positive *radical flank* effects created by more radical tactics (Haines 1984), and some established groups, recognizing this effect, deliberately aid direct-action groups (Rootes 2006). This relationship is rarely without tension: leaders of more moderate groups may resent ceding media attention, while leaders of more radical groups resent the allies who bargain on their behalf. At the same time, ongoing relationships between relatively moderate and radical groups influence each partner (Maney 2007). Zald and McCarthy (1980) focus on competition among movement organizations for resources, participants, and legitimacy as a source of tactical differentiation. Insofar as the potential pool of movement supporters is heterogeneous, movement organizations develop different "products" to appeal to different types of potential supporters (6). When resources appear plentiful, groups can define themselves with slight differences in ways that don't threaten their allies or downplay common purposes. As available resources shrink, competition within the market increases and groups will increasingly differentiate themselves from others more starkly, emphasizing distinctness rather than common purposes (Meyer and Imig 1993). Zald and McCarthy suggest that movement organizations will cooperate, however, when they develop distinct but compatible task specializations, allowing them to combine resources to achieve common goals with "similar tactical formulas" (1980, 11).

Internal Organizational Influences

Movement strategies are most frequently formulated by activists within social movement organizations (SMOs), and the organizational structures, emotional climates, resources and ideologies of SMOs shape their view of available strategic options as well as their choices. Like environmental dynamics and the structures of movement communities, internal organizational characteristics act as filters for strategies. As Jo Freeman (1979) argues, we can think about strategic decision making by SMOs as limited by certain factors. In her model, strategic decisions are affected by available resources, constraints on the use of resources, SMO structure and internal environment, and expectations about potential targets.

Resources are clearly central as groups can only select tactics they can support with sufficient money, numbers of people, expertise, and commitment. Yet as Freeman (1979, 179) states, all resources come with constraints, which form "a kind of filter between resources and SMOs." Beyond material resources, values, ideology, past experiences, reference groups, and relations with targets, groups will place some issues, alliances, and tactics off limits (Turner 1970; Freeman 1979). Strategies are always formulated in interaction with actors both inside and outside the organization. As activists create organizations, their structures and rules of governance operate as both constraints and resources. Organizational structures, particularly those that support effective leadership teams, can build strategic capacity (Ganz 2000; Reger and Staggenborg 2006). They provide opportunities for participants to learn skills and develop leadership qualities so that new leaders are continually trained. They feature a division of labor that disperses responsibilities efficiently while maintaining accountability and preventing the burnout that comes from overreliance on select individuals. They provide forums for internal debate, education, and decision making about mobilization and collective action strategies. They give leaders authority, but they also keep them accountable to their constituents. Such organizational features are often matters of some contest. In some SMOs, for instance, leaders deliberately limit their supporters to giving money, affording one or two leaders maximum autonomy in making strategic decisions (Kretschmer and Meyer 2007).

Although some organizational features such as the ability to develop leadership teams increase strategic capacity generally, others make SMOs better suited to certain types of strategies than others. Organizational variations include the extent and type of formalization or bureaucratization; professionalization of leadership; grassroots participation; centralization and hierarchy in decision-making structures; links among organizational levels, such as chapters and national headquarters; and forums available for decision making and deliberation. These features influence strategic choices of venues, tactics, and demands by limiting resources, information, and input from participants, and by affecting the ability to recognize and respond to environmental threats and opportunities.

Organizational and strategic choices shape subsequent strategic options, although how they do so is not always clear. Some analysts suggest that centralization and bureaucratization lead to a decline in insurgency, as oligarchic leaders become more conservative in their tactics and more focused on organizational maintenance (Michels 1915; Piven and Cloward 1977). Others point to the more positive association of bureaucracy and centralized decision making with movement survival and success, but suggest a connection between formalized organizational structures and a preference for institutionalized arenas and tactics (Gamson 1990; Staggenborg 1988). In the environmental movement, Rucht (1995) shows how the highly centralized Greenpeace engaged in professionally orchestrated, carefully planned and targeted tactics, which led the organization to avoid party politics and political positions that would threaten favorable media coverage and public sympathy. In contrast, the extremely decentralized Earth First! engaged in controversial direct action and civil disobedience tactics unencumbered by concerns with favorable media coverage and the need to attract mass donations (80). Comparing two feminist organizations, Staggenborg (1989) finds that formalization of offices and division of labor are associated with efficiency in decision making and task performance and an ability to engage in large-scale, externally targeted projects, while informal and decentralized organizations, which benefit from greater participant input, are less stable but tend to produce a wider range of innovative tactics.

Both organizational structure and ideology affect a group's ability to respond effectively to environmental challenges. In her study of the framing battles of gay rights activists and their Christian Right opponents over an anti-gay voter initiative, Dugan (2004) shows that the gay rights campaign failed to respond effectively to its opponents in part because a handful of leaders made decisions without consulting widely. This situation might have been remedied by an organizational structure that nurtured a diverse leadership team. In a study of Greenpeace and Friends of the Earth, Carmin and Balser (2002) find that experience, core values and beliefs, environmental philosophy, and political ideology all act as filters that shape perceptions of the potential efficacy and acceptability of particular tactics such as electoral participation or direct action. SMOs that rely on external funding and have inclusive boards of directors and director interlocks with elites and policy bodies are likely to adopt strategies in line with those linkages and dependencies (Dreiling and Wolf 2001). Whether or not an organization has tax-exempt status, runs a political action committee, or relies on public support or grassroots members—all influence its strategic choices (McCarthy, Britt, and Wolfson 1991; Dreiling and Wolf 2001).

Conclusion

Activists do not make strategic decisions abstractly but within particular contexts in interaction with other actors in a multiorganizational field. Decisions about demands, tactics, and arenas are not made anew, but within the constraints created by previous decisions and environmental and organizational structures. Studies of movement strategies are important as a means of understanding what routes of influence are possible for collective actors based on these constraints. In some instances, movement actors can shift the structure of constraints by, for example, structuring their organizations differently, cultivating different alliances, or changing elite perceptions. In other instances, they need to figure out how best to work within structural constraints. Studies of strategic decision making should consider these structural constraints and the ways in which activist choices can alter them over time. A meaningful understanding of activist agency only comes from a realistic assessment of what is possible.

Strategic action involves series of interactions with authorities, supporters, bystanders, opponents, media, and potential allies that takes place within environmental, community, and organizational contexts. We summarize the set of related decisions activists make in terms of demands, arenas, and tactics. We propose using these elements of strategy as visible expressions of strategic negotiations that also involve targeting, timing, framing, and other strategic choices. We are not suggesting a mechanical framework for the study of strategy. Any empirical study needs to depict the complexity and emotionality of strategic choice and the ongoing interactions involved in collective action. To capture this complexity, we need to understand how a changing web of relations in a multiorganizational field of actors constrains and enlarges strategic options over time.

The focus on a strategic field of actors that shapes available choices should allow us to develop a meaningful theory of social movement strategy as well as a series of propositions to guide empirical research on strategy. For example, if a movement is characterized by extensive ties among active organizations, we would expect innovation within that movement to come from the entry of new organizations to the field. We hope that our effort to conceptualize key elements of strategy and influences on strategic decision making will stimulate new theory and research.

Notes

We presented earlier versions of this chapter at the American Sociological Association, Collective Behavior/Social Movement Section's Workshop, "Movement Cultures, Strategies, and Outcomes," August 9–10, 2007, Hofstra University, Hempstead, New York, and at the Social Movement/Social Justice Workgroup at the University of California, Irvine, February 22, 2008. We thank participants in these settings and Greg Maney for their comments.

1. In identifying these three strategic elements, we recognize other ways of thinking about the components of strategy. Ganz (2004, 181), for instance, identifies "targeting, timing, and tactics" as key elements. In our scheme, targeting and timing can be analyzed with regard to demands, arenas, and tactics. Our goal is to provide a parsimonious conception of the major negotiations involved in movement strategy.

References

Amenta, Edwin, Neal Caren, and Sheera Joy Olasky. 2005. "Age for Leisure? Political Mediation and the Impact of the Pension Movement on U.S. Old-Age Policy." *American Sociological Review* 70:516–38.

Andrews, Kenneth T. 2002. "Movement–Countermovement Dynamics and the Emergence of New Institutions: The Case of 'White Flight' Schools in Mississippi." *Social Forces* 80:911–36.

Armstrong, Elizabeth A., and Suzanna M. Crage. 2006. "Movements and Memory: The Making of the Stonewall Myth." *American Sociological Review* 71:724–51.

Ash, Roberta. 1972. *Social Movements in America*. Chicago, Ill.: Markham.

Banaszak, Lee Ann. 1996. *Why Movements Succeed or Fail: Opportunity, Culture, and the Struggle for Woman Suffrage*. Princeton, N.J.: Princeton University Press.

Barkan, Steven E. 1979. "Strategic, Tactical, and Organizational Dilemmas of the Protest Movement against Nuclear Power." *Social Problems* 27:19–37.

Bernstein, Mary. 1997. "Celebration and Suppression: The Strategic Uses of Identity by the Lesbian and Gay Movement." *American Journal of Sociology* 103:531–65.

Brand, Karl-Werner. 1990. "Cyclical Aspects of New Social Movements: Waves of Cultural Criticism and Mobilization Cycles of New Middle-Class Radicalism." In *Challenging the Political Order: New Social and Political Movements in Western Democracies,* edited by Russell J. Dalton and Manfred Kuechler, 23–42. New York: Oxford University Press.

Carmin, Joann, and Deborah B. Balser. 2002. "Selecting Repertoires of Action in Environmental Movement Organizations." *Organization and Environment* 15:365–88.

Curtis, Russell L., Jr., and Louis Zurcher Jr. 1973. "Stable Resources of Protest Movements: The Multi-organizational Field." *Social Forces* 52:53–61.

Dreiling, Michael, and Brian Wolf. 2001. "Environmental Movement Organizations and Political Strategy." *Organization and Environment* 14:34–54.

Dugan, Kimberly B. 2004. "Strategy and 'Spin': Opposing Movement Frames in an Anti-gay Voter Initiative." *Sociological Focus* 37:213–33.

Engel, Stephen M. 2001. *The Unfinished Revolution: Social Movement Theory and the Gay and Lesbian Movement*. Cambridge: Cambridge University Press.

Freeman, Jo. 1979. "Resource Mobilization and Strategy: A Model for Analyzing Social Movement Organization Actions." In *The Dynamics of Social Movements: Resource Mobilization, Social Control, and Tactics,* edited by Mayer N. Zald and John D. McCarthy, 167–89. Cambridge, Mass.: Winthrop.

Gamson, William A. 1990. *The Strategy of Social Protest*. 2nd ed. Belmont, Calif.: Wadsworth.

Gamson, William A., and David S. Meyer. 1996. "Framing Political Opportunity."

In *Comparative Perspectives on Social Movements: Political Opportunities, Mobilizing Structures, and Cultural Framings,* edited by Doug McAdam, John D. McCarthy, and Mayer N. Zald, 275–90. Cambridge: Cambridge University Press.

Gamson, William A., and Gadi Wolfsfeld. 1993. "Movements and Media as Interacting Systems." *Annals of the Academy of Political and Social Science* 528:114–25.

Ganz, Marshall. 2000. "Resources and Resourcefulness: Strategic Capacity in the Unionization of California Agriculture, 1959–1966." *American Journal of Sociology* 105:1003–62.

———. 2004. "Why David Sometimes Wins: Strategic Capacity in Social Movements." In *Rethinking Social Movements: Structure, Meaning, and Emotion,* edited by Jeff Goodwin and James M. Jasper, 177–98. Lanham, Md.: Rowman & Littlefield.

Gerhards, Jurgen, and Dieter Rucht. 1992. "Mesomobilization: Organizing and Framing in Two Protest Campaigns in West Germany." *American Journal of Sociology* 98:555–95.

Gerlach, Luther, and Virginia H. Hine. 1970. *People, Power, Change: Movements of Social Transformation.* Indianapolis, Ind.: Bobbs-Merrill.

Gornick, Janet C., and David S. Meyer. 1998. "Changing Political Opportunity: The Anti-rape Movement and Public Policy." *Journal of Policy History* 10:367–98.

Haines, Herbert H. 1984. "Black Radicalization and the Funding of Civil Rights, 1957–1970." *Social Problems* 32:31–43.

Jasper, James M. 2004. "A Strategic Approach to Collective Action: Looking for Agency in Social-Movement Choices." *Mobilization* 9:1–16.

Keck, Margaret E., and Kathryn Sikkink. 1998. *Activists beyond Borders.* Ithaca, N.Y.: Cornell University Press.

Kitschelt, Herbert P. 1986. "Political Opportunity Structures and Political Protest: Anti-nuclear Movements in Four Democracies." *British Journal of Political Science* 16:57–85.

Klandermans, Bert. 1992. "The Social Construction of Protest and Multiorganizational Fields." In *Frontiers in Social Movement Theory,* edited by Aldon D. Morris and C. McClurg Mueller, 77–103. New Haven, Conn.: Yale University Press.

Kriesi, Hanspeter, Ruud Koopmans, Jan Willem Duyvendak, and Marco G. Giugni. 1995. *The Politics of New Social Movements in Western Europe.* Minneapolis: University of Minnesota Press.

Kretschmer, Kelsy, and David S. Meyer. 2007. "Platform Leadership: Cultivating Support for a Public Profile." *American Behavioral Scientist* 50:1395–412.

Maney, Gregory. 2000. "Transnational Mobilization and Civil Rights in Northern Ireland." *Social Problems* 47:153–79.

————. 2007. "From Civil War to Civil Rights and Back Again: The Interrelation of Rebellion and Protest in Northern Ireland, 1955–1972." *Research in Social Movements, Conflicts, and Change* 27:3–35.

McAdam, Doug. 1983. "Tactical Innovation and the Pace of Insurgency." *American Sociological Review* 48:735–54.

McCarthy, John, David W. Britt, and Mark Wolfson. 1991. "The Institutional Channeling of Social Movements by the State in the United States." *Research in Social Movements, Conflicts and Change* 13:45–76.

Michels, Robert. 1915. *Political Parties.* New York: Free Press.

Meyer, David S. 2007. *The Politics of Protest: Social Movements in America.* New York: Oxford University Press.

Meyer, David S., and Steven A. Boutcher. 2007. "Signals and Spillover: *Brown v. Board of Education* and Other Social Movements." *Perspectives on Politics* 5, no. 1: 81–93.

Meyer, David S., and Catherine Corrigall-Brown. 2005. "Coalitions and Political Context: U.S. Movements against Wars in Iraq." *Mobilization* 10:327–44.

Meyer, David S., and Douglas R. Imig. 1993. "Political Opportunity and the Rise and Decline of Interest Group Sectors." *Social Science Journal* 30:253–70.

Meyer, David S., and Suzanne Staggenborg. 1996. "Movements, Countermovements, and the Structure of Political Opportunity." *American Journal of Sociology* 101:1628–660.

Meyer, David S., and Sidney Tarrow, eds. 1998. *The Social Movement Society.* Lanham, Md.: Rowman & Littlefield.

Meyer, David S., and Nancy Whittier. 1994. "Social Movement Spillover." *Social Problems* 41:277–98.

Oliver, Pamela E., and Gerald Marwell. 1992. "Mobilizing Technologies for Collective Action." In *Frontiers in Social Movement Theory,* edited by Aldon D. Morris and C. McClurg Mueller, 251–72. New Haven, Conn.: Yale University Press.

Piven, Frances Fox, and Richard A. Cloward. 1977. *Poor People's Movements: Why They Succeed, How They Fail.* New York: Vintage Books.

Reger, Jo, and Suzanne Staggenborg. 2006. "Patterns of Mobilization in Local Movement Organizations: Leadership and Strategy in Four National Organization for Women Chapters." *Sociological Perspectives* 49:297–323.

Rohlinger, Deana A. 2006. "Friend and Foe: Media, Politics, and Tactics in the Abortion War." *Social Problems* 53:537–61.

Rootes, Christopher. 2006. "Facing South? British Environmental Movement Organisations and the Challenge of Globalisation." *Environmental Politics* 15:768–86.

Roth, Silke. 2005. "Sisterhood and Exclusionary Solidarity in a Labor Women's Organization." In *Emotions and Social Movements,* edited by Helena Flam and Debra King, 189–206. London: Routledge.

Rucht, Dieter. 1990. "The Strategies and Action Repertoires of New Movements." In *Challenging the Political Order: New Social and Political Movements in Western Democracies,* edited by Russell J. Dalton and Manfred Kuechler, 156–75. New York: Oxford University Press.

———. 1995. "Ecological Protest as Calculated Law-breaking: Greenpeace and Earth First! in Comparative Perspective." In *Green Politics Three,* edited by Wolfgang Rudig, 66–89. Edinburgh: Edinburgh University Press.

Skrentny, John D. 2006. "Policy-Elite Perceptions and Social Movement Success: Understanding Variations in Group Inclusion in Affirmative Action." *American Journal of Sociology* 11:1762–815.

Smith, Miriam. 1999. *Lesbian and Gay Rights in Canada.* Toronto: University of Toronto Press.

Staggenborg, Suzanne. 1986. "Coalition Work in the Pro-choice Movement: Organizational and Environmental Opportunities and Obstacles." *Social Problems* 33:374–90.

———. 1988. "The Consequences of Professionalization and Formalization in the Pro-choice Movement." *American Sociological Review* 53:585–605.

———. 1989. "Stability and Innovation in the Women's Movement: A Comparison of Two Movement Organizations." *Social Problems* 36:75–92.

———. 1993. "Critical Events and the Mobilization of the Pro-choice Movement." *Research in Political Sociology* 6:319–345.

———. 1998. "Social Movement Communities and Cycles of Protest: The Emergence and Maintenance of a Local Women's Movement." *Social Problems* 45, no. 2:180–204.

Tarrow, Sidney. 2005. *The New Transnational Activism.* New York: Cambridge University Press.

Taylor, Verta, and Leila J. Rupp. 2002. "Loving Internationalism: The Emotion Culture of Transnational Women's Organizations, 1888–1945." *Mobilization* 7:141–58.

Taylor, Verta, and Nella Van Dyke. 2004. "'Get Up, Stand Up': Tactical Repertoires of Social Movements." In *The Blackwell Companion to Social Movements,* edited by David A. Snow, Sarah A. Soule, and Hanspeter Kriesi, 262–93. Oxford: Blackwell.

Tilly, Charles. 1978. *From Mobilization to Revolution.* Reading, Mass.: Addison/Wesley.

Turner, Ralph H. 1970. "Determinants of Social Movement Strategies." In *Human Nature and Collective Behavior: Papers in Honor of Herbert Blumer,* edited by Tamotsu Shibutani, 145–64. Englewood Cliffs, N.J.: Prentice-Hall.

Zald, Mayer N., and John D. McCarthy. 1980. "Social Movement Industries: Competition and Cooperation among Movement Organizations." *Research in Social Movements, Conflicts and Change* 3:1–20.

2

Choice Points, Emotional Batteries, and Other Ways to Find Strategic Agency at the Microlevel

James M. Jasper

For years, activists have asked me what works of social science they should read that would make them better activists. It's always been an embarrassing question because there is so little to recommend. I used to suggest Saul Alinsky's *Rules for Radicals* (1971), although a few years ago, when I reread it, I realized that even he mostly provided vague bromides. Other scholars recommend Gamson's *Strategy of Social Protest* (1975), or Piven and Cloward's *Poor People's Movements* (1977). These are important books, to be sure, but they only deal with the effects of violence and disruption. Posing the question in this dichotomous way—do certain tactics succeed or not?—strips out complex issues about political contexts, trade-offs, and decision making.

Because they have decisions to make, people outside the academy care about strategy. The willingness of economists and political scientists to address strategy and decision making is largely what has given them such influence, even though most of their models of choice are, to a sociologist, willfully naïve. People listen to the disciplines that talk about choices rather than those that emphasize constraint or limits. It is time we had something to say that is relevant to decision makers such as activists. It is time we examined choices.

This is not to say we should become advocates. Our job as scholars is not to advise activists but to gather evidence to help us develop the most accurate explanations of social life. If, as citizens, we then use those theories to promote our favorite causes, that is great. That is our role as citizens. However, the best thing we can do for activists and for ourselves as scholars is to understand the world around us as thoroughly as possible. Yet how well do we understand that world if our work has no resonance with decision makers?

I loosely follow Max Weber in thinking that what we can offer decision makers is not "the right answer" in a given circumstance (because they usually have a better sense of what should be done than we do), but some considerations about the likely costs and benefits and risks of each possible choice. By knowing what has happened in similar circumstances (always only roughly similar), we can provide a list of risks to look out for. Choice A comes with a list of risks, choice B with a different list. In some cases, the trade-off is such that it cannot be eased. In others, there are tricks for dealing with adverse consequences. It is more realistic for scholarly advisors to provide a checklist of common mistakes for activists to avoid than to come up with the one right choice. This is no trivial role, as success frequently results from exploiting others' mistakes.

Sociologists often talk about agency as opposed to structure, but we still understand structure much more completely. It is the founding intuition of our discipline. This is why our interactions with decision makers matter. If they don't recognize their own situations and dilemmas in what we write, we probably have not gotten at agency, and we probably have not properly defined action. It is hard to imagine a robust concept of agency that excludes the players' own points of view.

Indeed, all good work on social movements already touches on strategic action. It exists when activists try to recruit new members, when they withdraw into more expressive action rather than engaging their opponents, when they adapt frames and narratives for various audiences, and when individuals join or defect. Everything participants do has some strategic element. Yet sociologists rarely use the language of strategic action and engagement, and so our many insights have never congealed into a framework or theory of strategy.

Despite a surge of work on decision making in other fields, there is still no self-conscious sociology of decisions—or more broadly, a sociology of strategy. It apparently goes against the structural impulse at the heart of the discipline. As a result, we have allowed game theory, derived from neoclassical economics and mathematics, to monopolize the language and thinking of strategy studies, even though we regularly complain that its models of human motivation are misguided. Whenever I tell people I am studying strategy, they inevitably—and wrongly—assume that I have become some sort of game theorist.

Some Basics

By strategic action, I mean simply a situation in which individuals or groups try to get others to do what they want them to—whether or not it is against the will of the other (Jasper 2004, 2006b). I emphasize the latter because most strategic action is aimed at changing others' desires, about persuasion rather than coercion. We try to preempt resistance rather than to suppress it. Words, force, and money—the three major means in strategic action—work in different ways. Still different social sciences tend to adopt one of them as an exemplar for all, misrepresenting the others in the process. If political science is traditionally about coercion and economics about money, then sociology should be the discipline for persuasion. However, as central as persuasion is, restricting ourselves to it probably gives too much away to the other disciplines, as well as leaving all three with partial visions of strategic engagement.

So what should we aim for in an approach to strategy? First, we need to look at the interplay between players' projects and the constraints facing them. Sociologists have always specialized in the constraints, although they often misspecify them by seeing them as structures. Effort and constraint, or action and order, or agency and structure must be studied together. We cannot see the constraints on people until we grasp what they are trying to do.[1]

Second, our approach to strategy also has to be interactional. Players engage one another, they anticipate, they react. We must thus incorporate expectations that entail some psychology and culture, and thus also emotions. Our expectations about others depend on our own experience with them, but also on their broader reputations (which are often highly stereotyped representations). Scholars know little about the work that goes into the construction of political reputations—by the players themselves, by their allies and opponents, and by the media and authorities (Fine 2001; Jasper and Young 2006). Reputations are not simply cognitive constructions; they are also emotional ones. We know how to feel about other players because of prior interactions, our observations, and their reputations.[2]

Any new framework for understanding strategy today has to be cultural and interpretive, recognizing humans as thinking, feeling, caring actors with a rich variety of ends and means, and as at least capable of rationality even when they do not refine that capacity very much. But rationality in a much broader sense than the rational choice conception of it as a kind of emotionally neutral calculation or maximization of a single goal. The very labels "rational," "irrational," and "nonrational" are almost never useful because action is embedded in so many complex contexts. If we understand those contexts, action almost always makes sense. I hope that an emotion-laden theory of strategic agency will help us move beyond outmoded debates over rationality.[3]

In reacting against overly calculating, economic models, we do not want to end up with an overly socialized conception of human action, as sociology tends to do (Wrong 1961; Campbell 1996). Too often, "communication" is our paradigm of human interaction, so that we see people as trying to maintain a shared definition of a situation, to protect and reinforce local norms, to help each other to maintain their dignity as participants, and so on. But much of the time, players are not easily defined by their immediate social settings. They take projects with them from setting to setting. They create new settings to pursue their ends. They reinterpret and rework settings. Most of all, they try to dupe others into thinking that this is one kind of situation when it is really a different kind of situation. They are not always trying to attain communicative agreement, even though they are trying to have an effect on others by miscommunication or by deception. Sociological models are poorly equipped to recognize this.

To give the communicative model its due, another important aspect of a sociology of strategy is that players are audiences for one anothers' words and actions. They're not calculators; they're interpreters. They constantly interpret everyone's words and actions, including their own. This also means that they're not only acting and talking, they're also constantly interpreting and describing their own actions and words for others—we're doing this now, we meant this, we're trying to accomplish that. They interpret history even as they are making it. What people say they are doing can be as important as what they really are doing, even when their words are meant to hide the reality. The world of strategy is a thoroughly cultural world, but that doesn't mean that people take at face value what others do and say.

We need a better understanding of rhetoric and performance (Alexander, Giesen, and Mast 2006), for rhetoric is to culture what strategy is to action: a way to emphasize agency and purpose without losing sight of constraints. The insights of ancient rhetoric have been rediscovered here and there, as in Francesca Polletta's use of metonymy (2006; chapter 3, this volume), but much work remains to be done.

I also want to emphasize that strategy includes goals. Movement scholars have all too often assumed some particular motivation—that people know what they want and are just waiting for a window of opportunity to open in order to go after it. A realistic strategic approach should expect diverse motives to be determined empirically rather than posited deductively. We don't want to assume that players have any single motive, especially one that we as observers know in advance. A single goal to maximize is good for mathematical models, bad for our grip on reality. We often conclude that protestors have made a mistake or acted irrationally when we have simply not understood what they were trying to do, or how they were juggling several goals, or switching between goals. We tend to miss the many clashes among goals as well as the conflicts between individual and group goals. As part of our oversocialized vision, we have a hard time seeing not only how individuals defect from team goals, but also the many ways that individuals pursue personal goals and group goals at the same time. We need to examine which goals are widely shared, which can be assumed, which are not shared, and which need to be carefully constructed by organizers. Christian Smith (2003) rightly complains that social scientists do not address motivation, and when they do, they tend to ignore moral motives. Less helpfully, he proceeds to replace material motives with moral ones, yielding another monomotive model.

Like game theory, a sociology of strategy needs to incorporate both individuals and collectives as players. I call these simple players and compound players, respectively. But unlike game theory, it has to recognize that the two are not formally the same. Collectives are always composed of individuals who have varying degrees of allegiance to the collective's goals. Compound players, because they also at least potentially contain factions, are arenas as well as players. Sociology has a lot to contribute to understanding these problems of coordination and communication, of collective identity and solidarity. The relationship between particular individuals and the groups to which they belong (beyond their identification with the group) is one of the great understudied research topics in the field of social movements.

Perhaps the greatest advantage of a more strategic approach to social movements is that it should force us to specify as concretely as possible the various players in a field of struggle. This includes the salient simple players within compound players along with the compound players (factions) within other compound players. We need to understand the capacities and goals of each, who is being targeted by each action and statement, and who is positioned to respond in what ways. We need careful catalogs of players (including, to the extent possible, potential players), much like the ones business strategists advise their corporate clients to construct when they think about strategy (Porter 1980). This should be the starting point of any study of contention, thus preventing later confusion.

Elsewhere, I have laid out this basic vocabulary for talking about strategy in social movements (Jasper 2004)—a vocabulary that includes terms like players and arenas; rhetoric and audiences; dilemmas and choices; resources, skills, and positions; and goals. I have also discussed these in book-length detail, although not applied to social movements (Jasper 2006b). Here I would like to briefly discuss different kinds of constraints followed by a more extensive discussion of some microlevel mechanisms that exemplify the work that I think we need to do to understand strategic agency.

What Are Constraints?

Sociologists have mostly studied strategy—if at all—as though it were primarily about constraints, and especially constraints of a structural, unbending kind. This approach assumes—wrongly—that we already know what the players want, so that we only need to examine what prevents them from getting it, rather than how they develop their goals or how players are created. We cannot understand constraint or structure unless we understand the intentions of those being constrained. We also need to understand the intentions of those doing the constraining because they provide the greatest source of constraint in any political setting.

We need to distinguish different kinds of constraints. As a rough approximation, there are strategic constraints, imposed by other players; physical constraints imposed by resources; cultural constraints imposed by our own understandings and the understandings of others (see Polletta, chapter 3, this volume); and finally the rules of the arenas. Rules and resources come closest to structural constraints in that they are difficult to change.

The very metaphor of a structure implies that they are immovable and rigid. Yet constraints aren't always or even primarily structural; most of the time so-called structural constraints actually hide other players, enforcing or reinterpreting existing rules, trying to create new rules, building up resources and alliances, repackaging existing tropes and images, and actively trying to foil other players. Structures don't do anything by themselves, which is why they are so often a misleading metaphor for social science. Social and natural science differ here. You can break a social norm or a government's law; you cannot break the laws of physics. The most structural constraints operate largely when other players enforce them, and through processes of interpretation. As the philosopher Charles Taylor (1993, 57) puts it, "A rule doesn't apply itself."

If any of these factors impose constraints, they do so at the microlevel. Concrete individuals and groups succeed or fail to achieve their ends through interactions with others. Even structural constraints, like laws, emerge from local interactions among legislators, lobbyists, staffers, and others. They are enforced in microsettings, as when a king gives a command, his military commanders choose whether to obey it, and foot soldiers must decide whether to comply.

The main problem with the current idea of constraints is that they tend to dichotomize strategic choices into those that are possible and those that are not. This follows from the root metaphor of a structure: you can walk through a door but not a wall; a window of opportunity is either open or closed. But this is a misleading view of strategic options, which generally fall along continua: from less costly to more, from less risky to more, and from lower potential payoffs to greater ones. In what I call the *Risk Dilemma* (Jasper 2006b, 18), potential costs and risks are often correlated with potential benefits, so that players must decide how much they are willing to risk. The expected values of low-risk, low-cost, low-payoff choices may roughly equal those of high-risk, high-cost, high-benefit options. This is one reason strategic decisions are so hard. Some players are willing to take risks that others are not. One of the main things we would like to know, in fact, is why different players value costs, benefits, and risks so differently—a key to understanding martyrs, fanatics, and others. In a dichotomized view of strategic choice, this psychological, cultural, and rhetorical realm disappears.

It is one thing to call for us to pay more attention to strategy, another to outline concepts that can help us do that. It is microlevel mechanisms that must do the real work in our explanations.

Micromechanisms

In my view, an approach centered on strategic agency has an additional advantage to those I have discussed: it encourages us to stick to the microlevel, or at least to begin there. Even structuralists like McAdam, Tarrow, and Tilly (2001) have admitted that we need to start afresh, building up from causal mechanisms to broader explanations. Their failure is due to their unwillingness to go down far enough to the microlevel interactions that make up social life (Koopmans 2003).

A mechanisms approach, often associated with rational choice theory (e.g., Elster 1998), recommends dropping down to a more concrete level of reality in order to find building blocks that are less controversial but that nonetheless describe common linkages between events (Stinchcombe 1991). Typically, in social science, this means finding individual-level concepts that can help us understand institutions. It might also entail a search for psychological mechanisms such as emotions that help account for individual actions and projects (Elster 1999). The advantages of disaggregating complex processes into component mechanisms is that we can see what is really going on, avoiding general laws on the one hand and mere description of cases on the other (Hedström and Swedberg 1998).

Only once we have developed an extensive tool kit of micromechanisms can we look beneath the broad metaphors that have long crippled the study of social movements. These include the idea of a "culture," corresponding roughly to the scope of a "society," a "nation," and a "state," or even the notion of a "social movement." Of course these are all fictitious constructions, although a nation and a state at least have some laws to define their boundaries. A movement is primarily a self-proclaimed collective identity that organizers hope will have various rhetorical effects on several audiences, including attracting new recruits, retaining and encouraging existing participants, and demanding that news media, authorities, and opponents take them seriously. Any claim to be a coherent movement can be deconstructed, much as the women's movement and the gay rights movement were deconstructed by those who saw difference within each movement. They are a necessary fiction for mobilization (Gamson 1995).

In place of such metaphors, I recommend a combination of more concrete entities: cognitive processes, cultural meanings, emotions, decisions, individuals and their interactions, resources, and rules. It is these entities that we actually study, not a movement. This microlevel approach will also allow us to join two dimensions of social life long kept apart by disciplinary turf battles and intellectual tastes: the study of purpose (or strategy) and the study of culture (or meaning and passion). It is also at this level that we can hope to see agency that is based on individual projects and actions. Collective agency remains mostly a metaphor. Otherwise, as Emirbayer and Mische (1998, 964) complain, "If structural contexts are analytically separable from (and stand over against) capacities for human agency, how is it possible for actors ever to mediate or to transform their own relationships to these contexts?"

Efforts to locate processes at the macrolevel only make the microprocesses implicit rather than explicit, preventing careful scrutiny. For example, protest groups may well borrow repertoires from each other (Polletta, chapter 3, this volume), but they do so one decision at a time, or as an activist moves from one group to another, or as organizers observe events—in other words, through microlevel interactions. We don't really understand imitation or the waves of protest it may trigger without understanding these microprocesses.[4]

I think we know a lot about cognitive and cultural mechanisms, beginning with different kinds of frames, but also including symbols, worldviews, ideologies, and other components of what is normally studied under the rubric of culture (Jasper 1997 catalogs many of these). We are beginning to know more about emotions, although I will still address one category of emotional dynamics below. Scholars have also addressed some of the components of morality, although not so much their emotional underpinnings. Resources have been extensively recognized and discussed, although laws and other rules less so. Finally, despite the explosion of research on decisions and decision making in fields outside sociology, there has been little explicit research or theory into decisions in social movements. I will address then two types of microlevel mechanisms that might help explain strategic agency: choice points, and one category of emotional mechanisms that I call emotional batteries. These kinds of mechanisms should be familiar to activists because this is the level of day-to-day discussions, activities, and tactical choices.

Choice Points

Let me give some examples of mechanisms that I hope are micro, observable, and important to strategy. The first are from a large list of strategic dilemmas that I have developed and partly published elsewhere (Jasper 2004, 2006a). The others are from a list of emotional mechanisms (Jasper 2006a; Goodwin and Jasper 2006).

Choice points are simply moments or situations when compound or simple players face alternatives, when they could do something different from what they in fact do. Each alternative has a list of risks, costs, and benefits associated with it—one reason the options are often difficult to compare. To make the matter more complex, not all choice points are recognized as such. A player may not stop to think about alternatives at all, for psychological or cultural reasons (forms of bounded choice), or simply because of lack of time and awareness. Indeed, most choice points are dominated by routines that are not carefully examined. Yet even when a player is unaware of making a choice, there are still unconsidered alternatives. In other words, there are still underlying trade-offs, with potential risks, costs, and benefits. One of the unanswered questions of movement research is why some trade-offs are faced as choices and dilemmas, and some are not. Having a list of dilemmas that recur across different settings can help us, as analysts, see effects and possibilities that participants themselves might not see. It's a place where we can advise activists if we want to, by telling them what choices were made in other, parallel situations.

We know little about how decisions are made in protest groups. Even staples of social psychology, such as Asch's findings about social pressure, Milgram's about deference to authority, and Janis's about groupthink, have rarely been applied to social movement decisions. Some of the best efforts (e.g., Ganz 2000) have been diverted by a search for successful decision making rather than a careful study of actual decision making across settings. Janja Lalich (2004) has interestingly documented the internal group dynamics of Heaven's Gate and the Democratic Workers Party, although here too an animus against destructive leaders guides her analysis. However, Lalich and Ganz—starting from condemnation and admiration, respectively—provide any number of mechanisms we might trace in all kinds of groups.

There are different kinds of strategic dilemmas or choice points. Some are mostly *Internal Dilemmas,* over how to build your team, how leaders should act, what they should symbolize to members, how permanent your organization should be, and so on. Basic internal dilemmas include the *Organization Dilemma* over how much formal bureaucracy to develop (Jasper 2004); the *Extension Dilemma* over how broad a team to build, recognizing that large size also brings diversity (Jasper 2006b); and the *Dilemma of Whose Goals?*, which recognizes that players always pursue multiple goals at the same time (Jasper 2006b).

Let me describe several additional and less obvious internal choice points. The *Dilemma of Inevitability* deals with how to motivate the members of your team. An ideology can promote confidence if it suggests that history or God is on your side. It also helps protestors deal with the ridicule of others. Animal rights activists, for instance, have several famous quotes to the effect that all important ideas appear preposterous when they first appear. The epigraph to Tom Regan's *The Case for Animal Rights,* for example, is from John Stuart Mill: "Every great movement must experience three stages: ridicule, discussion, adoption." At the same time, an ideology of inevitability may undermine the sense that action is urgently needed. Social change will happen without you. Many recruiting and fund-raising arguments try to find a middle way, conveying that, with a little work now, victory is certain. In another animal rights example, pamphlets often emphasize horrendous scientific tests that are no longer in use, thanks to the movement itself. But they cannot boast too much of this success without undermining their implication of urgency. It is important to take some credit for success so that potential supporters don't think your cause is hopeless (Jasper and Nelkin 1992). One hundred years ago, this dilemma caused considerable debate among the Marxists of the Second International.

The *Band-of-Brothers Dilemma* highlights the affective bonds crucial for keeping a movement together. The risk is that instead of identifying with the movement, individuals may bond with some smaller part. If you use the affective loyalties of personal networks to recruit people, they may retain primary loyalties to those other individuals, not the movement. An affinity group may decide to move from one issue or movement to another, just as many groups that had formed to fight civilian nuclear energy moved intact to the movement against nuclear weapons (Epstein 1985). Or two people may fall in love and withdraw into a private dyadic world (Goodwin 1997). Affective loyalties are an important glue for movements (Hirsch 1986), but they are hard for leaders to control and channel along the right paths. Arlie Hochschild pointed to a similar effect in her famous study of flight attendants (1983, 115): "Once established, team solidarity can have two effects. It can improve morale and thus improve service. But it can also become the basis for sharing grudges against the passengers or the company."

Coordination and alliances imply some division of labor, which inevitably means that some participants have more influence on decisions than others. One result of the structural paradigm has been to downplay the role of leaders in social movements in favor of aggrieved communities and recruitment networks (Barker, Johnson, and Lavalette 2001). In any research concerned with strategy, on the other hand, leaders return to center stage for they make most of the choices.

In the *Leadership Distance Dilemma*, should the leader be lofty and unique—a kind of superhuman saint—or a regular type, one of the guys? A leader may choose between lofty or colloquial rhetoric to indicate whether she is special or typical. The larger the movement or organization, the more important the Leadership Distance Dilemma becomes. One risk of elevating leaders is that subsequent revelations of their humanity may do great damage. Another risk is that successors will look inadequate. As Weber pointed out, charismatic leaders must be protected more than bureaucratic ones. Many leaders combine elements of the two, as in Ralph Nader's legendary simple lifestyle that made him seem even more saintly. The flip side of this combination is usually stubbornness, as we saw in the U.S. presidential elections of 2000. Another example is the simultaneous divinity and humanity of the paradigmatic charismatic as seen with the founder of one of the most successful religious movements in history, Jesus Christ.

The Ambitious-Leader Dilemma. We want strong and competent leaders. However, if they seem too ambitious, we worry that they may substitute their own goals for those of the group, in which case they become something like powerful allies instead of leaders (Michels [1915] 1962). This was the lesson that many American activists drew from the 1960s, when the media helped create stars like Jerry Rubin and Abbie Hoffman, who gained publicity but distorted the New Left's message in doing so (Gitlin 1980). Movements of the 1970s such as the antinuclear movement worked hard to keep prominent leaders like these from emerging (Epstein 1991). Like allies or the media, leaders become threatening to the extent they are powerful, thereby combining undesirable and desirable traits. They may pay too much attention to external audiences, for instance, at the expense of internal ones. In movement cultures that favor strong authority figures such as the religious right, leaders' ambitions may not pose the same dilemma as they do for more egalitarian movements as leaders are sometimes admired for their success even as they abandon the group's goals.

Others dilemmas are external, over how to have an impact on other players. I'll revisit briefly one central external dilemma—*Naughty or Nice*. Do you try to please those in authority or do you defy them, try to disrupt things, and break the laws and the norms (Jasper 2006b)? This is the classic strategic question that motivated Gamson, Piven and Cloward, and many others—a question that is still not fully resolved because, as a dilemma, it cannot be. For some groups, intimidation and disruption work. For others, they bring on the end of their own team. It is even possible for naughty actions to do both at the same time. Those who intimidate opponents into concessions may taint themselves in the process, sacrificing themselves as players but still gaining what they wanted. Scott Roeder, for instance, went to prison for murdering abortion provider George Tiller, but he also shut down the doctor's clinic.

Naughty techniques usually need specific and immediate goals. You can intimidate a corporation into recognizing a union or a legislature into passing a bill. However, the cost is in broader public opinion or in arousing a reaction from authorities. In other words, the short-run gain has to be important and relatively irreversible because there is usually long-run damage to your reputation. A lot of players have tried to work this dilemma by having a distinct radical flank that plays rough so that the mainstream can distance themselves from the extreme actions but perhaps still benefit from them—the bad cop alongside the good.

Of course, this just opens up a whole new field of struggle. Can you keep your distance, or does the whole team or coalition get branded as extremist? You have to work hard to manage public impressions. In a way, what a strategy of intimidation can do is split apart your opponents' coalition so that individuals or organizations defect because they're bearing too great a cost. The rest of the coalition will put a lot of pressure on them not to defect. A good example is the American antiabortion movement, which has scared more and more physicians away from performing abortions. The dangers, whether real or perceived, are just too high for a lot of doctors to face. And the pro-choice movement, at the same time, pressures them to keep practicing.

We rarely find a dilemma in its pure form. Most often, several dilemmas are woven together. For instance, *Naughty or Nice* frequently interacts with the *Extension Dilemma* over how large a team or alliance to build. The more extensive the team or alliance is, the more powerful it is, but also the more diversity it will have in both tastes in tactics and goals. Large teams are more likely to develop factions over many issues, but especially over favored tactics. The larger the team, the more likely there will be moderates and radicals, or those who favor nice tactics and those who favor naughty ones. Choices about who to include on your team are often choices about tactics because different groups and individuals favor different tactics.

Some dilemmas have to do with time, especially the short run versus the longer run—what I have called the *Today or Tomorrow Dilemma* (Jasper 2006b). The *Innovation Dilemma* is another time-oriented choice point especially relevant to those seeking social change (Jasper 2010). New strategic techniques can be especially effective as they catch other players off guard, but they have risks. For one, your own team may not be able to pull off the innovation because they themselves are not used to it either. With familiar tactics, you are at least aware of whether you have the know-how and the resources to carry them off. The dilemma also applies to changing cultural meanings. If you move too far, you are more likely to lose your audiences, but of course you don't get as far. If familiarity with your characteristic moves or meanings gives confidence to your opponents, it also reduces anxiety on your side. In trying some new line of action, you may overreach.

In addition to internal, external, and time dilemmas, there are dilemmas over means, over ends, and over trade-offs between means and ends. There are dozens of strategic trade-offs, dilemmas, and choices. The exact list is less important than the logic behind them. Further research, I hope, will tell us more about how various kinds of players recognize and deal with many different kinds of choice points. By examining the same dilemma as it is faced (or ignored) by various players, we can better understand how decisions are made and actions taken.

Emotional Batteries

Choices are obviously strategic, but so are emotions that permeate social and political life. I have also tried to catalog these into different types with different sources and effects (Jasper 2006a). Urges such as hunger, the need to sleep, and addiction tend to crowd out other goals. These goals are relatively unaffected by culture and are rarely the basis of political action. Reflexes tend to be quick to appear and quick to subside; they are the paradigm of universal "programmed emotions" (Ekman 1972), including anger, fear, joy, sadness, disgust, and surprise. Longer lasting than our urges or reflex emotions are our affective allegiances such as love, trust, and respect, along with their opposites. As Heise (1979) and others have shown, these attachments make up part of our culture. Moral sentiments such as pride, shame, compassion, and outrage are also part of our culture—feelings that we learn from those around us, and that deeply affect our politics. Finally, moods such as resignation, elation, or sadness lie somewhere between the short run and the long run. We carry them with us from one setting to another; they tend to change our level of energy for action in important ways. All these types of emotions, even urges, can affect our ability to carry out strategic action.

Some emotions are closely connected to goals. Others are more associated with means. Some are broadly mobilizing or demobilizing (Jasper 2006c). Affects provide many of our goals—punishing those we hate, helping those we love, avoiding those we fear.[5] Moral emotions are also a form of end, desired for their own sake. Moods primarily affect our means through our ability to act, although some moods are desired ends, such as the joy of collective effervescence (Collins 2004). Reflex emotions are also mostly about means and sometimes, in the case of fear and anger, prevent us from carrying out the actions necessary for achieving longer-term goals. Urges are immediate ends. As such, they too can derail the action necessary for other, long-term projects.

As just one example, I want to discuss moral emotions. These emotions differ from urges and reflex emotions although they are close to a kind of mood. As Spinoza argued, we do the right thing partly because it makes us feel good. In many ways, morality is an emotion—something we have lost sight of in the wake of Kant's stark distinction between the two. Morality consists of emotions of approval and disapproval. As William Gamson has pointed out, moral emotions are what really move people into action, even when they consist of negative impulses such as fear of disapproval or fear of sanctions.

The most obvious is indignation or outrage, the "hot cognitions" that motivate so much protest (Gamson 1992). These cognitions help trigger moral shocks when we find that the world is not living up to our moral expectations or when it is more threatening than what we had believed (Jasper 1997). Not all moral shocks lead to action, or at least action beyond tsk-tsking or complaining aloud. We need to find human agents to blame for what has happened, but even more, as a generation of scholars has demonstrated, we need to find the infrastructure for action. Sufficient moral shock may impel us to help create that infrastructure, to mobilize those resources, to absorb heavier costs, rather than just taking advantage of those that already exist. Scholars need to learn more about why some are willing to bear heavier burdens than others to right a wrong, just as organizers must learn to inspire that willingness.

A second common moral emotion is pride in doing the right thing and feeling good about participation. Deontological pride is what we feel and why we feel so good when we have done something morally sound or unusual. It may include some smugness as we compare ourselves to those we consider morally inferior, as well as some relief that we did not do the wrong thing even though we were tempted. Often, too, moral pride allows us to feel like agents rather than like victims. The promise of deontological pride helps get us involved in protest, and the satisfaction it delivers keeps us there, often despite enormous costs. Conversely, when we don't do what we believe to be right, we feel bad, ashamed. Activists try to find ways to shame people into action, often by suggesting that others are watching them. A central component of shame is this sense of being watched.

Less obvious is retribution—the satisfaction of setting things right, again often at great cost. Retribution can be simple revenge against those who have wronged us. Revenge is certainly one of the most common motivations in human history. Alternatively, retribution can be more abstractly a punishing of wrongdoers, a pride in justice. Exacting revenge is satisfying because it places us in the character of the hero—powerful, active, and good (Jasper and Young 2006). It reverses any victimhood we may have felt.

Running throughout these examples, and perhaps one of the basic dynamics of protest, is an interaction between negative emotions and positive; between a sense of threat, outrage, fear, and indignation on the one hand, and hope, joy, and thrill on the other. It's the contrast—the interplay between the good and the bad—that compels action, that gives a sense of urgency, and so on. Shame must become pride, resignation transformed into confidence. Wrongs must be righted.[6]

This dynamic is like a moral–emotional battery that, by separating positive and negative charges, gives us a shock—some energy that can help move us. It is the contrast between the positive and the negative states of affairs that propels us, or at least captures our imagination. We don't have to follow anthropologist Claude Lévi-Strauss in thinking that binary oppositions are hardwired into the human brain for us to recognize their power in capturing human choices and dilemmas. Emotional pairings like these are at the core of agency as they propel us from the present into the future (on the centrality of temporality to agency, see Emirbayer and Mische 1998). Jeffrey Alexander (2006) makes binaries of good and bad central to the rhetorical operations of the civic sphere.

These emotional dynamics are normally intentional and strategic. Activists carefully package words and images to shock others. Animal protectionists, for example, thoughtfully juxtapose gruesome images of animals in pain with happy stories of animals saved or animals living naturally in order to heighten the binary oppositions behind emotional batteries (Jasper and Poulsen 1995). Audiences, too, may train themselves to respond to certain rhetoric and imagery, developing the "right" sensibilities. There is pride in feeling the right way as well as in doing the right thing.

Conclusions

These are just several examples of the dozens or hundreds of strategic, emotional, cognitive, and moral mechanisms that we can find at the microlevel from which we can build up to bigger explanations. We start with something small—a decision taken at a meeting, a speech made to a crowd, the defection of a leader, individuals interacting with one another. From there, we trace some ramifications—the decision engages a group with other groups, the media, authorities, and others. Or the speech recruits new members, is framed in a certain way by the media (which consist of various strategic players too, such as reporters, editors, and owners, all with their own means and ends and routines). A defecting leader is transformed from a hero into a villain on one side, but on the other is portrayed as a convert to the light. Each of these actions leads to reactions and reactions in turn, in complex sequences that, although impossible to fully anticipate, are not impossible to trace. Scholars have not described these interactions because they have not looked for them.

If rational choice and game theories have long dominated strategy to the exclusion of culture, then culturally oriented scholars have too easily dismissed the building blocks game theory offers: players, arenas, choices. Humans are driven by both passion and purpose, and the two need to be combined in models of social movements. Creativity may lie at this intersection of passion and purpose as players improvise in the face of shifting interactions with others. They respond in new ways to old dilemmas.

With an awareness of what kinds of strategic trade-offs players might face, we are also able to see when decisions are not made, when routines are followed without debate. We can see when tastes in tactics make a group stick with the same means even though there are untried alternatives. We can see when hatred for opponents makes one goal (e.g., punishing them) more salient than attaining the original goals. We can see when opportunities for success or for recognition suddenly bring new goals or tactics to the fore. By describing potential choice points, scholars can offer activists a map of when to think about alternatives and thus innovations that might, in turn, give activists more creativity.

Many scholars will balk at the idea of hundreds of potential mechanisms. They cling to the old fantasy, often in modified form, of a general theory based on the hope that we can reduce reality to a handful of basic processes and structures. Instead, we need a tool kit approach in which we deploy a wealth of tools as needed. In this case, the more tools the better. What use is parsimony if it distorts our understanding of social movements? Movements are complex. Our tools should be too.

My focus on strategic agency is not meant as a Panglossian view that people can get what they want. On the contrary, I believe that too much research on social movements adopts an implicitly Whiggish vision of history in which progress eventually triumphs; technologies, affluence, human rights, political participation all spread together around the world, inexorably, despite occasional defeats. This is an inspiring political vision, to be sure. But it may be wrong. My focus on strategic dilemmas is meant to reflect a view of the world as more tragic, in which there are often no good choices, only least bad ones, in which oppression is as prominent as the battle against it, in which the best choices may not be good enough. Opponents of social justice, globally in the last thirty years, have exhibited more initiative and success than its supporters. Far from suggesting that protestors get what they want, a focus on strategic agency can explain why they rarely do. After all, authorities, opponents, and other players are equally striving to exert their own strategic agency. They usually have more resources and positions in arenas with which to do so.

I have tried to avoid talking about strategies in favor of strategic choices, actions, interactions, and so on. In business schools, strategies are simply long-term plans. In military usage, they are what is done in advance of the battle. Such devices are important enough, but what we need to focus on is the realm of interactions. These are strategic, not strategy.

With a strategic lens we can see people doing things, better see agency and constraints on it, see the actions of protestors and of other players equally, and see interactions that actually lead to various outcomes, bad as well as good. Attention to strategic agency at the microlevel seems to me the most promising way to bring together what we already know about protest, to make sure it is concrete and relevant, and to move research forward in promising directions. This volume should provide just that kind of push.

Notes

1. A strategic perspective, in my view, is rightly skeptical about concepts such as false consciousness or a third form of power that dismiss people's intentions.

2. Several recent writers have called for a relational approach, but this seems to me to structuralize interaction, portraying it as though it were trapped in an ongoing relationship of some sort. The term *interactive* allows for more agency. Daniel Cefaï (2007) does a thorough job of recovering our field's interactionist and pragmatist roots.

3. The idea of bounded rationality would have made these debates obsolete long ago had not rational choice theories revived them.

4. Sidney Tarrow's effort to portray aggregations (waves) as structures (cycles) seems to me to hide the causal mechanisms at work.

5. Different kinds of fear appear in different types. Some are reflexes. Others are abiding affects. Still others are moral in nature.

6. This is partly, in a way, a kind of updating and potential specification of old relative deprivation models.

References

Alexander, Jeffrey C. 2006. *The Civil Sphere*. New York: Oxford University Press.

Alexander, Jeffrey C., Bernhard Giesen, and Jason L. Mast, eds. 2006. *Social Performance: Symbolic Action, Cultural Pragmatics, and Ritual*. Cambridge: Cambridge University Press.

Alinsky, Saul. 1971. *Rules for Radicals: A Pragmatic Primer for Realistic Radicals*. New York: Random House.

Barker, Colin, Alan Johnson, and Michael Lavalette. 2001. *Leadership and Social Movements*. Manchester: Manchester University Press.

Campbell, Colin. 1996. *The Myth of Social Action*. Cambridge: Cambridge University Press.

Cefaï, Daniel. 2007. *Pourquoi se Mobilise-t-on? Les Théories de l'Action Collective*. Paris: Editions La Découverte.

Collins, Randall. 2004. *Interaction Ritual Chains*. Princeton, N.J.: Princeton University Press.

Ekman, Paul. 1972. *Emotion in the Human Face*. Elmsford, N.Y.: Pergamon.

Elster, Jon. 1998. "A Plea for Mechanisms." In *Social Mechanisms,* edited by Peter Hedström and Richard Swedberg, 45–73. Cambridge: Cambridge University Press.

———. 1999. *Alchemies of the Mind*. Cambridge: Cambridge University Press.

Emirbayer, Mustafa, and Anne Mische. 1998. "What Is Agency?" *American Journal of Sociology* 103:962–1023.

Epstein, Barbara. 1985. "The Culture of Direct Action." *Socialist Review* 82, no. 3: 31–61.

———. 1991. *Political Protest and Cultural Revolution*. Berkeley: University of California Press.

Fine, Gary Alan. 2001. *Difficult Reputations*. Chicago: University of Chicago Press.

Gamson, Joshua. 1995. "Must Identity Movements Self-Destruct?" *Social Problems* 42:390–407.

Gamson, William A. 1975. *The Strategy of Social Protest*. Homewood, Ill.: Dorsey Press.

———. 1992. *Talking Politics*. Cambridge: Cambridge University Press.

Ganz, Marshall. 2000. "Resources and Resourcefulness." *American Journal of Sociology* 105:1003–62.

Gitlin, Todd. 1980. *The Whole World Is Watching*. Berkeley: University of California Press.

Goodwin, Jeff. 1997. "The Libidinal Constitution of a High-Risk Social Movement: Affectual Ties and Solidarity in the Huk Rebellion." *American Sociological Review* 62:53–69.

Goodwin, Jeff, and James M. Jasper. 2006. "Emotions and Social Movements." In *Handbook of the Sociology of Emotions,* edited by Jan E. Stets and Jonathan H. Turner, 611–35. New York: Springer.

Hedström, Peter, and Richard Swedberg. 1998. *Social Mechanisms.* Cambridge: Cambridge University Press.

Heise, David. 1979. *Understanding Events.* Cambridge: Cambridge University Press.

Hirsch, Eric L. 1986. "The Creation of Political Solidarity in Social Movement Organizations." *Sociological Quarterly* 27:373–87.

Hochschild, Arlie. 1983. *The Managed Heart: Commercialization of Human Feeling.* Berkeley: University of California Press.

Jasper, James M. 1997. *The Art of Moral Protest.* Chicago: University of Chicago Press.

———. 2004. "A Strategic Approach to Collective Action: Looking for Agency in Social Movement Choices." *Mobilization* 9:1–16.

———. 2006a. "Motivation and Emotion." In *Oxford Handbook of Contextual Political Studies,* edited by Robert E. Goodin and Charles Tilly, 157–71. Oxford: Oxford University Press.

———. 2006b. *Getting Your Way: Strategic Dilemmas in Real Life.* Chicago: University of Chicago Press.

———. 2006c. "Emotions and the Microfoundations of Politics: Rethinking Ends and Means." In *Emotions, Politics and Society,* edited by Simon Clarke, Paul Hoggett, and Simon Thompson, 14–30. New York: Palgrave Macmillan.

———. 2010. "The Innovation Dilemma: Some Risks of Creativity in Strategic Agency." In *The Dark Side of Creativity,* edited by David H. Cropley, Arthur J. Cropley, James C. Kaufman, and Mark A. Runco, 91–113. Cambridge: Cambridge University Press.

Jasper, James M., and Dorothy Nelkin. 1992. *The Animal Rights Crusade.* New York: Free Press.

Jasper, James M., and Jane Poulsen. 1995. "Recruiting Strangers and Friends: Moral Shocks and Social Networks in Animal Rights and Antinuclear Protest." *Social Problems* 42:493–512.

Jasper, James M., and Michael Young. 2006. "Political Character Types: Defining Identities in Public Dramas." Paper presented at the annual meeting of the American Sociological Association, Montreal, August 11.

Koopmans, Ruud. 2003. "A Failed Revolution—But a Worthy Cause." *Mobilization* 8:116–19.

Lalich, Janja. 2004. *Bounded Choice: True Believers and Charismatic Cults.* Berkeley: University of California Press.

McAdam, Doug, Sidney Tarrow, and Charles Tilly. 2001. *Dynamics of Contention.* Cambridge: Cambridge University Press.

Michels, Robert. (1915) 1962. *Political Parties.* New York: Collier-Macmillan.

Polletta, Francesca. 2006. *It Was Like a Fever.* Chicago: University of Chicago Press.

Porter, Michael. 1980. *Competitive Strategy.* New York: Free Press.

Piven, Frances Fox, and Richard Cloward. 1977. *Poor People's Movements.* New York: Pantheon.

Smith, Christian. 2003. *Moral, Believing Animals.* Oxford: Oxford University Press.

Stinchcombe, Arthur L. 1991. "The Conditions of Fruitfulness of Theorizing about Mechanisms in Social Science." *Philosophy of the Social Sciences* 21:367–88.

Taylor, Charles. 1993. "To Follow a Rule . . ." In *Bourdieu: Critical Perspectives,* edited by Edward Lipuma, Moishe Postone, and Craig J. Calhoun, 45–60. Chicago: University of Chicago Press.

Wrong, Dennis. 1961. "The Oversocialized Conception of Man in Modern Sociology." *American Sociological Review* 26:183–93.

3

Three Mechanisms by Which Culture Shapes Movement Strategy: Repertoires, Institutional Norms, and Metonymy

Francesca Polletta

The problem for those who want to theorize the role of culture in strategy is this: how do you get at how culture limits movements' strategic options without representing activists as stupid, mystified, blind, or somehow limited in their ability to see strategic imperatives and opportunities that analysts can see? After all, if activists' beliefs are jeopardizing their success, why not just change those beliefs? This is not to say that activists aren't sometimes stupid, they aren't sometimes missing vital pieces of information, and they aren't susceptible to urban myths and sacred cows. That all goes without saying—for activists, just as the rest of us. The challenge, I believe, is to get at cultural constraints that operate no matter how smart and savvy activists are. Those constraints can be overcome, just as a deficit of funding or the demobilizing efforts of a repressive regime can be overcome. Often they are not overcome, however, with predictable consequences.

I suggest three analytical strategies for getting at how culture sets the terms of strategic action. *Collective action repertoires* are understandings shared by activists and authorities in a particular historical period about what strategies, tactics, and organizational forms are appropriate and effective. By tracing the rise and eclipse of particular repertoires, we can account for why strategies that seem obvious now simply were not obvious at other times. *Institutional norms of cultural expression* shape how activists make claims in diverse contexts—in court, to the media, in the legislature, and so on. Investigating those norms can help us to understand why activists are sometimes compelled to frame their message in ways that end up alienating potential participants or otherwise undermining their efforts. *Metonymy* is a figure of speech in which one word or image is invoked for another. Studying the emergence and operation of metonymies in activist groups' tactical discussions can shed light on the processes by which a tactical common sense is created—one that both opens up and forecloses options.

There are other ways to capture culture's constraining role. I choose to focus on repertoires, institutional norms, and the trope of metonymy because each one captures something that is easy to miss about how culture operates. Together, they help us to understand not only the formation of movement strategy, but also how culture operates inside and outside movements.

First, let me say what is wrong with how we tend to think about culture and strategy. When I say "we," I do not mean all of us all the time, but I think we are all guilty of it some of the time. We tend to see culture and strategy as opposed. Cultural commitments lead people to behave in ways that are consistent with their values. Strategic ones lead people to behave in ways that are instrumental in furthering their goals. A cultural commitment demands that you treat everyone as equals. A strategic one demands that you let the people who know better make the decisions. Culture dictates that if you are nonviolent, then you do not cut fences to enter and occupy a nuclear power plant site; strategy may dictate that you do. Activists juggle strategic commitments and cultural ones, sometimes favoring one, sometimes the other, and sometimes they are stymied by their inability to do simultaneously what is right and what is effective.

The problem with thinking about strategy this way is that it misses, first, the fact that culture can be strategic. This is not only in the sense that culture can be used strategically, á la theories of collective action framing, but also in the sense that cultural commitments can have instrumental benefits. For instance, a firm commitment to egalitarianism may, under certain conditions, serve to unify the group. A preference for a kind of cool, affectless rationality may legitimize the group in the eyes of some audiences (Einwohner 2002).

Seeing strategy and culture as opposed also misses the fact that what counts as strategic is cultural. Let me illustrate. In his sophisticated ethnographic account of the demise of the antinuclear Clamshell Alliance in the early 1980s, Gary Downey (1986) describes a split between people in the group he calls egalitarians, who were committed to strict consensus, and people he calls instrumentalists, who were willing to relax the requirement of strict consensus in the interests of political efficacy. The two sides clashed in a debate about whether to illegally occupy the Seabrook nuclear plant. According to Downey (1986, 370), some members "implicitly emphasized egalitarianism [at the expense of instrumentalism] . . . by arguing that a plant occupation was not successful if it did not produce a 'grassroots movement.'"

Why was galvanizing local activism seen as the expression of an egalitarian commitment rather than an instrumental one? In fact, Downey, tells us, initially it was not seen that way. The conflict between instrumentalists focused on stopping the construction of the Seabrook nuclear power plant, and egalitarians committed first to eradicating domination within their own ranks developed over time. Labeling the competing commitments as "instrumental" and "egalitarian" makes it difficult to see why galvanizing a local movement was considered at odds with an instrumental commitment. More important, the formulation obscures the shift through which the practices associated with an egalitarian commitment came to be seen as at odds with an instrumental one.

But here is the tricky part. We could just describe that shift, tracing activists' changing perceptions of what was strategic or ideological, what was a risk, and what was an opportunity. We could just describe how activists construct the rational. We want to do more, though. We want to explain why activists construct what is rational the way they do, and why those constructions change. We want to know why spurring grassroots mobilization was originally seen as strategic and came to be seen, by both sides in the debate, as ideological. Or why, to draw an example from my own work, consensus-based decision making, which in the early 1960s was seen as a practical organizing strategy, is now often seen as an ideological self-indulgence (Polletta 2006).

To better account for, rather than to simply describe, the role of culture in activists' strategic decision making, we need to pay fuller attention to the institutionalized *sources* of the understandings that shape activists' strategic decision making and to the observable *mechanisms* by which some options are ruled out and some ruled in. I say *institutionalized* sources because the culture that we use most is the culture that is familiar, that is part of the way we do things, conduct relationships, talk about politics, express emotions, and so on. The culture that matters is not free-floating, but rather anchored in familiar relationships, rules, and routines. I say *observable* mechanisms by which options are ruled in and ruled out to draw our attention to discursive and organizational processes instead of simply locating those mechanisms inside actors' heads.

Those are broad injunctions. Let me turn now to three analytical strategies, or more precisely, three loci of cultural constraint. Again, I focus on these three—repertoires, institutional norms, and the trope of metonymy—because they allow me to make three points about how we should study culture and strategic action, both in movements and more generally. The first is that we should resist thinking of culture as operating only at the level of micro-interaction. This is why repertoires are useful. The second is that we should resist thinking about culture only in terms of texts, rather than also rule-governed performances. This is where institutional norms are relevant. The third is that we should resist thinking about meaning as achieved through consistency and clarity. This is where metonymy is relevant.

Repertoires

In any given historical period, challengers are likely to make use of a limited range of strategies, tactics, and claims. As Charles Tilly (1999, 419) puts it,

> existing repertoires incorporate collectively-learned shared understandings concerning what forms of claim-making are possible, desirable, risky, expensive, or probable, as well as what consequences different possible forms of claim-making are likely to produce. They greatly constrain the contentious claims political actors make on each other and on agents of the state.

Repertoires are those shared understandings. Tilly insists that a repertoire is not a fixed menu of options. Rather, he emphasizes the extent to which claims that are considered realistic, appropriate, and effectual are developed through the interaction of challengers and authorities. Still, the fact that we can identify coherent sets of claims-making routines, which differ across historical periods—and which do not include other, hypothetically possible, routines—is evidence of cultural constraint.

What stands behind those repertoires? Why does one repertoire dominate rather than another? Tilly's (1998) answer, in the case of the emergence of a modern repertoire of protest in the nineteenth century, is that the state's relationship to its subjects changed. When the state's war-making projects required that it extract substantial resources from its subjects, it became a target, in turn, for subjects' demands. Protest became increasingly national, modular, and centered on electoral politics. Food riots and local skirmishes over taxation yielded to strikes and demonstrations in which people massed at formal seats of governmental power with banners and signs indicating their identity and interests. The electoral rally replaced the feast day processional, the formal meeting the charivari.

In Tilly's account, the national state played a critical role in establishing the repertoire of contention that subsequently bound both the state and protesters. In Michael Young's (2006) account of a later repertoire, in antebellum America, the state played virtually no role. More than 150 years before the so-called lifestyle politics of the new social movements, temperance reformers and abolitionists were encouraging citizens to publicly swear off the products of industries connected with the slave trade and to give emotional testimonials about the evils of drink at the same time as they fought to outlaw slavery and alcohol. Young attributes the rise of this "confessional mode of protest," a repertoire that fused bids for self- and social transformation, to the intersecting drives of two sets of religious institutions. In the 1830s, mainstream Protestant churches were creating a vast network of benevolent societies aimed at eradicating national sins like Sabbath breaking and drinking. Upstart Methodist sects were popularizing a revivalist style that focused on public confession. Reformers drew on these schemas of special sins and public confession to produce the first social movements in the United States with truly national scope.

The development of protest forms, strategies, targets, and issues associated with the rise of new digital technologies may be another new repertoire in the making. In this view, the Internet has made it easier to do the traditional tasks of mobilization, such as recruiting participants, staging demonstrations, communicating with the authorities, and so on. It has also changed what protest looks like in more fundamental ways (Bimber, Flanagin, and Stohl 2005; Earl and Kimport 2008; Shirky 2008; Yang 2009). The network logic of the Internet has become a model of and a model for transnational protest, Jeffrey Juris (2008) argues. An Internet-based logic is reflected in activists' preference for autonomy and diversity over unified fronts, horizontal coordination over centralized control, and temporary coalition over permanent organization. New digital technologies have not only helped activists to bridge the gap between radically democratic aspirations and the tactical demands of mobilization, but they have produced also political ideals in their own right.

Each of these accounts draws attention to the emergence of a distinctive way of protesting—to historically new claims, strategies, organizational forms, and targets. They attribute the emergence of new repertoires to diverse historical developments—in Tilly's account, to the centralization of the nation-state, and with it the need for citizens' allegiance; in Young's account, to the institutional needs of two major religious denominations; in the diverse accounts of the rise of Internet mobilization, to the spread of new communications technologies.

Repertoires pattern mobilization; they constrain activists' strategic and tactical options. Just how they do that is not yet clear. Tilly's answer was that activists are always innovating, always pushing at the boundaries of given repertoires. The boundaries kick in where authorities declare performances illegal or otherwise impermissible. At a time of rapidly changing political opportunity, those holding power are likely to enforce rigid repertoires, and challengers to develop more flexible ones (Tilly 2006). This is probably right, but there is also undoubtedly more to activists' assessment of where the line between acceptable and unacceptable lies. For one thing, activists' ability to predict authorities' response likely varies. Douglas Bevington (2009) shows that the major environmental organizations were unwilling to engage in controversial litigation in the 1980s because they feared losing influence with congressional policy makers whom they lobbied on environmental policy. However, when outsider biodiversity groups pursued such litigation and won, it proved not to be at the cost of favorable congressional actions. In other words, the major groups' proximity to policy makers may have led them to misjudge the risks of challenge.

Activists' understandings of what is appropriate are also likely shaped in relation to groups other than authorities—other activists, for example. One can imagine that in the new environment of horizontally networked transnational protest that Juris describes, top-down, centralized organizations have a rough time recruiting young people, even though such organizations may be more effective and, in some cases, more democratic, than determinedly horizontal ones (Polletta 2002). In short, we need a better understanding of how activists themselves produce the line between the inside and the outside of a prevailing repertoire (see, for an example of such an understanding, Connell and Voss 1990). We also need a better understanding of how repertoires change over time (e.g. Clemens 1996; Steinberg 1999). When are repertoire innovations incremental, and when are they more radical? Finally, in addition to repertoires of claims-making strategies, we should pay attention to how appropriate emotional motivations for protest spread, producing, again, not just one episode of protest or even one movement, but potentially a variety of them (Haskell 1985a, 1985b).

Although some of these questions require more microlevel analysis of how activists appraise tactical options, one of the virtues of the concept of repertoire is that it encourages macrolevel analysis. The emphasis is less on a single movement or movement organization's decision making than on how logics of collective action spread across issues, groups, and regions. The concept of repertoires encourages us to pay attention to diverse movements operating at the same time (Haskell 1985a, 1985b; Young 2006), to relations over time between movements and authorities (Tilly 2006), and to the logics or schemas underpinning geographically dispersed episodes of claims making (Wood 2007; Juris 2008).

Institutional Norms

A second analytical strategy for getting at cultural constraint focuses not on texts but on performances, and more specifically, on the norms of cultural performance. The argument here is that culture constrains not by limiting what people can think but by limiting what they can say. Institutional conventions of cultural expression and evaluation shape the claims one can easily make. Institutional conventions are the rules for interacting within a particular setting such as a court, a college seminar, or a scientific lab meeting. Some conventions are formalized; others are not. For example, a judge can tell a story in court; a defendant may be penalized for doing so. A plaintiff in small claims court may be encouraged to tell a personal story and then penalized nonetheless because her story does not demonstrate the clear lines of cause and effect that judges, even small claims court judges, expect (Conley and O'Barr 1990).

Routines of news reporting, courtroom interaction, fund-raising appeals, and talk show performance encourage activists to present some complaints and not others; to invoke certain kinds of justifications; to display certain emotions; and to present certain people as spokespersons. In her study of activism by adult survivors of child abuse, Nancy Whittier (2001) found that when survivors gathered in movement conferences and at marches, speakers told stories of personal fortitude. They described fear and self-loathing yielding to grief, anger, and finally to the strength that came from casting off shame. With titles like "Sing Loud, Sing Proud," and "Courageous—Always Courageous," movement magazine articles and workshops encouraged participants to emphasize their recovery rather than the details of their abuse. When survivors appeared in court, however, they were encouraged to focus on the fear, grief, shame, and hurt produced by their abuse. These kinds of emotional performances were required, Whittier writes, to prove that the survivor was a victim deserving of compensation. Advice articles in movement magazines warned those going to court that the experience would be demeaning. They should be prepared to tell their stories in the ways expected of them and should avoid betraying their anger or pride, but should also find outlets outside court in which to tell other parts of their story. On television talk shows, another place in which child abuse activists appeared frequently in the 1980s, survivors focused more on the abuse and its traumatizing effects than on the survivor's eventual recovery. Accompanied by therapists, guests often cried while clutching stuffed animals or speaking in childlike voices.

Whittier argues that by eliciting pity and horror in audiences, survivors' stance on talk shows may have made it more difficult for audiences to identify with them. By representing themselves as passive and powerless (an image reinforced by the presence of therapists), survivors may have repelled others suffering from abuse who might have been mobilized by expressions of focused anger and stories of personal overcoming.

Certainly, one can refuse the conventions of cultural performance. Survivors could have been angry on talk shows and prideful in courtroom hearings. But doing so would have been risky. Culture shapes strategy in the sense that abiding by the rules of cultural expression yields more calculable consequences than challenging them. For example, feminists who brought workplace discrimination suits in the 1980s were encouraged to put women on the stand who could testify to their experience of aspiring to a higher-paying but traditionally masculine job and not getting it. This was despite the fact that individual stories could not demonstrate *patterns* of disparate treatment. Feminists could have refused to frame their claims in terms of individuals' experiences of discrimination. However, when they did, they were much more likely to lose their cases (Schultz 1990). Judges sometimes berated them for just that. A judge in the famous Sears case said the plaintiffs might have won if they had produced "even a handful of witnesses to testify that Sears had frustrated their childhood dreams of becoming commission sellers" (Schultz 1990, 1809).

What was wrong with having individual women testify to their experiences of discrimination? It was not only that activists had to sign onto a strategy that was fundamentally illogical. By arguing that women had the same aspirations as men, aspirations that were frustrated by sexist managers, plaintiffs also left unchallenged the idea that aspirations are only shaped in childhood rather than shaped in the labor market and by how a job is advertised. Why would a woman think herself eligible for a job that was presented as a man's job? That was the question that plaintiffs should have been able to ask, but were not.

It is hardly surprising, moreover, that conventions of cultural expression enter into activists' own tactical calculations. The animal rights activists whom Julian Groves (2001) studied discouraged women from serving in leadership positions because they believed that women were seen by the public as prone to emotionalism. That would cost the movement credibility. Activists spent little time debating whether women were in fact prone to emotionalism, however, or whether emotional accounts were more or less effective than rational arguments. Their calculations were strategic, but they were based on gendered assumptions about reason and emotion. The anti–gulf war activists observed by Stephen Hart (2001) relied on a pragmatic, nuts-and-bolts style in their internal discussions. Discussions of participants' personal commitments or broad ideological visions were effectively ruled out of order. However, this constrained discursive style served them less effectively than did the expansive discourse characteristic of faith-based organizing groups, in which participants' ethical commitments were threaded through all discussions. Ironically, a discourse valued for its pragmatism proved less effective than one valued for its moral depth.

Are activists dumb if they don't recognize that discussions of faith and principle build commitment to the cause? That nuts-and-bolts tactical discussions are boring? That emotional appeals can be effective? They are not dumb; however, they are in some ways averse to risk. Activists have a stake in hewing to convention where it serves them and challenging it where it does not serve them. Aside from the fact that the conventional can easily seem natural, the conventional also yields predictable results. Challenging the norms of cultural expression, however necessary to securing real change, is a gamble.

Metonymy

Although I shifted in the last section from talking about cultural constraints operating out there in institutional norms to talking about how activists conceptualized those constraints in their internal discussions, I want to move now to an even more microinteractional level at which culture operates: in conversation. Observable conversational mechanisms operate to advantage some tactical options over others. In the absence of those mechanisms, we can assume, additional options would be available. Let me talk about metonymy, one such mechanism.

Metonymy is common figure of speech whereby one word or image is invoked for another. So we might refer to a decision made by "the crown" rather than the king, or describe journalists as "the press." Often, the object used in a metonymic relation denotes a whole cluster of objects. So when we say, "Washington is wary of recent Palestinian moves," we do not have a single person or organization in mind but rather a cluster of organizations that together represent Washington—State Department and national security officials, congressional representatives, the president, perhaps the pundits who comment on national affairs. Metonymy is similar to metaphor in involving the substitution of one thing for another. The difference, according to standard literary theory, is that in metonymy, the relationship between the two things is conventional, already known. Kings wear robes, but we don't refer to a decision handed down by "the robe." The use of metonymy indicates that the relationship between the two objects—the one referred to and the one or ones denoted—has taken on the status of common sense.

What makes metonymy useful for students of movements is that its use in movement groups' tactical decision making sheds light on how cultural associations shape strategy (Polletta 2006). We know that movement groups adopt targets, tactics, and strategies not only because they have a good likelihood of being effective and because they are consistent with the group's express ideological commitments, but also, often, because they are symbolically associated with people or things that are attractive for other reasons, or are symbolically opposed to people or things that are unattractive for other reasons.

Sometimes groups are explicit about the role of symbolic association. For example, feminists are often self-conscious in their rejection of bureaucratic organizational forms on account of the masculinist associations of such forms. However, many times the symbolic associations that shape strategic choice operate more implicitly. The emergence of metonymic structures in activists' discussions should alert us to the fact that such associations have become commonsensical. For example, when union officials in the 1960s farm workers' movement considered the possibility of launching boycotts and marches, they rejected such tactics as "not the union way" (Ganz 2000). "Union way" stood metonymically for a variety of things: political secularism; an unwillingness to engage in moral and emotional appeals; most importantly, an approach that was not that of the civil rights movement or a religious campaign. However, the effect of that metonymic association was to refuse tactics that could have energized the labor movement.

Of course, such associations can be challenged, and sometimes they are. Doing so is risky, though. As a kind of shorthand, metonymies both assume the existence of a group for whom the shorthand makes sense, and they signal membership in the group. That makes them difficult to challenge because to do so can be interpreted as a sign of one's ignorance and possibly one's insecure place in the group. It is always possible to think outside canonical narratives and the tropes on which they rest. To articulate those alternatives is risky, whether in a congressional hearing or in a group of like-minded activists.

As another example, in the early years of the militant Southern civil rights group, the Student Nonviolent Coordinating Committee (SNCC), making decisions by consensus and rotating leadership was seen as a practical organizing tool, a way to train people for political leadership (Polletta 2006). It was also seen as a distinctively Southern black strategy, in contrast to the parliamentary style characteristic of Northern white activist groups. Its Southern black associations were part of its appeal to Northern white New Leftists. Between 1964 and 1965, however, consensus-based, nonhierarchical decision making—participatory democracy—came to be seen as impractical, ideological, and self-indulgent. This was neither because SNCC's instrumental needs changed nor because its formal ideological commitments changed—two explanations that have been commonly offered. In SNCC workers' discussions during this period, participatory democracy increasingly came to be metonymically associated with the group's programmatic morass and with the dominance in the organization of Northern whites. I say metonymically associated because no one actually said how a more centralized organization would generate programmatic ideas. In fact, one could make a plausible case that a decentralized and nonhierarchical structure promoted the individual initiative that had been the source of SNCC's best ideas. Rather, at a time when the group was both desperate for effective direction and increasingly uncomfortable with the group's white membership, organizational structure stood in for these thorny problems. People did occasionally challenge the association of participatory democracy with programmatic paralysis on the one hand and the domination of whites on the other. They tended to be responded to in one of two ways, however. Either their challenges were ignored and discussion simply moved on, or challengers were seen as defending whites, whether themselves or other whites.

Metonymies can operate benignly, of course. However, they often have the effect of limiting the array of options worth considering. For SNCC workers, and, I argue, for activists long after, participatory democracy came to be seen as principled rather than pragmatic, aimed at personal self-liberation rather than political change, and white rather than black. The explicitly political benefits of the form were lost.

In a similar way, the alternative health care workers whom Sherryl Kleinman (1996) studied insisted that meetings of their collective should be recorded in careful minutes, even though no one actually ever used or referred to the minutes, because doing so was a sign that they were a serious organization. As a result, they ended up spending a great deal of energy demonstrating that they were like the mainstream organizations they explicitly disavowed. When anticorporate globalization activists today dismiss twinkling (wiggling one's fingers in agreement with a speaker) and vibe watchers in consensus decision making as Californian—that is, as apolitical and unconcerned with effective change—they foreclose the question of whether such techniques might in fact speed up decision making. In sum, tracing the establishment of metonymic structures in tactical debates can help us to understand how a tactical common sense is created and how it then shuts down possibilities as well as opening them up.

Conclusion

How do we get at the role of culture in shaping strategic possibilities without representing activists as strategic dopes or ideological dupes? Assume that, like the rest of us, activists are rational, creative, and practical. But, also like the rest of us, they are, among other things, more comfortable with the familiar than the unfamiliar, attuned to the norms of the institutional settings in which they operate, and fearful of seeming out of the loop in front of people they respect. The virtue of each of the concepts I have outlined is that they alert us to the institutionalized sources of the culture that shapes strategy and to the mechanisms by which it does so—*repertoires* by demonstrating broad historical variation in the use of strategies; *institutional norms* by drawing attention to the trade-offs that activists face in challenging convention; and *metonymy* by showing how cultural associations and oppositions are turned into common sense.

These are not the only ways that culture shapes strategic action—in addition, that is, to activists' formal principled commitments. We can talk instead about tastes in tactics (Jasper 1997); about logics of appropriateness (Clemens 1996); about linguistic tropes such as enthymemes (Feldman and Skoldberg 2002); about social epistemologies of emotions (Polletta 2001). Some of these concepts overlap with the ones I have been describing; they operate variously at macro-, meso-, and microlevels; and they, too, have the virtue of directing attention to the observable mechanisms by which culture limits not what people can aspire to, but what they can easily say.

This does not mean that challenges to mainstream culture always, willy-nilly, reproduce the status quo. Rather, for activists, the punch line is that important targets for movement work may be easily missed. Here is one: rather than only trying to challenge meaning, activists should challenge the social organization of meaning—the standards that define what counts as authoritative meaning. In his study of activism around AIDS, Steven Epstein (1996) shows that activists succeeded in gaining formal representation on federal research review committees. Just as important, they also gained recognition for AIDS patients' personal accounts of their illnesses as authoritative knowledge in drug research. Refusing the conventional antinomies of subjective and objective knowledge, reason and emotion, and science and folklore, they sought and won legitimacy for personal experience as a form of authoritative knowledge. In a similar vein, activists might work to gain authority for storytelling in contexts where statistics are called for and to gain authority for statistics where storytelling is expected.

The other target for movement work—and this is less banal than it seems—is the metonymies that structure activists' own tactical common sense. All groups engage in shorthand, and group shorthands are as much about signaling membership as expediting tasks. The challenge is to ensure that such shorthands do not have the effect of trading scrutiny for unity, challenge for being in the know.

The message for people who study activism is that paying attention to culture does not mean trading explanation for description. It does not mean focusing only on microinteraction at the expense of the large forces and structures that people confront. It does not mean treating people simply as vehicles of cultural tropes that are beyond their control. Rather, it sheds light on important dynamics both of innovation and constraint—dynamics that operate outside movements as well as in them.

References

Bevington, Douglas. 2009. *The Rebirth of Environmentalism: Grassroots Activism from the Spotted Owl to the Polar Bear.* Washington, D.C.: Island Press.

Bimber, Bruce, Andrew J. Flanagin, and Cynthia Stohl. 2005. "Reconceptualizing Collective Action in the Contemporary Media Environment." *Communication Theory* 15:365–88.

Clemens, Elisabeth. 1996. "Organizational Form as Frame: Collective Identity and Political Strategy in the American Labor Movement, 1880–1920." In *Comparative Perspectives on Social Movements: Political Opportunities, Mobilizing Structures, and Cultural Framings,* edited by Doug McAdam, John D. McCarthy, and Mayer N. Zald, 205–26. New York: Cambridge University Press.

Conley, John M., and William M. O'Barr. 1990. *Rules versus Relationships: The Ethnography of Legal Discourse.* Chicago: University of Chicago Press.

Connell, Carol, and Kim Voss. 1990. "Formal Organizations and the Fate of Social Movements: Craft Association and Class Alliance in the Knights of Labor. *American Sociological* Review 55:255–69.

Downey, Gary L. 1986. "Ideology and the Clamshell Identity: Organizational Dilemmas in the Anti–Nuclear Power Movement." *Social Problems* 33:357–71.

Earl, Jennifer, and Katrina Kimport. 2008. "The Targets of Online Protest: State and Private Targets of Four Online Protest Tactics." *Information, Communication and Society* 11:449–72.

Einwohner, Rachel L. 2002. "Bringing the Outsiders In: Opponents' Claims and the Construction of Animal Rights Activists' Identity." *Mobilization* 7:253–68.

Epstein, Steven. 1996. *Impure Science: AIDS, Activism, and the Politics of Knowledge.* Berkeley: University of California Press.

Feldman, Martha, and Kaj Skoldberg. 2002. "Stories and the Rhetoric of Contrariety: Subtexts of Organizing (Change)." *Culture and Organization* 8:275–92.

Ganz, Marshall. 2000. "Resources and Resourcefulness: Strategic Capacity in the Unionization of California Agriculture, 1959–1966." *American Journal of Sociology* 105:1003–62.

Groves, Julian. 2001. "Animal Rights and the Politics of Emotion: Folk Constructions of Emotion in the Animal Rights Movement." In *Passionate Politics: Emotions and Social Movements,* edited by Jeff Goodwin, James M. Jasper, and Francesca Polletta, 212–29. Chicago: University of Chicago Press.

Hart, Stephen. 2001. *Cultural Dilemmas of Progressive Politics: Styles of Engagement among Grassroots Activists.* Chicago: University of Chicago Press.

Haskell, Thomas. 1985a. "Capitalism and the Origins of the Humanitarian Sensibility, Parts 1 and 2." *American Historical Review* 90:339–61.

———. 1985b. "Capitalism and the Origins of the Humanitarian Sensibility, Part 3." *American Historical Review* 90:547–66.

Jasper, James M. 1997. *The Art of Moral Protest: Culture, Biography, and Creativity in Social Movements.* Chicago: University of Chicago Press.

Juris, Jeffrey S. 2008. *Networking Futures: The Movements against Corporate Globalization.* Durham, N.C.: Duke University Press.

Kleinman, Sherryl. 1996. *Opposing Ambitions: Gender and Identity in an Alternative Organization.* Chicago: University of Chicago Press.

Polletta, Francesca. 2001. "The Laws of Passion." *Law and Society Review* 35:467–93.

———. 2002. *Freedom is an Endless Meeting: Democracy in American Social Movements.* Chicago. University of Chicago Press.

———. 2006. *It Was Like a Fever: Storytelling in Protest and Politics.* Chicago: University of Chicago Press.

Schultz, Vicki. 1990. "Telling Stories about Women and Work: Judicial Interpretations of Sex Segregation in the Workplace in Title VII Cases Raising the Lack of Interest Argument." *Harvard University Law Review* 103:1749–843.

Shirky, Clay. 2008. *Here Comes Everybody: The Power of Organizing without Organizations.* New York: Penguin.

Steinberg, Marc. 1999. *Fighting Words: Working-Class Formation, Collective Action, and Discourse in Early Nineteenth-Century England.* Ithaca, N.Y.: Cornell University Press.

Tilly, Charles. 1998. *Popular Contention in Great Britain, 1758–1834.* Cambridge, Mass.: Harvard University Press.

———. 1999. "Now Where?" In *State/Culture: State-Formation after the Cultural Turn,* edited by G. Steinmetz, 407–20. Ithaca, N.Y.: Cornell University Press.

———. 2006. *Regimes and Repertoires.* Chicago: University of Chicago Press.

Whittier, Nancy. 2001. "Emotional Strategies: The Collective Reconstruction and Display of Oppositional Emotions in the Movement against Child Sexual Abuse." In *Passionate Politics: Emotions and Social Movements,* edited by Jeff

Goodwin, James M. Jasper, and Francesca Polletta, 233–50. Chicago: University of Chicago Press.

Wood, Lesley J. 2007. "Breaking the Wave: Repression, Identity and the Seattle Tactics." *Mobilization* 12:377–88.

Yang, Guobin. 2009. *The Power of the Internet in China: Citizen Activism Online.* New York: Columbia University Press.

Young, Michael. 2006. *Bearing Witness against Sin: The Evangelical Birth of the American Social Movement.* Chicago: University of Chicago Press.

II
Activist Engagement and Movement-Relevant Research

4

Raising Public Awareness of Domestic Violence: Strategic Communication and Movement Building

Charlotte Ryan, Karen Jeffreys, and Linda Blozie

In mass-mediated societies, social movement organizers augment direct organizing with media and other public relations work, hoping that increased visibility will reinforce strategic alliances, influence public attitudes, and, subsequently, forward desired changes in social institutions. Scholars have documented recurring obstacles that social movement organizers confront when attempting to communicate via mainstream media. Drawing on our sustained organizer–scholar collaboration, we map movement–media interactions on a mesolevel to develop a participatory and dialogic approach to communication that supports movement building (Barker-Plummer 1996).

We first explain how reflective organizers with the Rhode Island Coalition against Domestic Violence (RICADV) and activist–scholars in the Movement and Media Research Action Project (MRAP) established a working relationship. We review recognized obstacles to mass media movement interaction then outline three common U.S. models of movement–media public relations: independent media, social marketing, and media advocacy. We focus on social marketing and media advocacy and describe these models' distinct and shared deficiencies, highlighting their limited sense of agency— a curious failing because social movements intend to increase agency.

We then trace our collaborative efforts to integrate insights from social movement theory into the existing models to produce a more effective model of strategic communication that we call participatory communication for social change. We note the commonalities between our participatory model and Freirian-based participatory communication practices in the Global South. Scholars have long assumed that social movements might benefit from greater familiarity with social movement theories; we demonstrate that collaboration between social movement organizers and scholars can enhance both social movement theorizing and practice.

Media, Public Relations, and Communication

Media is "the space of politics in the information age," says social theorist Manuel Castells (2004, 371). Recognizing this, social movement organizers in mass-mediated societies often integrate public relations strategies into organizing strategies in hope that increased visibility will reinforce existing strategic alliances and influence public attitudes. Deeper and broader support, they expect, will strengthen their organizing for social and political changes.

Systemic obstacles, however, complicate organizers' efforts to communicate with their publics via mainstream media (Herman and Chomsky 1988; Croteau and Hoynes 1994, 2001; Herman and McChesney 1997). Although organizers recognize the barriers to routine media access, they hesitate to give opponents free reign in such an important arena. They operate from the "hope . . . at least of breaking the appearance of unanimity which is the greater part of the symbolic force of the dominant discourse" (Bourdieu 1999, viii).[1] To some, public relations may appear a minor variation on movement–media interaction. In fact, public relations is far more comprehensive than media, encompassing all efforts to relate to one's publics. After constructing their organization's internal communication systems (meetings, minutes, newsletters, Listservs), organizers consider venues for communicating with publics targeted in the movement's overall organizing strategy. The mix of selected venues is both constituency and issue specific. In some organizing campaigns, organizers may prefer to communicate via face-to-face meetings, lobbying days, e-mail, phone, or Internet, as well as to piggyback on other communication networks (Castells 2004). For other campaigns, organizers may disseminate information via temples, mosques, or church bulletins of sympathetic religious communities. An organizer's public relations toolbox also includes demonstrations, vigils, picket lines, festivals, marching bands,[2] and other forms of public display. These means of relating to publics are valuable communication in their own right, but they also stimulate mass media coverage. Interestingly, mainstream public relations practitioners increasingly appropriate word-of-mouth communication tactics that have long been movement strong suits (Levison, Frishman, and Lublin 2002; Parsons, Maclaran, and Tadajewski 2008).

In keeping with communication studies (Heath 2004), we conceptualize public relations as the building of working relationships with strategically targeted publics—in other words, allies, potential allies, or institutional figures to be influenced. So conceived, public relations is central to what organizers do. They build sustainable networks, create collective experiences, and foster the flow of ideas, emotions, and other resources. To support this work, organizers establish appropriate communication infrastructure, including media databases, strategic communication and media plans, messaging caucuses, framing and evaluation tools, and phone and e-mail protocols. Taken as a whole, this communication infrastructure systematizes how organizers talk politics—that is, how they engage in dialogue with targeted publics. "It's like a bread slicer," mused Angela Nash-Wade, RICADV's outreach coordinator and a veteran organizer in both the civil rights and women's movements. "After you've seen it work, you wonder, 'How did we ever do this before?'"

Movement public relations, in sum, is not an end in itself. Rather, it supports strategic movement building—the intentional, focused networking and accumulation of relationships and resources in service of a shared social and political agenda. This broader understanding of communication permeates communication studies[3] and is reflected in social movement studies. Ferree et al. (2002, 20), for instance, fold media opportunity into the broader concept of "discursive opportunity."

We build on a decade of scholar–activist collaboration between the RICADV and MRAP. We wanted to address the power inequalities in mass media systems—inequalities insufficiently addressed by the two approaches to public relations commonly used by U.S. social movement organizations: social marketing and media advocacy. To that end, we developed and tested a participatory model of movement–media interaction.

Our synthesis draws from studies of independent media, from structural and cultural critiques of market-driven mass media (Barker-Plummer 1995, 1996; Frey and Carragee 2007), and from participatory communication strategies common in the Global South (Riaño 1994). The resulting strategic public relations model applies our general worldview of consistent democracy within the mass media arena.

We first review how U.S. activists have conceptualized movement communication in a media-saturated society. We describe, contrast, and critique social marketing and media advocacy approaches in some depth. We next sketch our successful collaboration, extracting from our reflexive practice a dialogic and participatory model that addresses existing models' limits. The resulting movement-building approach to communication draws from three traditions. From cultural studies and political economic analyses, we incorporate the sensitivity to power inequalities. We integrate radical media's signature attention to autonomy, internal democracy, and commitment to giving voice to those directly affected by inequality. To these two elements, we add media studies' attention to mass media as a historically specific institutional arena with its own dynamics, routines, discourse, and norms. Social marketing and media advocacy communication models have excelled at applying this institution-specific knowledge.

We first construct, in other words, an egalitarian, participatory, dialogic communication platform, making it the basis of our own communication with each other. Then we add to this foundation social marketing and media advocacy practices. The resulting model has built-in tensions that we elaborate on throughout the chapter, and we turn our concentrated attention to them in the final pages.

The Collaborators and Their Methods

In 1985–86, a small group of Boston-based graduate students and faculty studying movement–media interaction formed the Movement and Media Research Action Project. In our first years, we attempted to develop exchanges that translated existing movement research into communication tools for movements, with framing being the most salient example. Simultaneously, we began to combine research for social movement groups with teaching and service. We also interviewed social movement activists about their communication efforts, integrating added insights into writing and workshops (Ryan 1991, 1996; Gamson and Goodson 2000). Eventually, we crafted a mission statement that read, "MRAP works with underrepresented and misrepresented communities to identify and challenge barriers to democratic communication, develop proactive messages and strategies, and build ongoing communications capacity."

Over time, MRAP has evolved into a collective actor in its own right. Although many MRAP members published in scholarly venues and worked in academic departments, in our collective persona as MRAP, we worked for social movements, forming partnerships to bridge the usual university–community divides. When we act as MRAP, we become more than an aggregate of individuals with shared interests. We work as a small collective actor implementing our mission via our social practice—thinking, collaborating, and reflecting as a conscious change agent in concert with movement partners.

In its first decade, MRAP ran workshops with over 200 organizations. It had taken between five and seven years for the more successful movement organizations to establish the communication capacity that in turn strengthened their media standing. We decided, therefore, to focus on organizations able to commit the time and resources necessary to build their media capacity. One of these organizations was the statewide RICADV, whose lead organizer, Karen Jeffreys, had collaborated previously with MRAP's codirector, Charlotte Ryan.

Born of the women's movement, the RICADV works to end domestic violence in its state.[4] In 1996, Jeffreys joined RICADV as its communication coordinator, joining an able team of organizers—outreach coordinator Angela Nash-Wade, civil rights activist and filmmaker Alice Trimieu, and popular educator Zulma Garcia. These seasoned organizers shared an ideology of consistent democracy with three core values—equality, diversity, and respect—that formed the basis of a working culture by which they governed themselves internally and related to allies and reporters. By the end of 2002, seven years after we began to work to systematize communication, RICADV dominated its media market. In other words, the coalition had developed the media capacity needed to gain media standing. Conducting a content analysis of shifting coverage of domestic violence murders over that seven-year period, MRAP was able to measure RICADV's rising media standing quantitatively (Ryan, Anastario, and Jeffreys 2005).

Documenting RICADV's rise in media standing was a mutually beneficial goal. RICADV wanted to know whether its efforts had measurable impact; this would influence how we utilized our labor power. Tangible gains would also boost RICADV's ability to attract resources from government and foundations. MRAP wanted to know whether our models of media–movement interaction worked. If a social movement actor established a sophisticated, sustainable intervention manipulating the norms and dynamics of the media arena, could they gain standing in journalists' eyes as a reliable, valued, and trusted source? At what cost?

To measure changes in media standing and in media capacity, we looked for ways to collect data that would meet academic standards yet be convenient, useful, and interesting for RICADV. We ultimately agreed on several methods that can be adapted by other theorist–activist teams.[5] We hired a service to clip all news coverage containing trigger phrases such as "domestic violence," "domestic abuse," and "battering" (RICADV selected the phrases). To measure media standing, RICADV and MRAP interns coded the articles, noting sources used and their relative location in each article. A rise in the use of RICADV-related sources and/or a rise in their location constituted a rise in media standing. A second measure of media standing was content specific. At RICADV, Jeffreys filed all press releases and advisories. By comparing advisories against resulting news coverage, MRAP could document whether RICADV's frame was being used. Rising utilization of RICADV's frame also represented rising media standing. To measure media capacity, we used a similar measure; we tracked the growth in RICADV's media database. Increased database size and the frequency of reporter contact—both variables that RICADV chose to study—measured rising media capacity.

RICADV and MRAP also both wanted to know which RICADV communication practices had produced rising standing as measured in news coverage. To do this, however, we needed to be able to see how RICADV actually conducted media work. We crafted yet another collaborative method to accomplish this. Taking a campaign focus, MRAP and RICADV participants constructed case studies of successful media campaigns using meeting minutes, press releases, and news coverage to identify all participants and to establish a time line. The resulting collaborative history traced RICADV's media planning and communication practices, measuring these against news outcomes. Our sustained partnership allowed us to see how growth accrued over time.

Movement–Media Interaction: Lessons from Literatures

Mass media form our time's "master forum—*the* major site of contest politically" (Gamson 1998, 59). If media coverage is critical for establishing and advancing political and social agendas (Edelman 1988; Curran 2002; Alimi 2007a; Castells 2007; Graber 2007), then inequalities in media access and control threaten the future of democracy (Herman 1995; Aufderheide 1999; McChesney 1999; Gans 2003).

Over the last half century, media systems have become ever more tightly bound to the market-driven imperatives of a transnational economy (Herman and McChesney 1997; McChesney 1999; Croteau and Hoynes 1994, 2001). In the case of media, this is doubly problematic in that those controlling media rationalize other social inequalities (Schiller 1996; Herman and McChesney 1997; McChesney 1999; Kellner 2005).

Recognizing media as the staging ground for political battles, politicians and others jockey over "agenda setting, policy enactment and implementation and the acquisition of political power" (Andrews 2002, 106). Journalists act as gatekeepers, choosing which ideas and debates gain traction (Bennett 1990) and who gains status as a reliable source (Gans 1979; Soley 1992). Movement organizers, although operating from the challenged end of the power spectrum, also seek media attention to increase visibility for their social and political change objectives (Gitlin 1980; Ryan 1991; Rohlinger 2002; Shepard and Hayduk 2002; Morris and Staggenborg 2004; Alimi 2007b). Although clearly media visibility may forward their strategic agenda, many organizers lack detailed understanding of media operations. They ask expert partners to gather and share useful concepts, approaches, and cases. This was one of RICADV's most recurring requests of MRAP.

Finding and distilling relevant literature was no small task. Relevant research is scattered throughout political science, sociology, planning, marketing, political economy, cultural studies, and especially communication. Literature on movement–media interaction crosses not only disciplines but continents. We found much useful literature emerging in the Global South (Waisbord n.d.; Riaño 1994; White, Nair, and Ascroft 1994; Dagron 2001; Servaes 2002, 2008). Sorting through this unruly thicket, we found much of use, but also that much about movement–media interaction remained underspecified and that few studies tracked groups over time (Klandermans 1992). Additionally, new media are reworking conventional understanding of media relations (Dichter 2005; Castells 2007).[6]

In our collaboration, MRAP and RICADV wanted to explore how organizers could exercise effective agency in encounters with mass media—a goal that serves theorists and practitioners alike. We found existing models of movement public relations tended to be overdetermined or underdetermined, failing to capture how skillful organizers, by understanding social contexts, could exercise more effective strategic choices (Jasper 2004). We shared Morris and Staggenborg's (2004, 188) view that power-laden media structures constrain movement options but do not determine them:

> Social structures cannot deliberate, imagine, strategize or engage in decision-making; human actors, navigating a matrix of social structures, initiate these activities. Strategic decisions figure prominently in determining movement outcomes, and social movement leaders are primary decision-makers, within social movements. . . . Because some choices are more effective than others the quality of decision-making can determine success or failure.

In other words, strategy, leadership, and collective decision making are interrelated (see also Ganz 2000). In the same spirit, we link strategy, leadership, and collective decision making in a participatory public relations model, showing how the public relations process builds internal movement relations. In mapping existing media power relations, deciding on outreach, and shaping message, collective leadership is consolidated even as it trains a new generation.

MRAP/Charlotte Ryan also reviewed studies related to the most common movement modes of interaction with media—critiques, engagement, and autonomy. Political economy and cultural studies of media illuminated structural inequalities. Mesolevel ethnographies and organizational behavior studies detailed newsroom practices. Feminist, Freirian, and learning community literatures yielded insights regarding internal democracy. Although success required fusing these modes, we describe them separately for heuristic purposes.

Critiques

Many studies of media–movement interaction explore how media institutions exercise power—more precisely, how players in media institutions contribute to the reproduction of inequalities of power. Like other resources, media resources are unequally distributed. Media systems' standard operating rules, reportorial practices, and cultures privilege existing power relations (Glasgow Media Group 1980, 1982; Bennett 1988; Herman and Chomsky 1988; Croteau and Hoynes 1994, 2001; Hoynes 1994; Mort 1992; Schiller 1996; McChesney 1999; Bagdikian 2000). Of value are studies of how individual movements relate to media (Gitlin 1980; Barker-Plummer 1995; Shepard and Hayduk 2002), how access constricts to once public spaces (McChesney 1993; Hoynes 1994; Starr 2000; Klinenberg 2007), and how routine news practices normalize the underreporting of challenges to authority. Particularly well studied is mass media's underrepresentation of movement protests (McCarthy, McPhail, and Smith 1996; Oliver and Myers 1999; Oliver and Maney 2000; Myers and Caniglia 2004; Smith et al. 2001).[7]

Engagement

To understand how media outlets operate, we reviewed mesolevel studies that analyzed daily news operations. These included observational or historical studies describing how reporters and editors' standardized practices and news criteria (Gans1979; Knightley 2002). A subgenre details the microcultures that shape coverage of specific topics such as labor (Glasgow Media Group 1976, 1980, 1982; Mort 1992; Martin 2004), racism (Entman and Rojecki 2001), and domestic violence (Pagelow 1981; Meyers 1997). Most conclude that news norms favor the powerful, the famous, the trivial, and the negative (Croteau and Hoynes 2001). Even when stories probe social problems, they focus on the human interest level, obscuring structural inequalities (Underwood 1993)

These studies dance on a tightrope between over- and underdetermination. Both macrocritiques and organizational studies detail how movement agency is constricted by mainstream media cultures and structures. Yet there is room for agency. In the actual negotiation between a specific reporter and a specific movement organizer, leadership skill, strategic sophistication, and collective decision making all come into play. Agency grows when skill becomes part of the movement's working culture, not the private property of a sole leader. Skillful movement organizers, in other words, widen political space in mass media outlets by maneuvering within the constraints well described by scholars. Collectivizing learning and resources is critical for sustaining and building on success.

Here the organizer and partnering theorist share a teaching role. MRAP/ Charlotte Ryan and RICADV/Karen Jeffreys worked together to distill media successes and failures into cautionary tales and best practices. We had to plan how to integrate these into RICADV's infrastructure and news routines so they would inform collective decision making. To this end, we organized formal workshops and campaign summary sessions, as well as informal conversations and lunches. With others, we planned conferences, curricula, and networks through which we could share what we had learned with the entire domestic violence movement and ultimately with other movements.

We learned how social movement organizers could more effectively work with mainstream reporters and editors whose gatekeeping routines privilege sitting authorities. For instance, espousing norms of objectivity, mainstream journalists promise "just the facts" (Golding and Elliott 1979, 175). If including opinion, they apply the balance norm, juxtaposing divergent points of view from two recognized sources (Goldenberg 1975; Gans 1979). Ryan (1993) found that even highly regarded independent media outlets such as National Public Radio apply a relatively mechanical balance norm. They generally cite the leading politician in a given battle and her or his leading opponent. By using sources with preexisting standing with whom they often have prior relationships, journalists reinforce their truth claims, routinize their work, and avoid costly lawsuits. Often facing speedup or layoffs, reporters are acutely aware of deadlines and productivity quotas.

To meet objectivity and balance norms, RICADV documented every claim scrupulously and developed collaborations with professional pollsters and academic researchers. We became adept at developing story ideas that served mainstream news conventions while providing interesting twists more likely to succeed. Although Ortner (1996) might call this gaming, we call it establishing a mutually beneficial working relationship. We recognized that developing working relationships with journalists could end up producing only superficial coverage changes—what Philips (1976) labels "novelty without change." To achieve deeper change, RICADV needed to combine media work with policy initiatives and direct organizing. To support the organizing, we turned to the third mode of movement–media interaction: the autonomous sphere.

Autonomy

Although new media hold promise for expanding democratic communications (Couldry and Curran 2003; McCaughey and Ayers 2003; Dichter 2005; Karaganis 2007), maintaining citizen access is an ongoing struggle (Ruggiero 2003; Klinenberg 2007). One well-traveled approach has been the creation and development of autonomous media (Downing 2000; Barker-Plummer, Kidd, and Rodriguez 2005; Kidd 2003; Lewis and Jones 2006). Movement organizers have much to learn from these hard-won free spaces. Of particular import are the internal infrastructures and communication systems that underpin collaborative power analysis, decision making, and framing processes (Grassroots Policy Project, http://www.grassrootspolicy.org). RICADV's work stressed strong relational ties (Diani 2000), coalition building (Bystydzienski and Schacht 2001), and collective identity processes (Kurtz 2002). When combined, these elements formed a platform from which movement organizers could "create effective strategies and frames" (Morris and Staggenborg 2004, 191) in mass-mediated arenas.

Before launching a mass media campaign, independent media offer rare opportunities for organizers to talk politics with activists who share their worldview. Radio (Lewis and Jones 2006) and the Internet (Kidd 2003) offer exemplary free spaces. Not to be ignored, however, are movement communication formats and networks that are not mass-mediated, such as face-to-face meetings and blogs (Castells 2004, 2007).[8] Corporate marketing's attention to viral marketing tactics, in fact, replicates communication patterns common in well-networked communities and social movements.

Collaborative Theorization

For many years, progressive social movement organizations focused on building independent media and exposing how corporate control of mass media had undermined democracy. Independent media and media criticism represented mutually reinforcing efforts to break the appearance of consensus. However, given the often limited reach of independent media and the centrality of mass media systems for talking politics, some organizers continued to engage with mass media.

In targeting mass media, social movement organizers had not forgotten about underlying power inequalities. To the contrary, they were acutely aware that they lacked government and corporate entities' easy access to mass media. Given the mass media's power to shape (and narrow) agendas and to name whose accounts count, social movement organizers recognized the value of achieving media standing as an addition to independent communication capacity (Ferree et al. 2002).

The complexities of adapting corporate public relations tactics to very different movement purposes has been undertheorized—a problem further complicated by the fact that movement communication practices are heterogeneous. Different organizations within the same movement may adopt disparate public relations strategies that are often poorly executed with insufficient infrastructure. For example, RICADV surveyed domestic violence coalitions in each U.S. state and territory and found that most states have no articulated public relations strategy. Only fourteen had staff dedicated to communication work.

Although there are many probable causes for the fragmented nature of communication work, we recognize that this condition speaks to, at least in part, the lack of a sustained dialogue between social movement organizations and theorists. Ideally, theorists would work with organizers to distill social movement experiences into generalizable lessons. Theorists could embed lessons in historical context and compare them with movement experiences in other places. Sustained collaboration, however, is the exception rather than the rule.

Another probable cause is the reactive and overextended nature of U.S. social movement organizing, as organizers bounce from crisis to crisis. Overextension, insufficient resources, and short-sighted urgency—all contribute to movements' failures to reflect, then deepen and store learning about communication's relation to overall movement-building strategies. Although lacking partnering theorists, overextended leaders and organizers do distill lessons from their own experiences, but they often lack the resources to do so systematically and then share these lessons with others. The public relations model we outline below is RICADV–MRAP's partnered effort to learn to theorize collaboratively in ways that serve both movement organizers and theorists. Our mesolevel of abstraction is deliberate (Staggenborg 2002), as is our attention to the particularities of the contested arena (Barker, Johnson, and Lavalette 2001).

Two Common Models

When seeking access to mass media, social movement organizers commonly use two public relations models: social marketing and media advocacy. We describe these models noting how they intersect and diverge. We summarize the models' limits as foundations for social movement public relations strategy and then explain how we learned to address these limits through collaborative learning/theorizing that occurred in iterative cycles of dialogue, action, and reflection.

Social Marketing

U.S. social movement communication strategies reflect, for better or worse, marketing's saturation of contemporary culture—a development over a half century in the making. Paralleling the post–World War II explosion of the U.S. advertising industry, social marketing pioneered the application of marketing concepts to social issues. Brotherhood could be marketed as easily as soap (Wiebe 1952). Like traditional marketing, social marketing stresses a consumer orientation and voluntary exchange in a free market. While acknowledging possible problems of fit, Walsh et al. (1993) stress the potential advantages of adapting marketing methods to promote social causes. They highlight social marketing's rigorous audience/market research tools and its attention to strategic planning and evaluation. They conclude that communicators promoting social change have much to gain from social marketing's systematic analysis of desired audiences and translation of messages into formats attractive to those audiences. Mothers Against Drunk Driving's designated driver campaign, Friends Don't Let Friends Drive Drunk, exemplifies effective social marketing that empowers individuals and peer groups to proactively prevent driving while intoxicated without requiring institutional or policy change.

Media Advocacy

Media advocacy builds on social marketing techniques but presents itself as an advance that addresses some of social marketing's limits. Most commonly, media advocates promote a policy change or other institutional reform that will improve conditions for a whole class of individuals. At times, these reforms pinpoint the underlying structural inequalities. For example, focusing on individual behavior change, social marketers urged individual consumers to stop smoking. In contrast, media advocates proposed policy changes (taxes and class action suits) that would penalize tobacco companies for their profit-driven deception of millions of smokers. Public awareness of smoking's negative effects was raised at the same time (Pertschuk 2001).

Many media advocates number themselves among social marketing's outspoken critics (Wallack et al. 1993). Most commonly, media advocates argue that social marketing's emphasis on individual behavior change rather than policy changes reduces those targeted to passive recipients of messages promoting individual change. Some advocates of social marketing reject such criticism as overdone, claiming that social marketing, although typically practiced in the manner criticized above, does not inherently function in this manner (Walsh et al. 1993). Social marketing research, they argue, grounds itself in classic sociological methods—focus groups, surveys, polls, and evaluation research—that serve useful roles in any change effort, including efforts to make structural change. The problem rests not in marketing's methods but in those who have lacked the vision and will to dedicate the resources needed to apply social marketing tools to social change. Indeed, social marketing advocates suggest that media advocacy represents not an independent model, but an improved, second-generation social marketing model that applies social marketing tools to the policy arena. Media advocacy, they argue, shares social marketing's focus on individuals, although media advocates ask individuals not simply to change behaviors, but also to function as individual citizens voting or otherwise pressing for public policy reform.

Difference in emphasis noted, social marketing and media advocacy share significant common ground. Both models accept social theorists' claim that mass media form critical convening systems of modern life essential for public discourse (Castells 2007). Both are mission driven, setting clear strategic goals. Both involve expert use of social science tools—market research, polling data, and focus groups—to analyze targeted audiences and to plan, execute, and evaluate strategic interventions. Both generally propose that their audiences—individuals defined by their historical and social environment—take action. We summarize these differences and commonalities in figure 4.1.

Limits and Omissions of Market-Driven Public Relations Models

Many social movement organizations that engage in social marketing, media advocacy, or other forms of mass media engagement also maintain their own media outlets or work with independent media. Additionally, most agree with media theorists who warn that the corporate media's narrowing of public discourse presents a significant threat to democracy (Gans 2003). Even when all three approaches (independent, critique, and engagement) are present, however, they represent parallel but disconnected silos of activity. Functioning in this fragmented fashion, organizers engaged in mainstream media do not integrate the critique of corporate media. Nor do they take advantage of independent media's potential to test and develop movement communication capacity.

Although media advocacy extends social marketing into the policy arena, the models share problematic assumptions, limitations, and omissions. Neither addresses systematic inequalities in media power. Neither insists that those directly affected be represented at all stages of communication planning. Nor does either model require that those directly affected be supported to build communication infrastructure that they control.

Both models' ignoring of structural media inequalities leads to questionable tactics. Rather than building self-sufficiency and tackling obstacles that silence marginalized group, both rely on experts to run focus groups and develop messages. RICADV and MRAP appreciate the role of experts, and RICADV campaigns routinely utilize expert services. Without conscious attention to structural inequalities and to the role of the disempowered in building a movement that challenges those inequalities, social marketers and

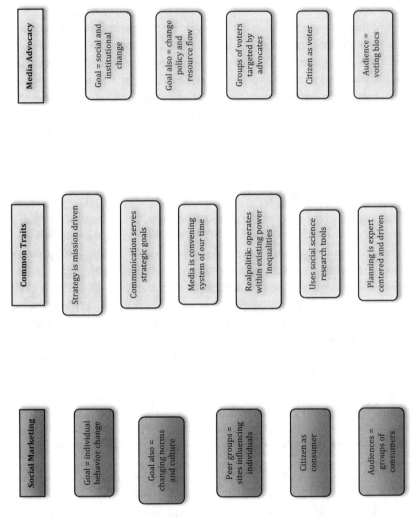

Figure 4.1. Comparison of Publicity Models Commonly Used by U.S. Social Movement Organizations

media advocates can substitute themselves and their opinions for those of the very groups they purport to serve. The word *advocate*, after all, comes from the Latin *advocare*, "to speak for another." Failing to attend to empowerment, neither model addresses the unintended consequences of expert-driven initiatives—that the knowledge workers who shape public relations strategies may marginalize the very groups that they hope to serve. Moreover, in the absence of a mass base of support, both models' dependence on government or foundation grants can exacerbate marginalization as researchers fit proposals to match grant makers' scope of interest.

In sum, neither the social marketing nor the media advocacy model takes, as a core assumption, the need to empower those directly affected. In failing to do so, each model becomes complicit in reinforcing existing inequalities of power. Both models lack the ideological foundation needed to break through what Freire (1994, 14) calls "the culture of silence." Neither acknowledges the enormous structural barriers to change and the concomitant need for marginalized individuals to form collective actors to challenge those barriers. Neither model engages in the planning necessary to support and sustain organizing of those directly affected by inequalities. Taken in isolation, the models' net effect is to limit the social movement organization's ability to use public relations strategies to challenge existing inequalities and/or to promote equality.

By 1995, after a decade of collaboration with organizers experimenting with social marketing and media advocacy, MRAP had developed the above critique. We knew we wanted to build a power-sensitive model, both in the sense of being sensitive to inequalities in power, but also sensitized to empowering marginalized groups. We thought that classic social research tools could help, and we were convinced that mass media access was important for social movement growth. In our partnership with RICADV, we found the agent and the opportunity to develop and test a third model. We describe the experiment and then the resulting model.

A Decade with RICADV, 1996–2005

In 1979, Rhode Island–based feminists founded RICADV with a mission of ending domestic violence in that state. By 1996, RICADV had built a network of domestic violence prevention agencies serving each of Rhode Island's six counties. It also provided sponsored a speakers' bureau of domestic violence survivors called Sisters Overcoming Abusive Relationships (SOAR). Despite these significant achievements, RICADV had not achieved media standing. Reporters did not recognize the organization as an authoritative, reliable source of information regarding domestic violence (Ferree et al. 2002).

Despite occasional news coverage, RICADV could not regularly and recurrently educate publics about domestic violence via mass media. Rhode Island media coverage of domestic violence typified researchers' findings that news stories commonly sensationalized domestic violence incidents, framing them as unpredictable, private tragedies (Pagelow 1981; Meyers 1997).

Arguing that this privatized framing obscured the root causes of domestic violence and slowed change efforts, RICADV domestic violence movement activists—organizers, advocates, victims, and survivors—began to challenge this privatization of domestic violence through multiple channels, including mass media. In 1996, RICADV director Deborah De Bare garnered funding to expand communication work. She hired organizer Karen Jeffreys, charging Jeffreys to develop public relations strategies that would strengthen RICADV's organizing, service, education, and lobbying. With expanded public relations, RICADV hoped to influence public attitudes and transform social institutions.

From the outset, Jeffreys began to link independent organizing with outreach to mainstream media. She approached SOAR, offering to help them expand organizing of domestic violence victims, witnesses, and survivors. With increased RICADV support, SOAR began to evolve into a collaborating but independent organization that could, if needed, set its own agenda. Jeffreys then worked with coalition member groups serving each region of Rhode Island to maximize statewide collaboration while increasing each group's control of local media outreach. To provide media research and training, Jeffreys recruited MRAP coordinator Charlotte Ryan, with whom she had collaborated previously.

Over the following ten years (1996–2005), RICADV became the leading source of news regarding domestic violence in Rhode Island—a top fifty media market (Ryan, Anastario, and DaCunha 2006). RICADV gained far more than organizational visibility, however. Its framing of domestic violence now permeated Rhode Island media coverage (Ryan, Anastario, and Jeffreys 2005). This coverage, coupled with RICADV–scholar research collaborations, strategic outreach, and organizing activities, increased public awareness of domestic violence.

RICADV collaborative organizing with Rhode Island post offices illustrates the growth. Backed by Rhode Island postal workers (among them a domestic violence survivor), U.S. Postal Service district manager Don Marshall and RICADV decided to promote the "Stop Family Violence" stamp as part of the October 2005 Domestic Violence Awareness Month. A portion of the revenue from the stamp's sale would support groups working to stop domestic violence. In additional to selling the stamp, all Rhode Island post offices displayed educational materials about domestic violence and collected cell phones as another way to raise funds for local domestic violence services. RICADV engaged in additional organizing and public relations efforts.

As a result of the campaign, Rhode Island boosted sales of its stamps by 2,694 percent in October 2005, outselling every other district in entire country.[9] As further evidence of deepened popular support, in the same year (2005), RICADV defeated the National Rifle Association (NRA) by successfully lobbying for the passage of a gun control bill long stalled in the Rhode Island legislature. To win its bitter two-year battle with the NRA, RICADV had united survivors, their families and friends, news editorial staff, police, and even some NRA members.

A Third Model

As RICADV and MRAP worked to establish RICADV's media standing, a third model of strategic communications organizing slowly emerged. We entered the collaboration with a critique of existing models and with the limits of fragmented practice. Although we had pieces of a new model, it would be a gross exaggeration to say we shared a conceptual framework and language. We were committed from the outset to drawing more generalizable lessons, but we did not always agree on what lesson to draw from any given success or failure. We argued about whether or not we were simply improving social marketing and media advocacy models or were developing a distinct model. We argued about which components of existing models we would preserve and about what to name our new approach. For months on end, we would agree to disagree about the conceptual model even as we continued to work and reflect on our progress.

Through many iterative cycles of dialogue, action, and reflection, we described our work in terms that we found acceptable. It took three more years to distill our approaches into a model we could share with other movements. During this distillation period, we came to see the broad parallels between the model we developed and models used in the Global South based on the writings and teachings of Paulo Freire (1994). To affirm this resonance, we began to call our approach by the label common in the Global South: participatory communication for social change. Work still remained, however, to adapt a Global South model to the conditions of the Global North.

Participatory Communication: An Integrated Movement Building Approach to Media

To social marketing and media advocacy methods, participatory communicators apply a more consistent empowerment lens. They analyze existing power relations, then develop strategic responses that incrementally strengthen the capacity of marginalized constituencies to mobilize on their own behalf. Identifying mobilization of the marginalized as an essential component of democratic change, participatory communicators celebrate "the right and power to intervene in the social order and change it through political praxis" (Freire 1994, 13).

Participatory communicators begin by asking, "How can communication work support marginalized groups as they challenge inequalities of power that underlie adverse outcomes?" The explicit goal of participatory communication models is to empower those directly affected by inequalities of power. Power represents sustained capacity to operate within those institutions to set social agenda, to allocate resources, to make and enforce laws, and to decide what things mean. When acting alone, individuals rarely can surmount inequalities of power embedded in social, political, economic, and cultural institutions.[10] To become empowered as change agents, individuals need to form collective actors that strategically focus on reshaping society's priorities, rules, resource allocation, and meaning making.

Working in the popular education and Freirian traditions, RICADV's participatory model emphasized dialogue, relation building, and grassroots empowerment. It is not simply good on process, however. Beginning with an analysis of structural inequalities, the model insists that those directly affected by these inequalities be part of change efforts (White, Nair, and Ascroft 1994; Dagron 2001). Social movement scholarship adds the importance of building a collective actor to guide that work. In the participatory model, collective efforts to make social change revolve around collaborative communication— identifying a problem, brainstorming suggestions, evaluating action alternatives, mobilizing allies, or resolving internal or coalition conflicts. The model operationalizes Gandhi's concept of being the change one wants to see.

RICADV's collective framing caucus exemplifies a participatory approach whereby everyone becomes a messenger. Staff and active members caucus to prepare campaign messages. Having seen their ideas included, they become more active messengers and more active participants in subsequent framing caucuses. The framing caucuses followed by post-media-event reflections form a regular space for talking politics, an organizational routine that interns replicate in future settings. One former RICADV intern, Titus Dos Remedios (2003, 2), adapted the caucus to his work organizing public school students:

> We run this conflict resolution program with kids at the middle school, and the kids wanted to propose all these changes to make the school safer. So two days after I had learned to do a media caucus, we did one with the kids to prepare them to talk to the principal. And the kids loved it. They

were so well prepared. After the kids left, the principal said, "Wow, the kids were so eloquent!"

RICADV's approach not only shifted communication to a collective context in which staff and members collaborating in preparing messages, but it also extended that collaborative spirit into coalition work. By 2002, RICADV was engaged in eight or more institutional arenas at any given time, including direct organizing of those directly affected along with mobilizing grassroots allies, courts, hospitals, police, service coalitions, political bodies, media, and academia. Although each arena was chosen for its potential to further RICADV's strategic goal of ending domestic violence, each arena had unique characteristics and arena-specific relationships needed to be cultivated.[11] RICADV's organizers insisted that consistent democracy grounded in its core values of equality, diversity, and respect needed to be its signature in coalition work as well. Thus, RICADV's political strategy permeated its relations with its publics in both coalition and media work. Communication involved media, but much more.

In sum, RICADV organizers built a collective actor that developed public relations strategies integrating independent media, media criticism, and engagement with mainstream media. In forging public relations strategy, RICADV organizers attempted to use media to build its movement, but also to challenge media as a critical social arena in itself. We summarize core elements of the participatory model in figure 4.2.

Discussion

Over the course of ten years, RICADV developed its media capacity, dramatically raised its media standing, and ultimately increased its ability to move a political agenda. RICADV's progress interests social movement scholars and activists for several reasons. First, RICADV's gains did not represent a national trend. Most state coalitions in the same time period did not report comparable gains. Second, RICADV documented its public relations efforts extensively, so that its rising media standing and political clout can be considered in their relation to the organization's public relations strategies. Finally, by sustaining recurring cycles of dialogue, action, and reflection, RICADV and scholar partner MRAP were able to discuss and link conceptual and practical issues that often evolve in isolation. We first discuss the added value of a participatory communication model for U.S. social movement organizations that choose to incorporate mainstream media as outlets critical for reach their desired constituencies. We then summarize what we learned regarding the potential added value of scholar–activist collaboration.

Ten Components	Description	Illustration
1. Challenge power inequalities by organizing	Organizers challenge power inequalities by building social networks to sustain collective resistance.	Karen Jeffreys joins RICADV in 1996, encouraging survivors and coalition members to add organizing to service provision. She taps previous networks to involve MRAP.
2. Build a sustainable collective actor	Assume group not individual action. Generally speaking, individuals can oppose and resist, but not change systems/relations.	RICADV organizers establish basic internal communication systems—meetings, protocols, and caucuses—so all can contribute to a shared vision.
3. Those directly affected by inequality need their own powerful actors	Those directly affected by inequality form collective actors that are at the center of decision making.	While continuing to cooperate with RICADV, domestic violence survivor group SOAR establishes its own priorities, leadership, and decision-making processes.
4. Embed shared worldview in shared organizational routines	Shared values (e.g., respect, diversity, and equality) underlie participatory processes for negotiating priorities and resolving conflicts that permit transparency, reflexivity, and accountability.	RICADV works with a consultant to write cultural agreements addressing diversity conflicts and a detailed decision-making rubric—who makes which decisions.
5. Strategize—detailed power and empowerment analyses inform work plans	Power analysis and shared values guide group's mission and vision from which strategy flows. Group strategy fits historical conditions with group resources	To serve mission—end domestic violence in Rhode Island—RICADV maps power and strategic response. Strategy is then translated into individual work plans.

Figure 4.2. (continued)

Ten Components	Description	Illustration
6. Long view and infrastructure	Because movement building is a long-term project, groups build infrastructure—sustainable systems and practices that break long-term goals into incremental steps.	Citing experiences with hundreds of groups, MRAP cautions that success will take five to seven years. RICADV expects faster progress but builds media systems.
7. Form a reflexive learning community	Reflect on collective experience as learning communities. With reflection part of routine, the collective actor measures results and makes strategic adjustments.	Organizational consultant and writer Deborah Linnell introduces learning community approaches; retreats and group debriefings encourage learning from practice.
8. Establish prefigurative relations	Daily work embodies group's core values, the collective actor forms a (relatively) free or safe space.	RICADV uses cultural agreements and retreats to deepen internal challenges to racism and other inequalities.
9. Framing is dialogic and dynamic	Framing involves dialogues over strategy. These begin inside movement organizations, then extend to supporters, potential allies, the unconvinced, and even opponents. It means reworking relationships.	Karen Jeffreys establishes a media caucus to encourage group conversations. Listening becomes more important.
10. Social networks are governed by the same values as the core organization	In coalition negotiations, RICADV applies its core values of respect, equality, and diversity.	RICADV creates a broad coalition including police, NRA members, and others to control handguns.

Figure 4.2. Strategic Communication for Movement Building

Collaborative theorizing is slow. We must attend to the interests and needs of both organizers and theorists. From the organizers' perspective, it took five years to clarify that we had developed a new public relations model suited to a mass-mediated society. We became confident that participatory communications approaches were effective when RICADV began to grow in membership and visibility, and had the capacity and power to make structural change, outstripping the growth of sister coalitions working hard under similar conditions. A second measure of our model's efficacy was that its predictive value for planning strategy. We could analyze situations and anticipate what all the social actors would do. More often than not, we were right. Reviewing our prior interactions with reporters and our statements in prior settings, RICADV organizers found we had often anticipated every reporter's questions. Finally, we were assured when the interns from RICADV translated our approaches to other organizations and issues and achieved independent successes.

Also critical to the model's success was the establishment of synergy between what many movement organizations used as three noninteractive processes—media critique, independent media,[12] and engagement with mass media. We combined these processes so that our approach benefited from power critiques, autonomous media practices, and engagements with mainstream institutions. Their melding is central to a participatory model that resonates with Global South communication approaches.

The final results may obscure the messiness of our actual learning process. We learned as much from glorious failures as from successes. Our model crystallized through engaging in dialogues with each other, with MRAP, and with reporters and communication practitioners. We refined it further as we organized workshops for sister coalitions and as we read studies of movement–media interaction from various disciplines, especially communication.[13] Organizers' expressed need for models and theories with predictive value catalyzed our theorizing. For organizers, anticipating media–movement interaction is not an academic exercise; it matters.

One key insight is our deepened understanding of power in relationship to movement public relations strategies. In contrast to social marketing and media advocacy, participatory communication's highlights three power-sensitive components of communication activism—the driving force of change; the core change agent; and the change process. By driving force, we mean that structural inequalities of power create the pressure for social change. To address that pressure, participatory communication moves beyond media advocacy (speaking publicly for another in ways that inadvertently maintain the silencing of those directly affected by inequalities of power). Instead, it seeks to build the collective capacity of marginalized communities to speak for themselves. In other words, it is not sufficient to use marginalized individuals as spokespersons, a practice that often reduces emerging movement leaders to poster children delivering expert-determined canned phrases. To function as change agents, marginalized constituencies need to form their own collective organizations within broader movements. Finally, on a process level, participatory processes can be used to renegotiate power relations. Policy campaigns seek finite gains, in the process building collective actors with growing power to negotiate for change. Communication networks become a critical component of movement-building (Diani 2000; Castells 2004). Participatory approaches also strengthen the horizontal relationships that Castells (2007) flags as one hallmark of a network society.

In response to Morris and Staggenborg's (2004, 191) question, "How do leaders and leadership teams create effective strategies and frames?" a participatory approach to public relations stresses that a social movement organization must establish basic organizational infrastructure and decision-making processes. Although detailed treatment of such prerequisites is beyond our scope here,[14] RICADV stressed the need for a clear mission (in this case, to end domestic violence). It worked to establish internal decision-making structures that would maximize broad, active participation. It studied the power dynamics that characterized domestic violence politics and from there developed a strategic plan that allowed it to use its resources effectively. The net result was that RICADV successfully expanded its grassroots base, achieved policy goals, and changed media coverage (Ryan, Anastario, and Jeffreys 2005).

MRAP entered its collaboration with RICADV citing the mantra, "Media strategy grows from political strategy." RICADV's success reflects its strategic leaders' consistently skillful navigation in three arenas: policy, media, and grassroots organizing. RICADV's organizers routinized how they gathered and institutionalized group experience so that lessons informed group practice. They developed routines for resolving conflicts and for supporting new leadership. In short, the organizers took infrastructure seriously.

MRAP provided collective support for Charlotte Ryan as she executed her RICADV responsibilities. Her tasks included introducing RICADV to relevant movement experiments from other times and settings, collaborating in RICADV reflection sessions, documenting RICADV's losses and advances in accessible formats, and experimenting with replicable models. Ryan relied on the MRAP seminar to gain needed distance and to systematically reflect on the organizing.

Scholars typically achieve distance by concluding fieldwork and then reflecting on the experience. In an ongoing involvement, the discipline of a weekly reflection in seminar was invaluable. Unlike academic conferences, where competitive individualism may swamp collaborative impulses, MRAP's job was to help Ryan as the involved researcher to provide sophisticated, exacting support to RICADV. Each MRAP member contributed from her or his experience and knowledge base. The collective result outstripped what an individual could produce. In an academic culture, which generally demeans practice even as it prattles about praxis, MRAP attempted to build a culture of respect in which all would contribute with the understanding that together we are more than alone; we saw genius as a collective noun.

Our sharing can be concrete. MRAP's members have mastered multiple literatures—political science, communication, cultural studies, political sociology, women's studies, globalization studies, organizational behavior, and movement studies. MRAP also accumulated resources—space, student labor, computers, library access, funding, and scholarly connections. Although any academic could gather comparable resources, the cumulative work when added to field work becomes unsustainable. As a cooperative of like-minded activist scholars, MRAP, despite limits and flaws, made possible an atypical theoretical practice.[15]

In encouraging collective leadership, strategizing, and framing, the RICADV–MRAP collaboration also systematized reflection, a development relevant to our claim that activist–theorist partnerships can contribute to theorizing. Organizing remains largely an oral culture. Organizers' workdays are long, and few write down what they learn. Supporting the translation of organizers' insights from spoken work to writing is critical, as is making movement theory accessible to organizers. This latter effort is slowed by the scholastic turn in social movement studies,[16] with jargon impenetrable to all but the initiated ensuring that only academics read movement theory (Bevington and Dixon 2005). The resulting absence of shared texts and vocabulary slows collaborative theorizing.

Although we see the resulting chasm as socially constructed and not inevitable, developing the shared conceptual framework for collaborative theorizing takes time and resources. In our case, it took years to tease out how our communication work intersected with and diverged from the social marketing and media advocacy models of movement public relations. It took more time to develop the participatory communication model presented. We were greatly helped by Global South theories, although these needed adaptation to distinct U.S. conditions. Imagine our pleasure when we happened on Riaño's (1994) suggestion that U.S. democratic social movements, particularly the U.S. civil rights, labor, feminist, and LGBTQ movements, were likely sites for participatory communication projects resonant with

Freirian-influenced models from the Global South. Echoing Global South communicators, U.S. movement organizers had created public relations strategies that synergistically melded autonomous communication systems with critical engagement with mass media.

The last point stresses what scholars add to activist experience. Being in close proximity with activists as they articulate and execute strategies has enormous value for scholars. If collaboration with MRAP supported RICADV's efforts to draw lessons from practice and link them to other traditions, MRAP benefited from watching as RICADV actually tried to apply those lessons in practice. MRAP's ability to create theory with predictive value grew as we became more familiar with the institutional dynamics of the arenas in which movements play. We came, for instance, to understand which sources reporters perceive as real people and which illuminated some troubling dynamics between reporters and movement spokespersons. Most dramatically, we retreated from a heavily structured understanding of framing that parsed myths, logics, images, anecdotes, arguments, and cognitive mind-sets. Recognizing that frames are the result of, not the impetus for, social relationships, we attend more carefully to framing as dynamic, a fluid meaning-making process that emerges as people engage in dialogue, building on their preexisting cultural understandings. This definition places agency (organizers and collective process) in fuller view.

Conclusion

Sensationalized stories treating domestic violence murders as unpredictable, private family tragedies obscure the causes of domestic violence and slow efforts at change. RICADV, working with MRAP, successfully challenged this privatization of domestic violence. We used participatory public relations strategies to augment direct organizing, coalition building, service provision, and organizing for structural changes. We influenced public attitudes in Rhode Island, increased resources for organizing, and subsequently transformed several critical Rhode Island social institutions. RICADV achieved measurable gains in both media standing and in power to effect political change.

Our collaborative relationship ensured that our joint work would have greater possibilities to be shared with other movements. By 2002 (year 7), RICADV's progress was recognized by other states. By 2004, MRAP had quantified RICADV's progress. Charts showing a rise in RICADV's media standing were greeted by thunderous applause at a 2004 national convention. Fourteen states signed on to create a shared curriculum, and all states and territories expressed interest in being trained in RICADV–MRAP's approaches.

RICADV and MRAP's collaborative theorizing over ten years systematized RICADV's ability to talk politics. As a result, RICADV's public relations strategy became more firmly anchored to its movement-building strategy. RICADV's public relations strategies resonate with practices of Global South activists who treat communications as movement building in the media arena. Above all, the added value of activist–scholar collaboration rests in our increased ability to rejoin action and theorizing in iterative cycles of dialogic planning, action, and reflection. We note that both scholars and activists need to locate themselves in collectives to sustain engagement.

Notes

1. Bourdieu (1990) proactively extends Bertold Brecht's (1964, 4) remark: "Anybody who advises us not to make use of such new apparatus just confirms the right of the apparatus to do bad work; he forgets himself out of sheer open-mindedness, for he is thus proclaiming his willingness to have nothing but dirt produced for him."

2. See, for instance, the Leftist Marching Band (http://leftistmarchingband.org) and the Festival of Activist Street Bands (http://honkfest.org).

3. For those interested in interdisciplinary approaches, communication scholarship offers vast conceptual and methodological resources that are, to date, underutilized in social movement studies.

4. The network of domestic violence coalitions in each U.S. state and colony represents a major accomplishment of the women's movement.

5. A fuller treatment of collaborative methods is beyond the scope of this chapter.

6. Regarding media transformation, see the Social Science Research Council Media Research Hub (http://www.ssrc.org).

7. Beyond our scope is the extensive literature on methodological issues in media–movement studies. See, for instance, Earl et al. (2004).

8. We do not address the rise of the blogosphere and its impact on organizing, a critical development that arose after we completed the work we describe here.

9. In a letter to RICADV dated November 18, 2005, the U.S. Postal Service district manager reported that their joint organizing and public relations had pushed domestic violence stamp sales from $3,608 in September 2005 to $97,213 in October 2005.

10. Note, however, the cultural centrality of Horatio Alger myths eulogizing individuals who succeed against all odds.

11. A single campaign may demand expertise in multiple social arenas—thus the need for collective, not solo, efforts. Collaborating scholars and activists may tap multiple organizational and theoretical fields, such as organizational theory, political economy of mass media, and cultural studies.

12. We recognize that many social movement groups routinely meld independent media work and media critique. However, these two approaches, used in isolation from mainstream media outlets, can lead to movement isolation from constituencies beyond the already committed. Some social movement organizations tag on a mass media strategy. However, in the process, they may drop many of the valuable cautions and power analysis tools of media criticism.

13. We urge movement scholars studying communication to read communication scholars studying movements. See, for instance, Frey and Carragee (2007).

14. Also beyond our scope here are discussions of the individual skills of the organizers involved.

15. Perhaps hesitation to embrace academic–activist partnerships is related to many scholars' automatic adoption of an individuated work model. Yet when one looks at recent advances in social movement theory, many result from sustained collaborative relations.

16. We use this term precisely to evoke the pedantic excesses of the medieval scholastic tradition.

References

Alimi, E. 2007a. "Discursive Contention: Palestinian Media Discourse and the Inception of the 'First' Intifada." *Harvard Journal of Press/Politics 12*:71–91.

———. 2007b. *Israeli Politics and the First Palestinian Intifada: Political Opportunities, Framing Processes and Contentious Politics.* New York: Routledge.

Andrews, Kenneth T. 2002. "Creating Social Change: Lessons from the Civil Rights Movement." In *Social Movements: Identity, Culture and the State,* edited by David S. Meyer, Nancy Whittier and Belinda Robnett, 105–20. New York: Oxford University Press.

Aufderheide, Patricia. 1999. *Communication Policy and the Public Interest.* New York: Guilford Press.

Bagdikian, Ben H. 2000. *The Media Monopoly.* 6th ed. Boston: Beacon Press.

Barker, Colin, Alan Johnson, and Michael Lavalette. 2001. *Leadership and Social Movements.* Manchester: Manchester University Press.

Barker-Plummer, Bernadette. 1995. "News as Political Resource: Media Strategies and Political Identity in the U.S. Women's Movement, 1966–1975." *Critical Studies in Mass Communication 72*:306–24.

———. 1996. "The Dialogic of Media and Social Movements." *Peace Review* 8:27–34.

Barker-Plummer, Bernadette, Dorothy Kidd, and Clemencia Rodriguez. 2005. "Media Democracy from the Ground Up: Mapping Communication Practices in the Counter Public Sphere." Social Science Research Council. http://www.ssrc.org.

Bennett, W. Lance. 1988. *The Politics of Illusion.* New York: Longman.

―――. 1990. "Toward a Theory of Press–State Relations in the United States." *Journal of Communication* 40:103–27.

Bevington, Douglas, and Chris Dixon. 2005. "Movement-Relevant Theory: Rethinking Social Movement Scholarship and Activism." *Social Movement Studies* 28, no. 3:185–208.

Bourdieu, Pierre. 1990. *In Other Words: Essays toward a Reflexive Sociology.* Stanford, Calif.: Stanford University Press.

―――. 1999. *Acts of Resistance.* New York: New Press.

Brecht, Bertolt. 1964. *On Theater.* New York: Methuen Books.

Bystydzienski, Jill M., and Steven P. Schacht, eds. 2001. *Forging Radical Alliances across Difference: Coalition Politics for the New Millenium.* New York: Rowman & Littlefield.

Castells, Manuel. 2004. *The Network Society: A Cross-cultural Perspective.* Northhampton, Mass.: Edgar Elgar.

―――. 2007. "Communication, Power, and Counter-power in the Network Society." *International Journal of Communication* 1:238–66.

Couldry, Nick, and James Curran. 2003. *Contesting Media Power: Alternative Media in a Networked World.* Lanham, Md.: Rowman & Littlefield.

Croteau, David, and William Hoynes. 1994. *By Invitation Only: How Media Limit Political Debate.* Monroe, Me.: Common Courage Press.

―――. 2001. *The Business of Media: Corporate Media and the Public Interest.* Boston: Pine Forge Press.

Curran, James. 2002. *Media and Power.* London: Routledge.

Dagron, Alfonso G. 2001. *Making Waves: Stories of Participatory Communication for Social Change.* New York: Rockefeller Foundation.

Diani, Mario. 2000. "The Relational Deficit of Ideologically Structured Action." *Mobilization* 5:17–24.

Dichter, Aliza. 2005. "Together, We Know More: Networks and Coalitions to Advance Media Democracy, Communication Rights and the Public Sphere, 1990–2005." Social Science Research Council. http://www.ssrc.org.

Dos Remedios, Titus. 2003. Interview with Karen Jeffreys and Charlotte Ryan. Unpublished manuscript, Department of Sociology, Boston College, Chestnut Hill, Mass.

Downing, John D. H. 2000. *Radical Media: Rebellious Communication and Social Movements.* Thousand Oaks, Calif.: Sage.

Earl, Jennifer, Andrew Martin, John D. McCarthy, and Sarah A. Soule. 2004. "The Use of Newspaper Data in the Study of Collective Action." *Annual Review of Sociology* 30:65–80.

Edelman, Murray. 1988. *Constructing the Political Spectacle.* Chicago: University of Chicago Press.

Entman, Robert M., and Andrew Rojecki. 2001. *The Black Image in the White Mind: Media and Race in America.* Chicago: University of Chicago Press.

Ferree, Myra M., William A. Gamson, Jürgen Gerhards, and Dieter Rucht. 2002. *Shaping Abortion Discourse.* Cambridge: Cambridge University Press.

Freire, Paulo. 1994. Preface to *Participatory Communication: Working for Change and Development,* edited by Shirley A. White, K. Sadanandan Nair, and Joseph R. Ascroft, 12–14. New Delhi: Sage Publications India.

Frey, Lawrence R., and Kevin M. Carragee, eds. 2007. *Communication Activism: Communication for Social Change.* 2 vols. Cresskill, N.J.: Hampton Press.

Gamson, William A. 1998. "Social Movements and Cultural Change." In *From Contention to Democracy,* edited by Marco G. Giugni, Doug McAdam, and Charles Tilly. 57–77. Lanham, Md.: Rowman & Littlefield.

Gans, Herbert J. 1979. *Deciding What's News: A Study of CBS Evening News, NBC Nightly News, Newsweek and Time.* New York: Vintage.

———. 2003. *Democracy and the News.* New York: Oxford University Press.

Ganz, Marshall. 2000. "Resources and Resourcefulness: Strategic Capacity in the Unionization of California Agriculture, 1959–1966." *American Journal of Sociology* 105:1003–62.

Gitlin, Todd. 1980. *The Whole World Is Watching: Mass Media in the Making and Unmaking of the New Left.* Berkeley: University of California Press.

Glasgow Media Group 1976. *Bad News.* London: Routledge and Kegan Paul.

———. 1980. *More Bad News.* London: Routledge and Kegan Paul.

———. 1982. *Really Bad News.* London: Writers and Readers.

Goldenberg, Edie. 1975. *Making the Papers: The Access of Resource-Poor Groups in Metropolitan Press.* Lexington, Mass.: Lexington Books.

Golding, Peter, and Philip Elliott. 1979. *Making the News.* London: Longmans.

Graber, Doris A. 2007. *Media, Power and Politics.* 5th ed. Washington, D.C.: CQ Press.

Heath, Robert L. 2004. *Handbook of Public Relations.* Thousand Oaks, Calif.: Sage.

Herman, Edward S. 1995. *Triumph of the Market.* Boston: South End Press.

Herman, Edward S., and Noam Chomsky. 1988. *Manufacturing Consent: The Political Economy of Mass Media.* New York: Pantheon.

Herman, Edward S., and Robert W. McChesney. 1997. *The Global Media: The New Missionaries of Corporate Capitalism.* London: Cassell.

Hoynes, William. 1994. *Public Television for Sale: Media, the Market, and the Public Sphere.* Boulder, Colo.: Westview Press.

Karaganis, Joe. 2007. "Structures of Participation in Digital Culture." Social Science Research Council. http://www.ssrc.org.

Kellner, Douglas. 2005. *Media Spectacle and the Crisis of Democracy.* Boulder, Colo.: Paradigm Press.

Kidd, D. 2003. "Indymedia.org: A New Communication Commons." In *Cyberac tivism: Online Activism in Theory and Practice,* edited by Martha McCaughey and Michael D. Ayers, 47–69. New York: Routledge.

Klandermans, Bert. 1992. "The Case for Longitudinal Research on Movement Participation." In *Studying Collective Action,* edited by Mario Diani and Ron Eyeman, 55–75. London: Sage.

Klinenberg, Eric. 2007. *Fighting for Air: Conglomerates, Citizens and the Battle to Control America's Media.* New York: Holt.

Knightley, Phillip. 2002. *The First Casualty: The War Correspondent as Hero, Propagandist and Mythmaker.* Baltimore: Johns Hopkins University Press.

Kurtz, Sharon. 2002. *Workplace Justice: Forging Multi-identity Movements.* Minneapolis: University of Minnesota Press.

Jasper, James M. 2004. "A Strategic Approach to Collective Action: Looking for Agency Is Social Movement Choices." *Mobilization* 9:1–16.

Levison, Jay C., Rick Frishman, and Jill Lublin. 2002. *Guerrilla Publicity: Hundreds of Sure-fire Tactics to Get Maximum Sales for Minimum Dollars.* Avon, Mass.: Adams Publishing.

Lewis, Peter M., and Susan Jones. 2006. *From the Margins to the Cutting Edge: Community Media and Empowerment.* Cresskill, N.J.: Hampton Press.

Martin, Christopher R. 2004. *Framed! Labor and the Corporate Media.* Ithaca, N.Y.: Cornell University Press.

McCarthy, John, Clark McPhail, and Jackie Smith. 1996. "Images of Protest: Estimating Selection Bias in Media Coverage of Washington Demonstrations, 1982–1991." *American Sociological Review* 61:478–99.

McCaughey, Martha, and Michael D. Ayers. 2003. *Cyberactivism: Online Activism in Theory and Practice.* New York: Routledge.

McChesney, Robert. 1993. *Telecommunications, Mass Media, and Democracy.* New York: Oxford University Press.

———. 1999. *Rich Media, Poor Democracy.* Urbana: University of Illinois Press.

Meyers, Marian. 1997. *News Coverage of Violence against Women: Engendering Blame.* Newbury Park, Calif.: Sage.

Morris, Aldon, and Suzanne Staggenborg. 2004. "Leadership in Social Movements." In *The Blackwell Companion to Social Movements,* edited by David A. Snow, Sarah A. Soule, and Hanspeter Kriesi, 171–96. Malden, Mass.: Blackwell.

Mort, Jo-Ann.1992. "How the Media Cover Labor: The Story That's Not Being Told." *Dissent* 39:81–85.

Myers, Daniel J., and Beth Caniglia. 2004. "All the Rioting That's Fit to Print: Selection Effects in National Newspaper Coverage of Civil Disorders, 1968–1969." *American Sociological Review* 69:519–43.

Oliver, Pamela E., and Gregory M. Maney. 2000. "Political Processes and Local Newspaper Coverage of Protest Events: From Selection Bias to Triadic Interaction." *American Journal of Sociology* 106:463–505.

Oliver, Pamela E., and Daniel J. Myers. 1999. "How Events Enter the Public Sphere: Conflict, Location, and Sponsorship in Local Newspaper Coverage of Public Events." *American Journal of Sociology* 105:38–87.

Ortner, Sherry B. 1996. *Making Gender: The Politics and Erotics of Culture.* Boston: Beacon Press.

Pagelow, Mildred D. 1981. *Woman Battering: Victims and Their Experiences.* Thousand Oaks, Calif.: Sage.

Parsons, Liz, Pauline Maclaran, and Mark Tadajewski. 2008. *Nonprofit Marketing.* London: Sage.

Pertschuk, Michael. 2001. *Smoke in Their Eyes: Lessons in Movement Leadership from the Tobacco Wars.* Nashville, Tenn.: Vanderbilt University Press.

Philips, E. Barbara. 1976. "Novelty without Change." *Journal of Communication* 26:87–92.

Riaño, Pilar. 1994. *Women in Grassroots Communication.* Newbury Park, Calif.: Sage.

Rohlinger, Deana A. 2002. "Framing the Abortion Debate: Organizational Resources, Media Strategies and Movement–Countermovement Dynamics." *Sociological Quarterly* 43:479–507.

Ruggiero, Greg. 2003. *Microradio and Democracy: (Low) Power to the People.* New York: Open Media.

Ryan, Charlotte. 1991. *Prime Time Activism: Media Strategies for Grassroots Organizing.* Boston: South End Press.

———. 1993. "Tilting Center: A Study of National Public Radio." *Extra!,* April/May.

———. 1996. "Media War over Welfare." *Peace Review* 8:13–20.

Ryan, Charlotte, Mike Anastario, and Alfredo DaCunha. 2006. "Changing Coverage of Domestic Violence: A Longitudinal Experiment in Participatory Communication." *Journal of Interpersonal Violence* 21:209–28.

Ryan, Charlotte, Michael Anastario, and Karen Jeffreys. 2005. "Start Small, Build Big: Negotiating Opportunities in Media Markets." *Mobilization* 10:111–28.

Schiller, Herbert I. 1996. *Information Inequality: The Deepening Social Crisis in America.* New York: Routledge.

Servaes, Jan. 2008. *Communication for Development and Social Change.* Thousand Oaks, Calif.: Sage.

———, ed. 2002. *Approaches to Development: Studies on Communication for Development.* Paris: UNESCO.

Shepard, Benjamin, and Ronald Hayduk. 2002. *From ACT UP to the WTO: Urban Protest and Community Building in the Era of Globalization.* London: Verso.

Smith, Jackie, John D. McCarthy, Clark McPhail, and Boguslaw Augustyn. 2001. "From Protest to Agenda Building: Description Bias in Media Coverage of Protest Events in Washington, D.C." *Social Forces* 79:1397–423.

Soley, Lawrence C. 1992. *The News Shapers: The Sources Who Explain the News.* New York: Praeger.

Staggenborg, Suzanne. 2002. "The 'Meso' in Social Movement Research." In *Social Movements: Identity, Culture and the State,* edited by David S. Meyer, Nancy Whittier and Belinda Robnett, 124–39. New York: Oxford University Press.

Starr, Jerold M. 2000. *Air Wars: The War over Public Broadcasting.* Boston: Beacon Press.

Underwood, Doug. 1993. *When MBAs Rule the Newsroom.* New York: Columbia University Press.

Waisbord, Silvio. n.d. "Family Tree of Theories, Methodologies and Strategies in Development Communication." Rockefeller Foundation. http://www.communicationforsocialchange.org.

Wallack, Lawrence, Lori E. Dorfman, David H. Jernigan, and Makani Themba-Nixon. 1993. *Media Advocacy and Public Health: Power for Prevention.* Newbury Park, Calif.: Sage.

Walsh, Diana C., Rima E. Rudd, Barbara A. Moeykens, and T. W. Moloney. 1993. "Social Marketing for Public Health." *Health Affairs* 12:104–19.

White, Shirley A., with Sadanandan K. Nair and Joseph R. Ascroft, eds. 1994. *Participatory Communication: Working for Change and Development.* New Delhi: Sage Publications India.

Wiebe, G. D. 1952. "Merchandising Commodities and Citizenship on Television." *Public Opinion Quarterly* 15:679–91.

5

Mobilizing the Generation Gap: Transnational Coalitions and Insider/Outsider Strategy in the Climate Action Network

Anna-Liisa Aunio

On December 8, 2005, the twenty-fifth anniversary of John Lennon's death, a group of attendees at the United Nations Climate Change Conference in Montreal gathered in the main hall and, to the tune of the Beatles' "We All Live in a Yellow Submarine," began singing, "We all live in a carbon-intensive world, a carbon-intensive world, a carbon-intensive world." Dressed in pajamas, lying on cushions and pillows, and surrounded by pictures from John Lennon and Yoko Ono's famous Montreal bed-in, this group staged their own bed-in to pressure governmental delegates in the climate change negotiations and commemorate the anniversary of Lennon's death. After discussing the importance of the Kyoto Protocol in their lives, they then sang a rendition of "Give Peace a Chance": "All we are saying is cut greenhouse gas, / All we are saying is give youth a chance." At the end, they played "Imagine" and issued this press release:

> Just as the Vietnam War was a defining issue for previous generations, climate change is the issue that will define our generation. Youth comprise a majority of the world's population, and they will feel the impacts of flooding, droughts, increased disease prevalence, lack of food security, and other impacts of climate change. According to Rosa Kouri, National Director of the Sierra Youth Coalition, "governments need to stop asking what this will cost them, and start asking what this will cost us. This is no time to play politics, we are all in bed together.

Interestingly, this group staged the protest not as members of Greenpeace, Friends of the Earth, or as environmentalists per se, but instead invoked their generational position within the environmental community as well as the conference generally. Although most were members of one or several environmental organizations, attended the meetings as NGO observers, and sported badges stating that they were members of the Climate Action Network (CAN), they presented themselves as outsiders to the system and engaged in more disruptive, creative, and extrainstitutional tactics. This role and these activities were embraced by other, more established actors within CAN. In fact, many senior insider activists and leaders spent most of their time using less disruptive institutionalized tactics with the hope that contentious activities would be carried out by the youth within their ranks. Climate activists thus mobilized the generation gap to create and use insider and outsider identities to push the climate change negotiations forward. By the time youth staged a similar bed-in at the negotiations in Copenhagen in 2009, it was clear that the strategic construction of these identities ultimately contributed to the emergence of a global youth climate movement, a drastic expansion in the number and diversity of NGOs participating in the climate change regime, and a dramatic shift to extrainstitutional contention emphasizing climate justice. Explaining how these activists mobilized the generation gap as an insider–outsider coalition is thus key to key to understanding the explosive growth in international climate activism after 2005.

To many researchers, this apparent construction of insider and outsider roles based on generational difference and their cooperation as an explicit strategy of social change may come as a surprise. In most studies of social movements, the relationship between insiders and outsiders is characterized as adversarial and acrimonious. Although recent scholarship on transnational mobilization leads us to expect that insiders and outsiders may be cooperating more in transnational contention (Meyer and Corrigall-Brown 2005; Murphy 2005; Levi and Murphy 2006; Tarrow 2005), the relationship is still rendered as a function of fixed ideological or geographical distinction between organizations (Brown and Fox 1998; Sikkink 2005; Tarrow 2005). However, in this case, climate activists cooperated with one another and strategically created a division of labor as insiders and outsiders based on generational identities. Moreover, these activists employed outsider—or extrainstitutional and contentious—tactics both inside and outside the institution's walls. Thus, although most studies define insiders and outsider by their action within or against international institutions (Bandy and Smith 2005), both insiders and outsiders in this case strategically used tactics appropriate to the context. These activists thus challenged conventional wisdom on the division between insiders and outsiders and in the process redefined the boundaries between institutional and extrainstitutional contention.

I focus on CAN at the 2005 Climate Change Conference and draw on my use of participant observation as an activist scholar. Beginning in 2005, I participated in CAN and was fortunate enough to watch the relationship between the old and new guard unfold. As I demonstrate, older and younger CAN participants constructed their generational difference as a politically salient tool to mobilize political will before and at the conference. They also interpreted what these roles entailed by defining what contained and contentious tactics meant in particular contexts. By participating, I was able to discern when members of CAN adopted their roles and how they constructed institutional and disruptive action in the context of the UNFCCC negotiations. More importantly, however, by embracing my experience as an activist and bringing it to bear on this research, I was able to see strategy develop—that is, the opportunities and constraints that activists perceive, the corresponding choices they face, and the path that they take. Although some admonish researchers to cultivate an outsider perspective to the subject matter, an insider perspective offers a broad view on strategic choice within movements. In this case, we thus gain a better understanding of the relationship between institutional and extrainstitutional action, as well as a more dynamic understanding of how coalitions and movements change over time.

I begin by providing a theoretical framework for insiders and outsiders in movements and coalitions. After discussing my data and methods, I then define and discuss the role of the old and new guard within CAN in creating the insider/outsider dynamic within the coalition in 2005. Although I argue that this case has significant insights for scholarship on transnational contention, I also believe that the benefits of movement-based research may help us, as sociologists, become more relevant to the activists and movements that we profess to explain. As such, this study of CAN may be beneficial not only to scholars, but also to activists. Attention to roles and tactics, as well as respect for differences within coalitions, may help activists learn to navigate change within the social movement field and thus strengthen their capacity to effect social change.

Insider/Outsider Coalitions in Transnational Politics

The distinction between insiders and outsiders—between reformers and radicals, between institutional and extrainstitutional action—is not new to either activists or scholars. In social movement theory, the relationship between insiders and outsiders has traditionally been associated with tactics and/or goals. On the one hand, those inside the system seek to reform it through more institutional methods like lobbying; they usually have access to resources and elite partners, and they employ professional staff. On the other hand, those outside the polity participate in contentious activities and are most often cast as challengers to institutions (Tilly 1978; Gamson 1990). Questions about the relationship of these institutional and extrainstitutional actors to the rise, maintenance, and decline of social movements have long been at the heart of scholarship on contentious politics (McAdam, Tarrow, and Tilly 2001). Most often, we conceive of insiders and outsiders with reference to organizational identity. More importantly, we have typically characterized insiders and outsiders as players with fixed, stable identities that are at odds with one another.

Interestingly, studies of transnational activism have recently begun to emphasize a contested but potentially more cooperative relationship between insiders and outsiders. Rather than ideological perspective or tactical repertoire, however, these studies often constitute insiders and outsiders as a function of their organizational size and location. They are collaborating in transnational spaces, Tarrow (2005) argues, because of increasing internationalization,[1] wherein the growth in the number and complexity of international institutions such as the U.N. act as flash points for activists; they present both threats and opportunities for action. Although conflict and mistrust may pervade the collaboration, in some cases, insiders and outsiders have succeeded in carrying out coordinated action and built long-lasting coalitions. In their analysis of multilateral development banks, Brown and Fox (1998) argue that participants of insider–outsider coalitions understand how their knowledge bases can complement one another. Insiders and outsider may also partner, however, with the recognition that both institutional and extrainstitutional action is necessary to achieve particular goals. As such, some argue that these coalitions can combine both institutionalized tactics and more contentious tactics, as well as shift more easily up and down from the international context to the national (Sikkink 2005; Tarrow 2005).

Whether as adversaries in the same movement field or as uneasy partners in coalitions, what all of this research emphasizes is the relationship between insiders and outsiders predicated on a fixed, predetermined identity associated with activists' organizational affiliation, location, or ideological position. Their designation as insiders and outsiders in these analyses is defined by established categories in social movement research of institutional and extrainstitutional action or ideology. Their relationship, once established, persists over time. However, insiders and outsiders, as well as the institutional and extrainstitutional designation that defines each as such, are neither fixed nor stable (Tarrow 2005). By constituting the relationship between insiders and outsiders as predetermined attributes of organizations that persist, no studies have thus far considered that insider and outsider identities could be strategically cast and played by activists. As such, no research on transnational contention has considered the insider–outsider coalition as a dynamic relationship between players who self-consciously understand the benefits of both institutional and extrainstitutional action and seek to create these boundaries in order to gain particular advantages. If CAN, for example, is assessed by these standards, these approaches do little to help us understand why the insider–outsider dynamic emerged in 2005, after CAN had been operating as a coalition for sixteen years. Additionally, they also do little to help us understand why the insider–outsider dynamic emerged based on generational identities within the coalition. Further, they cannot explain how activists interpreted their roles as insiders and outsiders both within and outside of the convention. Finally, they do little to help us understand how these divisions shaped the relationship between institutional and extrainstitutional action after 2005. Thus, although this work is helpful in interpreting the empirical reality of an increase in the number of coalitions and identifying why organizations may coalesce around international institutions, it does little to account for change, context, and strategy over time.

To explain the emergence of insider and outsider roles within CAN, we need to consider the role of strategy within transnational coalitions. The insider–outsider dynamic emerged within CAN at the 2005 Climate Change Conference. Activists who played other roles in other locales saw their generational position as a newfound strategy to both use institutional and extrainstitutional tactics within and outside the convention walls. As a consequence, the insider–outsider dynamic aided older members of the network, but also enabled new participants to meaningfully participate in the CAN coalition. CAN successfully extended the coalition to encompass new members—members who brought media attention and a human face to the issue of climate change.

In creating this relationship, the old guard and the new guard redefined the boundaries between institutional and extrainstitutional action. In this case, old guard activists defined their actions as institutionalized in two predominant ways: first, they socialized state actors by defining the environmental position and thus norm within the UNFCCC, and second, they socialized new recruits into the complex negotiation process. In this respect, because many have been active and present at negotiations every year, the old guard acts as the most continuous and stable institutional memory for international negotiations. New guard youth constructed two roles as well: first, they created, participated in, and publicized contentious activities within and outside of the convention hall, and second, they framed action on climate change as an issue of climate justice, thereby bridging northern and southern interests to create and sustain broad support for action. They were, in this process, the moral voice of the meeting (Jasper 1997), which placed pressure on the negotiations to move forward and thus did the "emotion work" (Hochschild 1979, 1983, 2003) of the mobilizing effort.

Examination of this case is both empirically and theoretically significant to research on transnational coalitions and movements. Empirically, the number of coalitions in transnational politics has grown significantly in recent decades. Insider–outsider coalitions emphasize the ways in which action across borders is increasingly common. Their relationship has become explicitly identified to explain an increase in the number and type of transnational coalitions active in both national and international arenas (Brown and Fox 1998; Bandy and Smith 2005; Sikkink 2005; Tarrow 2005).[2] In her analysis of the Yearbook of International Associations, Smith (2005) found that a coalition organizational structure accounted for just 25 percent of transnational social movement organizations in 1973. By the year 2000, that number rose to 60 percent. The collaborative use of contentious action and institutionalized tactics may, in fact, be the new modus operandi for activism in transnational spaces (Tarrow 2005). Yet although movement scholars admonish us to consider and examine the interaction of "the established and the new" (McAdam, Tarrow, and Tilly 2001, 8), explaining the relationship between insiders and outsiders, and between institutional and extrainstitutional action remains a blurry proposition in transnational politics (Tarrow 2005). This case is a start in clarifying the relationship and extending our understanding of what the content of insider and outsider means in transnational spaces. Below, after a brief discussion of my data and methods, I discuss how participants created these roles at the 2005 Montreal conference.

Data and Methods

I focus here on the United Nations Framework Convention on Climate Change (UNFCCC), a convention that was introduced at the Rio Earth Summit in 1992 and went into effect in March 1994.[3] The primary goal of the convention is to reduce greenhouse gas emissions to a level that does not interfere with the Earth's climate system.[4] The Convention of Parties (COP), constituted by all ratifying parties, meets for two weeks once a year in November or December to evaluate and amend the framework. In 1997, industrialized countries agreed to set timetables and targets in the Kyoto Protocol. After a contentious international debate, the protocol went into effect in 2005 without U.S. participation. In 2005, I attended my first COP meeting after the Kyoto Protocol's entrance into force. This was the first of many COPs focused on negotiating a post-Kyoto regime—a process that culminated in a contentious and unsuccessful COP in Copenhagen in 2009. Of these, Montreal proved to be pivotal to expanding NGO participation and movement mobilization. The conference location in Montreal, funding from the host Canadian government, and the significance of the conference with regard to launching a post-Kyoto round of talks in the face of U.S. opposition all set the stage for the potential entrance of a significant number of new participants. Youth were prominent among these new participants.

I began participating in the coalition through previous activist work I had done and my connections to an influential member of the coalition, Elizabeth May, the veteran director of the Sierra Club of Canada.[5] In September 2005, she took me in tow to a three-day activist training weekend in preparation for the Montreal conference. In December 2005, I became more involved in CAN through their daily meetings, strategy sessions, and planning for an International Day of Action. Though established in 1989 as predominantly a northern coalition, CAN now includes 700 member organizations from over ninety countries. They are recognized as insiders within the institutional framework. They are even recognized as an official constituency, representing all environmental NGOs at meetings.

CAN's institutionalization and status as a constituency enables coalition members to strictly police membership and enforce closed participation at meetings. Neither nonmember NGOs nor researchers are allowed to attend daily meetings at conferences and are in particular restricted from attending overall strategy sessions. Over the course of the three sessions, because I was accredited through CAN, I was able to participate in any and all meetings. In addition, I joined the technology working group and followed this track of the negotiations with a small group of CAN members in order to better understand the negotiations and the CAN process within working groups. Finally, at the 2007 conference, members entrusted me to serve on the editorial board for the daily edition of *Eco.* This was significant because the editorial board is charged with ensuring that all articles accurately reflect the CAN perspective. By participating in this group and the late-night sessions that accompanied it, I became an insider in the CAN coalition from 2005 to 2008. Overall, I logged over 600 hours in the field at CAN-related events.

To complement this, I also conducted in-depth, semistructured interviews with a sample of forty-five key informants from accredited NGOs at the UNFCCC. These included CAN members as well as youth participants at the three conferences. Although my fieldwork covered three conferences, here, I will focus only on the 2005 conference in Montreal. It was at this conference that the insider–outsider relationship between older CAN members and newer CAN volunteers emerged.

At the core of this project is the question of the role of the activist scholar and the issue of movement-relevant research. For many social movement scholars, the process of becoming part of the academy—how we are socialized into the institution of academia—removes us ever more from the direct line of fire that shapes many activists' lives. Thus, while many of us begin our training with commitments to various principles and direct movement participation, when we conduct research, we invariably feel accountable to leave who we are and what we stand for waiting in the wings. The navigation of our personal principles and professional lives becomes, in this regard, a terrain of contestation itself. For me, as a longtime activist and recent scholar, the division between roles and navigation of both arenas became a complicated proposition during the course of my research. In effect, my academic training drew me closer to an outsider relationship to the subject at hand. I was, in this regard, called to be the value-neutral researcher. However, willingly or not, I was an insider to this project. Moreover, I became more of one as time progressed. Though I initially had difficulty with this role, I eventually came to realize that it had significant benefits that I never anticipated. Most importantly, I realized that being engaged in the movement helped me understand the lifeworld of many youth within the coalition. Doing so opened doors to understanding how CAN dealt with change, how participants defined themselves within the coalition, and what consequences it had for their relationship to one another and to mobilization broadly.

Although the value-neutral position of the researcher has many advantages, being an activist scholar taught me that this position also has its costs. In effect, we lose the capacity to understand what it means to be embedded in a community and within a movement. We also then lose the creative, dynamic perspective that being a movement insider offers us. This has an impact on our ability to actually remain relevant to the activists and movements we choose to study and, in some cases, remain committed to. In this regard, although there has been a renewed call within social movement theory to produce research that both reflects and can be applied to activists' work, the fulfillment of this call has, in practice, proven more theoretical than real. This is a serious issue within this field. If, as sociologists, we are to analyze, interpret, and explain movements with precision, how is it that most activists find us irrelevant to their work?

In studying social movements, the movement-based, activist perspective enables researchers to gain better, rather than more limited, theoretical and practical perspectives on activism. I argue, in particular, that we gain a better purchase on strategy within movement spaces; and as others argue, strategy is the key to understanding the dynamism of collective action. It is also crucial to remaining relevant to those movements we purport to understand and explain.

Below, I discuss each group—which I call the old guard and the new guard—within CAN. I then delineate how they acted as insiders and outsiders through their participation in the 2005 Montreal conference.

The Old Guard of CAN: Insider Knowledge, Experience, and Strategy

The old guard of CAN emerged from the long-term, heavily institutionalized, environmental organizations in industrialized countries. The coalition began with, and is still dominated by, organizations from the Global North. Many of its activists have been working for organizations or committed to environmental issues for decades. This, as well as the scientific rationale for environmental problems, has created a wealth of long-term expertise and partnerships between environmental organizations and researchers, tantamount to an epistemic community in relation to the politics of climate change (Haas 1992). Elizabeth May (2005a), director of the Sierra Club of Canada, wrote that these individuals constituted an

> elite corps of top-notch NGO climate negotiators. I have been working on this issue since 1986, but I have not been in the U.N. negotiation system as have Bill Hare, a scientist at the Potsdam Institute who works for Greenpeace International, Jennifer Morgan from World Wildlife Fund—International, Alden Meyer from the Union of Concerned Scientists in Washington DC, and a handful of others. Luckily for me, one of my best friends, someone I hired to work on climate for Sierra Club of Canada right after Rio. . . . Louise Comeau . . . is one of those who covered all the COPs for a long time. . . . So between Bill, Jennifer, Alden and Louise I have a lot of senior U.N. experience on which to rely.

May describes these individuals as carrying "senior U.N. experience," although only one old guard member (not mentioned by her) worked briefly for the United Nations Environmental Program. This designation is based on their continued participation in the negotiations over the course of the convention. In this respect, the old guard cuts across many different kinds of organizations because activists have known one another or been active in the same U.N. circuit over time (Lahusen 1999). In fact, much of the old guard elite group has been working on climate change research and campaigning through the CAN for close to twenty years. These activists are defined by more than age. They hold a wealth of experience from accumulated years and various positions associated with a range of environmental organizations. In short, for the old guard, environmentalism has proven to represent more than a personal cause; it is also a career choice and professional calling, a vocation.

Most of the elite CAN members began their vocational training as outsiders participating in protests, campaigns, and demonstrations within the national context. However, the primary way in which elder CAN elites garnered legitimacy within the convention walls was to call on the collective weight of their experience and expertise. As such, old guard CAN members used their status as a strategy to socialize state actors into the convention framework and, most importantly, to chart the environmental course within the negotiations. Beginning in 2005, however, older CAN members also shaped their relationship to newcomers strategically. Recognizing the central role that extrainstitutional action plays in creating political will, CAN old guard members also successfully socialized the new guard in two ways. First, they helped youth navigate the alphabet soup of the UNFCCC meetings. Second, and more importantly, they also socialized these new recruits into the critical role that outsiders play in mobilization. They succeeded in doing so because of their own experience on the front lines of the action as well as their ambivalence toward their status as insiders to the convention. In this regard, the old guard redefined the boundaries of insider/outsider identity by focusing on generational difference and positively used that difference in a complementary fashion by adopting institutional and extrainstitutional tactics based on these identities.

Charting the Environmental Course

Studies of international institutions suggest that they are central in shaping states' behavior (Meyer et al. 1997; Boli and Thomas 1999). States become socialized to new norms through participation in these venues. Environmental protection, for example, became a norm for which states could be held accountable with the expansion of international environmental accords such as the UNFCCC (Frank et al. 1999). They are important within international venues in creating, interpreting, and communicating what environmentalism means in the messy context of negotiations. CAN elite members engaged in institutionalized action in this regard by creatively constructing and reconstructing the environmental position in accordance with the current state of play at international meetings. Within the UNFCCC, CAN old guard members engage in this action predominantly through organizing daily meeting sessions at negotiating sessions and organizing working groups to track the negotiations. This smaller political group, dominated by experienced CAN members, sets the tone for and manages the progress of these working groups. They even sell proposals to other members on sensitive issues. The goal of each working group is to develop a CAN position on the issue if and when necessary.[6]

Participating in these working groups and developing a position produces insider knowledge in four ways. First, it serves as a research and thought exercise for members of the working group to understand the full implications of the issue, the proposals on the table, and the roles and positions of governments or governmental blocs. Working group members must think through, to their logical conclusion, all of the aspects of different scenarios in order to figure out what a proper environmental position might be—that is, an environmental position that also takes account of other significant issues such as social justice. Second, and as a consequence, developing this position is a consensus-building exercise for the group itself. Working groups interpret and respond to developments within the convention walls and float their ideas within the daily meetings to the CAN membership. Obtaining feedback and developing a consensus position through these meetings provides a forum for organizations to work out conflicts and reinforce commitment to the coalition. Third, the working group drafts an article for this position for the daily *Eco*— CAN's daily report on the proceedings.[7] Most delegates pick up the *Eco* as well as *Earth Negotiations Bulletin* in the morning at the same time as they retrieve the daily program outlining that day's agenda for the meetings.[8] As such, CAN's position is disseminated to most delegations, and in many cases, it initiates discussions in the hallways. With this, the statement becomes an official position of the coalition and, by extension, of all environmental NGOs. Finally, CAN members use this position in their interactions with other NGOs and specific governments. Lobbying is the most visible part of this process, though much of the institutionalized action takes place behind closed doors.

By building consensus, establishing a position, and discussing the potential avenues of action for particular governments and groups, CAN effectively charts the environmental position on the issue. In doing so, veteran members of CAN disseminate the environmental position to define a potential course of action and position themselves as the primary arbiters of the aims of the convention. When asked what the roles of the different constituencies within the UNFCCC were, Barbara Black, the NGO liaison officer at the UNFCCC replied, with reference to CAN, "They are using a lot of this information [from research organizations] to take care that everyone is involved at the political level, either regionally through lobbying the EU, nationally, or internationally, they are trying to ensure that the aims of the convention, in the way that they feel, are kept firmly on track" (interview with the author). Notably, in her interview, she only discusses the role of keeping the convention "firmly on track" with reference to CAN.

Socializing State Actors

The advantage of this strategy for many insiders is the potential power it gives them with state delegations. Because they have been doing so for a long time and with such consistency, many governments and the U.N. itself often rely on CAN for analysis of the issues and a sense of historical perspective with reference to the framework. Louise Comeau notes:

> Often, the problem isn't that government officials don't care about the issues; it's that they just don't know about them. Elections bring in new administrations, and with new administrations you get staff turnover. That's when institutional amnesia sets in. So I started a series of briefings. I'd get in there and educate these new officials—give 'em the confidence that they could talk about the issues with authority. (interview with the author)

During the Montreal Climate Change Conference, the Canadian prime minister, Paul Martin, made personal calls to heads of state to push the negotiations forward and was advised not by Environment Canada, but by Jennifer Morgan, an old guard climate expert from World Wildlife Fund International. This extends to international delegations. A twenty-six-year veteran of Greenpeace, Steve Sawyer, who now leads the Global Wind Energy Council, relates the following:

> When we go into these international meetings, we're invariably the most knowledgeable people in the room. So we end up educating the government officials on the issues. This is especially true when we're dealing with governments from the developing world. So you could say that part of what we do is to define the problem and its various possible solutions. (interview with the author)

Here, Sawyer is addressing both the collective experience of CAN in relation to specific delegations as well as their capacity to do problem definition. Of course, this is not true of all governments or delegations. Governments that are more inclined toward CAN's perspective are more likely to engage CAN organizations and expertise. Regardless, states less inclined toward CAN proposals often must still engage the issues with consideration to their positions.

Although CAN members are certainly not the only actors within the convention, the institutionalization of the coalition, the continuity of the old guard, and the consensus building within the coalition communicates a unified sense of purpose, collective memory, and mission that can more easily be transmitted within and outside of the convention walls. The overall impact of their insider knowledge and status has been to provide a collective sense of institutional memory for the UNFCCC. Individuals who participate in an institution's events, daily routines, and rituals actively create a collective memory that is integral to legitimizing the way to do things. Thus institutions are reproduced not only by practices encoded in documents and bureaucratic rules, but also by institutional memory or the collective interpretation of the rules, rituals, and values of the institution by those who practice them. They are fundamentally cognitive. As Wendt (1992, 399) argues, "Institutions come to confront individuals as more or less coercive social facts, but they are still a function of what actors collectively 'know.'" In this regard, institutional memory is an expression of the proper way to do things: "I was there," and "I remember when. . . . " These carry weight. Individuals who were there at the beginning can claim more normative authority than newcomers. CAN, and in particular the collective experience of the old guard, acts as the longest-running and consistent institutional memory for the framework. This collective know-how carries weight with other actors whether they support CAN's positions or not. It also benefits newcomers and did benefit youth in 2005. New participants become socialized into the institutional proceedings and thus can navigate international spaces much more quickly.

This position was not without its costs. Although CAN insiders garnered legitimacy as a function of their experience and expertise, many members privately expressed doubt about the coalition's efficacy in communicating and building political will for action on climate change. More than one participant at the Activist Training Weekend remarked that the United States was able to reject the Kyoto Protocol because organizations focused far too much on the negotiations and not on building political will at home.[9] In addition, the issue and CAN itself faced many of the north–south tensions demonstrated in other studies of transnational coalitions and movements (Brown and Fox 1998; O'Brien et al. 2000). In this respect, old guard activists have had a difficult time framing climate change in such a way as to bridge north–south issues and attract broad public support in the transnational arena. Overall, they had admittedly been unable to put a human face on climate change.

Overwhelmingly, this ambivalence reflected a conflicted relationship to their role as insiders and recognition of the critical role of outsiders to mobilizing political will. Although they recognized the legitimacy garnered from their insider status within the convention, many, like Rob Bradley, also thought that they had invariably drifted too far away from their roots in the fulfillment of their role and become too native (interview with the author). Participants had two reactions to this ambivalence. First, many continuously recalled their activities and roles in the action to legitimate and substantiate their status as activists and differentiate their work as part of a movement, distinct from the advocacy work that other NGOs did. In relation to this, interviewees within the old guard overwhelmingly stressed their connection to the front lines and their past as outsiders as evidence of experience and connection to environmentalism as a movement. Some discussed growing up in the movement, whereas others pointed to particular events that granted them street credibility (author's interviews with Shane Rattenbury, Zeina Al'Haij, and Gina Sanchez). Most expressed nostalgia for or a desire to return to the front lines but stated that their transition to becoming insiders was a function of necessity and a logical consequence of experience. They commented, in this regard, that they were (unfortunately) more effective when a bit removed from the action.

The second reaction to this ambivalence was to question the efficacy and even viability of environmentalism as a movement in the contemporary and international context. Some expressed discomfort with being identified as an activist or associated with an environmental movement (author's interviews with Morag Carter, Zoë Caron, and Louise Comeau). Others linked the problem to one of the paid, professionalized movement organizations. One long-term supporter, John Michael, remarked at the 2005 conference that the problem with environmentalism was one of the paycheck: "Too many people," he argued, "are getting paid to do this. We need more people like you to bring energy and life into things again" (interview with the author).

The New Guard Emergence: Outsider Strategy

With the entrance of youth at the 2005 conference, conflicted old guard members saw an opportunity to inject new life into their efforts. Similar to the term "old guard," "youth" did not just imply age. Although the old guard had a wealth of experience working for a variety of environmental NGOs over time, most youth were expected to be relatively inexperienced and un-affiliated—that is, without professional knowledge or position. Essential to this was often their status as students and volunteers (i.e., not paid staff) within larger organizations, or as part of grassroots (i.e., small and local) coalitions. Volunteer status, for many of the old guard, inherently meant that they were more independent or able and free to decide individually on their position. This, of course, meant that they could adopt the most extreme position even if it was politically untenable. For many, this also inherently meant unencumbered, meaning unmarried and without children. For some, it even meant lack of a serious relationship. This implied a belief in the necessity of moving around without restraint, of being able to take risks and go to places without consideration of home, family, or job. Greenpeace, for example, only sent individuals for action at locations if they were able to be arrested. In this respect, the youth constituted a group with the most "biographical availability" (McAdam 1983, 70) for action. They had the least restrictions on their lives and the most free time to commit to the cause.

Although youth had attended previous COP conferences from the beginning of the convention, never before did they represent such a strong and independent voice, organize specifically as youth, or consider themselves a separate and special constituency within the convention walls (Revkin 2005). Over the course of the two weeks, over 500 youth organized within the convention. Outside, thousands participated in the march. They did so in part through the active support of established NGOs, though many were affiliated with local organizations or campaigns that were active on college campuses. Old guard members played a facilitating role in youth arriving at the conference and assisted their participation in the conference. Beginning in 2005, CAN members brought expertise and a sense of institutional memory to the framework, and as a consequence, they established the normative framework for which progress on the convention track could be measured. New guard youth learned from their older members what progress meant and brought an emotional, creative energy to demanding those results. In so doing, they succeeded in garnering media attention and focusing that media attention on the consequences of the negotiations for future generations. The basis of this relationship began with old guard members. They established a cooperative relationship by extending the benefits of socialization and the lessons of institutionalization to youth.

Socializing New Members

Many scholars recognize the role of socialization within insider–outsider coalitions (Tarrow 2005), but few have discussed the ways in which insiders help outsiders navigate the institutional spaces. Though the old guard had a history of doing capacity building for new organizations and members of the coalition, the large number of youth in 2005 as well as their status as volunteers produced a different strategy of socialization. Old guard members sought to use their expertise to help youth navigate the negotiations with ease, but they also encouraged their participation in the coalition as a distinct group. This was a first for CAN. All other members of the coalition work in CAN's name at the international sessions. However, youth both worked with CAN and actively constructed their role as outsiders vis-à-vis old guard members. There were thus two major aspects to the social learning strategy adopted by older members. First, old guard CAN members socialized new recruits into the overall structure and operation of the international negotiations. New recruits looked to the old guard to help them understand the alphabet soup of U.N. negotiations, the history of the climate regime, the positions of various governments, and the science behind climate change. Leading up to the conference, CAN International began mobilization by hosting an Activist Training Weekend workshop. Organizations registered to participate, and young recruits could apply to attend. Many youth received subsidies to defray the cost of their attendance for travel from CAN Canada or CAN International. Elizabeth May (2005b) from Sierra Club Canada developed a guide to the negotiations for new participants entitled "A Planetary Citizen Guide to Global Climate Change Negotiations—or—How to Use a MOP" and created a safe zone for volunteers to ask basic questions by hosting daily evening briefings for the duration of the conference. One youth activist likened his two-week experience to a "crash Ph.D. programme" on climate (May 2005c).

Second, within the UNFCCC negotiations, CAN old guard included youth in the environmental NGO constituency, but also encouraged them to remain independent and to adopt the role of outsiders. In this respect, old guard members socialized youth in the distinction and significance of extra-institutional action to mobilization. When the youth thus secured a meeting with the Canadian delegation and asked the old guard for advice on what kinds of questions they should ask, Elizabeth May responded:

> Look, don't get involved with all of the "Article 3.9" this and "draft proposal" that. We [the old guard] do it only because we have to. You can become like the Borg [a *Star Trek* reference] after a while doing it; pretty soon you are all connected to this techno-speak. You don't have to do it. Talk passionately about why you care about this issue and why you think they are screwing things up for you.[10]

May is clearly looking to the new guard to talk passionately and to provide the moral imperative for governments to act quickly. She contrasts this with the need for the older generation to do "techno-speak."

Youth embraced both the opportunities that old guard CAN members offered them as well as their unique role in the negotiations. They recognized this, in part, as a way of becoming involved in the negotiations as students and volunteers with much less experience and knowledge than many CAN members. In so doing, they chose not to follow the working groups on substantive issues and contribute to the overall effort by emphasizing the big picture. When asked about the main difference between youth and CAN members, Zoë Caron responded,

They [CAN] very much rely on the experts in the group, which is very understandable. I mean, they work all year round on these issues and then come here and have twelve days to do what they can. . . . I think that's why they have their own group and we have our own group, because youth come here with the same goals in mind, but we go through more of a process of figuring out how we're going to do that each time. . . . Our main focus is bringing to light or bringing to the table that, just to consider the reality of the issue and more the overall, I guess, arching issue as opposed to technicalities of SBSTA [Subsidiary Body for Science and Technical Advice] or whatever they are working on. There's a lot of youth here who don't necessarily grasp that right away and don't want to grasp that. (interview with the author)

Here, Caron, like Elizabeth May, reflects on the relationship between old guard and new guard. When asked what the youth brought to the picture that other groups did not, Rosa Kouri, president of the Sierra Youth Coalition, replied,

I think that we have a really unique place to speak as victims, I think, on the issue of climate change, where it seems like it's distant, it seems like it's removed, but young people are really going to be the victims—all young people are. That's a big piece of it. Just being able to speak from that very sincere place that this impacts us. . . . Right, we can be a lot more real— I think we have a lot more freedom than our adult colleagues in NGOs. That's really good, we have more freedom. And we have more fun, like we emphasize a lot more creativity in tactics, which is actually really brilliant. . . . Young people get it, like we just, I mean, I don't know if it's because we're the generation raised in . . . the highest and strongest part of consumer culture—advertising culture—but we get it. (interview with the author)

Here, Kouri stresses the youth's particular position with reference to the older NGOs—the ability to be more free, or independent as a consequence of their unofficial affiliation with CAN and many environmental NGOs. She also, however, touches on the central aspects of the youth's work as outsiders coming up with and executing innovative tactics and "speaking as," or framing their effort as victims of climate inaction. Youth considered themselves outsiders in this regard because they engaged in activities that would place pressure on the negotiations and they were at a structural disadvantage with reference to the big-budget, professional environmental organizations. The old guard viewed these actions as complementary and even synergistic to their work (author's interview with Morag Carter).

Tactical Innovation

Creativity is central to mobilization. From the civil rights era forward, tactical innovation has often been associated with building movement momentum (McAdam 1983). Although youth were involved in planning the first International Day of Climate Action outside the convention, much of the creative, innovative work took place within the convention meeting itself. The tactics they used were innovative in two ways. First, youth shifted effortlessly between inside the conference hall to outside the hall. Within the conference walls, youth staged daily interventions designed to attract media and build support. The bed-in was just one example. Youth participants also provided fortune cookies to delegates with climate fortunes such as "You will pass article 3.9" and "You will think first of youth in negotiations" within the conference walls. To demonstrate solidarity, they wore T-shirts throughout the conference with "Stop Asking What It Is Going to Cost You and Start Asking What It Is Going to Cost Us" emblazoned on both front and back. At particular times, they engaged in more direct action against particular targets. On one occasion, the youth delivered a survival kit that contained gas masks to the U.S. delegation as it was on its way to a meeting. One member was subsequently ejected from the conference hall. Outside, they organized directly in front of the conference location. One of their most successful actions was to set up a makeshift ice rink and launch a "Save Hockey" campaign. As the unusually warm winter day made the ice melt, participants found it more and more difficult to play and, accordingly, drove their point home.

The second way that youth were innovative with reference to their tactics was their use of optimism and humor. Indeed, they created a "radical flank effect" (Haines 1984, 32) as a function of advocating for, rather than against, the institution. This was a function of the fact that these outsiders were protesting the inaction at the international level on the issue and attempting to push the negotiations forward; that is, they were attempting to strengthen the international framework rather than to tear it down. In much of the analyses of outsiders thus far, the presumption is that they are protesting outside the conference halls and against international institutions, as is the case with the global justice movement (Bandy and Smith 2005). In this case, mobilization around the 2005 Montreal conference was predominantly aimed at assuring that the United States would not stand in the way of future talks. Because activists were acting in defense of the institutional framework, they were again granting more room for protest and contentious activities within the conference walls. They used this space to creatively respond to the negotiations.

They found, through trial and error, which tactics were more successful. Here, Caron describes the failure of one of their actions and the relationship to their overall tactics:

> I found that the actions that were really serious and depressing weren't effective at all. People were like, "I don't want to see that, that's just old." And so one of our actions was—we didn't do very many, but one was, we had four stories; we had four people talk about how they were personally affected by climate change and we had, like, slow, kind of depressing music playing in the background. And it was sad, and I'm sure some people were affected by it, but it just wasn't—like who wants to watch that. That's the story that you always hear: how bad things are. But putting a spin on the story makes it a little more lighthearted and reminds you that it's about people. (interview with the author)

Spin is not just about tactics; youth also needed to develop an innovative frame to bring together their constituency and attract potential adherents.

Framing

Through participation in the 2005 conference, youth established a shared frame that underpinned disparate actions. They did so by highlighting their role as outsiders with reference to their structural position within the conference and in relation to older members of CAN. Because they stressed their economic and structural disadvantage, they were able to frame their participation as a function of their status of being at risk of experiencing and paying for the consequences of climate change. Above, Kouri makes reference to their "unique place as victims." The "future generations at risk" frame resonated broadly within the coalition, the conference, and the media. This had two consequences. First, the at-risk frame helped to bridge north–south differences within the climate change regime and motivated united action at the conference. Youth began with the proposition that "the most severe impacts of climate change are predicted to occur in the coming decades, and as youth, we will experience the lion's share of climate changes devastation."[11] Youth then linked their at-risk status to the at-risk status of others through solidarity: "We youth stand in solidarity with low-income, people of color, and Indigenous communities who are disproportionately impacted by climate change in three critical ways: by compromising health, imposing economic burdens, and endangering cultures."[12] Throughout the conference, youth wore armbands to visibly demonstrate their solidarity. The youth then extended their claim to solidarity by extending the possibility to the delegates. Youth thus mobilized broadly as direct beneficiaries of government's action (or inaction) on climate change. In contrast to environmental groups that spoke for the environment and mobilize conscience constituents, youth were able to claim legitimacy as those affected by the decisions within the conference walls. Suddenly, climate change had a human face.

Because the frame was successful within the coalition and conference, it garnered a great deal of media attention. The bed-in was covered on a host of television news networks, including CNN, the BBC, and the CBC.[13] In addition, Andrew Revkin (2005), a journalist for the *New York Times,* wrote an article highlighting the conference's importance to "their generation." Both Kouri and Caron indicated that their tactics were aimed at attracting media attention. Kouri referred to their actions as scripts, or dramatic performances specifically aimed at the camera and emphasized their capacity to "get it" with reference to the media (interview with the author). Attention was not limited to the news, however. Perhaps the most important means of bringing attention to the issue and their work was the youth's use of media—most importantly, the Internet. At the conference, youth participants launched a website (http://itsgettinghotinhere.org) as a clearinghouse of the youth climate movement. The website is unique in its direct connection from youth to their audience. On the site, individuals log in as representatives of the youth movement and blog about what they are doing with reference to climate change from 160 countries in the world. During the 2005 conference, the site received several thousand hits per day and was the primary way in which participants communicated their feelings and perceptions about the negotiations. The site has since become a suggested source on the web by the *New York Times.* In this respect, Kouri discusses the youth's ability to get it, not only in terms of highlighting their actions within the conference walls, but also with reference to their use of the Internet to get their message out (interview with the author).

The overall effect of these tactical and framing innovations produced by the youth was to bring a human, emotional perspective to the issue of climate change. Their role in this regard was both symbolic and affective. They did emotion work that some scholars argue is a necessary but insufficient requirement for mobilization (Hochschild 1979; McAdam and Aminzade 2001, 2002). It is significant to note, however, that youth identified their grievances but focused on motivating action by emphasizing their ability to do so through optimistic and often humorous tactics. This strongly affected youth participants. They most often characterized the 2005 conference as an inspiring experience that motivated them to continue involvement. This also affected older, more experienced CAN members. When asked about the participation of youth in the international negotiations, one old guard member responded,

> I think that they have brought an incredible level of energy and optimism. One of the things that happens in these negotiations is that, it's very easy to become cavalier and cynical, whereas when there are fresh faces, young blood, lots at stake for the youth delegation that are here and it propitiated incredibly well, it's really refreshing, it's really heartening. I really appreciate it. (author's interview with Morag Carter)

Although it is unlikely that their tactics and frames influenced the trajectory of the negotiations in 2005, the extrainstitutional work that the youth performed facilitated mobilization inside and outside the convention hall.

This affected a significant expansion in mobilization from 2006 to 2009. After the 2005 conference, youth in Canada established the Canadian Youth Climate Coalition and continued to carry out actions in Canada. This was just the beginning: an international youth climate movement, encompassing local and national organizations in over 100 countries, emerged out of the 2005 conference. In 2009, they became officially recognized as a constituency in their own right in the UNFCCC negotiations. Though they embrace this distinct identity, however, they still have access to CAN meetings and maintain their relationship to CAN by framing their activities in much the same manner as they did in 2005. In addition, by framing their "at-risk" status in terms of intergenerational equity, youth amplified southern NGOs and developing countries' long-standing calls for climate justice aimed at both northern countries and NGOs (Pettit 2004). This contributed to the expansion of climate change mobilization, and in particular the emergence of the climate justice movement. This movement, formed by the convergence of justice and environmental movements, expanded year by year after Montreal until, in 2009, it brought an historic number of NGOs together both inside and outside the walls. These new participants mobilized both northern and southern NGOs and in turn dramatically expanded CAN's membership from 350 organizations in 2005 to 700 organizations in 2010. In doing so, they also adopted the new guard's fluid approach to extrainstitutional tactics by carrying out contentious actions inside and outside the convention walls.

Ultimately, the sheer number of NGOs, accompanied by contentious activities both inside and outside ultimately led to the disenfranchisement of many NGOs, the closure of the negotiation process to a few parties, and subsequent limitations on civil society participation in COP meetings (Fisher

2010; McGregor 2011). In this respect, both the tactics and the frames adopted by youth in 2005 shaped the expansion of mobilization on climate change after Montreal. This reflects some scholars' observations that some frames are successful because they mobilize people, whereas others help activists achieve particular policy outcomes. There may even be a trade-off between the two (Staggenborg and Lecomte 2009).

Conclusion

Within the CAN, old guard and new guard activists certainly recognized their different statuses and generational differences. At the 2005 Climate Change Conference in Montreal, however, these two groups transformed their differences into complementary, politicized identities through the adoption of particular roles: insiders and outsiders. These identities helped define a division of labor among coalition members. Old guard CAN members adopted the role of institutionalized insiders and defined this role with reference to their capacity to act as socializing agents, often ambivalently, and as an institutional memory for state actors and new members of their coalition. New guard youth learned from the older members and brought an emotional, creative energy to demanding results in the interests of their generation. By acting cooperatively, activists thus both garnered media attention and mobilized a broad audience without compromising their ability to act as drafters of text, advisers, and lobbyists to delegations. In the process, they creatively redefined the boundaries of institutional and extrainstitutional action and used this action to contribute to the coalition's goals. This cooperative differentiation thus also expanded the coalition to encompass a large influx of newcomers and extended activism on climate change from traditional environmental groups to new constituencies and new locales In this respect, adopting insider–outsider roles strategically broadened activism on climate change across borders into new communities, a choice that contributed to the overall growth of the coalition, mobilization on climate change, and the formation of new organizations, coalitions, and movements.

This dynamic is not new to activists. Saul Alinsky, in his 1971 organizing manual, *Rules for Radicals,* highlights the strategic nature of adopting these roles. However, this comes as a surprise with reference to current theories on insider–outsider dynamics and coalitions in contentious politics. In classic literature, movement insiders and outsiders often been characterized as at odds with one another even though they may be in the same multiorganizational field (Klandermans 1992). In his classic study of black radicalization and the civil rights movement, Haines (1984) demonstrated that the emergence of more radical organizations created a radical flank effect. More

moderate organizations experienced an upsurge in financial support as radical organizations gained momentum. The positive benefit to more moderate groups, in these cases, was unintended. In the more cooperative terrain
of transnational activism, researchers argue that insider/outsider coalitions
emerge on the basis of these identities as authentic and persistent attributes.
Yet as this case demonstrates, activists that recognize the complementary nature
of institutional and extrainstitutional action may construct these roles self-
consciously. Moreover, they may do so within established coalitions as a
strategy to integrate new constituencies and to expand the range of repertoires, tactics, and frames available to activists.

Without the perspective of the activist in this case, these insights would
have been overlooked, as they were in Alinsky's time. Without attention to
the insider–outsider dynamic in this case, we would have missed one of the
ways in which CAN and activism on climate change significantly expanded
after 2005. Moreover, we would have overlooked the ways in which activists
creatively interpreted these roles within and outside the convention's walls,
thus redefining the boundaries between institutional and extrainstitutional
action in the process. As a result, current scholarship may also be missing
some of the more creative, innovative aspects of transnational mobilization.
As such, I emphasize the significance of movement-based research in expanding our capacity as researchers to explain contentious politics.

The insights garnered from the movement perspective will ultimately
also help us to become more relevant to activists in the future. In this case,
for example, the success the insider–outsider relationship within CAN was
not uncontested territory. With the influx of new activists and the generational divide between members, there were often conflicts about whether
and how youth should participate in the coalition as well as the conference.
In fact, the temptation to create a new constituency with its own status in
order to separate from CAN and thus eschew its ties to the coalition often
loomed on the horizon. Ultimately, however, CAN and youth succeeded in
navigating this terrain by establishing and respecting each other's roles within
the coalition. As such, the significance of appreciating each other's strengths
and defining roles according to the context may prove fundamental to building strong relationships through coalitions. Activists may gain some perspective from these insights. There is often a natural tendency to encourage new
participants in any organization or movement to adopt the well-worn steps
of the established guard. Doing so, however, may have unanticipated costs.
It may prove instead to be more beneficial to provide space for new groups
to find a place within existing coalitions, to encourage and accommodate

change, and thus to expand and strengthen the movement's efficacy overall. CAN's success in doing so defines one potential path for activists to take to accomplish this. Attention to the ways in which a division of labor based on insider and outsider roles benefit cooperation may thus help to define a course of action for activists embark on, particularly as they increasingly work across borders.

Notes

1. Tarrow (2005, 8) identifies three aspects of internationalization: increasing horizontal relationships between states and NGOs, increasing vertical links from the local to the international, and creating enhanced formal and informal structures that facilitate the formation of networks and open up space for transnational activism.

2. Levi and Murphy (2006, 654) define coalitions as "collaborative, means-oriented arrangements that permit distinct organizational entities to pool resources in order to effect change."

3. The others are the Convention on Biological Diversity and the United Nations Convention to Combat Desertification. Together, they are known as the Rio Conventions.

4. Greenhouse gases are those considered responsible for contributing to climate change and global warming. UNFCCC recognizes six: carbon dioxide (CO_2), methane (CH_4), nitrous oxide (N_2O), hydrofluorocarbons, perfluorocarbons, and sulfur hexafluoride (SF_6).

5. May started the Sierra Club in Canada in 1989 and stepped down in 2006 to run (successfully) for the leadership of the Canadian Green Party.

6. This section is based on extensive field notes from participation in a CAN working group as well as daily meetings.

7. *Eco* newsletters for UNFCCC meetings may be found at http://www .climatenetwork.org.

8. *Earth Negotiations Bulletin* is a daily summary of developments within the negotiations created by the International Institute for Sustainable Development. It is designed as a nonpartisan, independent, and objective report of the negotiations.

9. Field notes, September 22, 2005.

10. Field notes, December 6, 2005.

11. Field notes, December 3, 2005.

12. Field notes, December 10, 2005.

13. Field notes, December 9, 2005.

References

Bandy, Joe, and Jackie Smith, eds. 2005. *Coalitions across Borders: Transnational Protest and the Neoliberal Order.* Lanham, Md.: Rowman & Littlefield.

Boli, John, and George M. Thomas. 1999. "INGOs and the Organization of World Culture." In *Constructing World Culture: International Nongovernmental Organizations since 1875,* edited by John Boli and George M. Thomas, 14–49. Stanford, Calif.: Stanford University Press.

Brown, L. David, and Jonathan A. Fox. 1998. "Accountability within Transnational Coalitions." In *The Struggle for Accountability: The World Bank, NGOs, and Grassroots Movements,* edited by Jonathan A. Fox and L. David Brown, 439–84. Cambridge, Mass.: MIT Press.

Fisher, Dana R. 2010. "COP-15 in Copenhagen: How the Merging of Movements Left Civil Society Out in the Cold." *Global Environmental Politics* 10, no. 2: 11–17.

Frank, David John, Ann Hironaka, John W. Meyer, Evan Schofer, and Nancy Brandon Tuma. 1999. "The Rationalization and Organization of Nature in World Culture." In *Constructing World Culture: International Nongovernmental Organizations since 1875,* edited by John Boli and George M. Thomas, 81–99. Stanford, Calif.: Stanford University Press.

Gamson, William A. 1990. *The Strategy of Social Protest.* Belmont, Calif.: Wadsworth.

Haas, Peter. 1992. "Introduction: Epistemic Communities and International Policy Coordination." *International Organization* 46:1–36.

Haines, Herbert H. 1984. "Black Radicalization and the Funding of Civil Rights, 1957–1970." *Social Problems* 32:31–43.

Hochschild, Arlie Russell. 1979. "Emotion Work, Feeling Rules, and Social Structure." *American Journal of Sociology* 85:551–75.

———. 1983. *The Managed Heart: Commercialization of Human Feeling.* Berkeley: University of California Press.

———. 2003. *Commercialization of Intimate Life: Notes from Home and Work.* Berkeley: University of California Press.

Jasper, James. 1997. *The Art of Moral Protest: Culture, Biography, and Creativity in Social Movements.* Chicago: University of Chicago Press.

Klandermans, Bert. 1992. "The Social Construction of Protest and Multiorganizational Fields." In *Frontiers in Social Movement Theory,* edited by Aldon D. Morris and Carol McClurg Mueller, 77–103. New Haven, Conn.: Yale University Press.

Lahusen, Christian. 1999. "International Campaigns in Context: Collective Action between the Local and the Global." In *Social Movements in a Globalizing World,* edited by Donatella della Porta, Hanspeter Kriesi, and Dieter Rucht, 189–205. New York: St. Martin's Press.

Levi, Margaret, and Gillian Murphy. 2006. "Coalitions of Contention: The Case of the WTO Protests in Seattle." *Political Studies* 54:651–70.

May, Elizabeth. 2005a. "Day 5—Climate Conference." *Citizen Shift,* December 3. http://citizenshift.org.

———. 2005b. "A Planetary Citizen Guide to Global Climate Change Negotiations—or—How to Use a MOP." *Citizen Shift*, November 15. http://citizen
shift.org.

———. 2005c. "Day 8—Climate Conference." *Citizen Shift*, December 3. http://
citizenshift.org.

McAdam, Doug. 1986. "Recruitment to High-Risk Activism: The Case of Freedom
Summer." *American Journal of Sociology* 92, no. 1:64–90.

McAdam, Doug, and Ronald Aminzade. 2001. "Emotions and Contentious Politics."
In *Silence and Voice in the Study of Contentious Politics,* edited by Ronald R.
Aminzade, Jack A. Goldstone, Doug McAdam, and Elizabeth J. Perry, 14–50.
New York: Cambridge University Press.

———. 2002. "Introduction: Emotions and Contentious Politics." *Mobilization*
7:107–9.

McAdam, Doug, Sidney Tarrow, and Charles Tilly. 2001. *Dynamics of Contention.*
Cambridge: Cambridge University Press.

McGregor, Ian. 2011. "Disenfranchisement of Countries and Civil Society at COP-
15 in Copenhagen." *Global Environmental Politics* 11, no. 1:1–7.

Meyer, David S., and Catherine Corrigall-Brown. 2005. "Coalitions and Political
Context: U.S. Movements against Wars in Iraq." *Mobilization* 10:327–44.

Meyer, John W., John Boli, George M. Thomas, and Francisco O. Ramirez.
1997. "World Society and the Nation State." *American Journal of Sociology*
103:144–81.

Murphy, Gillian. 2005. "Coalitions and the Development of the Global Environmental Movement: A Double-Edged Sword." *Mobilization* 10, no. 2:235–50.

O'Brien, Robert, Anne Marie Goetz, Jan Aart Scholte, and Marc Williams. 2000.
*Contesting Global Governance: Multilateral Economic Institutions and Global
Social Movements.* Cambridge: Cambridge University Press.

Pettit, Jethro. 2004. "Climate Justice: A New Social Movement for Atmospheric
Rights." *IDS Bulletin* 35:102–6.

Revkin, Andrew. 2005. "Youths Make Spirited Case at Climate Meeting." *New York
Times,* December 9. http://www.nytimes.com.

Sikkink, Kathryn. 2005. "Patterns of Dynamic Multilevel Governance and the
Insider–Outsider Coalition." In *Transnational Protest and Global Activism,* edited
by Donatella della Porta and Sidney Tarrow, 151–73. Lanham, Md.: Rowman
& Littlefield.

Smith, Jackie. 2005. "Globalization and Transnational Social Movement Organiza-
tions." In *Social Movements and Organization Theory,* edited by Gerald F. Davis,
Doug McAdam, W. Richard Scott, and Mayer N. Zald. New York: Cambridge
University Press.

Staggenborg, Suzanne, and Josée Lecomte. 2009. "Social Movement Campaigns:

Mobilization and Outcome in the Montreal Women's Movement Commmu-
nity. *Mobilization* 14, no. 2:163–80.

Tarrow, Sidney. 2005. *The New Transnational Activism.* New York: Cambridge University Press.

Tilly, Charles. 1978. *From Mobilization to Revolution.* Reading, Mass.: Addison/Wesley.

Wendt, Alexander. 1992. "Anarchy Is What States Make of It: The Social Construction of Power Politics." *International Organization* 46:391–425.

6

Local Strategies for Global Change: Working for Human Rights and Economic Empowerment in the Midwest

Jackie Smith

A growing chorus of scholar activists is helping us recognize the value of doing engaged scholarship.[1] The previous two chapters in this section add to this chorus, illustrating some important lessons gained from using more participatory methods in our study of social movements. What is interesting about this recent flowering of discussion about the public and political roles and responsibilities of social scientists—what some have called public sociology or engaged scholarship—is that it has taken place simultaneously in a number of social science disciplines, beginning in the mid- to late 1990s, and that it coincides with a rising global tide of social movement activity. No sociologist worthy of the label would call this a coincidence. Clearly, we are part of the societies we study, and no method can fully purge our own life experiences and perspectives from our research. Our ideas and research questions are inescapably shaped by the ongoing public and professional discourses to which we happen to be exposed as our personal biographies meet history (Mills 1959). By acknowledging and embracing this reality, we can enhance our skills as social analysts while also helping address the persistent inequalities plaguing social relations.

The strategic choice to be active is one that must be borne in mind as one works to secure adequate time in one's life for engaged scholarship. Work in the academy has become increasingly demanding. This parallels the global trend of expanding marketization and commodification of the social world (Aranowitz 2000). Our commitment to education makes our profession more of a vocation (i.e., an integral part of our identities) than a job. As a result, drawing boundaries between our work and our personal lives becomes more difficult. Many of us are footloose—ready to move for a job in our field or to uproot ourselves for a better opportunity in the academy. Many academics justify their lack of political engagement by defining their teaching as political work. However, as Peters (2005) reminds us, this form of activism cannot be seen as completely fulfilling our responsibility to share our knowledge and skills with the larger community. Consequently, many academics are only marginally involved in community life outside their campuses. The choice to be active is therefore a part of one's personal strategic path, but it is also structured by the way we tend to be embedded in the larger structures of our society, including ones that reproduce inequality and oppression.

In thinking about strategy from this perspective, we might recast Meyer and Staggenborg's definition in chapter 1 to read: "For [scholar] activists, strategy refers to choices about claims, issues, allies, frames, identity, and presentation of self, resources, and tactics." I explore my choice to identify as a scholar activist as part of a larger collective process of strategizing on how to better articulate ourselves with movements. The ways academics are asked to think about their identities in relation to movements as well as their positioning within the larger power structures that movements seek to transform are relevant to the larger political struggles that we are seeking to understand, whether we acknowledge it or not. The fact that our profession pushes us to distance ourselves from social movements is a source of power for those who prefer the status quo. By failing to question professional norms and social relations, we reinforce existing power relations.

But we should nevertheless be asking why scholars have been such prominent actors in so many movements in history. How do our positions in society affect our roles and possible contributions to social movements? After considering these questions, I discuss how my research on transnational activism has shaped my efforts to translate models of activism from the global political arena into my own local context. Finally, I explore the lessons learned from this experience and the larger implications for social movement strategy and scholarship.

Scholars and Social Change: Standpoint as Theory and Strategy

As I walked around the World Social Forum (WSF) Territory in Porto Alegre, Brazil, during the 2005 gathering of the WSF, I was surprised to feel like I was at an academic conference rather than at an activist gathering.[2] Indeed, some prominent scholars in my field were in Porto Alegre and participating in sessions that grappled with ideas about the impact of economic changes on local and national communities. Discussions among participants often referred to social science concepts and authors such as Immanuel Wallerstein, Antonio Negri, David Harvey, Noam Chomsky, and Paulo Freire. More than once, I bumped into a member of a research team conducting surveys of WSF participants. I myself was there as a delegate from a group called Sociologists Without Borders, and my formal participation in the forum involved work with similar academic groupings to improve coordination among scholar activists working on global justice issues.

These observations correspond with others that attested to the large presence of highly educated activists in contemporary activism on global issues. For instance, Schönleitner (2003) reports that more than 70 percent of participants in the first WSFs in Porto Alegre had attended some college, mostly in the social sciences.[3] Soule and Condo (2005) report that student- and youth-led protests in the United States were more likely than other protests to address international issues. Further, students have played central roles in contemporary activism on labor rights and antisweatshop campaigns, particularly in helping to globalize labor solidarity struggles (e.g., Ross 2004).

In many ways, the prominence of intellectuals and students in global justice activism is not surprising. Scholars' positions provide them with exceptional opportunities and capacities that can encourage participation in movements (Wiltfang and McAdam 1991). Moreover, because education is highly correlated with income and class, we can assume that this category of people is more likely to travel internationally and to have the leisure to become informed about and engaged with global problems. Also important is the weakness of radical labor unions committed to building a constituency for transnational labor solidarity. Within the labor movement itself, committed internationalists have tended to be somewhat removed from rank-and-file activists and organizational agendas, at least in the West (Herod 2001). This has left an institutional vacuum that denies workers an accessible and routine source of education about globalization and its effects on working people and on less privileged communities. People with ties to universities also tend to have more access to the substantial resources needed to attend international meetings as well as to maintain regular contacts with activists and groups outside one's home country. Courses in the social sciences on globalization, economics, and political institutions can also expand the potential support for transnational movements by helping students understand the substance of global contention and the processes through which global policy and other social changes can happen.

Another explanation for the disproportionate participation of students and intellectuals in the global justice movement is that the professional activities in which these individuals are involved are more likely to give them access to information and experiences that extend beyond their local community origins. Students and scholars tend to leave their local communities in search of knowledge and experiences. In the process, they cultivate a spirit of inquiry that makes them open to new and different experiences and ideas. Such experiences, coupled with analytical training, help them to articulate broadly shared visions for social change and allow them to understand the differences and commonalities across different local cultures and sectoral groupings.[4] Thus, they are particularly well positioned to serve as brokers, or translators between different groups, making them important players in processes of coalition building that are central to any social movement (e.g., Bandy and Smith 2005).[5] Their important role in helping cultivate transnational ties reflects this reality (Tarrow 2005).

As many conservative think tanks and pundits have pointed out, universities are also settings where critical thinking about global processes has been encouraged.[6] Universities are spaces that foster the development of what Rochon (1998) calls critical communities. Critical communities, he notes, are important incubators of social movements because they provide supportive social settings and networks in which critical ideas about the state of social affairs and ideas about alternatives can evolve and spread. According to Rochon (1998, 161), the critical community "creates a map of the social and political world. Movement mobilization occurs when large numbers of people are able to locate themselves on that map" (also see Wuthnow 1989; Coy, Woerhle, and Maney 2008).

The overrepresentation of highly educated people in global justice activism is not inconsistent with more general patterns of political participation. Those with more formal education are consistently more likely to vote and engage in other forms of political participation than less educated citizens. Although education overlaps to an important degree with class advantages, it operates differently from simple measures of people's access to economic resources. Analyzing variation in participation in national-level politics, Verba and colleagues concluded that the factors that prevent people from participating in national politics include a lack of motivation, capacity, and access to relevant social networks (Verba, Schlozman, and Brady 1995). Motivation is shaped by people's interest in the subject, which in turn is conditioned by the information they have on the subject. It is also affected by people's sense that by acting they can actually make a difference. Capacity is determined to a large extent by their available resources. One needs at least time and information, as well as money, to be active in politics. Also, the study by Verba and colleagues concluded that people who had developed skills that are relevant to political engagement—either in their workplace, or in church or other civil society activities—were also more likely to be politically active than those who lacked such skills. This finding demonstrates the need in democracies to create dispersed and widely accessible spaces where all people can learn how to be engaged citizens. Finally, people have to be invited to be politically active; most people need to either be urged by families and friends to vote or be active in political parties, or they need to be invited to participate in a social movement event. Relatively few politically active people start their political careers without some access to social networks that encouraged this kind of action (e.g., McAdam 1988).

If motivation, capacity, and networks are important for helping people to become active and engaged citizens, then it is clear that universities or other places that enable people to expand their understandings of different countries and of global interdependence will be crucial to any effort to build a more democratic global polity. As decisions of increasing importance to the daily lives of citizens are taken in intergovernmental bodies that are further and further removed from people's experiences, those concerned with global democracy must work to help people understand the connections between global forces and their lived experience. Although neoliberal globalization has increasingly subjected a growing array of social institutions to global market forces, universities have become one of the few social institutions with substantial capacity and freedom (however limited) to systematically engage in this kind of work. Outside the United States, one finds more expectation that scholars be public intellectuals and correspondingly more space in the public and media arenas for scholars to embrace this role. Still, there is clearly a need for more work globally to expand the links between the academy and the larger society if either is to thrive. In today's academy, we clearly must choose between training students to become workers in a competitive global economy and to become critical, informed, and engaged citizens in a developing global society.

Scholar Activism and the WSF Process

The WSF process is arguably one of the most important political developments of our time. Begun in 2001 as an initiative of civil society leaders in Brazil and France, the WSFs have grown rapidly in their numbers of participants and in their geographic scope. The idea of the WSF process emerges from the fact that the WSF is not an event or an actor, but rather a series of convenings of the multiple actors involved in struggles for global economic and social justice at multiple levels between the local and global. The forums thus extend across time and space, providing opportunities for participants to engage in dialogue, learning, experimentation, and collective action aimed at advancing a global justice movement (Fisher and Ponniah 2003; Smith et al. 2007). The slogan that motivates the WSF process is "Another world is possible," and its charter of principles articulates its broad mission:

> The World Social Forum is an open meeting place for reflective thinking, democratic debate of ideas, formulation of proposals, free exchange of experiences and interlinking for effective action by groups and movements of civil society that are opposed to neoliberalism and to domination of the world by capital and any form of imperialism, and are committed to building a planetary society directed towards fruitful relationships among Mankind and between it and the Earth. . . . The alternatives proposed at the World Social Forum stand in opposition to a process of globalisation commanded by the large multinational corporations and by the governments and international institutions at the service of those corporations' interests, with the complicity of national governments. They are designed to ensure that globalisation in solidarity will prevail as a new stage in world history. This will respect universal human rights and those of all citizens—men and women—of all nations and the environment and will rest on democratic international systems and institutions at the service of social justice, equality and the sovereignty of peoples.[7]

Activists within the WSF are explicit in their desire to avoid forming new centralized organizations. An explicit ideology of horizontalism—valuing decentralized authority and radical, participatory democratic values—permeates the culture of the WSF. Although the open space idea is ambiguous and itself debated by activists, it reflects the strategic thinking that has emerged among activists from many sectors and parts of the world. By creating open spaces, the WSF process has encouraged a global proliferation of ideas and tactics while fostering a sense of unity around a shared set of values and a tangible movement arena (della Porta 2005; della Porta et al. 2006; Teivainen 2002).

Throughout its decade of existence, the WSF International Council has worked to decentralize the WSF process and extend it to local contexts. In addition to encouraging and supporting the formation of national and local social forums, in 2005, it began facilitating opportunities at the WSF for local and national groups to conduct self-organized workshops. In 2006, there was another move to promote horizontalism by holding a polycentric forum with sequential meetings in Venezuela, Mali, and Pakistan. This form evolved into the decentralized forums where activists are encouraged to organize local social forum activities during the same time as the WSF meeting. Now the world meeting will alternate with these decentralized actions to help strengthen the local–global connections. In 2009, the forum introduced a new experiment to enhance ties to local communities; this experiment was called Belém Expanded. Meeting rooms at the world meeting in Belém, Brazil, were set up to enable activists to link directly to local communities via the Internet, Skype, and other technologies. A website was set up to encourage organizers to hold sessions simultaneously in the global forum and local settings. The expanded idea has been incorporated into subsequent social forums, including the second United States Social Forum in Detroit, Michigan.

It is not surprising that the WSF has emerged at this particular historic moment. Many analysts believe that today's ecological and social crises are heralding major systemic changes in our world (Arrighi and Silver 2001; Harvey 2009; Wallerstein 2009). As in past eras of major revolutionary change, slowing economic growth and unavoidable social and ecological limits to capital accumulation has denied the world's capitalist class "the main hidden stabilizer of the system, the optimism of the oppressed" (Wallerstein 2004, 84–85). We are at a point in history where our society must choose between alternative paths for structuring global economic and social relations. Wallerstein portrays this fork in our historic road as the Spirit of Porto Alegre embodied in the WSF process confronting the Spirit of Davos, or the forces of global capitalism that converge annually at the World Economic Forum.

The strategic choice for engaged work has become even more urgent given the enormous scale of the multiple crises our world now faces. However, once one chooses to become part of this struggle, it is engagement with social movements that informs one's strategy—that is, the choices about "claims, issues, allies, frames, identity and presentation of self, resources, and tactics" for acting out the scholar activist role (Meyer and Staggenborg, chapter 1, this volume). Our sociological imaginations are important tools for helping us understand our own historical circumstances and the potential for our strategic choices to make a difference. Below I trace my own experiences of engaged scholarship in the Spirit of Porto Alegre, reflecting on strategic lessons for those seeking to bring the tools of social science to the task of helping to change the world.

My work on transnational social movements provided me a unique opportunity to observe the development of the WSF process and consider its implications and potential for furthering large-scale social change. I attended the first WSF in Porto Alegre, Brazil, having a sense that this event, like the 1999 protests against the World Trade Organization in Seattle, could become a major turning point for global activism.[8] At the time, there was widespread sentiment that the emerging movement for global economic justice needed to have its own space to articulate its ideals and visions for another world rather than to simply react against the visions being offered by governments and economic elites. In fact, many similar sorts of civil society forums had been organized in previous years, often alongside intergovernmental meetings such as the Group of Eight and World Bank/International Monetary Fund annual meetings and the United Nations global conferences.[9] The continuation and expansion of the WSFs, coupled with the spread of many hundreds of smaller-scale social forums at regional, national, and local levels, demonstrate the resonance for activists around the world of the WSF founders' invitation to meet in Porto Alegre. It suggests that activists in many places were thinking similarly about strategies for challenging neoliberal globalization. The major significance of the WSF process lies in that it has helped to create and expand spaces, both physical and conceptual, in which activists can work to strengthen activist networks and advance ideas for building another world.

My effort to understand the WSF process, the strategic thinking among activists, and the potential of this movement for bringing about large-scale social change led me to engage in participant observation in various social forum settings where I adopted a number of different roles. I began attending the forums by participating mainly in workshops aimed at considering the role of scholar activists in the process. Although many of the scholars and intellectuals were attending sessions on a variety of specific issues, many also wanted to think more broadly about their place in the movements and about how they could be more effective in contributing to social change efforts. I participated in these conversations at the WSFs in Porto Alegre (2005), at the European Social Forum (2004), and at local social forums in the United States. A few of the participants had also attended other international meetings where this theme was discussed. I worked to try to distill some basic themes from all of these discussions that I attended, using the learning and cross-national communication process that I believe WSF founders had sought to encourage. Here, my training in social science analysis and the opportunity I had as a scholar to take time to review notes taken on numerous meetings over several years and provide an analysis of themes and synthesis of ideas was certainly important. Clearly, many nonacademics in social movements also have skills, if not always the time and opportunity, to do this work. The WSF process explicitly invites and encourages this analysis and synthesis, thereby supporting engaged scholarship while also helping break down class barriers to participation in global-level political advocacy.

A 2005 WSF workshop on social movements and the academy synthesized a series of conversations held at earlier social forums, producing a list

of three key ways that scholar activists can best contribute to the global justice movement: (1) by resisting neoliberalism on campuses, including threats
to the rights and security of campus workers and to public access to higher
education; (2) by defending the knowledge commons from further privatization and commodification via more restrictive copyright protections; and
(3) by supporting civil society at local, national, and global levels. Although
scholar activists aren't the only ones who can advance these goals, they are
better placed and have more resources for working on the first two aims and
can contribute to the third in very particular ways. This conceptualization
was useful for me as well as others in our workshop because it helped us think
strategically about our skills and their potential place in this emerging global
social movement. Activists often choose the activities they engage in on the
basis of their personal interests and social positions. This schema encourages
some thought about appropriate divisions of labor and about the best uses
of the unequally distributed resources and skills in this diverse movement.

I have drawn on this schema (focusing largely on the work of supporting civil society) as I have shifted my attention from the global sites of the
WSF toward the local context where I live. Partly in response to the WSF
movement toward decentralization, and partly in response to my own desire
to cut back on my international travel (and the carbon footprint it generates),
I have been working in my local community to try to apply the WSF's principles and visions in South Bend, Indiana. In this community, like others
across the United States, there is little motivation to think or do much about
global politics that seem so far removed from local experiences. There is also
limited capacity in terms of knowledge of global problems and institutions,
and popular misconceptions and xenophobia often work against efforts to
generate movement action on global issues. I decided to follow the call of the
WSF International Council to try to bring the WSF process into our local
community as a way of inviting people to learn more about their world and
the people in it while also helping them see that they are part of a larger network of activists and organizations concerned about creating a more humane,
just, and sustainable world. In 2007, following public "report-backs" on the
first United States Social Forum that my students and I did for members of our
community, we decided to launch a local social forum process in our region.

Michiana Social Forum and Global Human Rights

Participating in the Michiana Social Forum (MSF) helped me better understand the challenges and the potential of applying the WSF principles to local
settings. It also helped me better appreciate the need for and difficulties of
translation across the global–local divide. Finally, working to carry out the

WSF ideals has highlighted for me even more the significance of the fact that WSF organizers have deliberately crafted this as a process, rather than as simply a conference or even a series of conferences. The idea of embarking on a process implies a commitment to ongoing and evolving patterns of interactions and relations. Such interactions and relations lead in unanticipated directions as activists respond to particular organizing contexts and work to expand and strengthen coalitions. The WSF is thus distinct from much social movement activism in that it privileges relationships and movement building over achieving specific political goals. It can be seen as a global attempt to remedy the widespread inequities in motivation, capacity, and access that have denied so much of the world's population an effective political voice (Verba, Schlozman, and Brady 1995).

My work in the MSF has shown me that translating the WSF ideals into a local context requires extensive and time-consuming work to build trust with community leaders and to frame issues in ways that resonate with local concerns and ongoing policy debates. The key projects that I have helped facilitate through the MSF are: (1) events that aim to bring together diverse groups in the community while encouraging attentiveness to larger themes of global social justice and human rights; (2) networks of activists providing regular contributions of letters to the editor to the local newspaper as well as radio and newsletter opinion/editorials encouraging greater global awareness and appreciation for economic and other human rights;[10] and (3) a community currency initiative aimed at bringing lessons from other activist groups and enacting models of economic transformation in our locale.

This choice of activities reflects an emerging strategy for implementing our local social forum process and translating lessons from global to local. It did not begin with an outline or detailed map. Rather, my activist colleagues and I have been making the path by walking. My work studying other global movements has proved useful in guiding our steps and linking our local actions with those around the world.

The Local Context

Michiana is the name for the region of around 800,000 people living in north central Indiana and southwest lower Michigan. It includes the counties surrounding the city of South Bend, the largest city in the region, home to about 100,000 residents (300,000 in the metropolitan area). In the past, it was a major industrial area, drawing power from the St. Joseph, or *Sakiwäsipi*, River. Studebaker automobiles and the Oliver Chilled Plow were produced here, and remnants of these factories remain in the downtown. The automobile industry remains an important one, and two United Auto Workers locals are still active in the city. The leading industries today are health care and education. The city is home to the University of Notre Dame as well as to a state university campus and several smaller Christian colleges. The nearby city of Elkhart, Indiana, was once a leader in musical instrument manufacturing and has produced many of the horns played by top jazz and band musicians. It later became the center of recreational vehicle manufacturing, but it now is suffering some of the nation's highest unemployment as that industry collapses.[11] South Bend's population is more diverse than much of the rest of the region. Just over half (56 percent) of city residents are white, nearly 35 percent are African American, and over 8 percent are Latino (mainly from Mexico). Large immigrant populations also live in other Michiana cities, although their numbers are dwindling as manufacturing industries close. Nearly 17 percent of the population of South Bend lives below the poverty line. The area has been particularly hard hit by the housing crisis, and foreclosure rates are among the highest in the country. Cities in Michiana tend to be somewhat segregated by class and race, and tensions have increased as the immigrant population has grown. International migrant workers have been terrorized in recent years by regular workplace raids by U.S. immigration and customs enforcement.

The MSF Process

Within this context, we worked to organize a week of action in response to the WSF's call for actions around the world in lieu of a global meeting of the WSF in 2008. Our main activity for the week was a forum that provided information about the WSF process and invited discussions about how to build and strengthen local coalitions for economic and social justice in the region. In addition, we participated in a labor protest action on behalf of local housing authority workers, attended a peace rally, and hosted a press conference on the Blue-Green Alliance between labor and environmental groups. Probably one of the most important lessons I have learned through this whole process is that patience is essential. Timetables and even tactics must remain flexible as one pursues the work of building diverse and inclusive local coalitions. The process of helping local organizers understand the larger themes and goals of the global justice movement requires time-consuming work to build interpersonal trust even more than it requires information sharing. Our work would have been easier if our region had a more radical activist culture, but we did find some important resources in a strong labor presence and a large population of residents who are part of the Mennonite and other historic peace church traditions. Local coalitions of activists working to oppose the wars in Iraq and Afghanistan as well as to strengthen ties between labor and the larger activist community ultimately made our social forum possible and helped to sustain it after our initial event.

In moving beyond our first MSF, we drew on the WSF principles and on the lessons and experiences of activists and analysts in the WSF process. Our local social forum participants, for instance, decided at our first MSF to organize around a Human Rights City initiative in order to help attract a wide array of groups working on various social issues in our region. The idea of the Human Rights City is one that I had seen discussed by various groups at previous WSFs (see the People's Movement for Human Rights Learning, http://www.pdhre.org), and I had noted how useful human rights discourse seemed to be at uniting groups in the WSF settings. Locally, we found residents receptive to this idea when we presented it at our first MSF, and it has been a key focus for our subsequent organizing work.

To carry forward our Human Rights City idea, we planned to celebrate the sixtieth anniversary of the Universal Declaration of Human Rights with a party in fall 2008.[12] We worked with our local Jobs With Justice chapter and with the county's human rights commission to organize the party, which was held in a local union hall.[13] We also enlisted a student to design a layout for a pocket-sized version of the Universal Declaration of Human Rights text that included a Spanish summary translation. We continue to distribute these as part of our efforts to raise community awareness of human rights. A local bank printed a few thousand copies of our pocket declaration, and we've found this a useful tool for inspiring people to know their rights and in some cases to become more active in social justice work.

It took some effort to get a diverse array of people to attend the Universal Declaration of Human Rights anniversary celebration, but we managed to attract around 200 people on a snowy Saturday. The party helped inform people about the human rights issues in our community. Speakers representing immigrants, racial minorities, labor, and gay and lesbian groups spoke about local challenges for various rights. After more than two years of organizing, we're starting to get more multiracial and multiclass involvement, but this remains one of the key challenges for our organizing effort. The WSF process is not alone here, as many other movements face similar obstacles. However, what is unique about the WSF process is its explicit commitment to confronting the processes and practices that serve to exclude relatively powerless groups. The constant effort to expand the WSF's inclusiveness has shaped the process itself and encouraged our own local groups to put coalition and trust building at the center of our work. This contrasts more traditional organizing that focuses on organizing events, activities, or organizations, with coalitions being means to these ends.

The human rights celebration helped generate an ongoing effort to work with the county's human rights commission to develop a human rights speakers bureau. The bureau is now training volunteers to speak in schools and community groups about human rights. A team of volunteers has been writing letters to our local newspaper on human rights themes. This aims to expand human rights discussions in the community and to challenge dominant discourses that would deny rights to particular groups. These activities also allow us to build trust among community activists and to expand our coalition as we actively work to support other groups' campaigns and demonstrate their links to human rights. For instance, we supported the work of another coalition group to convince local legislators to pass an ordinance that would allow legislators to grant tax abatement only to those businesses that provide minimally acceptable wages to their workers and that can demonstrate that they are making specific, positive contributions to the community. The prevailing discourse had been that legislators must engage in a race to the bottom, providing tax breaks to any companies wishing to invest in our region.[14] MSF's campaign helped reinforce the human rights claims in this debate and contributed to the public pressure that eventually helped pass this legislation.

In sum, the WSF process provided an important model and a set of guiding principles for us to translate into our local context as we worked to create a truly inclusive and democratic community that places people over profit. The strategic lessons one might take from this case might be organized around our familiar conceptual categories of mobilizing structures, political opportunities, and framing. Indeed, social movement theory can offer many useful insights for activists, but I've found that being engaged with movements helps me better identify the theory that activists need while aiding the work of translation from academic to practitioner discourses.

The WSF process is explicit in its emphasis on building decentralized networks of organizations, movements, and individuals. The literature on the WSFs is permeated by network imagery. We therefore have adopted a networking strategy as we sought to develop a mobilizing structure consisting of ties to diverse local organizations and individuals. Although this strategy involves a risk that the project could fail if key activists get distracted or move away, it has the advantages of having few overhead costs (we just have a website and don't spend time running an organization) and of allowing for new activists to easily become engaged in the process. By serving as a site where coalition or alliance building is the main goal, new initiatives can be readily introduced. Relationships and trust have developed as a result of our collaborative activities, and I'm finding it easier to encourage fellow organizers to engage in political imagination and experimentation as a result.[15]

I've learned from my local work how the WSF process encourages and supports activists seeking opportunities in local and national settings to engage in projects that will help build bridges across diverse groups. Attending meetings of different community groups has helped sensitize activists in our MSF process to the various policy arenas and initiatives around which we might launch collective actions. Local labor struggles and legislative initiatives to protect against discrimination based on sexual orientation and to regulate local tax abatements provided strategic opportunities for MSF activists to support the work of particular groups while also introducing people in our region to larger human rights and social justice concerns. This work has won MSF respect and support among key allies.

In regard to framing, we began our work knowing that the antineoliberal message of the WSF had little resonance in this community. However, the values of community, human rights, and self-reliance did. Thus, we needed to repackage the ideological message for our local setting, but doing so within the framework of a larger global movement helped people see the tensions between highly resonant values such as social solidarity and environmental sustainability and the global economy. Because many in our region are connected somehow to agricultural production, they could readily find common cause with some leading peasant associations in the WSF such as Via Campesina. Also, youth and antipoverty activists could readily connect with the stories we told of their counterparts in places like South Africa and Brazil. The WSF process provided framing resources in the form of examples of similar communities and people in locales around the world, helping us put human faces on rather abstract economic policy debates. Also, the human rights framework and campaign ideas like the Human Rights City initiative were key framing resources we could draw from the global movement, taking care, of course, to adapt it to the local context.

One challenge we've had in the MSF process is expanding ties to low-income people and people of color. This work has been complicated also by the fact that the core MSF activists tend to be white and middle-class as well as secular. Many in the communities where we're organizing tend to be deeply embedded in church networks, so we're working to expand our ties to and the trust of church leaders. One strategy we've been exploring to help expand our appeal to these groups is to focus more on providing concrete projects to address economic insecurity faced by growing numbers of people in our community. Below, I discuss our current work to develop a community currency in Michiana, a project that is not formally connected to the MSF but that draws on the same networks of activists and organizing philosophy and that will likely expand the pool of participants in future MSF activities.

Building a Solidarity Economy

One of the biggest challenges activists face as they work to resist globalized capitalism is the widespread perception that there is no alternative for individuals or local communities but to engage in the globalized competition for trade and profits. The proponents of global markets and the policies that support them control the major media outlets and much of the political debate about appropriate economic policies. They run the corporations that employ many people, thereby exerting a disproportionate influence in public policy debates (Sklair 2001). Many organizers in the global justice movement are thus actively working to provide people with alternatives to global capitalism as they promote the idea that another world is possible. The notion of the solidarity economy as an alternative to the dominant capitalist model has captured the imaginations of many in the WSF process and the global justice movement more generally, and we're working to spread this idea locally in Michiana.

At a talk I gave at a local fair trade fair on the effects of economic globalization on our region, I discussed the ways that other communities like ours were responding to the challenges of deindustrialization, job losses and deunionization, urban sprawl, and environmental degradation. One such example was the use of community currencies such as Ithaca's Hours project, which circulates locally issued money to supplement U.S. dollars in small markets that tend to be marginalized by global and national markets. After my talk, several people wanted to learn more. Those conversations led to an effort to establish the Michiana Community Currency.

Understanding the logic of community currencies and their feasibility for a particular region is one thing, as is figuring out how to go from discussions among a small group of activists with highly varying levels of organizing experience and commitment; implementing our local currency is quite another. My work as a scholar has been helpful as we've sought models for implementing this initiative in our region, but I've had to rely on the work of other activists and my own activist instincts to determine what specific steps we need to move from point A to point B. What we're doing here is essentially trying to create new economic institutions within the framework of the existing capitalist, market-dominated ones. We are restructuring markets to encourage more local transactions and to reassign value to human labor and to our communities and natural environments. This has required substantial efforts at public education that we've done through public presentations, the production and distribution of a regular newsletter, developing and maintaining a website, and through one-on-one conversations. It has also required an effort to build an organization capable of ensuring that the necessary work gets done even when our core activists and leaders become preoccupied with their day jobs.

I have drawn on social movement scholarship to help me identify strategic opportunities and prioritize organizational goals. Again, we can use the notions of mobilizing structures, political opportunities, and framing to help us think about the strategies we've used in this project. In reviewing the experiences of other local currency initiatives, I quickly came to the conclusion that the successful ones are built on strong social foundations. We learned that the failure rate of local currencies mirrors that of all small businesses—about 80 percent. We knew that the odds were against us from the start, but we found it would be crucial to avoid the tendency to push for a quick move to print the new money without thinking much about the social context in which the money would flow. I have stressed the need for us to build a strong network of ties to diverse segments of our community before the actual printing of money. Building a commitment to work together to strengthen the local economy is essentially what will encourage people to trust the value of our local scrip and will entice them to use it and keep using it. Although it is more difficult to get volunteers to help in the hard work of network building as opposed to printing our own local money, we've emphasized this work and have used activities like a "name the money" survey and a design contest involving students to both move us toward launching our currency while also building networks of commitment to the larger economic solidarity project. Also, relationships we've built through the MSF process have helped expand the pool of supporters and resources for this initiative.

A new political opportunity emerged for us with the global financial meltdown in fall 2008 that focused people's attention on the economy. This heightened salience of economic crisis helped us win a small grant that helped pay a staff person to do some of the work that had been overwhelming me and other core leaders. It also helped gain us meetings with city and business leaders who have been grasping for ideas in these challenging economic times. Another important opportunity emerged when a group of local businesses launched an initiative in October called ShoLo to encourage residents to support locally owned businesses. ShoLo's aims strongly resemble those of our Michiana Community Currency project. So we've been working to build relationships with ShoLo's leaders and its network of local businesses. We produced an issue of the Michiana Community Currency newsletter with ShoLo and highlighted the ecological and social advantages of buying local. Copies of the issue have been distributed among ShoLo merchants to inform them of our work, and they have helped distribute the newsletter to their customers. Instead of simply asking them to join our initiative, we're showing them how we might work together for mutual benefit. In this way, we hope to engage in block recruitment to strengthen our base of support in the business community as well as among activists and other residents (Oberschall 1980).

Framing a project like this isn't easy, especially in the U.S. political context where cold war politics continues to marginalize discourse about alternatives to capitalism. However, the economic crisis opened some new space for us to encourage residents to think about possibilities for another sort of local economy. As policy makers in Washington seemed more concerned with saving banks and large corporations than local communities, we have offered residents a thoughtful and tested model for reorganizing local economic relationships that is having appeal in diverse circles. By providing an innovative idea for expanding local economic capacities and focusing on local needs, we're also encouraging a larger critique of the global capitalist economy.

I've found it important, however, to think strategically about the different interests and concerns of constituencies we're aiming to mobilize. These constituencies include business and government leaders as well as community activists, youth, senior citizens, and residents in a racially and economically segmented region. Mapping out these constituencies and actively working to discuss the project in ways that resonate with particular group interests has been vital to moving the project forward. Our newsletter and talks to different community groups have been key places where this framing work happens. Such work is essential both before our launching of our local currency and after it is issued.

Conclusion

In their contribution to this volume (chapter 1), Meyer and Staggenborg observe:

> Activists learn various strategies, assess their opportunities, and position themselves for new rounds of collective action in distinct contexts and as a consequence of their relationships with actors inside and outside the movement. This iterative process depends on the reactions of others engaging the same sets of issues and constituencies, which can alter the next round of opportunities and constraints.

Given this dynamic process of learning, articulating, and adapting strategies, social movement scholars should not be asking whether or not engaged scholarship is a legitimate practice. Rather, they should be asking whether we can even understand, analyze, and contribute to discussions about strategy without participatory research designs. If strategy develops and changes over time, the research tactic of parachuting in for short bursts of observations, interviews, or analyses of movement artifacts is unlikely to contribute much to our knowledge about movement strategies or their roles in social change.

I have learned several important lessons about strategy from doing local organizing work. These lessons are ones that I could not have achieved without direct engagement in efforts to make social change. First, the success of the WSF process and global civil society building more generally requires dedicated and creative leadership to help build bridges across geographic divides as well as the class, racial, cultural, and political divides that characterize our society. Scholars tend to have resources that are valuable to this kind of work, but it is important to keep in mind that many activists are also talented in this regard; they have much to teach even the most seasoned scholar activist. Second, I have learned to appreciate the potentially powerful discourses of resistance available in local settings. The language of human rights, local autonomy, and community solidarity can be a powerful tool for helping foster cooperation and collaboration across diverse groups within a given locale while also helping local activists appreciate the connections between local and global issues. Our role as scholars can serve as a resource in helping people reconceptualize problems in ways that prioritize human rights over other goals, helping challenge dominant frameworks in ways that are less threatening because they resonate with deep-seated (if obscured) values. Third, I've learned the importance of being patient, being committed to a long-term process, and being content with ambiguity. The WSF is more about relationships than events or collective actions, and I have learned to scale back expectations to allow the process of building relationships and trust to develop over time.

Traditional approaches to doing research and the demands of our academic profession work against us as we attempt to build the ties to community that can enhance our knowledge of movements and social change. This suggests that we need a strategy to change our profession if we believe that our professional work should involve efforts to help our society respond to the unsustainable and inhumane inequalities of our world. To quote a Sociologists Without Borders T-shirt, if "another sociology is possible," we need to identify the steps toward making it a reality. Many good ideas are emerging in debates on public sociology.[16] Certainly, expanding the spaces and incentive structures for academics to be engaged with and to use their skills in service of their communities should be a top priority. In addition, more (and more equitable) engagement with scholars and scholarship from other world regions is essential, but it is largely discouraged in everyday professional routines.

If another world is possible, many diverse groups must be part of the effort to make it a reality. Social scientists can play an important role here, but we need to free ourselves from the constraints our profession has imposed on us. Thus, in thinking about movement strategies in a global context, we come to the conclusion that we must also develop strategies for affecting our own disciplines and professional institutions to allow us to be more fully engaged and attentive citizens in an increasingly integrated global society.

Notes

1. See, for instance, Croteau, Hoynes, and Ryan (2005); Blau and Karides (2008); Blau and Smith (2006); and Clawson et al. (2007).

2. Feminist scholars emphasize the need for scholars to be conscious of their own positioning in relation to our research collaborators. By placing ourselves within the social narrative and interrogating and making explicit our own standpoint in relation to our research, we achieve strong objectivity, or the ability to better understand and assess the subtle ways power inequities affect social dynamics. See Hesse-Biber and Yaiser (2004).

3. Other studies confirm that global justice activists tend to have more formal education than the general population and protesters on other issues (e.g., della Porta 2005; Norris, Walgrave, and Van Aelst 2002; Walgrave and Verhulst 2004). Reports on a survey of participants at the 2005 WSF also support the contention that participants in this movement have high levels of formal education (Reese et al. 2008).

4. I don't want to suggest that formal training is a necessary criterion for defining intellectual leadership in social movements because some leaders develop these skills without such training. Certainly, the tools required for scientific inquiry can be helpful in the process of integrating and assimilating diverse ideas and experiences into a coherent collective vision.

5. At the same time, this tendency has led many activists to question the over-representation of middle-class voices and interests in the global justice movement. As the global justice movement matures and as more activists reflect and engage in critical dialogue on the problem of representation and inequality within the movement, there is evidence of change here.

6. Universities have been shaped in important ways by social movements, and the emergence of programs devoted to cross-disciplinary studies such as gender studies, peace studies, black studies, and even global or development studies emerged at least in part from the critiques offered by social movements of the 1960s (Rochon 1998). Conservative politicians have therefore sought to curb academic freedom and to limit public funding for higher education as a way of limiting criticism of government policy. For instance, an important response of the Nixon administration to anti–Vietnam War protests was to cut public subsidies for higher education.

7. See Fórum Social Mundial (http://www.forumsocialmundial.org.br/).

8. This hunch was only possible because I had embraced the role of scholar activist. I was therefore actively engaged in thinking about strategy and also attentive to strategic discussions among various movement actors. I should note that few other U.S. scholars attended either the World Trade Organization protests in Seattle or the first WSF in Porto Alegre, demonstrating how traditional methods prevent scholars from anticipating important developments in social movements.

9. The United Nations hosted a series of major conferences throughout the 1990s, including the U.N. Conference on Environment and Development in Rio de Janeiro in 1992 and the Fourth World Conference on Women in 1995 in Beijing (e.g., Friedman, Clark, and Hochstetler 2005).

10. I've written or delivered radio essays myself, but I have also actively encouraged other organizers to submit their work to local media outlets. We have created an editorial collective of area faculty and graduate students who will review activists' ideas for op-ed pieces and provide editorial suggestions. This helps boost residents' confidence about their ability to contribute to the public discourse articulated through local media outlets.

11. Elkhart's unemployment rate was 14.8 percent in December 2009.

12. The MSF consists of a core activist group and a larger network of supporters connected largely through an e-mail Listserv. It remains a loose and informal network with little formal organizational structure, but our Listserv of a couple hundred Michiana residents can be called on for actions. Between actions, we use the e-mail list to keep people informed about issues in the community that are relevant to social justice, such as a recent initiative to provide legal protection against discrimination based on sexual orientation. Most of the MSF core activists are university faculty or graduate students, or are involved in key labor and peace groups. The MSF process has been particularly helpful at fostering more connections among regional activist networks because the key contacts from outside South Bend tend to be from the activist cores of neighboring cities and towns.

13. Funded largely by labor associations, Jobs With Justice is a national organization that aims to build alliances among union locals as well as between labor and community groups.

14. The ordinance's detractors continue to claim that the ordinance will discourage new investment in the region. Activists' research showed that most tax abatements were given to businesses already active in the region and were not effective at attracting outside investors.

15. For instance, our current work to bring local activists to the second U.S. Social Forum in Detroit would not be possible without our having worked to build alliances with local labor and human rights groups before the event.

16. See Clawson et al. (2007), especially Stacey's (2007) list of things we must

do to make another sociology possible in "If I Were the Goddess of Sociological Things."

References

Aranowitz, Stanley. 2000. *The Knowledge Factory: Dismantling the Corporate University and Creating True Higher Learning.* New York: Beacon Press.

Arrighi, Giovanni, and Beverly J. Silver. 2001. "Capitalism and World (Dis)Order." *Review of International Studies* 27:257–79.

Bandy, Joe, and Jackie Smith, eds. 2005. *Coalitions across Borders: Transnational Protest and the Neoliberal Order.* Lanham, Md.: Rowman & Littlefield.

Blau, Judith, and Marina Karides. 2008. *The World and U.S. Social Forums: A Better World Is Possible and Necessary.* Leiden: Brill.

Blau, Judith, and Keri E. Iyall Smith. 2006. *Public Sociologies Reader.* Boulder, Colo.: Rowman & Littlefield.

Clawson, Dan, Robert Zussman, Joya Misra, Naomi Gerstel, Randall Stokes, Douglas L. Anderton, and Maichael Burawoy, eds. 2007. *Public Sociology.* Berkeley: University of California Press.

Coy, Patrick G., Lynne M. Woehrle, and Gregory M. Maney. 2008. "A Typology of Oppositional Knowledge: Democracy and the U.S. Peace Movement." *Sociological Research Online* 13, no. 3. doi:10.5153/sro.1739.

Croteau, David, William Hoynes, and Charlotte Ryan, eds. 2005. *Rhyming Hope and History: Activists, Academics, and Social Movement Scholarship.* Minneapolis: University of Minnesota Press.

della Porta, Donatella. 2005. "Multiple Belongings, Tolerant Identities, and the Construction of 'Another Politics': Between the European Social Forum and the Local Social Fora." In *Transnational Protest and Global Activism,* edited by Donatella della Porta and Sidney Tarrow, 175–202. Lanham, Md.: Rowman & Littlefield.

della Porta, Donatella, Massimiliano Andretta, Lorenzo Mosca, and Herbert Reiter. 2006. *Globalization from Below: Transnational Activists and Protest Networks.* Minneapolis: University of Minnesota Press.

Fisher, William, and Thomas Ponniah, eds. 2003. *Another World Is Possible: Popular Alternatives to Globalization at the World Social Forum.* New York: Zed.

Friedman, Elisabeth Jay, Ann Marie Clark, and Kathryn Hochstetler. 2005. *Sovereignty, Democracy, and Global Civil Society: State–Society Relations at the U.N. World Conferences.* Albany: State University of New York Press.

Harvey, David. 2009. "Organizing for the Anti-capitalist Transition." *Monthly Review* 61:243–61.

Herod, Andrew. 2001. *Labor Geographies: Workers and the Landscapes of Capitalism.* New York: Guilford Press.

Hesse-Biber, Sharlene N., and Michelle L. Yaiser, eds. 2004. *Feminist Perspectives on Social Research*. New York: Oxford University Press.

McAdam, Doug. 1988. "Social Networks and. Collective Action: A Theory of the Critical Mass." *American Journal of Sociology* 94:502–34.

Mills, C. Wright. 1959. *The Sociological Imagination*. New York: Oxford University Press.

Norris, Pippa, Stefaan Walgrave, and Peter Van Aelst. 2002. "Who Demonstrates? Anti-state Rebels, Conventional Participants, or Everyone?" Unpublished manuscript, John F. Kennedy School of Government, Harvard University, Cambridge, Mass.

Oberschall, Anthony. 1980. "Loosely Structured Collective Conflict: A Theory and an Application." *Research in Social Movements, Conflicts and Change* 3:45–68.

Peters, Cynthia. 2005. "Knowing What's Wrong Is Not Enough." In *Rhyming Hope and History: Activists, Academics and Social Movement Scholarship*, edited by David Croteau, William Hoynes, and Charlotte Ryan, 41–56. Minneapolis: University of Minnesota Press.

Reese, Ellen, Christopher Chase-Dunn, Kadambari Anatram, Gary Coyne, Matheu Kaneshiro, Ashley N. Koda, Roy Kwan, and Preeta Saxena. 2008. "Research Note: Surveys of World Social Forum Participants Show Influence of Place and Base in the Global Public Sphere." *Mobilization* 13:431–46.

Rochon, Thomas R. 1998. *Culture Moves*. Princeton, N.J.: Princeton University Press.

Ross, Robert J. S. 2004. "From Antisweatshop to Global Justice to Antiwar: How the New New Left Is the Same and Different from the Old New Left." *Journal of World Systems Research* 10:287–319.

Schönleitner, Günter. 2003 "World Social Forum: Making Another World Possible?" In *Globalizing Civic Engagement: Civil Society and Transnational Action*, edited by John Clark, 127–49. London: Earthscan.

Sklair, Leslie. 2001. *The Transnational Capitalist Class*. Cambridge: Blackwell.

Smith, Jackie, Marina Karides, Marc Becker, Dorval Brunelle, Christopher Chase-Dunn, Donatella della Porta, Rosalba Icaza, Jeffrey Juris, Lorenzo Mosca, Ellen Reese, Peter Jay Smith, and Rolando Vászuez. 2007. *Global Democracy and the World Social Forums*. Boulder, Colo.: Paradigm Publishers.

Soule, Sarah A., and Ann Marie Condo. 2005. "Student and Youth Collective Action in the United States, 1960–1990." Paper presented at the Democracy Collaborative Research Seminar on the Role of Youths and Universities in Mobilizing Social Movements, April, College Park, Md.

Stacey, Judith. 2007. "If I Were the Goddess of Sociological Things." In *Public Sociology*, edited by Dan Clawson, Robert Zussman, Joya Misra, Naomi Gerstel, Randall Stokes, Douglas L. Anderton, and Michael Burawoy, 91–100. Berkeley: University of California Press.

Tarrow, Sidney. 2005. *The New Transnational Activism.* New York: Cambridge University Press.

Teivainen, Teivo. 2002. "The World Social Forum and Global Democratisation: Learning from Porto Alegre." *Third World Quarterly* 23:621–32.

Verba, Sidney, Kay Lehman Schlozman, and Henry Brady. 1995. *Voice and Equality: Civic Voluntarism in American Politics.* Cambridge, Mass.: Harvard University Press.

Walgrave, Stefaan, and Joris Verhulst. 2003. "Worldwide Anti–War in Iraq Protest: A Preliminary Test of the Transnational Movements Thesis." Paper presented at the Second ECPR International Conference, September, Marburg, Germany.

Wallerstein, Immanuel. 2004. *World-Systems Analysis: An Introduction.* Durham, N.C.: Duke University Press.

———. 2009. "Crisis of the Capitalist System: Where Do We Go from Here?" *Monthly Review* 61:1–29.

Wiltfang, Gregory L., and Doug McAdam. 1991. "The Costs and Risks of Social Activism: A Study of Sanctuary Movement Activism." *Social Forces* 69:987–1010.

Wuthnow, Robert. 1989. *Communities of Discourse: Ideology and Social Structure in the Reformation, the Enlightenment, and European Socialism.* Cambridge, Mass.: Harvard University Press.

III
Formation and Development
of Strategy

7

The Politics of Coming Out: Visibility and Identity in Activism against Child Sexual Abuse

Nancy Whittier

In the early 1970s, gay liberation activists began to come out. Gay men and lesbians publicly disclosed their sexual identities in order to celebrate their identity, display their rejection of conventional sexual and political strictures, and create social change by challenging invisibility, stigma, and assumptions about the nature of homosexuality. In the following decades, coming out became a common way for social movement participants, and those who saw themselves as allied with those movements and their constituencies, to conceptualize identity disclosures, the relation between individual and collective experience and identity, and strategies for social change. People came out as feminists, as conservatives, as people of color who could pass for white, as Christians, Jews, and Muslims, and as survivors of childhood sexual abuse. Here, I use my research on activists against child sexual abuse to explore the relationship between identity strategies and social change.

Coming out is a movement strategy that includes public identity disclosure, internal group definitions of collective identity, and emotion-laden individual transformations of identity. I analyze coming out in order to theorize the relationship between collective and individual identities and movement strategy. I argue that identity transformations are not limited in their impact to individuals. Instead, coming out, as an identity strategy, targets individuals' identities, mainstream culture, institutions, and public policy. My point here rests on two main tenets. First, collective identity—the definition of a group that is constructed by that group—cannot be fully understood without understanding individual identity as well. Yet the links between the two are not straightforward and they can exist in tension or conflict with each other. Second, collective and individual identities are closely related to the state and to other social movements as well as to larger cultural themes. When people disclose stigmatized identities publicly, their own identities shift at both emotional and cognitive levels, and so do onlookers' identities and their beliefs about the group. Reciprocally, these new identities spur collective action. Identity strategies are not limited to targets of identity or emotion, however. Activists also use visibility as a strategy for influencing mainstream culture, institutions, and public policy.

Coming out emerged as a strategy and as a way of understanding identity display and change both because of internal movement reasons—ties to other movements, theoretical and tactical debates among participants—and in response to external contexts, particularly the use of identity and therapeutic discourses within the state and other institutions targeted for change. Coming out as a strategy for social change began in the gay and lesbian liberation movement, but it built on other social movements. The civil rights movement and subsequent Black Power, American Indian, and Chicano movements fostered the idea that pride in one's identity was a means of challenging a dominant culture that denigrated one's group. The woman's movement popularized the idea that so-called personal experiences were connected to larger inequalities. The feminist movements for legalization of abortion and against rape developed the speak-out, in which women told about their stigmatized experiences in order to show that ordinary women had such experiences and to challenge their invisibility. In all of these cases, speaking about identity and experience acquired political meaning because of its effects on individual emotions (reducing shame, promoting pride) and because the individual was aligned with a collectivity (Whittier 2001). By disclosing individual experiences and identities, participants declared their allegiance to a social movement that challenged dominant notions of their group's nature and position. In fairly short order, even people who did not directly participate in the social movement could adopt the identity strategy of coming out to make their own political statement, to attempt to change attitudes in their own circle of influence, and to declare allegiance to a social movement. Thus, coming out, like racial or ethnic pride, became a way that identity disclosure could be linked to social change outside of more conventionally defined collective action.

Like many other groups, survivors of child sexual abuse adopted coming out as a way of conceptualizing their own identity disclosures. Like other groups, they understood coming out on multiple levels. At the individual level, it referred first to acknowledging and understanding one's own experiences and coming to identify as a survivor, and second to disclosing one's identity both in daily life and in the course of movement activities. At the collective, movement level, it referred to public events at which individuals displayed their identity as a group such as demonstrations or speak-outs. Participants understood both individual and collective coming out strategically as a means of producing social change in the larger society and in individuals, changing the emotions associated with experiences of child sexual abuse. Because individuals' feelings about their own identities were one target for social change, activists understood individual transformations strategically as a positive and political outcome of coming out strategies.

Identity strategies include individual or group disclosure of identity with the aim of producing change in how individuals understand and feel about their identity, in how the group is defined in the larger culture, or in the policies of the state and other institutions. Activists against child sexual abuse used identity strategies in a variety of ways. First, they sought transformations of individual feelings and identity as a form of social change, not only the well-being of the individual. Second, individuals and groups came out publicly. Individuals disclosed their identities strategically in the course of daily life in hopes of affecting the institutions with which they interacted. Group came out through public events and displayed movement identities through public cultural projects, displaying a strong collective identity as survivors that drew together otherwise ideologically diverse individuals and groups. Third, organizations extended the politics of visibility into public policy as they developed public health campaigns that sought to bring the issue of child sexual abuse into the public eye.

The ways that the movement against child sexual abuse used identity disclosure strategies are virtually identical to those of GLBT movements and other movements that employ discourses and strategies of coming out. Thus, this case sheds light on the broader question of the links between individual and collective identity in movement strategy.

Theories of Identity and Social Change

Culture and identity have a central place in power and resistance. The beliefs of people on both sides of power inequalities in the legitimacy or inevitability of those inequalities are important for maintaining or overturning them. They are important both in terms of *individual identity*, or how individuals understand themselves, their experiences, and their social position, and *collective identity*, or how groups' shared characteristics are defined both by the groups themselves and by others. One key dynamic of social movements is individuals' affiliation with groups, which entails changes in individual identity as individuals rethink their selves in light of how social movements define the group. For example, as the gay and lesbian movement redefined sexual identity, individual lesbians and gay men affiliated with a collective identity that emphasized pride rather than shame. This also changed how those individuals thought about themselves.

Both scholars and activists have conceptualized the internalization of domination in terms of identity or the definition of a group and its political place (Collins 1990). However, what identity is and the relationship between domination and resistance in identity strategies is widely disputed. Theorists and activists have been critical of social movements that focus on identity strategies, including coming out, labeling these strategies "identity politics." For queer theorists and postmodern theorists of gender, identity categories are a means of fixing behavior in definable units. Normal and abnormal are established by means of dichotomies of categories (Seidman 1996; Valocchi 2005). The legitimacy of the superior group is maintained by making the boundaries of these categories seem fixed and natural (Butler 1990; Berlant and Warner 1995). Queer and poststructuralist theories critique the idea that people can understand their selves through a straightforward narrative, arguing instead that personal history is continually reconstructed (Esterberg 1997). In addition, they criticize the idea that experience is straightforward, that its meaning is easily accessible and transparent to the individual, and that experience has particular epistemological authority (Scott 1991). All of these raise important questions about how to understand activism oriented toward redefining a group's own experience and claiming and displaying a self-defined collective identity.

Most sociological theorists of gender and sexuality agree that the ways that groups are defined and differentiated from each other serve to naturalize their apparent differences and their hierarchical relationship, although they tend to give greater credence to structural and institutional factors and to the weight of history (Lorber 2005). In contrast to queer theory's contention that only the *deconstruction* of identity categories can be truly liberatory, however, they view challenges to the *content* and *position* of those categories as important. Both groups of scholars tend to be critical of collective action oriented toward identity, seeing it as either reinforcing domination by playing into authorities' use of identity categories as a means of oppression, or avoiding more substantive political challenge (Brown 1995). These critiques are linked to a larger critique of a putative therapeutic turn in feminism and other social movements (Brown 1995) and to the use of therapeutic means of social control by the state (Rose 1990; Polsky 1991; Nolan 1998). In this view, activists' focus on changing identity and emotion is not merely a distraction from political goals, but a capitulation to the expansion of state power into the self.

Collective and individual identity have also been the objects of considerable work in social movements (Melucci 1985; Taylor and Whittier 1992; Bernstein 1997; Polletta and Jasper 2000). This work has shown the importance of collective identity for mobilization, its status as a goal in itself, and its strategic public deployment. A parallel smaller literature deals with individual identity in social movements, showing how participation affects individual identities (Stryker, Owens, and White 2000) and how diverse individual identities interact with collective identity (LeClere 2007; Reger, Einwohner, and Myers 2008). A third related literature on emotions in social movements examines the changes in feelings that result from movement participation and how movements attempt to change emotions of both participants and targets (Taylor 1996; Goodwin, Jasper, and Polletta 2001; Whittier 2000; Flam 2005).

The literatures on the therapeutic state and analyses of identity in feminist and queer theory have remained largely separate from social movement analyses of identity and the state (Whittier 2002). I attempt to draw on insights from each to examine identity strategies in relationship to the state, mainstream culture, and other institutions. Coming out is activists' attempt to regain the self, to politicize it, and to define it for themselves. When activists come out, they publicly display a politicized, redefined version of what it means to be part of their group, and they declare that their individual fates—both their position in hierarchies and their happiness—are bound up with the fate of the collectivity. They thus reject the notion that happiness can be achieved outside of social transformation, but they see the route to social transformation as involving both collective and individual identity strategies. To achieve it, they both appropriate and challenge therapeutic discourse and technique to define and control that collective identity.

In contrast to the idea that identity strategies are at best a retreat from politics, I argue that activists develop and refine identity strategies with an eye toward achieving social change in individuals, culture, and institutions. Although changing how individuals think and feel about themselves is a social change goal in itself, these changes also facilitate collective action by groups that are stigmatized or invisible. Reciprocally, when groups engage in collective coming out—what I call visibility politics—they open up space for individuals to redefine their own identities and to come out in their own spheres of influence. Thus, the strategy of coming outpoints to the political nature of identity politics as well as to the interplay between individual and collective identities. The external forces that critics of identity politics point to—the rise of therapeutic techniques for social control, the surveillance and policing of identity categories—are precisely the forces that activists seek to confront. These forces along with the influence of earlier social movements account for the rise of identity strategies and visibility politics (Whittier 2009). Identity strategies respond to the ways that the state and other institutions attempt to construct and define identities, and they attempt to shape individuals' beliefs and feelings about themselves in different ways.

As activists develop identity strategies, they consider the existing views of their group within particular contexts and calibrate their identity disclosures to achieve maximum impact. This impact stems from the ways that identity disclosure can establish credibility (Coy and Woehrle 1996; Nepstad 2001), affect the emotional responses of viewers, and bring the issue into public view. Identity strategies are not always effective, of course, and it is difficult to measure their success, but in this regard, they are no different from any other movement strategy (Giugni, McAdam, and Tilly 1999).

Methods and the Case

This chapter is drawn from a larger study of organizing against child sexual abuse in the U.S. over the past thirty years (Whittier 2009). The social movement against child sexual abuse initially emerged out of feminist antirape efforts. Over time, the movement has transformed and now is enormously diverse in perspective, with considerable variation in political affiliation, organizational structure, strategies, and tactics. Adult survivors of child sexual abuse have organized both in self-help groups and in activist groups oriented toward changing the perception and treatment of adult survivors of child sexual abuse, prosecuting offenders, and reducing the occurrence of child sexual abuse. Other groups for legal and treatment changes in child protective services, the prosecution of offenders, and training children in assault prevention. Here, I focus primarily on organizing by adult survivors using a variety of visibility tactics.[1] They have worked to change subjectivity and emotion through self-help organizations, public visibility projects, and groups focusing on public health.

Self-defined survivor activists range from those who see child sexual abuse as inextricably linked to feminism, antiracism, and queer liberation to conservative evangelical Christians who see shoring up the traditional family as the best prevention for child sexual abuse. They vary between coalition and disagreement. Movement tactics are a complex mix of policy-oriented, cultural, and individual activism. They include service provision (i.e., treatment or support for adult survivors, child victims, or offenders), direct action and demonstrations, legislative campaigns (e.g., around community notification laws or extensions on statutes of limitations), self-help and support groups, public health campaigns, art, and theater. There are several visible national organizations and countless grassroots groups.

A countermovement, led by a national organization, the False Memory Syndrome Foundation, politicized the survivors' movement even as membership in organizations shrank from its heyday in the 1980s and early 1990s (Davis 2005; Whittier 2009). From the late 1990s to the early 2000s, activists sought to provide emotional support to survivors and worked to end child sexual abuse by both engaging with policy issues and bearing witness to the pain it caused. It included organizations that worked with the state to take a public health approach to preventing child sexual abuse, essentially shifting the emphasis on visibility from individual coming out to community-wide publicity efforts.

Data include forty-five in-depth, semistructured interviews with participants, documents from numerous movement organizations, participant observation at movement events, and data on federal grant funding and mainstream media coverage.[2]

Individual Identity Change as a Movement Strategy

Activists sought to change how people who had been sexually abused understood and felt about the experience so that they would feel unashamed and would blame the abuse on the abuser rather than on themselves (Whittier 2000). Many activists sought to promote political explanations for child sexual abuse, including male domination, children's disempowerment, and societal silence and discomfort. Understanding child sexual abuse in these ways, they believed, would help those who had experienced it to recover from its aftereffects (Whittier 2009). The movement's major tactic for promoting individual identity change was self-help in which peer-led groups discussed their experiences of child sexual abuse, attempted to help each other cope with and change their feelings about those experiences, and worked to reduce invisibility and stigma associated with child sexual abuse. These groups saw their work as political because of its effects on individuals, its challenge to the dominance and approaches of professional psychotherapy, and the impact of survivors' increased visibility on mainstream views of child sexual abuse (Whittier 2009). They engaged in both therapeutic efforts to change how individuals felt about and coped with their histories of abuse and attempts to change cultural and political responses to the problem. Most groups that promoted self-help also engaged directly with treatment facilities, professionals, the state, or religious institutions. They included large national organizations, local groups that met in churches or women's centers, and many newsletters and publications.

Self-help groups focused on changing individual identity both by transforming individuals' emotions and by constructing and displaying a different

collective identity for survivors of child sexual abuse. Several national organizations and countless local groups promoted self-help for survivors of child
sexual abuse, and resources were plentiful for people who wanted to start their
own self-help groups. For example, at an annual conference of VOICES, a
national organization promoting self-help, the National Black Women's Health
Project sponsored a workshop on how to start and run a self-help group (Green
1998). The NBWHP itself facilitated self-help groups focused on emotional
and physical health issues for African American women in many cities and
combined encouragement for individuals with advocacy for social change.
Explaining the goals of self-help, the presenter noted that it "doesn't stop with
the self" but "expands to help the world."[3] Similarly, the Healing Woman
Foundation aimed to "teach women that: They are not alone; Healing is Possible; [and] When they are ready, they can make a difference by taking their
healing into the world. Our goal is to create a strong, organized, vocal community of women survivors of childhood sexual abuse and their supporters,
who can speak out about violence against women and children."[4]

Participants were diverse in class, age, religion, sexual orientation, and
political ideology. Yet participants and publications talked about survivors
as a unified group and emphasized commonalities over differences of status
or of type of abuse. The common language of coming out facilitated the connection. The notion of coming out assumed not only a shared collective identity, but also a shared individual experience of overcoming shame and silence
to speak out publicly about child sexual abuse.

The overall goal of self-help organizations at the individual level was
emotional change (Whittier 2000). Organizers attempted to allow conference or group attendees space to express their painful feelings, but also to
encourage them to move through them. The value placed on accepting and
expressing one's genuine feelings means that even nonnormative or undesirable emotions were overtly welcomed. I heard attendees at one conference
discuss their conflicted feelings of love and hate for an abusive father, for
example, or their despair that they would ever "feel like a survivor instead of
a victim." At the same time, organizers wanted to promote feelings associated with resistance and consistent with the movements' understanding of
how the emotional trajectory from damage to healing occurs.[5] These changes
in individual identity and emotion were linked to a collective identity and
to coming out strategies that made individual and collective identities publicly visible.

Organizations encouraged individuals to come out publicly as an important strategy for changing both participants and targets. Most activists saw
disclosure of identity or declarations of allegiance to the collective identity

of "survivor" as transformative for individuals' own identities and for those who heard the disclosures. Many organizations hybridized individual healing and public coming out. For example, SESAME (Survivors of Educator Sexual Abuse and Misconduct Emerge) aimed to "increase the public's awareness of Educator Sexual Abuse by breaking our silence in a strong, united voice," "foster the recovery of victims and survivors through mutual support," advocate for "Student Sexual Harassment policies, regulations, and laws," and promote "proper boundaries between school staff and students" through codes of ethics.[6] Publications framed as healing oriented also regularly published updates and calls to action regarding policy issues. They melded therapeutic discourse with externally oriented politics partly because the therapeutic focus appealed to a broader audience, what leaders termed "beginning survivors." In this way, they drew on hegemonic discourses that had greater emotional resonance in order to broaden their appeal (Maney, Woehrle, and Coy 2005). They also used therapeutic discourse because they viewed changing the self as an important and a political goal and saw therapeutic techniques as a strategy for achieving that change.

Conferences typically included a mixture of workshops on healing for individuals and collective issues, underscoring the links between individual identity and collective identity as well as the emotional dimensions of both. For example, at the 1998 VOICES conference, plenary talks were given by Illinois attorney general Jim Ryan, and *Courage to Heal* author Ellen Bass, representing the dual foci of the group on policy and individual transformation. A workshop presentation at the same conference entitled Take Control and Stand Triumphantly as a Conqueror exhorted survivors not only to "take control" of their own lives (a message consistent with a focus on individual identity), but also to take control of their communities by becoming involved in advocacy organizations. The premise of the talk, as well as the comments afterward, was that survivors could not become involved in "advocacy" (including coming out) without changing their individual identities, and that, conversely, involvement in political work would affect individual identities (furthering "healing").[7]

For some activists, encouraging others' recovery from sexual abuse was their own political contribution; one that they saw as inseparable from other kinds of social change. For example, an African American woman who facilitated self-help groups for women through a multiracial, mixed-class church, explained how her political view of incest had emerged:

> The first part was helping women to see that they were not alone and that they no longer needed to be isolated or ashamed. . . . I didn't really think

of what needed to happen in society. But then as I worked for the issue more and more I said, "Wait a minute. As we change, we need to help change the world." . . . So then I began to look at what supports our environment that incest can live in. And then it was like: the patriarchy. Uh-huh. It began to hook up with my feminism. So then, after that, it was like, "Ok, this is an oppression." I began to name it as oppression and injustice. And so at that moment, I looked around and said, "Oh, the same kind of changes that are necessary for me to be free as a Black woman are the same kind of changes it takes [to end] incest."

A white woman in her thirties similarly described the connections between her own healing and politics:

I feel very fortunate about that [having feminist political frameworks to understand incest] because oftentimes I was able to have the power and the passion about healing myself that I did because I knew I was part of a bigger chain. Like a link in the chain that was trying to create freedom for people. And by me telling the truth about my life and by me healing, I was taking political action. Like, when I couldn't heal for me, I could heal for, you know, for justice.

Both of these respondents viewed multiple forms of oppression as interconnected, influenced by feminist intersectionality theories (Collins 1990). They used intersectional analyses to connect child sexual abuse to other forms of inequality, building a collective identity with deliberately permeable boundaries (Taylor and Whittier 1992). Respondents who did not share their feminist or progressive politics also prioritized shared experiences of child sexual abuse over differences of politics, religion, sexuality, or class (Whittier 2009).

In sum, because activists saw child sexual abuse as having political causes, they saw its effects on individuals as a form of political injustice and saw changing how individuals felt and viewed themselves as political change. Activists understood individual identity, individual identity disclosure, collective identity disclosure, cultural transformation, and social policy change as connected to each other. Similarly, feminist theories of the political stress that we can't understand change in institutions without seeing it as linked to change in other areas, and that definitions of politics that exclude cultural or personal change are inadequate for capturing the scope of change in gender and sexuality (Collins 1990). Because the survivors' movement saw speaking out as political, it extended the notion of coming out into a politics of visibility that included public art and speak-outs.

Public Identity Disclosures: Individual and Collective Identity Collective Action

In addition to transforming the emotions of individuals, the groups engaged in a politics of visibility that sought to change attitudes and feelings of others. The survivors' movement used strategies that emphasized public identity disclosure in several ways. At the individual level, activists came out in daily life about their experiences of child sexual abuse. At the collective level, they organized demonstrations, speak-outs, conferences under the theme "To Tell the Truth," and they made art—written word, performance, and visual—to express their identities and emotions publicly and in efforts to transform observers' beliefs and emotions. The public disclosures that constitute the politics of visibility are disclosures of both collective identity—the movements' definition of what it means to be a survivor—and individual identity—individuals' own experiences and meaning-making. Participants believed visibility could change targets, and they also experienced their own identity disclosures as self-changing. Here, they borrowed from the ideology of coming out in GLBT communities that viewed public disclosure as an antidote to shame and invisibility.

Individual Coming Out Strategies in Institutions

Activists attempt to change the structure and practices of institutions from the outside, but they also change institutions by entering into them, either as direct participants or as influential voices or perspectives (Katzenstein 1998). In either case, to achieve their influence, activists must be open about their agenda. For participants in the survivors' movement, as for gay and lesbian activists and AIDS activists (see Epstein 1996), this entailed coming out. When they are open about having been sexually abused as children, employees, bureaucrats, clients, or students believed that they could change their organizations and the individuals that they come in contact with. They established credibility on the issue (Coy and Woehrle 1996; Nepstad 2001), although this was not assured as some respondents worried about the influence of stereotypes of survivors as weak, victimized, and overly emotional. Nevertheless, they attempted to use the public collective identity of "survivor" to bolster their influence. When open and engaged movement participants are present inside the institutions that control or manage child sexual abuse, those institutions can change. Respondents reported talking with coworkers and supervisors about how to make their organizations more responsive to survivors of child sexual abuse, if relevant to the organization. In other kinds of organizations, respondents simply attempted to change participants' beliefs about child sexual abuse by talking about their experiences.

In some instances, activists came out more officially as speakers or trainers in community mental health centers, police departments, hospitals, or social services departments. Such programming provides a point of entry for grassroots activists into the state bureaucracies that manage and respond to child sexual abuse. When presenters included adults who were open about their own experiences of child sexual abuse, their presence was as important a message as any informational content. Such presentations allowed survivor activists to define their own experiences and identities and to declare these identities inside the very institutions that are charged with constructing and enforcing identities and beliefs about child sexual abuse.

Activists coming out within and in contact with institutions contributed to movement stabilization. This is partly apparent through funding opportunities. Several foundations, including the Women's Foundation in San Francisco and the Ms. Foundation for Women, developed programs for funding work against child sexual abuse as a result of staff or donors who talked about their own experiences of child sexual abuse. Beyond this, the actual impact of individuals coming out in institutions is hard to gauge as with many social movement outcomes. It was nevertheless an important movement strategy that activists promoted and discussed and engaged in deliberately. It is a reminder that movement strategies can be carried out by individuals, not just by collectivities, and that while some strategic activity is formal, other strategic activity is carried out by individuals within their daily lives without formal movement coordination. Many other coming-out strategies were collective, public, and coordinated by movement groups.

Speak-outs, Events, and Demonstrations

The feminist movements for legalization of abortion and against rape developed the speak-out, in which women told about their stigmatized experiences in order to show that ordinary women had such experiences and to challenge their invisibility. Take Back the Night marches and events against violence against women often included speak-outs, and some of my respondents reported participating in those. For example, Arthur first spoke publicly about his childhood abuse by a priest at a 1980s speak-out organized by a rape crisis center.[8]

Speak-outs specifically against child sexual abuse first became nationally visible in 1992, when an activist in Santa Fe, New Mexico, organized a local speak-out, attended by 500 people, under the name To Tell the Truth (Miller 1992). The concept spread rapidly, and a coordinated national effort organized To Tell the Truth events in many localities in 1993 and every year since then. Speak-outs were personally transformative for participants, who reported feeling less shame and stigma after speaking openly about their experiences. Their collective nature enhanced this effect. As the organizer of the first event said, "The more people speak out, the faster we heal" (Miller 1992, quoting Mary Ann Benton). In addition to speak-outs, survivors came out at demonstrations and other events. One regular demonstration was a contingent in the San Francisco Gay Pride Parade organized by RunRiot, a local survivors' activist group. Participants carried signs, chanted and sang, wore stickers proclaiming their identity and various slogans, and handed out fliers about child sexual abuse to observers. Smaller demonstrations and events were also common. Amali's support group at Glide Memorial Church "did a Mother's Day performance . . . and we did a thing about being survivors. Poetry, a whole show. . . . And so there we were, and we were not anonymous."

The experience of being open publicly about having been sexually abused as a child changed people's sense of themselves. They felt that the simple act of openness enabled them to feel a sense of self, of ownership of their own experiences. Here we see the reciprocal relationships between individual and collective identity as well as between public disclosure and individual identity and emotion. At the most basic level, as Amali put it, "being involved with [activist] projects has raised my consciousness and allowed me to be in the world." Many, like Leslie, saw those changes in individuals as significant in themselves: "Even if we don't stop child sexual abuse, I think that there are numbers of people having that experience of . . . 'I'm public and I'm doing it.' I think that's just, in and of itself, a really profound thing. I mean, it *is* social change." Coming out was an inevitable feature of any public demonstration because participants felt that they were revealing their own identities as survivors.

Coming Out, Invisibility, and Mobilization

Without mass visibility, many respondents argued, it was impossible to mobilize survivors. At the most basic level, any form of collective action by survivors of child sexual abuse entails coming out. As Ella put it, "The invisibility of the survivor . . . plays against us." Kimberly expanded on this dilemma, making an analogy, as many respondents did, to the lesbian and gay and black civil rights movements:

> What really catapulted those other movements was when people, a massive group of people, came together and were visible. You know, whether it was ACT-UP with the gay movement . . . when they started marching in the street in numbers that people started saying, "Well, there's a lot of gay folks out here!" You know, or the Black movement, the civil rights movement,

showing folks that we won't sit at the back of the bus anymore. . . . The women's movement, the same thing.

By countering the invisibility of child sexual abuse, Kimberly believed, mass collective action by survivors could change how people conceptualize the issue:

> I believe we have to get there. We have to march on Washington by the millions. We have to come out of the closet, if you will. . . . There's nothing that identifies us as survivors in society if we don't say that we are. . . . Once we are visible, it exposes the insidious perpetration of violence that has persisted and continues to persist unchecked.

For Kimberly, as for other respondents, collective action entailed coming out. This was both its central problematic—how to mobilize a constituency to proclaim a stigmatized and personally painful experience publicly—and the source of its power. Activists believed coming out would raise awareness of child sexual abuse by making its prevalence visible. As one woman put it, "I think most people are shielded from it. So I try to unshield. I think people have to get unshielded if we're ever going to really stop it." Strategically, their aim was to make the frequency of child sexual abuse apparent and to illustrate the broad reach of its effects.

Protest Art

Art activism was a major component of the survivors' movement during this period and reflected the same kinds of visibility politics as other forms of coming out. Protest art is a common means by which movements communicate their new meanings publicly (Krouse 1993). Respondents who were artists or who promoted art activism hoped that the art would produce social change. For example, one organization brought an exhibit of three statues representing stages of response to and healing from child sexual abuse to conferences and workshops. The organization's founder contended that viewing the statues helped workshop participants to understand the issue in new ways and to transform their own emotions. She wrote, "Art becomes an organizing tool when it is put in service of a cause that needs to be publicized . . . [Our] art bypasses . . . resistance because it's about 'speaking up,' breaking silence, in a way that can be 'heard' first at a level of image, emotion, and experience."[9]

Activist art appeared in many venues, from newsletters that published poetry and drawings to musical performances and talent shows at conferences to independent theater performances and publications to arts shows at conferences or public settings. Songs, poetry, and visual art depicted the experience of abuse, the emotions felt by children and adult survivors, the brutality of offenders, or the indifference or cruelty of other adults. In addition to individual performances, collective public art projects flourished. The largest of these, the Clothesline Project, holds T-shirts depicting experiences of abuse and violence painted by visitors to the exhibit.

Artistic quality varied considerably, but is not the central point. At its core, the art aimed to break the artist's own silence, bring visibility to the issue, and transform how audience members think and feel about child sexual abuse. Visitors to one art exhibit, an organizational announcement wrote, were expected to experience a range of emotions, "sadness, fear, anger, repulsion, compassion, etc.," because "it is appropriate to feel angry about the rape and violation of innocent children." Such art was a route to social change precisely because it bore witness to atrocity; the announcement continued: "It is our belief that we contribute to the healing of child sexual abuse by our willingness to bear witness to its reality, in spite of our discomfort in doing so. . . . The Art of Healing is a forum for healing and empowerment, an opportunity for adult survivors to share with a strong, clear voice, to tell the truth, and to reclaim their power" (Survivors Healing Center, http://www .survivorshealingcenter.org/services.html). "Telling the truth" through art is a coming-out strategy in which individuals display their own identities and their allegiance to a collective identity in order to produce change in observers. Activist art did not aim primarily to produce moral shock (Jasper 1997), but rather to lead viewers to a deeper emotional understanding of the nature and effects of child sexual abuse, to highlight similarities between child sexual abuse and other forms of oppression, to formulate an analysis of child sexual abuse that blames perpetrators rather than victims, and to emphasize the strength of those who survive child sexual abuse. When activists talk about bearing witness, they emphasize the ways that silence and stigma make child sexual abuse possible and argue that child sexual abuse cannot continue when it is made visible.

The survivors movement is one among many that employ the politics of visibility. Identity disclosure, activist art, and demonstrations that bear witness to violence are common to women's, lesbian/gay, transgender, and antiracism movements, and vigils that bear witness to collective violence have been a major tactic of antiwar, human rights, and Holocaust remembrance groups. These strategies aim to change the individuals who participate and those who observe both cognitively and emotionally, bringing attention to issues that might otherwise go unspoken and dramatizing the problem in ways that bypass observers' preconceptions and evoke an emotional response. On a very different level, public health–style campaigns sought to do the same thing.

Collective Visibility Politics and the State: Public Health

Public health initiatives attempt to improve the health of groups of people through education campaigns or public policy initiatives, rather than improving the health of individuals one at a time through medical intervention. Public health campaigns focus on harm reduction—that is, reducing the incidence and impact of a problematic behavior rather than law enforcement or intervention by child welfare agencies. The idea is that when people are educated about the problems associated with a behavior, when people are given resources to change it, and when cultural acceptance of the behavior declines, the behavior itself will be less common. When public health campaigns address hidden or stigmatized issues, they use an institutional variety of coming-out strategies.

The campaigns aimed at preventing child sexual abuse were in some ways a natural extension of the politics of visibility. Activists saw widespread publicity about how to prevent child sexual abuse as another way of destroying the secrecy and stigma in which child sexual abuse flourishes. After successful public health campaigns on issues such as smoking, drunk driving, gun use, domestic violence, and eating habits, government funders and agencies, especially the Centers for Disease Control and Prevention (CDC), were enthusiastic about a similar approach to reducing child sexual abuse.

Activists against child sexual abuse found the public health approach appealing for several reasons. Many longtime activists were frustrated by the movement's lack of impact on the actual incidence of child sexual abuse. Although resources and responses to abuse after the fact had improved, prevention efforts had stalled.[10] Several groups in different areas independently came to the conclusion that they needed to use sophisticated marketing and community organizing techniques to attempt to reshape the public view of abuse and of how to intervene to prevent it. They were inspired by the ideas of visibility and coming out from their experience in the survivors' movement, by the success of other public health campaigns, and often by their own professional experience in marketing or business. Many organizations worked within the public health approach, sponsoring events such as a walk/run organized by Stop the Silence, and Mothers Against Sexual Abuse, which drew directly on Mothers Against Drunk Driving in its name, and distributing educational materials, referring victims and families to professionals for treatment, and working on relevant legislation.[11]

Focused on the insight that it was adults, not children, who needed to be the center of prevention efforts, one such group, Stop It Now!, coordinated several statewide campaigns with advertising about child sexual abuse and toll-free help lines to receive calls from people seeking advice about how to deal with abuse situations and offenders seeking help. It produced and distributed publications on topics such as adolescent sex offenders and how to intervene with an adult who shows sexually inappropriate behavior with a child. Another group, Generation Five, similarly focused on getting adults involved with prevention and on disseminating information widely. Instead of public service announcements, however, Generation Five emphasized community organizing and capacity building, running training programs for community leaders who could weave prevention efforts into their other work such as youth or domestic violence organizing, and focused on building a multi-ethnic and multicultural approach. Their focus emphasized visibility of individuals and the issue across racial and ethnic communities and organizations.

Such organizations built on the themes of visibility and survivor self-determination, but sought to establish child sexual abuse as an issue of health similar to smoking or drunk driving. For example, Stop It Now! framed child sexual abuse as a public health epidemic.[12] Their view is that the public health approach addresses the "root causes" of child sexual abuse by

> Develop[ing] awareness in potential abusers and encourag[ing] them to seek help.
>
> Challeng[ing] abusers to stop the abuse immediately and seek treatment through a helpline or on the internet.
>
> Work[ing] with families, peers, and friends on how to confront abusers.
>
> Join[ing] with others to build a social climate that says "We will no longer tolerate the sexual abuse of children."[13]

They thus see individual change in abusers and bystanders as linked to visibility and open discussion of the issue that in turn leads to social change. Similarly, Generation Five drew on alliances with domestic violence opponents who emphasized how "communities can help families to prevent violence and seek effective support by creating public discussions that counter the assumption that 'family business' should remain 'family business.'"[14]

These groups work to disseminate their view of child sexual abuse through polished and widely disseminated advertising and community outreach campaigns. These campaigns were the offspring of both mass media advertising and the visibility strategies of social movements such as ACT UP with its attention-getting poster campaigns. Stop It Now!'s print media campaigns focused on basic information, such as "sex with children is wrong," and encouraged people to speak up if they had suspicions about family members' behavior with children.[15] Public service announcements created by another group, Darkness to Light, appeared on several cable networks and publications (Darkness to Light 2005a; Lee 2005). Polished and compelling, they focused on the high rate of child abuse (one in six boys, one in four girls), using images such as six boys in baseball uniforms or four girls jumping to the popular song "Girls Just Wanna Have Fun," complete with a voice-over by the artist, Cyndi Lauper.[16] The commercials referred viewers to a national help line that connected callers to local help lines.

Through their media campaigns, the groups sought to enter mass culture on their own terms rather than accepting existing representations of child sexual abuse. Yet in order to make their own campaigns comprehensible, the groups could not avoid drawing on existing representations. Darkness to Light, for example, referred to abuse survivors as the "walking wounded," and in its literature, website, and public service announcements, it liberally sprinkled images of attractive, innocent, and vulnerable-looking children. Similarly, Stop It Now! ads used images of children playing to suggest both their innocence (which should be protected) and their vulnerability. These efforts to catch attention and remain readable undeniably made the ads more effective, but they also limited their ability to discuss the more structural and political elements of the groups' analysis, such as the overwhelming prevalence of familial abuse or the ways that institutions collude with concealing abuse. These are the dilemmas that face activist attempts to influence mainstream culture, including most forms of public coming out. Activists can only attain visibility within dominant culture if their messages are comprehensible within that culture, marginalizing those approaches that are the most challenging (Rochon 1998; Whittier 2009).

In addition to advertisement, organizations also used face-to-face campaigns that allowed them to present more challenging elements of their approach and emphasized personal identity disclosure and transformations for all parties—survivors of child sexual abuse, offenders, and bystanders. For example, Darkness to Light designed a prevention training program aimed at adults called Stewards of Children, available to organizations or online; it trained parents and adults who worked with children to be aware of signs of potential abuse, discuss issues of abuse, and exercise caution in allowing children to be alone with adults, using videos, discussion, and reading materials.[17] Mostly disseminated through organizations such as churches, YMCA/YWCAs, or Big Brother/Big Sister, the Stewards of Children program relied on facilitators trained by Darkness to Light to conduct the trainings.

Stop It Now!, in a quintessential visibility strategy, sponsored public dialogues between abuse survivors and offenders in an attempt to diminish community denial about the existence and nature of child sexual abuse and to raise hope that effective treatment for offenders was available. Pairing a survivor and a "recovering offender" who had been convicted and served his sentence, the dialogues included each participant's telling his or her own story, then questioning and commenting with the other. The dialogues neatly sidestepped skepticism about the legitimacy of claims of abuse by including a convicted sex offender who admitted his own actions and the strategies he had used to lure a victim and conceal the abuse alongside a survivor who could describe the similar strategies used by the (different) person who had abused her. The offender's testimony about his own treatment and recovery process also offered support for the group's advocacy of effective treatment and, of course, represented his own public coming out. Like other forms of coming out, these visibility projects sought to change audience beliefs and emotions about child sexual abuse, not simply raising awareness but promoting the movement's analyses of the issue.

The public health approach spread fairly rapidly among organizations, and they achieved a measure of visibility and political support. Whether the approach can reduce child sexual abuse remains unknown, but it allowed the organizations to achieve cultural visibility for their own messages at an unprecedented level. The approach was also compelling to government officials, particularly in the CDC. Stop It Now! presented its work many times to the CDC and the U.S. Justice Department. Generation Five also participated in meetings sponsored by the CDC. Their access to these agencies was unprecedented for child sexual abuse groups led by nonclinicians, but activist groups dealing with other public health issues such as drunk driving, breast cancer, and AIDS had paved the way (Epstein 1996).

Public health groups, like participants in self-help programs or speakouts, drew on the politics of visibility, but they shifted the focus from individual visibility to visibility of the issue, and from relatively unpolished (if formulaic) narratives (Davis 2005) to highly polished, professional-level advertisements. In the focus on building capacity, they formalized the process of individual transformation. They also relied on their personal experience of sexual abuse to help establish credibility and determine the organizations' direction. Virtually all such organizations were founded by survivors of child sexual abuse and incorporated the voices and ideas of survivors through focus groups and through quotes and vignettes in publications and advertisements. They thus show the connections between different models of coming out (informal within grassroots organizations and through advertising campaigns) as well as between individual, collective, and social change.

Conclusion

Coming-out strategies in self-help groups, art, and public health made up a strong politics of visibility in which individuals defined their identities and worked to influence how others thought and felt about child sexual abuse. They saw themselves as asserting their right to define their own experiences and trying to convey those experiences to others. In contrast to the notion of collective identity as emphasizing commonalities among group members (Taylor and Whittier 1992; Whittier 1995), survivors' visibility politics emphasized self-expression and individuality, focusing on expressing multiple perspectives as a means of healing and bearing witness. It asserted collective identity less and emphasized variation in individual identity more. The public health organizations also built on visibility politics, but they used different means, aiming to enter the mass media on their own terms through advertising and educational campaigns and focusing on visibility of the issue more than the individual. The politicized self-help movement emphasized individual identity change; the visibility activists emphasized public identity disclosure; and the public health activists emphasized the visibility of the issue as defined by the movement.

The goals of the movement against child sexual abuse were to prevent child sexual abuse, improve the treatment of people who had been sexually abused, and help those people to recover from the aftereffects of their childhood experiences. These goals required change in public policy, institutions such as law enforcement and medicine, mainstream culture, and individual beliefs and emotions. Correspondingly, their strategies for achieving these goals included individual and institutional change, advocacy, and emotional transformation. Individuals' thoughts, feelings, and behaviors were as important targets as cultural representations, policy, and legislation. Individual transformation was in a sense a precondition to mobilization because mobilization required individuals who had been sexually abused as children to come out. Beyond this, in emphasizing the visibility of the issue and of individual survivors (and offenders, in the case of the public health wing), activists sought to change interiority by changing beliefs about child sexual abuse, emotional responses to it, and interaction in daily life. They wanted people—survivors, offenders, and bystanders—to recognize abuse when it was occurring, to feel both outrage and empowerment to act, and to intervene when it did occur. They believed that these changes required public disclosure of individual and collective identities and visibility of the issue.

Coming out is as a strategy has significant limitations, some of which are at the heart of the critique of identity politics. For one, identity strategies limit the role of people who do not share the identity category—in this case, people who have not experienced child sexual abuse. The survivors' movement, like others, created identity categories for nonsurvivors, terming them allies or prosurvivors, but these categories carry sometimes restrictive assumptions about the perspective and experiences of those within them. Another limitation, central to the critique of identity politics, has to do with the pervasive power of existing definitions of the group. Institutions are dominated by a discourse that casts victims of child sexual abuse as seriously and permanently wounded and subject to interpretation and treatment by experts rather than themselves. Because credentials and authority in both the state and the mass media rest on standards of objectivity, the credibility of activists who speak based on their own experience is suspect. Activists have trouble disclosing identity on their own terms when they enter the mass media and can easily be cast in terms of the dominant definitions of the category (Whittier 2009). Finally, only some kinds of social processes and structures can be changed through coming out. To the extent that a movement relies on it to the exclusion of other tactics, or assumes that coming out will work in all situations, it can limit movement effectiveness.

To stop at these critiques, however, leaves us without a nuanced understanding of identity strategies. As I have shown, transformations in individual identity can provide a base for collective action and collective identity disclosure. In turn, collective identity disclosure can affect the individual identities of potential recruits as well as the cognitions and emotions of other observers. Activists deliberate about how to come out in order to persuade onlookers to think about an issue or group in a new way, and visibility strategies have clear social change goals. Further, identity strategies are used within institutions, both as individual participants disclose their identities and through advocacy or training. Finally, viewing public health campaigns as a form of visibility politics illustrates how identity strategies can be used at an institutional level. Like any other strategy, identity strategies are limited by cultural and political constraints. The outcomes that result rarely entail complete achievement of movement goals.

My aim here has been to examine the theoretical dimensions of identity strategies in more depth. Doing so emphasizes the connections between individual identity (including its construction, disclosure, and transformation), collective identity (including its construction, disclosure, and transformation), and visibility strategies that emphasize identity disclosure, including both those who emphasize the personal expression of identity (such as speak-outs and protest art) and those who emphasize the disclosure of a more formalized and homogenized expression of collective identity, such as the public health projects. Changes in individual participants affect the kinds of strategies that movements are able to, and choose to, undertake. Further, movement strategies not only affect outcomes, but also shape collective identity and the identities of individuals. Theorizing these connections and examining them in other movements, including those who do not articulate explicit identity strategies, will be a fruitful direction for further work.

Notes

1. I'll refer to this movement interchangeably as "the movement against child sexual abuse" and "the survivors' movement" (its self-label).

2. Data on federal grants come from the *NCCAN Clearinghouse Compendium of Discretionary Grants, Fiscal Years 1975–1995,* published in September 1996 by the National Center on Child Abuse and Neglect. My discussion of popular culture is based on an analysis of all articles about child sexual abuse indexed in the *Readers' Guide to Periodical Literature* from 1960 to 2005.

3. Field notes, 16th VOICES in Action Inc. Conference, Evanston, Illinois, July 24–26, 1998. Quotes are close paraphrases based on my notes.

4. Healing Woman Foundation flier, collected at the 16th VOICES in Action Inc. Conference, personal collection of the author.

5. Field notes, 16th VOICES in Action Inc. Conference; field notes, Incest Awareness Foundation Conference, New York City, January 30–31, 1999.

6. SESAME flier, collected at the 16th VOICES in Action Inc. Conference and the 1999 Incest Awareness Foundation Conference, personal collection of author.

7. Field notes, 16th VOICES in Action Inc. Conference, workshop by Holly Broach-Sowells.

8. All names are pseudonyms.

9. Donna Jensen, "People of Fire Grant Proposal," June 1999, personal collection of the author.

10. The success of the countermovement also had rendered many of the movement's earlier strategies ineffective by impugning the credibility of adult survivors. A focus on prevention sidestepped the countermovement's critique of memory by focusing on child sexual abuse itself.

11. Stop the Silence, Stop Child Sexual Abuse (http://www.stopcsa.org), annual race; Mothers Against Sexual Abuse (http://www.againstsexualabuse.org).

12. Stop It Now! (http://www.stopitnow.org), "Child Abuse: A Public Health Epidemic."

13. Stop It Now!, "The Key Premises of Our Work."

14. Generation Five (http://www.generationfive.org), "Defining the Problem."

15. Stop It Now!, "How Our Programs Work."

16. Darkness to Light (http://www.darkness2light.org), "Darkness to Light Media Campaign: Public Awareness about Child Sexual Abuse."

17. The online prevention program was funded by a $461,208 U.S. Department of Commerce Technologies Opportunity Program grant and a $250,000 Department of Justice grant. See Darkness to Light (2005b).

References

Berlant, Lauren, and Michael Warner. 1995. "What Does Queer Theory Teach Us about X?" *PMLA* 110, no. 3:343–47.

Bernstein, Mary. 1997. "Celebration and Suppression: The Strategic Uses of Identity in the Lesbian and Gay Movement." *American Journal of Sociology* 103:537–65.

Brown, Wendy. 1995. *States of Injury*. Princeton, N.J.: Princeton University Press.

Butler, Judith. 1990. *Gender Trouble*. New York: Routledge.

Collins, Patricia Hill. 1990. *Black Feminist Thought*. Boston: Unwin Hyman.

Coy, Patrick G., and Lynne M. Woehrle. 1996. "Constructing Identity and Oppositional Knowledge: The Framing Practices of Peace Movement Organizations during the Persian Gulf War." *Sociological Spectrum* 16:287–327.

Darkness to Light. 2005a. "Stewards of Children Now in Full Release." *Darkness to Light Newsletter* 10:1.

———. 2005b. "Darkness to Light Awarded Federal TOP Grant." *Darkness to Light Newsletter* 10:3.

Davis, Joseph. 2005. *Accounts of Innocence*. Chicago: University of Chicago Press.

Epstein, Steven. 1996. *Impure Science: AIDS, Activism, and the Politics of Knowledge*. Berkeley: University of California Press.

Esterberg, Kristen. 1997. *Lesbian and Bisexual Identities*. Philadelphia: Temple University Press.

Flam, Helena, ed. 2005. *Emotions and Social Movements*. London: Routledge.

Giugni, Marco, Doug McAdam, and Charles Tilly, eds. 1999. *How Social Movements Matter*. Minneapolis: University of Minnesota Press.

Green, Toylee. 1998. "Self Help Groups: How to Develop and Conduct." Presented at "Unlock the Voice . . . Free the Spirit," 16th VOICES in Action Inc. Conference, July 24, Evanston, Ill.

Jasper, James M. 1997. The Art of Moral Protest. Chicago: University of Chicago Press.

Katzenstein, Mary. 1998. *Faithful and Fearless: Moving Feminist Protest Inside the Church and the Military*. Princeton, N.J.: Princeton University Press.

Krouse, Mary Elizabeth. 1993. "Gift-Giving and Social Transformation: The AIDS Memorial Quilt as Social Movement Culture." Ph.D. diss., Ohio State University, Columbus.

LeClere, Danny. 2007. "The Problem with Queer and Single Identity Politics."

Unpublished manuscript, Department of Sociology, Smith College, Northampton, Mass.

Lee, Annie. 2005. "Letter from the President." *Darkness to Light Newsletter* 10:2.

Lorber, Judith. 2005. *Breaking the Bowls: Degendering and Feminist Change.* New York: Norton.

Maney, Gregory M., Lynne M. Woehrle, and Patrick G. Coy. 2005. "Harnessing and Challenging Hegemony: The U.S. Peace Movement after 9/11." *Sociological Perspectives* 38:357–81.

Melucci, Alberto. 1985. "The Symbolic Challenge of Contemporary Movements." *Social Research* 52:789–816.

Miller, Leslie. 1992. "Sexual Abuse Survivors Find Strength to Speak in Numbers." *USA Today,* August 27, D6.

Nepstad, Sharon E. 2001. 2001. "Creating Transnational Solidarity: The Use of Narrative in the U.S.–Central America Peace Movement." *Mobilization* 6:21–36.

Nolan, James, Jr. 1998. *The Therapeutic State: Justifying Government at Century's End.* New York: New York University Press.

Polletta, Francesca, Jeff Goodwin, and James Jasper, eds. 2000. *Political Passions: Emotions and Social Movements.* Chicago: University of Chicago Press.

Polletta, Francesca, and James M. Jasper. 2000. "Collective Identity and Social Movements." *Annual Review of Sociology* 27:283–305.

Polsky, Andrew J. 1991. *The Rise of the Therapeutic State.* Princeton, N.J.: Princeton University Press.

Reger, Jo, Rachel L. Einwohner, and Daniel J. Myers, eds. 2008. *Identity Work in Social Movements.* Minneapolis: University of Minnesota Press.

Rochon, Thomas R. 1998. *Culture Moves.* Princeton, N.J.: Princeton University Press.

Rose, Nikolas. 1990. *Governing the Soul: The Shaping of the Private Self.* London: Routledge.

Scott, Joan. 1991. "The Evidence of Experience." *Critical Inquiry* 17:773–98.

Seidman, Steven. 1996. Introduction to *Queer Theory/Sociology,* edited by Steven Seidman, 1–30. Oxford: Blackwell.

Stryker, Sheldon, Timothy Owens, and Robert White, eds. 2000. *Self, Identity, and Social Movements.* Minneapolis: University of Minnesota Press.

Taylor, Verta. 1996. *Rock-a-by Baby: Feminism, Self-Help, and Postpartum Depression.* New York: Routledge.

Taylor, Verta, and Nancy Whittier. 1992. "Collective Identity and Lesbian Feminist Mobilization." In *Frontiers of Social Movement Theory,* edited by Aldon D. Morris and Carol McClurg Mueller, 104–30. New Haven, Conn.: Yale University Press.

Valocchi, Stephen. 2005. "Not Yet Queer Enough: The Lessons of Queer Theory for the Sociology of Gender and Sexuality." *Gender and Society* 19:750–70.

Whittier, Nancy. 1995. *Feminist Generations: The Persistence of a Radical Women's Movement.* Philadelphia: Temple University Press.

———. 2001. "Emotional Strategies: The Collective Reconstruction and Display of Oppositional Emotions in the Movement against Child Sexual Abuse." In *Passionate Politics: Emotions and Social Movements,* edited by Jeff Goodwin, James M. Jasper, and Francesca Polletta, 233–50. Chicago: University of Chicago Press.

———. 2002. "Meaning and Structure in Social Movements." In *Social Movements: Identity, Culture, and the State,* edited by David S. Meyer, Nancy Whittier, and Belinda Robnett, 289–307. New York: Oxford University Press.

———. 2009. *The Politics of Child Sexual Abuse: Emotion, Social Movements, and the State.* New York: Oxford University Press.

8

Agreeing for Different Reasons: Ideology, Strategic Differences, and Coalition Dynamics in the Northern Ireland Civil Rights Movement

Gregory M. Maney

From its inception in 1920, the state of Northern Ireland has witnessed conflict between, on the hand, the mostly Protestant, Unionist majority of the population supporting a political union with Great Britain, and, on the other hand, the largely Catholic, Nationalist minority seeking the reunification of Northern Ireland with the other twenty-six counties of the island of Ireland. A deep desire to ensure the retention of British links, coupled with a recalcitrant, irredentist opposition produced political and economic institutions largely controlled by, and favoring, the Unionist majority. During the 1960s, a civil rights movement emerged, using nonviolent forms of collective civil disobedience to challenge the second-class citizenship status of Nationalist minority without raising the issue of partition. The movement demanded fundamental changes in housing allocation, the electoral system, and policing. Civil rights mobilization resulted in a violent backlash from the hard-line Loyalist segment of the Unionist population. This backlash, in turn, contributed to the renewal of an armed Republican campaign for Irish reunification. As the civil rights movement declined amid deepening factionalism and dwindling numbers, many promised reforms remained unimplemented or were reversed.

A triangulated, longitudinal analysis of the perspectives of those participating in two major coalitions within the civil rights movement in Northern Ireland offers preliminary answers to three research questions: What is the relationship between ideology and strategy? Under what circumstances is more than one strategy likely to be favored by large segments of the same movement? And finally, what factors explain the consequences of strategic differences for intramovement dynamics? Strategic differences within the movement reflected contrasting ideologies among participants. Variations in the social location of participants, popular awareness of alternative strategies deployed by other movements, a relative balance of power between ideological opponents, and a coalition-based model of organization all contributed to strategic multiplicity within the movement. Nonetheless, prominent activists with different strategies participated in mass civil rights marches during the early stages of contention. The quasi-institutionalized and flexible character of mass marches enabled those with opposing strategies to participate for very different reasons. Only when authorities and opponents responded to the marches did strategic differences produce tactical divergence.

Theory

I define strategy as actions intended to give rise to sequences of events that ultimately end with the achievement of the core objectives. This dynamic definition permits the possibility that activists have visions extending beyond the immediate social context and its attendant dilemmas. Since the seminal works of Gamson (1975) and Piven and Cloward (1977), several scholars have examined the effects of strategy on the outcomes of social movements (e.g., Amenta, Halfmann, and Young 1999; Ganz 2000; Bernstein 2003; Andrews 2004; Edwards and McCarthy 2004; McCammon et al. 2008). Yet the sources of strategy and processes of implementation have received less attention (Jasper 2004). Some observers have implied a single strategy for a social movement. As social movement scholars move away from the assumption that activists are human calculators who objectively recognize opportunities and constraints in their environments, however, we come to recognize the difficulties of creating a shared vision of the world and how to change it. Responses to strategic dilemmas are likely to vary depending on social location, beliefs, values, emotions, and group commitments (e.g., Robnett 2004). Large-scale agreement on strategies within movements with heterogeneous constituencies would be irrational given likely variations in goals and perceived interests.

The possibility of multiple strategies being pursued simultaneously by different activists raises questions regarding intramovement dynamics. Is it possible for a coalition of organizations to engage in coherent and coordinated collective action when its participants embrace different strategies? If so, under what circumstances is this action likely to occur? To date, these important questions have received little research attention. Understanding the effects of multiple strategies on intramovement dynamics requires developing a framework for understanding sources of strategic differences.

Ideology and Strategy

On the basis of a lively and productive discussion initiated by Oliver and Johnston (2000), I define ideology as systematically related, enduring, and generally applied beliefs regarding how the world does and should work as well as how the world does and should change. Some researchers suggest that the strategies of organizers reflect their ideologies. In her study on the Student Nonviolent Coordinating Committee, Polletta (1995, 2002) points out how certain opportunities to achieve their goals were bypassed because of the activists' assumption that these avenues of change were not possible. Conversely, she observed cases where activists believed that opportunities for change existed when in fact they did not. Other studies have emphasized how activists' beliefs, values, and group commitments guide tactical selection and innovation (e.g., Dalton 1994; Meyer 2004; Nepstad 2004).[1] Specifying ideological bases of strategy will help us to better understand strategic differences that arise among activists. Two interrelated components of ideology produce strategic differences: the goals of social change desired, and ontological assumptions regarding the underlying causes of social problems and, accordingly, how social change can be achieved.

Social Change Goals

Activists frequently differ in the type, depth, and specificity of goals that inform their participation in a movement. Differences in goal types frequently produce differences in strategy. For instance, activists seeking social integration will likely advocate cultivating broad alliances, while those wanting separation will probably reject such alliances.

Even activists sharing the same type of goal may nonetheless differ in terms of the depth of their ambitions (Downey and Rohlinger 2008). Some seek only limited reforms; others strive for comprehensive changes. Although not always the case, the depth of goal preferences is negatively related to degree of goal focus. Those pursuing limited changes tend to specify, in greater detail, what they wish to change than those wishing to make systemic changes (Gamson 1975). As with the type of goal being pursued, differences in the depth and specificity of goals often create conflicts over strategy. On the one hand, those who wish to make systemic changes often complain about having their visions vetoed by the lowest common denominator who seek specific limited changes. On the other hand, those seeking limited changes often perceive those with more comprehensive agendas as distracting focus from core issues or attempting to hijack the movement for illegitimate purposes. Differences in goals between activists reflect and contribute to different social ontological assumptions. Like goals, variations in ontological assumptions often give rise to differences in strategy.

Social Ontological Assumptions

Social ontological assumptions involve generalized beliefs regarding the source of a social problem and, by extension, what changes must take place for the problem to be solved. Distinctive assumptions encourage different strategic emphases. Further complicating matters, ideological differences can occur even among those who assume the same general sources of social problems. Activists focusing on symbolic changes can disagree over which facets of a dominant symbolic culture are most deeply associated with the social problem. Similarly, activists emphasizing structural changes can argue about the fundamental group basis of the social problem or which institution is primarily responsible. In addition, those who share the same assumptions regarding underlying causes of social problems may have very different assumptions about how social change takes place. For instance, some activists assume that change requires alliances across social cleavages. In contrast, others assume that movements will succeed only if they consist of those who have, in the words of Marx and Engels ([1848] 1998), "nothing to lose but their chains."

Contextual Sources of Strategic Multiplicity

I argue that three contextual factors increase the likelihood of multiple strategies reaching prominence within the same social movement. First, movements that draw its participants from multiple social locations are likely to experience strategic differences. Examples of social location include but are not limited to age, class, ethnicity, gender, race, religion, and sexual orientation. Differences in social locations give rise to different experiences, interests, and bases of solidarity (Fantasia 1988; Taylor and Whittier 1992). In the process, they also produce variations in attitudes, commitments, and rules of behavior—variations that can generate tensions over strategy (Friedman and McAdam 1992). Second, recent exposure to contrasting strategies used by other high-profile movements also encourages strategic multiplicity. This is especially likely with a heterogeneous movement, where participants differ in the extent to which they attribute similarities to participants in other movements (McAdam and Rucht 1993). Third, a relative balance of power between ideologically disparate elements within a movement can prevent one ideological block from resolving conflicts over strategic differences by imposing its preferences over the resistance of another. Ironically, attempts to be open, equitable, and inclusive in decision making are likely to contribute to ongoing differences over strategy. Given the probability of substantive disagreements, does strategic multiplicity doom a movement to factionalism, inertia, and failure?

Strategic Multiplicity and Coalition Dynamics

Scholars have emphasized how strategic differences lead to conflict within coalitions of social movement organizations (Staggenborg 1986; Benford 1993; Balser 1997). Given the seemingly endless list of possible strategies and their various permutations, it is a wonder that a large number of activists with strong, opposing ideologies ever agree on tactics. Yet they sometimes do for the simple reason that any given tactic can be viewed as being consistent with multiple strategies. Different people can agree to the same demand, target, or event for different, even contradictory reasons. A tactic will proliferate when actors with different strategies view it as likely to bring about expected sequences of events that conclude with the fulfillment of their objectives. I propose that two factors make this tactical convergence more likely: early stages of contention, and the use of quasi-institutionalized and flexible tactics.

Stage of Mobilization and Contention

Coalitions containing members with multiple strategies will be more likely to agree on (or at least not oppose the other's) tactics during the early stages of contention. Early stages of contention are characterized by conditions of uncertainty, where responses from authorities and opponents are not fully known. Activists can envision very different responses consistent with alternative sequences of contention. As a result, those with different strategies agree to participate in the same event for different reasons. By reinforcing conditions of uncertainty along with a sense of efficacy among activists, crisis framing in media coverage encourages continued support for a shared tactic.

Established patterns of responses from authorities and opponents, however, frequently expose long-standing differences in strategy. Studies of social movement trajectories have observed that movements begin to splinter at the height of their numbers and influence (e.g., Koopmans 1993; Tarrow 1998). As the ranks of a movement swell, targets are likely to develop more consistent responses to movement practices. Possible responses include repression, subversion, cooptation, channeling, facilitation, and concession. Each of these responses carries major implications for expected sequences of events and outcomes of contention. It is at such moments that differences in strategy are most likely to surface. For example, those believing that promised concessions have reasonably satisfied most of their objectives will likely oppose tactics that antagonize authorities and countermovements. In contrast, others may view concessions as a threat to their long-term objectives and inconsistent with their assumption that meaningful social change requires mass social upheaval. Accordingly, they will push for additional demands and the continuance of the tactics that brought about the concessions in the first place. It is at this point when accusations of moderates selling out and militants taking over become loud and shrill. In the ensuing struggle over strategy, tactics within a movement increasingly diverge. Thus, over their lifetimes, coalitions characterized by strategic multiplicity are likely to experience higher highs accompanying broad-based participation, and accordingly lower lows in terms of factionalism, conflict, and disillusionment.

Quasi-Institutionalized, Flexible Tactics

Different actors can assign different meanings to the same event. Tarrow (1998) distinguishes between three types of collective action: violence, disruption, and convention. Yet different activists often assign the same event to varying categories. Some may view events that destroy property as violent types of collective action while others view them as forms of disruption. Similarly, some may view marches through streets as disruptive while others view them as conventional.

Mixed reactions of authorities can contribute to opposing constructions of the same tactic. Authorities sometimes allow certain instances of a protest form while forbidding others. Such inconsistent responses are likely in cases where authorities encounter either innovative protest forms or familiar forms deployed by unexpected actors. The quasi-institutionalization of a tactic sends mixed messages as to whether or not the tactic is conventional or disruptive.

Those seeking limited reforms through institutional means will agree to participate in a protest if they see it as being conventional. Those seeking comprehensive changes through extrainstitutional means will support the protest if they see it as being disruptive. In cases of strategic multiplicity within coalitions, the former will emphasize and seek to safeguard the institutionalized aspects of the event form, while the latter will accentuate its disruptive aspects. The ability of different activists to make the same tactic more or less violent, disruptive, or conventional indicates that the tactic itself is highly flexible. In summary, quasi-institutionalized and flexible tactics are more likely to be agreed on by activists with different strategies than types that are either institutionalized, consistently and severely repressed, or unambiguous in their potential for disruption or violence. An examination of the civil rights movement in Northern Ireland offers a preliminary assessment of these assertions.

Method

Consisting primarily, though not exclusively, of Catholic Nationalists, the civil rights movement in Northern Ireland (ca. 1963–72) called for the extension and realization in practice of rights guaranteed to all British citizens (see the Appendix for a glossary of case-specific terminology). During my research, I identified fifty-five organizations participating in movement events based in Northern Ireland. I examined movement ephemera at four archives. I also read op-ed pieces, newsletter articles, historical accounts, memoirs, and biographies. Between 1998 and 1999, I also conducted semistructured interviews with thirteen key informants.[2] Strategy-related statements from these sources were entered into thematic files. What emerges from these sources is a movement characterized by strategic differences rooted in opposing ideologies.

A key methodological challenge involved controlling for factors other than strategic differences that might explain divisions over tactics such as different talents and resources, personality clashes, and power struggles. In the case of both coalitions studied (the Northern Ireland Civil Rights Association and the Derry Citizens Action Committee), those with different talents and personalities within the same ideological blocks nonetheless tended to make the same arguments for or against certain tactics. Moreover, power struggles also tended to fall along ideological and strategic lines.

With alternative explanations accounted for, the section below focuses on stages and forms of contention as factors influencing coalition dynamics. I created a file listing civil rights movement events in chronological order. By pinpointing the timing of specific tactics, the chronology allows for an assessment of the hypothesis that strategic differences are more likely to manifest themselves in later stages of contention and to contribute to a divergence in tactics.

The case also provides an instance of a quasi-institutionalized, flexible form of contention. In Britain, mass marches were widely regarded as a fundamental right of citizens. As part of the United Kingdom, residents of Northern Ireland were legally entitled to the same citizenships rights as residents of Britain. At the same time, the devolved, Unionist-controlled government of Northern Ireland routinely permitted mass marches by Unionists as part of annual celebrations. Mass marches by members of the Nationalist minority, however, were less frequently permitted. When allowed, the police placed heavy restrictions on their routes. Moreover, mass marches are typically flexible tactics in that organizers can choose whether or not to march through areas where residents will likely object and can choose whether or not to defy any ban imposed by authorities. To assess whether civil rights activists attached different meanings to civil rights marches, I created a specific file containing all comments made on the topic by source, date, and theme. The resulting triangulated, longitudinal analysis reveals that when civil rights activists in Northern Ireland engaged in similar tactics, they often did so for very different strategic reasons.

Findings: Ideology and Strategy

Leading figures within the two main coalitions of the civil rights movement in Northern Ireland possessed strong ideologies that differed in terms of their goals and ontological assumptions. These ideological distinctions contributed to fundamental differences in strategy.

Goals of Participants

Although those playing key roles within the civil rights movement in Northern Ireland often made the same demands (e.g., public housing allocated on the basis of need; one person, one vote), their primary objectives frequently differed. Three main goals that emerged from the data were civil rights for Catholics, socialism, and a united Ireland.

Full citizenship rights for the mainly Catholic Nationalist minority in Northern Ireland presented a primary motivation for many older middle-class activists. As cofounders of the Campaign for Social Justice, Conn and Pat McCluskey "just wanted to make sure that people had their fair share." Unionists often retained political control in areas where they constituted only a minority of the population. As chairman of the Irish Nationalist Party, James Doherty was acutely aware that "Derry was run by a [Unionist] minority." He viewed civil rights demands as "something intrinsically to be supported."

For other participants, a deep concern about poverty and exploitation served as the main reason for getting involved in civil rights agitation. As founder of the Derry Unemployed Action Committee, Eamonn Melaugh, participated to promote "a standard of living for everybody compatible with the rest of the United Kingdom and the twentieth century." A severe housing shortage existed, resulting in overcrowding and homelessness. High levels of unemployment, coupled with the failure to fully extend the benefits of the British welfare state to Northern Ireland, contributed to deep poverty among many Protestants and Catholics alike. Heavily influenced by the New Left in Great Britain, younger activists such as Eamonn McCann hoped that the civil rights movement would bring about better conditions for all workers.

At least through the latter part of 1969, most participants in the civil rights movement agreed to avoid discussing partition. Not surprisingly, some

Republicans stayed away from the movement because they did not see its relevance to their goal of reunification. In 1966, the Young Republican Association's support for tenant's rights generated hostility. According to one YRA member, "They declared, somewhat vainly, that 'issues such as housing and unemployment have nothing to do with republicanism'" (ÓDochartaigh 1994, 34).

Nonetheless, the goal of reunification did serve as a motivation for key figures in the civil rights movement. Beginning in the late 1950s, an organization based in Britain, the Connolly Association, launched a series of civil rights marches, the longest being from Liverpool to London. The marches followed the organization's publication of *Our Plan to End Partition*. The document argued for mobilizing the British public against repressive, undemocratic Stormont laws. In so doing, the British government would be forced to address the issue of partition. Well-known participants in the movement such as Roy Johnston, Fionbarra ÓDochartaigh, and Bobby Heatley were actively involved in the Connolly Association before returning to Northern Ireland. Although not overtly stated, the question of partition was, according to Heatley, "never far out of the picture." The Connolly Association also had ties with the Communist Party in Northern Ireland. A member of the party's executive committee and a Protestant, Edwina Stewart, saw the civil rights movement as "creating conditions favorable to reunification without civil war." Stewart and others sharing this goal had "the sophistication to realize the strategic advantage of not openly raising the issue of partition and not appearing anti-Protestant."

Although some participants valued these three goals equally, others did not. For example, the McCluskeys viewed questions of socialism and a united Ireland as "distractions from the main issues." Eamonn Melaugh believed that movement should have been about ending poverty and homelessness for all people, rather than Catholic emancipation or ending partition.

Social Ontological Assumptions

These contrasting priorities reflected and reinforced different assumptions regarding the bases of social inequality and promising paths to social change. Those prioritizing civil rights for Catholics assumed that ethnicity was the fundamental social dividing line in Northern Ireland. A prominent member of the middle class in Derry and heavily influenced by the civil rights movement in the United States, John Hume was the vice chair of the Derry Citizens Action Committee before being elected to parliament on a civil rights platform. In response to some activists' stressing socialist ideals, Hume declared that the civil rights movement is not, it never has been, and it has been repeatedly stated not to be a move-ment which seeks to promote either a socialist or a conservative society. It seeks only a just society, and the achievement of justice and democracy is surely a necessary first step in Northern Ireland to end forever the equa-tion of religion and politics before normal politics can take place. (Arthur 1974, 64)

Hume was not alone in his belief that progress toward a different basis for politics first required ethnic equality. Founded in 1963, the Wolfe Tone Soci-eties played a key role in the formation of the civil rights movement (Purdie 1988). Initiated by left-oriented republicans, Wolfe Tone Societies were dis-cussion and research groups that also included Communist Party members and trade unionists. Many in the Wolfe Tone Societies saw the sectarian privileges of Protestants in Northern Ireland as the primary stumbling block to a united Ireland (Feeney 1974). As long as working-class Protestants derived benefits from their ethnicity, they would be unlikely to cooperate with working-class Catholics, even if it was in their interest to do so. The path to a united, social-ist Ireland therefore required dismantling Protestant privileges.

Other participants, however, rejected the primacy of ethnicity as a social cleavage. Instead, they argued that class was the most significant dividing line in society and that class struggle was the main engine for social change. Focus-ing on dismantling sectarian institutions would simply divide the working class along ethnic lines. Only by organizing across ethnic lines could funda-mental citizenship rights be ensured. Alongside members of the New Left–oriented Derry Labor Party, members of the Derry Republican Club formed the Derry Housing Action Committee (DHAC) in February 1968. DHAC organized squats, blockades, and other forms of civil disobedience. In explain-ing these activities, DHAC's head, Matt O'Leary, stated,

> We are looking forward to overcoming the religious divisions. A number
> of politically conscious individuals are working to raise the struggle from
> a religious basis to a class basis and we want to develop a mass protest
> movement against the housing conditions, gerrymandering and unemploy-
> ment here. Religious divisions are a hangover from the past. ("Housing
> Protest in Derry Street," *Belfast Telegraph,* June 22, 1968)

By forging working-class unity, it was believed that the civil rights move-ment would reduce the significance of sectarianism.

Members of the New Left student group, the People's Democracy (PD), labeled the proponents of the ethnic equality perspective as "Green Tories" (*New Left Review* 1969, 15–16; McCluskey 1989, 86). At a rally in Strabane in July 1969, for instance, Bernadette Devlin chastised Irish Nationalist Party member of parliament (MP) Austin Currie and other speakers for not addressing unemployment in both communities. The attacks were strongly rebuked by John Hume among others (Arthur 1974).

Some activists even rejected the existence of ethnic inequalities in Northern Ireland. In a September 10, 1968, editorial in the *Derry Journal* arguing for the elimination of the Irish Nationalist Party, a member of the Derry Labour Party, Eamonn McCann, stated, "Since it represents an acceptance of the present sectarian divide in our society it can never strip away the layers of political camouflage and reveal the basic truth that our problems are those of class, not creed, and that the Protestant working class is, to put it bluntly, being conned into believing that it is, in any meaningful sense, a privileged section of society."

Differences in social ontological assumptions also existed among participants motivated by the same desire to end partition. Those assuming that ethnic equality had to precede working-class unity also frequently assumed that reforming the state was the key to a united Ireland. The head of the Connolly Association, Desmond Greaves, had a major influence on several people who become leading figures in the civil rights movement. According to Coughlan, Greaves

> advocated the imposition of a legislative straitjacket by the Westminster Parliament on the subordinate Stormont assembly that would at once outlaw discriminatory practices—so guaranteeing civil rights and freedoms for the Northern nationalist population—while at the same time permitting, and preferably encouraging, the devolved administration in the North to develop closer relations with the South. He saw such a constitutional initiative as the best way of enabling nationalists to take advantage of the divisions with unionism, encouraging an alliance in a reformed Stormont between nationalists and liberal unionists, isolating the unionist right and opening up a way in time to peaceful reunification with Dublin. (1991, 10)

Greaves had strong ties with members of the Communist Party in Northern Ireland. In 1962, the Communist Party in Northern Ireland issued *Ireland's Path to Socialism*. The pamphlet emphasized the democratization of Northern Ireland's political institutions as a prerequisite to achieving a united, socialist Ireland. The party played a key role in facilitating the emergence of the Northern Ireland Civil Rights Association (NICRA). In response to a suggestion by Greaves, in May 1965, party member Betty Sinclair organized a conference on civil liberties in Belfast (Coughlan 1991). Representatives from the Campaign for Social Justice, Sinn Féin, and the Northern Ireland Labour

Party attended (NICRA 1978). A series of these meetings eventually led to NICRA's formation.

Like the Communist Party in Northern Ireland, the Republican leadership during the mid-1960s also assumed that reforming Stormont was key to a united Ireland (Sinn Féin 1966; White 2006). Other Republicans involved in the movement, however, rejected the assumption that the Unionist-controlled state could be reformed. As a result, they envisioned a quite different sequence of events:

> The contrary attitude . . . was increasingly one which held that the six-county state could not be democratised, that by its very nature it was irreformable and that the major effect of civil rights struggle would be to show clearly the contradictions within the state, the colonial nature of its very existence and the clear responsibility which the British government has for the situation there. (Sinn Féin Education Department n.d., 2)

This attitude was shared by members of the New Left. A leading member of the PD, Michael Farrell (1976, 253), stated, "The PD, was firmly, if instinctively, convinced that the Unionist Party, being based on sectarianism and Protestant supremacy, could never dismantle the Orange State." It was expected that the inability of the state to reform itself when confronted would create the best conditions for fundamental social change. In an article entitled "People's Democracy: A Discussion on Strategy," a journalist from the *New Left Review* posed the following question: "Your central demands appear at first sight to be reformist—one man, one job and one family, one house. Why have you focused on these specific issues?" (*New Left Review* 1969, 4). Eamonn McCann responded thusly:

> Because the transformation of Irish society necessary to implement these reforms is a revolution. We are definitely in a pre-revolutionary situation in the north. The Unionist Party must give something to the pope-heads of Derry to get them off the streets, but if they give them anything the Unionist party will break up. So by supporting these demands in a militant manner, we are supporting class demands and we are striking hard against the ruling political party.

Disagreements over whether the Northern Ireland state could be reformed often stemmed from different assumptions regarding the sequencing of events in revolutions. For movement participants active in the Communist Party and the presplit Republican leadership, a successful revolution required the formation of a cross-class alliance with progressive members of the bourgeoisie (Feeney 1974). By facilitating alliances with moderate, middle-class

Unionist politicians, reforming Stormont would set the stage for a socialist revolution. The issue highlighted a deep ideological divide between the old left and the New Left. Through their journal, the *Northern Star,* the PD frequently attacked the two-stage theory of revolution. PD member Eamon O'Kane (1971) argued that the main thing preventing a direct transition from feudalism and imperial domination to socialism is the Communist Party and its strategy based on the two-stage theory: "In other words, the proletariat in alliance with the poor peasants could have carried through the tasks of the democratic revolution and the anti-imperialist fight under the leadership of the Communist Party if they had not been forced to commit suicide because of the doctrined stupidity of Comintern." The oppressed classes could successfully transform society from below on their own.

Findings: Contextual Sources of Strategic Multiplicity

The civil rights movement in Northern Ireland provides an example of how the three contextual factors discussed above contribute to strategic multiplicity within a movement. From an early stage, prominent organizational members of the two main coalitions—the Derry Citizens' Action Committee (DCAC) and NICRA—differed in terms of their social locations and their collective identities. Conflicts over strategy often fell along class and generational lines (see Maney 2000 for a detailed discussion). In particular, students and youth, particularly those from working-class backgrounds, tended to support strategies associated with international New Left student movements (Arthur 1974). In contrast, older middle-class members tended to support strategies associated with the civil rights movement in the United States (Dooley 1998). The open, inclusive, and democratic structures of both coalitions combined with a relative balance of power between disparate ideological elements increased rather than diminished fears of takeover by those with differing strategies.

Strategic Multiplicity and Coalition Dynamics

Ideological differences existed among prominent activists and organizations from the inception of both coalitions. Yet all of those discussed above participated in mass civil rights marches during the early stages of contention. They embraced the tactic for very different reasons.

Early Stages of Contention

In January 1968, British MP Paul Rose told Irish Nationalist Party MP Austin Currie during a meeting in the House of Commons, "no British government—including this Labour government—will intervene to remedy injustice in Northern Ireland unless you people there force it to do so" (Currie 1998, 16). Later that month, Currie predicted that "politics will move in a more militant direction" if reforms in Northern Ireland were not forthcoming ("Action Sought on 'Sealed Lips' Policy towards Ulster Affairs," *Belfast Telegraph*, January 29, 1968). In June, Currie joined the Brantry Republican Club in conducting a sit-in in public housing to protest discriminatory housing allocation in Caledon by the Unionist-dominated Dungannon Council (NICRA 1978).

Although it garnered extensive local publicity, the sit-in did not capture wider media attention. Viewing such attention as critical to securing British government intervention on behalf of Catholic civil rights, Currie advocated mass marches: "A prime objective of the proposed civil rights marches was to publicise internationally injustices to Northern Ireland and to force the British government to intervene to redress them" (1998, 16).

While the Campaign for Social Justice had previously focused on letter writing and lobbying, Currie's emphasis on the publicity potential of the marches fit well with their long-standing strategy. In "Northern Ireland: What the Papers Have to Say," the Campaign for Social Justice states,

> We feel that if our cause is to succeed, and it must succeed, we must draw the attention of all men of goodwill to the existing state of affairs in Northern Ireland. We trust you will bring our indignation to the notice of the British and Northern Ireland Governments and public opinion in the hope that the force of your opinion may change the current state of affairs. (2)

Accordingly, on July 27, 1968, during a meeting of the Northern Ireland Civil Rights Association in Maghera, along with Campaign for Social Justice member and councilor Michael McLoughlin, Austin Currie proposed a civil rights march from Coalisland to Dungannon.

Currie's help in organizing the Caledon sit-in earned him support among members of the DHAC. On August 16, 1968, DHAC invited Currie to attend a protest over the shortage of public housing. Unlike Currie, who emphasized civil rights for Catholics, leaders of DHAC stressed the need to build more housing for all working families. The *Derry Journal* quoted Eamonn Melaugh as stating, "If houses were not built, violence in Derry was not only a possibility but 'an inevitability'" ("Violence Inevitable if Houses Are Not Built," August 20, 1968). Committed to building a mass movement among the poor of all religions, DHAC readily supported Currie's call for what they termed "a human rights march" from Coalisland to Dungannon ("Housing Action Committee Supports Currie March," *Derry Journal*, August 16, 1968). Reflecting his broad-based commitment to socialist ideals, Melaugh had founded the Derry Unemployed Action Committee. Receiving NICRA's support for its slogan of "One Man—One Job," the action committee readily endorsed the march as an opportunity to spread its message.

Although those discussed so far saw civil rights marches as advancing their various strategies, others saw the marches as threats to theirs. Members of the Communist Party feared that the passions aroused by attacks by the police force, the Royal Ulster Constabulary, and Loyalist attacks on peaceful demonstrations would ignite minority rebellion and fall into the hands of Unionists eager to play the Orange card. Reflecting the party's plan to bring about an alliance with liberal Unionists, Betty Sinclair sought to ensure that marches were nonviolent and law-abiding. During the Coalisland to Dungannon march, Sinclair addressed crowd through a loudspeaker. According to the *Irish News* ("Batons Used on Marchers in Dungannon," August 26, 1968), she appealed for the crowd to comply with a ban on marching into the center of Dungannon:

> The object of the parade was to hold a peaceful meeting in Dungannon, and the whole purpose of the night's event was to demonstrate for Civil Rights, for jobs, and for houses, but the Government had decided if they marched into Market Square, they would bring the might of the law down on them. We are asking you to listen to the speakers, and what we have done today will go down in history, and in this way we will be more effective in showing to the world that we are a peaceful people, asking for our civil rights in an orderly manner.

Sinclair was not alone in this regard. According to the *Belfast Telegraph* ("Dungannon March 'Just the Beginning,'" August 26, 1968), "Speakers and stewards made repeated appeals for the marchers to control themselves. . . . Another speaker, who forgot to give his name, said: 'Cracked skulls will serve nobody's purpose.'"

Whereas Sinclair sought to steer the event clear of conflict with authorities, New Left activists participated precisely for this reason. Ideologically based tensions were palpably manifest as the former sought to minimize disruption while the latter tried to maximize it. According to the account of a police officer at the event, Sinclair was "loudly 'booed' by some of the marchers. I heard cries of 'Czechoslovakia,' 'Russia,' 'Jackboot' and one youth shouted 'Are you on the Pill?' At times her voice was drowned by the crowd and numerous scuffles took place round the platform" (PRONI 1968a). Those believing that change required disruption challenged the rerouting of the parade. A number of youth involved in the march surged toward the police cordon, but many were forced back by marshals. Those who did manage to reach the cordon were beaten back by the police, resulting in some throwing of stones, broken placards, and poles at the police. On the clash with police, Sinclair "intervened in an attempt to prevent any violence, called an end to the protest and suggested that before they disperse, those in the crowd should sing the civil rights anthem" (Dooley 1998, 51).

After the march, the Young Socialists issued a press release stating that it condemned "all those who spoke at the meeting. . . . Had they not sold their principles and instead continued leading the parade into the centre of Dungannon, then, perhaps, something could have been achieved in the name of civil rights" ("Batons Used on Marchers in Dungannon," *Irish News,* August 26, 1968). Reflecting the assumption that progress comes through conflict and destabilization, different organizers of the next civil rights march in Derry/Londonderry deliberately selected a route that they knew Unionists would not accept. The proposed march route went through the Diamond, a location at the center of the city holding particular symbolic significance to Unionists. In a society whose territorial status was hotly contested, the lead organizers recognized that the Unionists would never accede to the Nationalists' "occupying" the Diamond (interview with ÓDochartaigh). As expected, the minister of home affairs banned the proposed route. One of the main organizers of the march, Eamonn McCann (1993, 92), hoped that sight of the blood of those peacefully protesting social injustices would "tear the apathy out of the people of Derry."

Consistent with their strategy, Communist Party members on the executive board of NICRA opposed the route of the Derry march on the grounds that it would lead to violence and heighten sectarian divisions. Members of the New Left Derry Labour Party—backed by the Derry City Republican Club—vowed to hold the march with or without NICRA's endorsement. NICRA did endorse the march, due in part to support from those wanting to increase pressure on the British government to intervene.

As with the march in August, members of the Communist Party involved themselves in the march to prevent polarization. After reading out the order banning the proposed parade route, the Royal Ulster Constabulary county inspector warned about the peril to the safety of women and children. Police then cordoned off demonstrators from behind. During her speech, Sinclair again told marchers to go home. And as previously, Young Socialists in attendance pursued their confrontation-oriented strategy. After booing Sinclair, some threw placards, poles, and stones at the police. Whether they did so in response to police provocation is still a matter of dispute (Hansard 1968, 1017; Farrell 1976). What is not disputed is that the police moved in on demonstrators who were conducting a sit-in, clubbing them and hosing them with water cannons. Anticipating this response, McCann actually encouraged MPs to stand at the front of the march so that he could escape the brunt of the police attacks. Accordingly, the frontline MPs made credible, influential eye-witnesses for journalists. John Ryan, MP for Uxbridge, reported seeing "a woman, aged over sixty, having her spectacles removed by a policeman before being hit on the head by a baton. She was not one of the demonstrators. He saw children, covered with blood, being carried into a cafe" ("'I felt proud' Says Mr. Fitt," *Irish Press,* October 7, 1968). Film footage taken by an RTE television crew was broadcasted throughout the world. Soon thereafter, the British prime minister, Harold Wilson, requested a meeting with the Northern Ireland prime minister, Terence O'Neill, to discuss what had transpired.

Although some saw it before, certainly after October 5, most involved recognized that civil rights marches would yield sympathetic coverage and mass support for the movement. Even here, such effects were deemed advantageous for different reasons. John Hume (1998, 4) emphasized the reforms that resulted from the marches:

> The positive effect of October 5 was very strong. It had a worldwide impact through television. It led to the establishment of the Derry Citizens' Action Committee of which I was proud to be a member. Harnessing the maximum strength of the city against injustice, the DCAC achieved more change than had been achieved in the 50 years previous in 48 days in response to the massive national and international pressure created by the consequences of October 5.

Reticent before the march, most members of the Communist Party came to view the tactic as the way to build a mass movement to begin reforming Stormont. Rather than criticizing protesters for defying the law, as it had done in August, the party instead criticized police for enforcing the law. The day after the march, the party's executive committee issued a press release stating, "We declare our revulsion at the unprovoked police brutality, which was inflicted on members of a peaceful demonstration, and also on innocent bystanders" (PRONI 1968b). The statement went on to call for general involvement in the civil rights movement and demanded a public inquiry into police action and the sacking of the minister of home affairs.

In contrast, the events of October 5 reinforced the assumption among some participants that the negative publicity would help to smash Stormont rather than reform it:

> The civil rights cause that afternoon attracted the missing ingredient that was to turn our agitation into a mass movement literally overnight. This ingredient was the power of modern modes of communication, which brought

down the thud of the batons, the force of the water-canon, the cries of the people, and the blood on the tarmac into the living rooms of millions. The predictions of the few had become reality for the many, as the mask of a one-party police state slipped one afternoon to reveal its true undemocratic and ugly sectarian face. (ÓDochartaigh 1994, 26–27)

With marching being perceived as consistent with multiple, opposing strategies, leading members of the movement threw all of their weight into organizing the next march in Derry on November 16, 1968. Whereas the first two marches involved several hundred participants each, this march involved at least 15,000 people. The dynamics among participants of different ideological persuasions were nonetheless the same. Two leaders of the Derry Citizens Action Committee, Ivan Cooper and John Hume, negotiated with the police who had blocked off the planned march to the Diamond. Four marchers were allowed to climb over the barricade. Many in the crowd, including members of the PD, however, were not satisfied with this symbolic triumph and forcibly breached the barricades. A clash with police and Loyalist counterdemonstrators ensued for half an hour before the demonstrators occupied the Diamond. By producing political changes, media coverage of repression of civil rights marches was viewed as a promising development by those pursuing very different strategies. Nonetheless, these same changes soon led to splits over whether to continue the tactic.

The Unfolding of Strategic Differences

On November 22, 1968, at the urging of the British prime minister, the Northern Ireland prime minister, Terence O'Neill, announced a series of reforms that addressed some civil rights demands. The official statement by Stormont made it clear that the government hoped its concessions would lead to the end of mass marching (PRONI 1968c). Both DCAC and NICRA's executive boards welcomed the statement. While demanding further reforms, they nonetheless declared a moratorium on civil rights marches. From December 9, 1968, through most of March 1969, both coalitions abided by the moratorium. These decisions were supported primarily by those assuming that ethnic inequality was the fundamental social dividing line and that reforming Stormont was the key to achieving their objectives. Consistent with their goal of normalizing Northern Ireland politics, two elected DCAC leaders—Ivan Cooper (chair) and John Hume (vice chair)—argued strongly in favor of the moratorium. With increasing violence during and after marches and their success in prodding concessions from Stormont, both believed that the electoral arena provided the best forum for consolidating reforms and advancing the civil rights agenda.

For others supporting a moratorium on marching, the government's reforms opened the door to anticipated political alliances. Further marches were therefore not only unnecessary, but also threatened to undermine the position of liberal Unionists by raising fears that the Nationalist minority had more in mind than just civil rights. The decision to stop marching was justified on two bases: first, "the promised reforms must be given a chance to work, both for their own sake and for the credibility of the whole principle of civil rights demands," and second, "the chances of sectarian violence were growing by the day and anything which might diffuse the situation would be welcome" (NICRA 1978, 15). Betty Sinclair stated, "All we needed was time . . . a lull in which to see if Captain O'Neill is going to carry out the reforms he had promised" (Arthur 1974, 61).

For those prioritizing the immediate advancement of socialism, however, the moratorium was unacceptable. Members of the New Left belonging to DHAC, the Derry Labour Party, and PD vowed to continue marching. For Fionnbarra ÓDochartaigh (1994, 85–86), the reforms did not begin to address the needs of the poor: "The better-off Catholic middle class did not share the same sense of urgency, simply because they had a roof over their head that they could call their own, a car and annual holiday, etc. These economic disparities created a real gulf in terms of respective aspirations and tactics."

Most of these activists also believed that Stormont could not be reformed and that political destabilization held the key to achieving their objectives. Accordingly, they supported the continuance of marching. On December 9, 1968, a large PD meeting decided to call off a planned march to the Belfast city hall scheduled for December 11, 1968. In a subsequent, smaller meeting, held when most students were on winter break, PD members also affiliated with the Young Socialists pushed through motion to hold a march from Belfast to Derry in early January. Eoin Sweeney explained the rationale for the motion:

> All were going for at least one common reason: a reaction against the evasive platitudes with which O'Neill and his men tried to pass the can for his own misdeeds. . . . In marching we felt that we were pushing a structure (that contained the seeds of great violence among other things) towards a point where its internal proceedings would cause a snapping and a breaking to begin. (Arthur 1974, 40–41)

The cabal within the PD highlights strategic differences present not only within coalitions, but also individual organizations. The same tactic that initially brought those with different strategies together to march on October 5 in Derry/Londonderry now, at a later stage of contention, produced major conflicts. Along with the majority on the NICRA executive board, DCAC leaders Cooper and Hume opposed the Long March, fearing the violence that did in fact take place (Akenson 1973). The Communist and Republican leaderships of the time viewed the event thusly:

> As an exercise in marching it was either foolhardy or brave, but as part of an attempt to put political pressure on a Government to grant basic democratic reforms it succeeded only in raising the political temperature. The end result of the marching was a heightening of sectarian feelings. . . . The PD march helped to drive the Protestant working class into the arms of [Loyalists] Paisley and Bunting. (NICRA 1978, 17)

For the PD, however, "the march to Derry exposed to the world the old realities . . . concealed behind the 'new face' of unionism" (LHLPC 1969).

The split over whether to continue marching contributed to departures from the movement. In March 1969, four members of NICRA's executive board resigned in protest of the PD's growing influence and the decision to hold marches protesting the Public Order (Amendment) Act. In the words of Campaign for Social Justice cofounder Patricia McCluskey, the PD "were using us, we felt, as a facade, as a cover, and I felt things were getting out of hand" (Dooley 1998, 60).

Ideologically based differences in strategy resulted in irreconcilable differences over tactics at a later stage of contention. The Derry Citizens Action Committee disbanded after widespread and severe rioting throughout Northern Ireland in August 1969. By early 1970, the PD had opted out of NICRA. The group decided not to run candidates for the executive committee "because we felt that the vital work of broadening the struggle against the Unionists onto the economic front could best be done outside the CRA" (People's Democracy ca. 1970). Republicans in the movement who came to reject their leadership's recognition of Stormont and acceptance of constitutional politics formed Provisional Sinn Féin (White 2006). In the process, Communist Party and Official Sinn Féin candidates gained, by default, control of NICRA's executive board. Although greater strategic proximity produced a renewed tactical convergence, NICRA lost the central political significance that it was once accorded.

Conclusions

An analysis of the civil rights movement in Northern Ireland supports the assertion that a single tactic can be a multipurpose product of different strategies by organizers. Repeated tactics by two coalitions reflected short-term intersections of multiple strategies rather than the emergence of a single strategy. The same tactic was seen by different actors as giving rise to different sequences of events that would accomplish different objectives. Ironically, changes in the political context resulting from shared tactics contributed to subsequent disputes, as actors sought to respond to these changes in ways that assisted them in realizing their contrasting visions.

The findings make several contributions to our understanding of social movement strategy. First, they illustrate how differing goals and contrasting social ontological assumptions lead to incompatible strategies. Ideology filters the meanings of any given collective action, whether by movement actors, authorities, or opponents. Although scholars have increasingly recognized how political opportunities and threats are socially constructed, the basis of these constructions has not been theorized. The case examined here suggests that the meanings of events depend on the ideologies of those interpreting them. Once civil rights marches produced both concessions from the State and increasingly violent countermobilization, the tactic became viewed as a threat to the strategies of some while it continued to be viewed as an opportunity to advance the strategies of others.

Similarly, how activists responded to strategic dilemmas (Jasper 2004) depended on their ideologies. Those who thought Stormont could and should be reformed chose the "nice" strategy of declaring moratoria on mass civil rights marches. On the other hand, those who thought the opposite chose the "naughty" strategy and continued marching. Further research on the ideologies of activists should prove helpful in explaining responses to strategic dilemmas.

Second, although not as parsimonious as rational choice assumptions, specifying ideological bases of strategies has other advantages. The approach captures a deeper agency borne of passionate, principled convictions coupled with often sophisticated social analysis. In highlighting the carefully considered and complex envisioning that shapes decisions regarding collective action, such a specification pays greater respect to activists' creative and imaginative intellectual work than the cold, mechanical image of rational maximizers making decisions on the basis of perfect information about changes in their environment. Strategy is important to activists precisely because they work in circumstances that do not conform to the assumptions of rational choice theory. Rather than being constantly driven by material self-interest, activists must decide which goals they value most. Instead of knowing the costs and benefits of different actions, activists must try to anticipate what consequences their actions will bring.

Third, the chapter specifies and illustrates contextual factors encouraging strategic multiplicity within a movement. A movement composed of those occupying different social locations and possessing relatively equal levels of power are likely to experience strategic multiplicity. This is particularly the case when participants have contrasting strategic models with demonstrated effects at their disposal. Although the literature has presented horizontal, non-hierarchical connective structures as factors that help to sustain movements by facilitating cooperation, the findings suggest that these structures are likely to have the opposite effect on movements bringing together a wide array of actors. For ideologically diverse movements, capacities to implement effective strategies are diminished rather than enhanced by the formation of broad-based coalitions.

Fourth, past studies of intramovement dynamics have viewed strategic divides as insurmountable obstacles. The findings I present here suggest that coalitions can form and develop shared tactics even when prominent organizers advocate opposing strategies. Despite strong, opposing ideologies, leading members of the civil rights movement in Northern Ireland participated in civil rights marches over a four-month period. They did so because they believed that the marches could advance their strategies, even though these strategies differed markedly. Uncertainty regarding how authorities would respond ultimately helped to sustain the plausibility of different visions of sequences of events arising from the marches. The quasi-institutionalized character of mass marches in Northern Ireland also encouraged participation among activists seeking alternatively to minimize and maximize their potential for disruption and violence.

Rather than a shared sense of threat or opportunity serving as a source of unity, conditions of political uncertainty encouraged cooperation by allowing very different interpretations of the political environment to coexist. It was only when authorities issued concessions and opponents became increasingly violent that the differences in interpretation came into focus. This finding goes against conventional wisdom regarding intramovement dynamics. It suggests that coalitions characterized by strong ideologies and strategic multiplicity differ from other coalitions in that clear-cut responses from authorities and opponents contribute to negative rather than to positive intramovement dynamics.

Fifth, the study clarifies the character of the interplay between strategy and social context. Specifically, changes in the social context that arise in the course of contention are more likely to change tactics than strategies. As actors put strategies into practice, they assess the implications of tactics for their strategies. Tactics perceived to take advantage of opportunities to advance anticipated sequences of events and social outcomes are embraced. Tactics perceived to threaten the advancement of anticipated sequences of events and social outcomes are resisted or participated in so as to minimize their damage. Although actors can alter their strategies in response to changing conditions and lessons learned from contention (e.g., King and Cornwall 2005; McCammon et al. 2008), the case examined here suggests that strong ideologies can result in organizers persisting in trying to bring about envisioned sequences of events and outcomes. Although their visions may reduce them to irrelevance in the short term, their survival in the doldrums (Rupp and Taylor 1987) could provide the strategic foundations for those participating in subsequent waves of contention.

In addition to its contributions to scholarship, the study has particular relevance to activists. On the upside, it suggests that participating in coalitions with those with strong and even opposing ideologies can be constructive, particularly during the early stages of an issue campaign when the responses of authorities and opponents are uncertain. Cooperation is most likely when the coalition develops tactics that are seen as advancing multiple strategies.

On the downside, the findings suggest that after authorities and opponents establish their responses, continued participation in such coalitions is likely to be unproductive. Positive relations between organizations with different strategies may be better accomplished during such moments through informal, implicit agreements to establish separate niches (Downey and Rohlinger 2008). Nonetheless, ideologies and strategies are not immutable. Activists can focus on persuading others to rethink certain goals and ontological assumptions that get in the way of strategic consensus or, at least, coexistence. Although at times tedious and conducive to conflict, these discussions hold the long-term promise of transforming intramovement disputes into greater strategic capacity. Forums that facilitate dialogue promote not only recognition and tolerance of strategic multiplicity, but also the possibility of strategic convergence.

Appendix. Glossary of Case-Specific Terminology

Loyalists—Militant Unionists willing to use force if necessary to prevent reunification.

Nationalists—Mostly Catholic; favor the reunification of Ireland.

Northern Ireland—Six of the thirty-two counties of Ireland that are constitutionally linked with Great Britain as part of the United Kingdom since the early 1920s. The other twenty-six counties of Ireland are known as the Republic of Ireland, which was declared a sovereign, independent republic in the constitution of 1937 and reaffirmed by an act of parliament in 1949.

Partition—The political separation of Northern Ireland from the rest of Ireland; established under the Government of Ireland Act of 1920 and the Anglo-Irish (Irish Free State) Treaty of 1921.

Republicans—Militant nationalists historically more willing to use force if necessary to bring about the end of partition.

Reunification—Ending the partition of Ireland and returning to the rule of Ireland as one political unit as had been the case before the early 1920s.

Stormont—The parliament and/or cabinet of the Northern Ireland state.

Unionists—Mostly Protestant; favor retaining the existing status of Northern Ireland as part of the United Kingdom.

Notes

I thank Lorenzo Bosi and my coeditors for their helpful comments. Research was made possible through grants from the Irish American Cultural Institute, the University of Wisconsin, Madison, and the United States Institute of Peace. The views expressed here are solely my own and do not necessarily reflect those of the granting agencies.

1. Repertoires of action are only likely to solidify when the strategies, tactics, and organizational forms are consistent with prevailing ideologies. The literature has largely overlooked this relationship, attributing the formation of repertoires instead to either their fit with a regime type (existing or emerging), new technologies, emerging institutional needs, or cultural traditions (see chapter 3). These explanations are incomplete in that they neglect the importance of activists' assigning meanings to these circumstances in relationship to their goals and through the prism of their assumptions regarding how social change is best accomplished (for similar arguments, see chapters 10 and 12).

2. Quotations from informants provided in text are from responses to the interviews. For a listing of archives, secondary sources, and persons interviewed, see Maney (2000).

References

Akenson, Donald H. 1973. *The United States and Ireland.* Cambridge, Mass.: Harvard University Press.

Amenta, Edwin, Drew Halfmann, and Michael P. Young. 1999. "The Strategies and Contexts of Social Protest: Political Mediation and the Impact of the Townsend Movement in California." *Mobilization* 4:1–23.

Andrews, Kenneth T. 2004. *Freedom Is a Constant Struggle: The Mississippi Civil Rights Movement and Its Legacy.* Chicago: University of Chicago Press.

Arthur, Paul. 1974. *The People's Democracy, 1968–1973.* Belfast: Blackstaff Press.

Balser, Deborah B. 1997. "The Impact of Environmental Factors on Factionalism and Schism in Social Movement Organizations." *Social Forces* 76:199–228.

Benford, Robert D. 1993. "Frame Disputes within the Nuclear Disarmament Movement." *Social Forces* 71:677–701.

Bernstein, Mary. 2003. "Nothing Ventured, Nothing Gained? Conceptualizing Social

Movement 'Success' in the Lesbian and Gay Movement." *Sociological Perspectives* 46:353–79.

Coughlan, Anthony. 1991. "C. Desmond Greaves, 1913–1988: An Obituary Essay." In *Studies in Irish Labour History 1*, 1–24. Dublin: Irish Labour History Society.

Currie, Austin. 1998. "Breaching the Walls of Injustice." *Irish News* Souvenir Supplement, October 5, 16.

Dalton, Russell J. 1994. *The Green Rainbow: Environmental Groups in Western Europe.* New Haven, Conn.: Yale University Press.

Dooley, Brian. 1998. *Black and Green: Civil Rights Struggles in Northern Ireland and Black America.* London: Pluto.

Downey, Dennis J., and Deana A. Rohlinger. 2008. "Linking Strategic Choice with Macro-Organizational Dynamics: Strategy and Social Movement Articulation." *Research in Social Movements, Conflicts and Change* 28:3–38.

Edwards, Bob, and John D. McCarthy. 2004. "Strategy Matters: The Contingent Value of Social Capital in the Survival of Local Social Movement Organizations." *Social Forces* 83:621–51.

Fantasia, Rick. 1989. *Cultures of Solidarity: Consciousness, Action, and Contemporary American Workers.* Berkeley: University of California Press.

Farrell, Michael. 1976. *Northern Ireland: The Orange State.* London: Pluto.

Feeney, Vincent E. 1974. "The Civil Rights Movement in Northern Ireland." *Eire* 9:30–40.

Friedman, Debra, and Doug McAdam. 1992. "Collective Identity and Activism: Networks, Choices, and the Life of a Social Movement." In *Frontiers of Social Movement Theory*, edited by Aldon D. Morris and Carol McClurg Mueller, 134–73. New Haven, Conn.: Yale University Press.

Gamson, William A. 1975. *The Strategy of Social Protest.* Homewood, Ill.: Dorsey Press.

Ganz, Marshall. 2000. "Resources and Resourcefulness: Strategic Capacity in the Unionization of California Agriculture, 1959–1966." *American Journal of Sociology* 105:1003–62.

Hansard. 1968. Parliamentary Debates, House of Commons (Stormont). Vol. 70, no.17, columns 1015–17. October 16.

Hume, John. 1998. "It Was the Worst 'Example of Injustice' in That State." *Irish News* Souvenir Supplement, October 5, 4.

Jasper, James. 2004. "A Strategic Approach to Collective Action: Looking for Agency in Social Movement Choices." *Mobilization* 9:1–16.

King, Brayden, and Marie Cornwall. 2005. "Specialists and Generalists: Learning Strategies in the Woman Suffrage Movement, 1866–1918." *Research in Social Movements, Conflicts, and Change* 26:3–34.

Koopmans, Ruud. 1993. "The Dynamics of Protest Waves: West Germany, 1965 to 1989." *American Sociological Review* 58:637–58.

Linen Hall Library Political Collection (LHLPC). 1969. Civil Rights Organisations Box 1. Pamphlet entitled "Why PD?"

Maney, Gregory M. 2000. "Transnational Mobilization and Civil Rights in Northern Ireland." *Social Problems* 47:153–79.

Marx, Karl, and Frederich Engels. (1848) 1998. *The Communist Manifesto.* London: Verso.

McAdam, Doug, and Dieter Rucht. 1993. "The Cross-National Diffusion of Movement Ideas." *Annals of the American Academy of Political and Social Science* 528:56–74.

McCammon, Holly J., Soma Chaudhuri, Lyndi Hewitt, Courtney Sanders Muse, Harmony D. Newman, Carrie Lee Smith, and Teresa M. Terrell. 2008. "Becoming Full Citizens: The U.S. Women's Jury Rights Campaigns, the Pace of Reform, and Strategic Adaptation." *American Journal of Sociology* 113:1104–47.

McCann, Eamonn. 1993. *War and an Irish Town.* 2nd ed. Boulder, Colo.: Pluto Press.

McCluskey, Conn. 1989. *Up Off Their Knees: A Commentary on the Civil Rights Movement in Northern Ireland.* Galway: Conn McCluskey and Associates.

Meyer, Megan. 2004. "Organizational Identity, Political Contexts, and SMO Action: Explaining the Tactical Choices Made by Peace Organizations in Israel, Northern Ireland, and South Africa." *Social Movement Studies* 3:167–97.

Nepstad, Sharon Erickson. 2004. "Disciples and Dissenters: Tactical Choice and Consequences." *Research in Social Movements, Conflicts and Change* 25:139–59.

New Left Review. 1969. "People's Democracy: A Discussion on Strategy." *New Left Review* 55:3–19.

Northern Ireland Civil Rights Association (NICRA). 1978. *"We Shall Overcome": The History of the Struggle for Civil Rights in Northern Ireland, 1968–1978.* Belfast: NICRA.

ÓDochartaigh, Fionnbarra. 1994. *Ulster's White Negroes: From Civil Rights to Insurrection.* San Francisco, Calif.: AK Press.

O'Kane, Eamon. 1971. "The ICO and the 2 Stages Theory." *Northern Star,* no. 3 (February–March).

Oliver, Pamela E., and Hank Johnston. 2000. "What a Good Idea! Ideologies and Frames in Social Movement Research." *Mobilization* 5:37–54.

People's Democracy. 1970. Untitled article. *Northern Star.* 1:4.

Piven, Frances Fox, and Richard Cloward. 1977. *Poor People's Movements.* New York: Pantheon Books.

Polletta, Francesca. 1995. "Strategy and Ideology in 1960s Black Protest." Paper presented at the annual meeting of the American Sociological Association, Washington, D.C., August 19–23.

———. 2002. *Freedom Is an Endless Meeting: Democracy in America Social Movements.* Chicago: University of Chicago Press.

Public Records Office, Northern Ireland (PRONI). 1968a. CAB/9B/205c/7. Letter from RUC District Inspector George Ivan Sterritt to Inspector General dated August 28.

———. 1968b. CAB/9B/205/7. "Statement of Executive Committee of the Communist Party, (N. Ireland) on October 5th Civil Rights March—Derry City."

———. 1968c. CAB/9B/303/1. Untitled document stamped "Secret," dated November 22.

Purdie, Bob. 1988. "Was the Civil Rights Movement a Republican/Communist Conspiracy?" *Irish Political Studies* 3:33–41.

Robnett, Belinda. 2004. "Emotional Resonance, Social Location, and Strategic Framing." *Sociological Focus* 37:195–212.

Rupp, Leila J., and Verta Taylor. 1987. *Survival in the Doldrums: The American Women's Rights Movement, 1945 to the 1960s.* New York: Oxford University Press.

Sinn Féin. 1966. "Forward from 1966—Presidential Address of Tomas MacGiolla to the 61st Annual Ardfheis of Sinn Féin." November 27, Dublin.

Sinn Féin Education Department. n.d. *The Split.* Republican Lecture Series 1. Belfast: Sinn Féin.

Staggenborg, Suzanne. 1986. "Coalition Work in the Pro-choice Movement: Organizational and Environmental Opportunities and Obstacles." *Social Problems* 33:374–90.

Tarrow, Sidney. 1998. *Power in Movement: Social Movements, Collective Action and Politics.* 2nd ed. New York: Cambridge University Press.

Taylor, Verta, and Nancy Whittier. 1992. "Collective Identity in Social Movement Communities: Lesbian Feminist Mobilization" In *Frontiers of Social Movement Theory,* edited by Aldon D. Morris and Carol McClurg Mueller, 104–30. New Haven, Conn.: Yale University Press.

White, Robert W. 2006. *Ruairí Ó Brádaigh: The Life and Politics of an Irish Revolutionary.* Bloomington: University of Indiana Press.

9

Marketing for Justice: Corporate Social Movement Organizations

Belinda Robnett and Jessica Ayo Alabi

Corporate social movement organizations, an emergent form of social movement organization, differs from both professional and entrepreneurial movement organizations (McCarthy and Zald 1977; Staggenborg 1988) in that it is led by both a professional and an entrepreneur leader and it is not dependent on foundation support because philanthropy is a core organizational component. The coexistence of these two forms of leadership shapes the organizational structure and facilitates outreach strategies that include those associated with both entrepreneurial and professional social movement organizations (SMOs); it also blends a general membership approach and a cadre approach (Cloward and Piven 1984). Although the strategies of dissemination are largely controlled by the entrepreneur leader, much of the movement's message is controlled by the professional leader. The finance strategy of a corporate social movement is also distinct because it does not depend on outside benefactors or inside donors, but on inside philanthropist entrepreneur leaders who personally and through financial associations bankroll the movement (Ostrander 2005). Although the movement is subject to compromise because of the entrepreneur's financial interests, it is less subject to outside co-optation. Consequently, the movement organization can focus more on its strategy to market the movement than on its strategy of organizational maintenance.

Among academics and progressive activists, corporate entities are often viewed as almost antithetical to the attainment of social justice. Although an analysis of one organization may not constitute a trend in the formation of contemporary SMOs, it nevertheless provides an exception to our preconceived notions of who can generate a social movement and how political and social interests can be spearheaded by a corporate enterprise. Through an analysis of Hip-Hop Movement Connections (HHMC),[1] an SMO formed by a hip-hop mogul, Daniel Williams, we demonstrate the ways in which corporations can organize, market, and partner with professional and community organizations and leaders to build a national level social movement. We invoke the term *corporate* not because the explicit goal of the corporate entrepreneur who initiated the SMO was to seek a financial profit, but because the organization was founded by a corporate mogul and largely funded by his corporation and his business contacts.

It is not a stretch to assert that most social movements are initiated by entrepreneur leaders who are passionate about a cause and later seek outside foundation and perhaps corporate funding to support the mission. Although corporations sometimes sponsor social change campaigns, such as Dove's emphasis on "real women's bodies," these efforts are accompanied by explicit profit goals and are a part of a marketing plan to sell their products. HHMC, however, does not explicitly market its founder's products; nor is it a part of his corporate enterprises. Instead, HHMC is a not-for-profit organization that funds local social change efforts primarily in large urban cities and provides financial support for political organizing efforts. However, although the work of these local urban organizations is not directly controlled by personal donations, Williams and the other corporate donors would not participate if the organization's strategies were so radical that they compromised the sale of their products (i.e., hip-hop music). HHMC, along with its other corporate sponsors, undoubtedly benefits from the benevolent financial support it offers to local political groups, but it does not infuse the marketing of its products into the movement work.

A second way that the corporate SMO differs from more traditional SMOs is that it is built on a model of coleadership that includes both an entrepreneur leader who "initiates movements, organizations and tactics" (Kleidman 1986, 191–92) and a professional leader who "devotes full time to the movement," relies on outside resources, works for and speaks on behalf of a paper membership, and "attempts to influence policy toward" the constituency (McCarthy and Zald 1973, 20). In the case of HHMC, Williams partnered with Brian Green, former president of a major civil rights organization, to channel a cultural movement into a mass-based political movement. He has managed to do this through a complex blend of entrepreneurial and professional leadership, an organization that possesses both informal and formal characteristics, the utilization of a cadre and a membership base, insider philanthropic leadership, and strategic social change marketing through a corporate network that solicits the participation of hip-hop artists.

This research, therefore, addresses and complicates our theoretical understanding of social movement models and the implications for movement strategies. Typically, our conceptualization of movement leaders include entrepreneur leaders who initiate movements but resist formal organization (Staggenborg 1988) or, after initiating the movement, evolve into professional leaders (McCarthy and Zald 1977). Staggenborg (1988, 594) has suggested that entrepreneurs and professionals develop two distinct types of organizations: "In contrast to the professional manager who brings skills to an organization and expects to operate within an established structure, movement entrepreneurs may try to prevent the creation of an organizational structure in which decision making is routinized and, therefore, less subject to personal control."

This suggests that the corporate social movement model with both professional and entrepreneur leaders constitutes a third type of organizational model that completely resembles neither McCarthy's and Zald's (1977) model nor that of Staggenborg (1988). The corporate SMO is characterized by a coleadership model that includes a philanthropic entrepreneur leader and a professional leader. Here, we explore the ways in which the characteristics of these SMOs influence movement outreach, communications, and financial strategies.

Case Study

Daniel Williams is a multimillionaire corporate music executive who has served as chair of a record label and vice-chair of a hip-hop advertising agency, and who owns a communications company, two hip-hop fashion brands and clothing lines, and other corporate ventures. Initially, politicians, African American leaders, and civil rights veterans held summits with Williams because they believed he should be more responsible as a hip-hop mogul, not because they saw him as an activist.

In 2001, over 300 hip-hop artists, record executives, civil rights movement activists, African American politicians, and young people gathered in New York to attend a large summit to address concerns about ongoing violent feuds in hip-hop between West Coast and East Coast factions. Several African American organizations, including the Urban League and the Nation of Islam, had previously attempted to negotiate peace between East and West Coast rappers Tupac Shakur and Notorious B.I.G. Unfortunately, after peace summits on both coasts, both rappers were assassinated, and coastal conflict and violence continued to explode in hip-hop. Like others before, the summit primarily addressed violence and other negative aspects of hip-hop. This summit was different, however, in that Daniel Williams, who spearheaded the summit, decided to create an organization to sustain and implement the ideas developed. Thus Hip-Hop Movement Connection (HHMC), a nonprofit, nonpartisan, national hip-hop political organization, was born. Immediately, the headquarters opened in New York with a field office in Washington, D.C. Additionally, a board of wealthy, powerful people was appointed, and a veteran civil rights leader, Dr. Brian Green, who worked with Martin Luther King Jr., was selected to serve as president of the organization. The motto of HHMC is "Taking Back Responsibility," a response to African American critics like Jessie Jackson, Bill Cosby, Louis Farrakhan, and C. Delores Tucker, who accused hip-hop artists and supporters of glamorizing violence and behaving irresponsibly in their music. The conclusion of the 2001 Hip-Hop Summit was a sign of tangible change. Since its inception, HHMC claims to have registered millions of new young voters at various rallies, protests, and marches, as well as to have held forty-five successful summits on civic education and political awareness.

The board of directors is made up of famous and powerful people in the music industry, noteworthy scholars, and civic leaders. The music industry insiders have access to a long list of hip-hop artists. Williams invited power players in the music industry like Sean "Puffy" Combs, Jay-Z, and Jermaine Dupri to serve on the thirteen-member board, along with scholar Manning Marable and former president and CEO of the NAACP, Kwesi Mfume. Board members are not merely famous, multiplatinum hip-hop artists but are also members of Williams's personal circle of peers and friends. The board is made up of nine African Americans and four European Americans and meets at least once a year, as required by nonprofit board regulations.

The majority of the initiatives are introduced by Williams and Green, reviewed by the board for their support and participation, and implemented by volunteers and paid staff. It is clear, however, that board member participation is strategic and based on celebrity status and ability to draw participants. All board members may participate in the larger events, but the most famous are always in the forefront.

Literature Review
Leadership and Organizational Structure

Although a full discussion of the treatment of leadership in social movements is beyond our scope here, we wish to focus more narrowly on the relationships between movement leadership type, movement organization, and social movement strategies. In doing so, we find the work of Staggenborg (1988) and

McCarthy and Zald (1973, 1977) most relevant. McCarthy and Zald (1973) introduced the notion of a professional social movement. Although not submitting to "the tyranny of the iron cage" offered by the Weber-Michels's model, in which SMOs over time succumb to oligarchy, routinization, and institutionalization, they suggest that modern social movements may choose or advance toward professionalization. This model includes full-time leaders, cultivation of resources "outside of the aggrieved group," a paper-only or nonexistent membership base, leader representation of its constituency, and efforts to influence social, political, and economic policy (McCarthy and Zald 1973, 20). Later, McCarthy and Zald (1977) extended this model by suggesting that entrepreneur leaders who initiate movements also develop professional SMOs. Such organizations are formal with officers, paid staff, and standardized procedures that include specific bylaws and decision-making processes. The authors acknowledge that there are few prototypes of the model. Indeed, several studies indicate that many social movements are a mix of the professional SMO and other informal chapters or decentralized offshoots, as in the case of Pennsylvanians for a Biblical Majority with its professional state-level organization and local church supporters (Cable 1984; see also McFarland 1984).

Relying on her analysis of the U.S. pro-choice movement, Staggenborg (1988, 594) objected to the conceptualization of movement leaders in McCarthy and Zald's model, arguing that "nonprofessional leaders are more likely to initiate movements (as opposed to SMOs) and tactics than are professionals." She suggests a distinction between movement entrepreneurs and professional leaders. Movement entrepreneurs are likened to business entrepreneurs who prefer personal control and take risks without any guarantee of success. Such leaders strongly resist formalization, preferring optimum decision-making power in an informal structure. Her study failed to support McCarthy and Zald's expectation of the transition of entrepreneurial leaders to professional leaders. A professional leader may start an SMO, but she or he is not likely to start a social movement. This distinction is an important one that forms the basis of our analysis.

Organizational Structures and Outreach Strategies

It has been argued that entrepreneurial and professional leaderships and organizational forms lend themselves to distinct outreach strategies. On the one hand, the entrepreneurial model favors a cadre membership base where organizers are organized (Cloward and Piven 1984, 595). On the other, a professional model is more likely to focus on organizational maintenance and the cultivation of a paper membership base (Staggenborg 1988). Extending the work of these scholars, we suggest that a new model of social movement leadership and organization has emerged in which entrepreneur leaders and professional leaders team up. How, then, will this model influence communication strategies?

Communication Strategies

Members of social movements often struggle over control of the movement's message. In our case, the entrepreneur leader and the professional leader must negotiate framing of the movement's message. It is apparent that some tensions might exist in that Daniel Williams is a hip-hop mogul who has managed to amass a significant fortune. As noted by Negas (1999, 84), hip-hop is "a self-conscious business activity as well as a cultural form and aesthetic practice." Williams's interests may include an emphasis on economic prosperity and consumption, which is not inconsistent with much of hip-hop's identity. Brian Green, however, is a seasoned civil rights veteran whose interests may focus on a more traditional civil rights agenda such as equal protection under the law that Boyd (2002) has critiqued as outmoded and off-putting to the hip-hop generation.

That tensions might exist within hip-hop between economic and civil rights interests, capitalism, and consumerism versus economic equality and justice, would not be not surprising. Rose (1994, 36) asserts that "rap's contradictory stance towards capitalism" was also present in jazz, blues, and R & B. Our focus is thus on the ways that Williams's and Green's movement message represents an economic or civil rights framing. Although Staggenborg's research does not specifically address control over the movement's message, she does show that entrepreneur leaders are more likely than professional leaders to develop new tactics and strategies. Accordingly, we expect that Williams, as the entrepreneur leader, will have more control over the movement's message as a strategic innovation that can connect culture and politics to transform the consciousness of hip-hop youth.

Finance Strategies

We are not aware of research that addresses the finance strategies used when philanthropist/donors are not only insiders, but also the SMOs leader and board members. Although inside donors ensure less interference, what happens when there is little or no interference? Does the model of the corporate SMO's finance strategies enhance or compromise the organizations' ability to represent its purported constituency?

All social movements must engage in strategies of finance. They generally do so through fund-raising, often targeting individuals and/or foundations.

On the basis of their analyses of four social movement case studies, Ostrander, Silver, and McCarthy (2005) reconceptualize our understanding of the relationship between funders/philanthropists and SMOs. Prior studies had posited a funding dilemma in which SMOs are torn between insider-only funding and funding that threatens to alter or dilute their goals. According to Ostrander, Silver, and McCarthy (2005, 274), such models are based on a theory of social control in which "mobilizing money is inconsistent with organizing action" and such funders are outsiders who may "co-opt movement action." Insiders are viewed as preferable funders because they will not derail the movement. Similarly, channeling theory suggests that because of outsider funding practices, they unintentionally interfere with the goals of SMOs. The authors disagree with perspectives that render outside funding as negative and grantees as relatively impotent. Instead, they propose a relational model in which funders and activists negotiate terms of support. In this regard, the latter are not without agency. The negotiated terms rest on a continuum that may afford grantees total autonomy or varying degrees of compromise. Cress and Snow (2000) show that grantees make strategic choices about funding. Their study finds that activists strategically seek out funding from foundations that share their goals.

Cress and Snow's work also suggests that not all funders are movement outsiders who derail a movement's goals. Ostrander (2005) similarly argues that movement insiders can also be donors. In this regard, philanthropy theory has set up a false dichotomy between funders/donors as outsiders and activists as insiders. There are organizations such as the group Resource Generation, headquartered in Boston, that promote social entrepreneurship or venture philanthropy characterized by hands-on donor involvement. This organization and others such as the National Black United Fund mobilize or push for "indigenous philanthropy," which is, according to Carson (1999, 249), a "collective effort by [groups] to pool their financial and volunteer resources to address group concerns." There are clearly SMOs that maintain some control over their funding to prevent co-optation by external grantors.

Although the financial security of HHMC protects it from potential corruption by outside donors and foundations, it is prudent to understand how inside donors may also be influenced by other economic interests. Thus, the theoretical assumption that inside donors are always better comes into question. The focus of the organization also shifts from organizational maintenance to marketing. The movement is marketed through the strategic use of hip-hop artists. HHMC uses a top-down corporate–artist network model to implement its strategies and tactics. The top-down model solicits support from people who are at the top of corporate organizations and their networks, who have historically been white men or men of color who do not agitate the status quo of corporate industries. The network serves to garner the participation of hip-hop artists to mobilize youth. The network emanates from the record company executives on HHMC's board and the labels and artists they promote. This certainly provides incentive for artists to get involved and assures HHMC that it will always have a lineup that draws thousands of potential voters to its political rallies and summits because the organization promises contact with the musicians.

Methods

The data used in our study were obtained between June 2002 and September 2006 by coauthor Jessica Ayo Alabi (2007). The purpose was to explore efforts to organize and mobilize urban young people around political issues. HHMC was chosen because it is a primary national voice of the hip-hop generation, addressing important challenges facing urban youth. Although hundreds of hip-hop political organizations have developed throughout the United States, most of them are grassroots, community-run organizations. However, HHMC has acquired national recognition, massive participation, and a position at the forefront of the hip-hop political movement. Because the organization's leaders requested anonymity, we use pseudonyms for the name of the organization and the names of participants.

A multimethod approach to gather data was used, including: (1) engaging in passive observation at events including conferences, summits, concerts, and rallies in six cities—Los Angeles, Chicago, Las Vegas, San Francisco, Atlanta, and Philadelphia; (2) conducting eight in-depth, open-ended, semi-structured interviews of HHMC leaders; (3) conducting thirty-five casual, conversational interviews with participants through naturally occurring conversations, asking a small number of predetermined questions (Gillham 2000); and (4) gathering organizational documents from websites, articles, press releases, online discussions, and printed materials handed out at events. All this information was gathered to explore the coleadership effects of a professional leader and entrepreneur leader on organizational structure, strategies of recruitment, and strategies of finance.

The overall analysis incorporated grounded theory, noting themes and patterns in order to create broad summaries in the form of memos (Warren and Karner 2005). Memos were also used to interpret the data and to connect the data to the conceptual and theoretical discussions. An open coding method was used that allowed the categories to come from the data rather than preconceived categories (Warren and Karner 2005). By means of the inductive method, an analysis grid with respondents, events, and documents down the side and coding categories across the top was developed (Gillham 2000). The grid was then reviewed using focused coding (Warren and Karner 2005) to develop narrower categories, such as organizational characteristics (e.g., leadership, funding mechanism, decision-making process, division of labor) as well as strategies and tactics (e.g., recruitment, mobilization, mass demonstrations).

The Cadre and Paper Members Too: Outreach Strategies

Paper Membership and Marketing

The presidential election of 2004 gave birth to a plethora of youth voter mobilization campaigns, including the Young Voter Alliance (composed of a coalition of groups such as Young Democrats of America), the League of Pissed Off Voters, the League of Hip-Hop Voters, MoveOn Student Action, the National Stonewall Democrats, the National Coalition on Black Strategic Civic Participation with its Black Youth Vote Program, and Vote for Change (cosponsored by MoveOn PAC and America Coming Together). With this effort, new strategic forms of recruitment emerged, including reaching out to youth in nonpolitical settings such as "community centers, gyms, and nightclubs" (Shea and Green 2007, 198). Two important strategies included Internet use and music. Vote for Change sponsored a music tour consisting of thirty-seven concerts in thirty cities. Similarly, Music for America held concerts, solicited attendees' e-mail addresses, and later provided them with links to register to vote (Green 2004). HHMC also uses these outreach strategies.

HHMC's strategy of outreach and dissemination is heavily influenced by HHMC's corporate model in which Williams uses his business contacts to solicit the help of hip-hop artists. The top-down corporate–artist network advantages the organization such that they are able to get superstar rap artists to sit their panels for political summits, workshops, and rallies. HHMC then attracts new members and volunteers with the promise of contact with these musicians. Registering to vote is a requirement for free entrance to its star-studded summits and rallies. These members need an e-mail address and are connected to the state and country registrar in their residential area. When they have completed that process, they can print out their form and bring it to the HHMC event. The website includes the following invitation:

> Join Hip-Hop Vote today . . . Membership is free!
> All you have to do is to fill in this short membership form by signing up
>   as a member of "Hip-Hop Vote"!
> As a member you will receive:

—*great exclusive benefits*
—*personally you will get our special e-mail newsletter*
—*plus timely information on hip-hop artists' new releases*
—*if you are 17 and 34 or over we will give you access to the information online that you will need to vote!!!*
—*you will also be eligible for special discounts on the latest new clothing, shoe wear & gear*
All you have to do is just fill in the membership form with your information . . . do it now by signing up as a member of "Hip-Hop Vote"! Thank you for joining the Hip-Hop Vote and for hitting our website!

The most critical and active department pertaining to HHMC's political mobilization goals is Hip-Hop Vote, which is responsible for coordinating all HHMC's voter registration rallies, concerts, and summits. An important aspect of event planning for Hip-Hop Vote is volunteer training. Two or three months before a large rally, Volunteer Training Day is planned to train local volunteers in voting rights, Election Day operations, and voter registration regulations. Volunteers are invited to a VIP private after-party at a popular club or hangout of a popular hip-hop artist. For example, one HHMC flyer for volunteer training in Miami, Florida, reads:

> For taking part in the training your name will be added to our special VIP trainee invitation list and you will be given a VIP trainee ticket to the hottest party on Miami Beach at "The Mansion." Please distribute this information to any and all interested people who want to help with Hip-Hop Vote and who want to party with us this weekend.

Another coordination strategy for Hip-Hop Vote includes the Hip-Hop Vote Tour, which some have likened to the 1960s Freedom Rides. Yet unlike the Freedom Riders, these volunteers are lured with the promise of meeting hip-hop artists. They do not face the probability of violence or death. Although many may ride out of a conviction to increase minority voter registration, it is clear that the star-studded incentive provides a powerful lure. Volunteers are offered an opportunity to participate in an all-expense-paid trip for one month before the 2004 election, touring the country and encouraging urban youth to get out the vote. The Washington, D.C., flyer reads:

> Dear Volunteer: HHMC is looking for 100 volunteers to help staff and coordinate our upcoming nonpartisan Hip-Hop Vote Tour that will include state of the art tour buses reserved for the trip to key states and cities in the Midwest and the South. We will encourage millions of young voters to "Get out and Vote!" Join us for a week at a time or for the entire tour.

All expenses of the tour will be covered by HHMC. Hip-Hop artists and other celebrities will be joining the tour.

Both flyers demonstrate that the bulk of HHMC's organizational work is carried out by volunteers. However, the volunteers may or may not be interested in political organizing or the goals and objectives of the organization. Hip-hop parties and the opportunity to rub elbows with celebrity hip-hop artists greatly improve the possibility that HHMC will get the volunteers that it needs to carry out its objectives. Many of the volunteers are wannabe rap artists or entertainers looking for a window of opportunity or their big break in the industry.

The Cadre

In addition to paper members and those who want to become stars, there is a serious group of volunteers who function as bridge leaders at the community level who connect their local communities to the HHMC movement (see Robnett 1996, 1997). They are generally contacted by HHMC staff members or respond to advertisements seeking organizational support for HHMC events. Most of the bridge leaders are from grassroots organizations or nonpartisan voter registration initiative organizations such as the African American Voter Registration Education Project, the African American Voter Rep Project, the National Voter Coalition, Rock the Vote, Rap the Vote, and Americans Coming Together. They differ from the other volunteers who show up for the day to help fill bags with information sheets. Although they are not formal leaders, on the days of the events they are often recognized as the person in charge. For example, at a Los Angeles rally, participants, volunteers, and community activists who desired opportunities to speak on the platform were referred to a young woman in jeans and a HHMC T-shirt. She said she was from the African American Voter Registration Rep Project and had been working on the event for "twenty-four hours straight" (interview with Alabi). Everything of substance that happened during the event had to have her stamp of approval. She hurried around solving problems, talking to participants and volunteers, and even setting agendas and making closing comments.

Several of the bridge leaders that were interviewed during events had little knowledge of the internal workings of HHMC, as they were often leaders of local grassroots organizations who were contacted and solicited as partners. For example, the following are some of the bridge leaders' responses when asked, "How did you come to be involved in the political event or activity?" A bridge leader interviewed during the Atlanta rally said:

> I am very interested in some of the violence that's been going on around here. I don't think the youth understand what they are doing. I have been volunteering with the Inner-City Uplift program and we were contacted about the summit which needed some volunteers to help round up the youth and get them registered and involved in they communities. (interview with Alabi)

A bridge leader at the Los Angeles rally also emphasized getting youth involved: "This is just one of our many events we're doing to help young people get involved. I have been involved in politics my whole life and I know how important they are. We have to use whatever we can to draw young people in instead of pushing them away. I am a part of HHMC because I see the difference it makes in the lives of young people" (interview with Alabi). The financial options at HHMC's disposal allowed it to offer material incentives to participate. As one bridge leader at the Los Angeles Summit stated,

> I am actually with the kids from Watts from the Jordon Down Projects. They gave us these T-shirts and provided transportation for us to come down here. We work with the youth after school to try to help them get involved in the community, stay out of gangs and drugs and go to college. I think this is an important event, but I am worried about what will happen later. (interview with Alabi)

In some cities, HHMC hosted events, but no official or paid HHMC representative attended. This is important in understanding the use of celebrity status in division of labor. Formal leaders often only showed up to rallies to speak on the panel and conduct press releases. Sometimes they attended less than 20 percent of the event. Bridge leaders were in charge of follow-up activities and local interaction with participants after formal leaders returned to New York or Washington, D.C.

Connecting Cultural Messages to Political Messages: Communication Strategies

HHMC strategically connected cultural messages to political messages. It appears that although the messages are not exactly like those of the 1960s, with an emphasis on civil rights, the messages do not emphasize consumption or economic affluence. They are, in fact, more in keeping with those proposed by Brian Green during his tenure as president of a major civil rights organization. Thus, it does not appear that Williams unduly influences the proffered messages. There are three dominant messages conveyed by HHMC: injustice, demand for societal transformation, and hip-hop power. These messages are sequential in that the first is primarily cultural and builds on the preexisting grievances of urban youth. The second message shifts the acknowledgment of injustice to action, suggesting that society must be transformed to change the injustices. The final message links the cultural to the political, suggesting that through political engagement, those who are oppressed can gain power. The final message is also linked to economic empowerment that brings political power.

Injustice Message

The injustice message can be seen throughout HHMC, including in its goals, mission statement, purpose, demands through press releases, radio announcements, ads, and interviews. For example, for HHMC, "Taking Back Responsibility" translates into turning hip-hop into a powerful political force for urban youth. Williams believes that the power and positive aspects of hiphop music can be demonstrated by successfully achieving the following four goals stated in HHMC's mission statement: "(1) Harnessing the cultural relevance and power of Hip-Hop music to serve as a catalyst for social change; (2) Empowering youth through educational advocacy; (3) Proactively fighting the war against poverty and injustice using Hip-Hop as an influential agent of social change; and (4) Mobilizing the Hip-Hop vote." According to Green, "Every activity that HHMC does is fundamentally connected to one of these four goals and moving hip-hop into the direction of becoming a powerful political instrument. The music is so powerful and we intend to use that power!" (interview with Alabi). The overall thrust of the language used by Green and those used to articulate the goals of HHMC denotes the idea that fusing hip-hop with politics is new. From the vantage point of HHMC, hip-hop music has been deemed negative and irresponsible. Now the organization hopes to harness hip-hop music, turning it into something positive.

In addition, the list of demands, titled "What We Want," acknowledges the cultural messages of injustice that include educational inequality, unequal access and quality of health care, unequal treatment by the criminal justice system, unfair policing, voting rights tampering, and economic inequality. For example, #4 in the list of demands reads, "We want the highest quality of public education equally for all"; demand #7 reads, "We want the total elimination of police brutality and the unjust incarceration of people of color and all others." These demands resonate with potential participants who view both education and law enforcement agencies as unjust institutions. Other examples include interview responses from HHMC leaders to the question, "What issues are discussed at these types of events most often?" HHMC's president states: "All facets of social life are discussed. We don't just want the young people to vote, we want them to talk about what's going on in their communities. We have summits with specific issues like gangs, violence, money, and things that are important to the young people—the unfair treatment they get from the police that is suppose to protect them" (interview with Alabi). Similarly, HHMC's grassroots leader in Los Angeles responds with, "Voting and community problems and injustices we face every day" (interview with Alabi).

More evidence that emphasizes this injustice message includes the press release announcing HHMC's decision to help reopen the Emmett Till case. In 1955, Emmett Till, a fourteen-year-old boy visiting Mississippi from Chicago, was brutally beaten, mutilated, and lynched for allegedly whistling at a white woman. The press release indicated that HHMC was initiating an ad campaign that would show pictures of the brutalized youth, present a documentary of the torture and murder of the boy, and provide an interview with his mother. Other press releases announced the United Nations' recognition of the injustice and previewing of the documentary. During this previewing, the president of HHMC stated, "What happened to Emmett Till was an assault on all black people."

Societal Transformation Message

The second message, the demand for societal transformation, goes beyond calling for simple or complex reforms. Most often HHMC uses language that includes the terms *ending, elimination,* and *transformation.* The following excerpts from rally speakers and panelists include calls for a revolt, though the term *revolution* was never used in any of the documents, events, or interviews. A speaker at the Los Angeles rally stated: "If you want to end police brutality, you got to put an end to police training that makes you the enemy." A speaker at the Los Angeles summit put transformation in historical perspective: "We need to demolish unjust laws. The injustice we are facing isn't new. It's the same old injustice we've been facing for over three hundred years and now is the time to put an end to it." A Chicago summit speaker concluded: "Until racism ends and poverty is eliminated, the war against our people ain't over. My child still goes to a segregated school with all black kids in 2005 . . . in 2005? We need another Rosa Parks; this has got to stop!"

Several press releases dealt with HHMC's commitment to ending New York's Rockefeller Drug Laws, which were enacted in 1973 when Nelson Rockefeller was governor. The Rockefeller Drug Laws require harsh prison terms for the possession or sale of relatively small amounts of drugs; the law is believed to target African Americans, minorities, and youth unfairly. A press release that includes both the injustice message and the message of societal transformation notes, "The Rockefeller Drug Laws are unfair, unjust, and un-American, and that's why Governor Pataki should repeal these unfair laws now!" Perhaps the most typical use of this frame is articulated in several of the "What We Want" demands of HHMC. For example, demand #3 calls for "the total elimination of poverty," while demand #5 calls for "the total elimination of racism and racial profiling, violence, hatred and bigotry." Demand #8 echoes the press release, calling for "the end and repeal of all repressive legislations, laws, regulations and ordinances such as 'three strikes' laws; federal and state mandatory minimum sentencing; trying and sentencing juveniles as adults; sentencing disparities between crack and powdered cocaine use; capitol punishment." Demand #10 calls for transformation into a "Nu America": "We want the progressive transformation of American society into a Nu America as a result of organizing and mobilizing the energy, activism and resources of the hip-hop community at the grassroots level throughout the United States."

Hip-Hop Power Message

In addition to the injustice and the "demand for societal transformation" messages, HHMC constructs a hip-hop power message that relies heavily on redirecting potential participants to its organization as the official representatives of hip-hop power. For example, the following was the opening statement from HHMC leadership at one of the largest and most attended summits in Los Angeles: "The hip-hop community is so powerful and, while some of us have been very successful entrepreneurs, it's just as important to acknowledge that we are a part of a larger community." The founder of HHMC also emphasized strength in numbers: "MC Dollar's chairing the LA Hip-Hop Summit is an example of how this movement has many leaders and can't be stopped."

In several press releases and interviews, the hip-hop power message was also evident. Several summits were in New York, Atlanta, New Orleans, and Detroit, where HHMC announced the "One Mind, One Vote" campaign. The organization announced that it would target 20 million voters in five years in its voter registration efforts. Their goal was to mobilize the hip-hop vote and to exercise hip-hop power.

The demand for hip-hop power was evident in several of the "What We Want" demands of HHMC. Demand #12 states, "We want advocacy of public policies that are in the interests of hip-hop before Congress, state legislatures, municipal governments, the media and the entertainment industry." In demand #10, where HHMC calls for a "Nu America," HHMC is an integral part of this transformation as it flexes hip-hop power in statements like, "Nu America . . . as a result of organizing and mobilizing the energy, activism and resources of the hip-hop community at the grassroots level throughout the United States." This display of hip-hop power appears to be a call to recognize hip-hop and HHMC as power brokers in mainstream institutions.

Another example that demonstrates HHMC's construction of hip-hop power in dealing with mainstream U.S. institutions was HHMC's reaction to attacks of hip-hop culture and artists. In one of its press releases, HHMC announced its defense of hip-hop culture "before members of the U.S. Congress, the Federal Trade Commission and the Federal Communications Commission." As a motivational message, hip-hop power defines HHMC as the political mobilization vehicle towards societal transformation. It does this by creating awareness of hip-hop's powerful and enormously influential nature while simultaneously constructing HHMC as the conduit for that power.

Inside Philanthropic Leaders: Funding Strategies

HHMC hosts and facilitates massive political events and activities, making funding a vital component of their ability to be an effective organization. Because Daniel Williams is a multimillionaire, there are rarely financial challenges facing HHMC. The funding process of HHMC is formal because of its nonprofit status, but Williams's for-profit hip-hop business ventures also benefit from HHMC. One example of the formal financing structure is noted in a press release that announces a gift from HHMC's founder to HHMC. It states, "Daniel Williams, the Founder and Chairman of the Hip-Hop Movement Connection presented a donation of $100,000 to Dr. Brian Green, President/CEO of the Hip-Hop Movement Connection to help defray costs of staging the rally." In effect, because Williams leads HHMC and donates to HHMC, he recycles his money from for-profit businesses to nonprofit business. This is a common business/philanthropic model—consider, for example, Microsoft and the Bill and Melinda Gates Foundation. In this model, strict records are kept and strict regulations are followed. In addition, this formal financial record keeping ensures HHMC of the financial resources needed to carry out its tasks, even though it is a skeleton organization. With this formal financial certainty, there is no need for dues or fees. All HHMC events, including concerts, panels, summits, and rallies, are free, even when they headline a major recording artist. For example, the Atlanta and Detroit summits had artist lineups that rival concerts with $100 entry fees. Yet these summits attracted over 75,000 participants, who were admitted for free.

Inside Donors, Business Interests, and Marketing

Daniel Williams is also the founder of a multimillion-dollar communications corporation that supplies secured credit cards, cell phones, and other products

to the hip-hop community. Critics have characterized this corporate relationship as a conflict of interest. They argue that Williams's for-profit business partnerships that help to fund HHMC indirectly enjoy financial gains
from the political rallies and summits that HHMC sponsors. For example,
HHMC's organizational name is used in local community-partner events,
including the advertisements on local urban radio stations. Often volunteers
wear a HHMC T-shirt with the names of partners, local businesses, or corporate sponsors printed on them. All gifts and giveaways, such as information-
filled bags, had "HHMC" printed on them, along with the name of the
partner. Large, professionally created signs and banners bearing the HHMC
name and logo adorned all event entrances, sidelines, and stages.

The costs involved with hosting such a massive event are extraordinary,
but the formal donation structure ensures that securing the money and rap
stars is not an issue. Corporate sponsors such as Anheuser-Busch, Sony,
Chrysler, and Clear Channel Communications also donate to HHMC's political effort. This often bolsters the funding stream and the association with
other corporate products such as video games, radio stations, and popular
beverages. Sometimes these products and cosponsors give away prizes and
incentives to participants and volunteers, such as a PlayStation game console.
As mentioned earlier, the Hip-Hop Vote is able to lure volunteers with VIP
parties, all-expense paid tours, and the promise to meet celebrities in exchange
for their participation. This ensures that volunteers will always be obtain-
able. Although they have to attract volunteers via celebrity participation and
parties, having massive resources at their disposal makes recruiting relatively
easy. Also, because there is little overhead but major exposure and opportunities to mobilize participants, HHMC partners are eager and willing to co-
sponsor events.

Discussion and Conclusion

A new form of SMO—a corporate SMO—has emerged in the twenty-first
century, one that couples entrepreneur leaders with professional leaders and
business interests with liberal political mobilization. The corporate SMO has
several strategic advantages: (1) its outreach strategy combines a paper membership with a cadre capable of bridging the masses to the movement; (2) its
communication strategy accepts the philanthropic entrepreneur leader's control over the dissemination of the movement's message but allows for the message to be framed by the professional leader; and (3) its financial strategy is
less consumed with organizational maintenance and concerns of outside co-
optation than organizations dependent on multiple small donors or outside
benefactors. In this regard, it shares many similarities to, but also differs from,

a professional SMO as outlined by McCarthy and Zald (1973). Although they suggest the leadership is full time, only one of HHMC's leaders maintains full-time status. Professional SMOs are believed to receive a large proportion of resources from those outside of the constituency it purports to represent, but the bulk of HHMC's funding comes from inside donors. Like many professional SMOs, its structure is formal, but its decision-making process is informal, and generally all decisions are made by the entrepreneur leader and the professional leader. This suggests that like Staggenborg's assertion, entrepreneur leaders prefer informal structures for ultimate organizational control. In our case, however, it appears that a formal structure is in place that satisfies the needs of the professional leader and supports the financial infrastructure of the organization. HHMC has a paper membership, as do most professional organizations, but it also has a significant cadre. Similar to professional SMOs, it speaks on behalf of the aggrieved group and attempts to influence policy (McCarthy and Zald 1987; McAdam, McCarthy, and Zald 1988). Although corporate social movement mobilization has its benefits, several issues remain.

Ostrander (2005) and Ostrander, Silver, and McCarthy (2005) question the theoretical underpinnings that suggest a binary between funders and organizations. Yet both studies leave intact the theoretical belief that donations given by insider philanthropists/donors necessarily mean that the SMO will not be co-opted or compromised. We are concerned about the extent to which business interests may conflict with the interests of the movement. In what ways is this new configuration of SMO leadership with a philanthropic leader at its helm co-optable? To what extent do these events benefit the artists, particularly those who are on Williams's record labels? As Robert Allen warned us in 1969, the "privileged black bourgeoisie" often takes "control of organizations ostensibly dedicated to militant reform, to enabling black people to assume control over their own lives," but in the end come to serve only the needs of this "opportunistic elite" and become "simply an added burden strapped to the back of black America" (53–54). Yet if Williams's labels grow more successful, does this not reinforce the stability and independence of this organization thus supporting greater mobilization?

As far as we can ascertain, both interests are mutually advantageous. Although Williams markets his artists on behalf of the movement, the HHMC simultaneously draws masses of black youth to participate. Still, what we do not know is the extent to which Williams, his artists, and other corporate supporters financially benefited from their altruism. We are certain that Williams and other sponsors would not continue to support the movement should it radicalize and jeopardize the sale of their products. There is no evidence, however, to support the contention that Williams or HHMC compromised or co-opted the efforts of local groups. Given that HHMC contacts local groups to coordinate their efforts, it would seem that they are able to control the types of organizations and local leaders they support. We surmise that they are likely to exclude groups with whom they ideologically or strategically disagree.

A second concern of ours is the extent to which HHMC's political conscious-raising efforts are enduring. When youth participate in HHMC-sponsored events and register to vote, does this translate into enduring political awareness and participation? Does it increase their voting? We were also concerned about the extent to which HHMC's efforts create political change, although that was not our focus. We rely on HHMC documents pertaining to a few of their asserted successes.

For example, they claim that "on August 14, 2003, the Philadelphia Hip-Hop Summit registered over 11,000 voters, the largest number of young new voters registered ever at a single hip-hop event in the United States." The documents state that HHMC "fostered the establishment of grassroots Hip-Hop Summit Youth Councils in Queens, New York; Seattle; Baltimore; Kansas City; and Dallas. The Youth Councils engage youth in Leadership development activities at a local level." Another HHMC document states that they "joined with the Alliance for Quality Education, mobilizing 100,000 New York City public school students and top Hip-Hop recording artists to a protest rally at City Hall, which resulted in Mayor Bloomberg restoring $300 million in proposed cuts to the New York City public school budget. The National Federation of Teachers also partnered in this rally, and in part through the advocacy of the Hip-Hop community, they were able to finally negotiate a fair compensation contract for New York City public school teachers." Finally, the organization claims that it "recently organized a public awareness campaign on the unfairness of the Rockefeller Drug Laws in New York culminating in a public rally of over 60,000."

These claims strongly suggest that HHMC achieves many of its goals and is building a grassroots infrastructure to enhance youth involvement.[2] We have also examined voting data among African American youth. Although the connection to the HHMC is only suggestive, we do know that multiple efforts were made to engage youth in politics and to get them to vote in the 2004 election. As compared to the 2000 presidential election, current population survey data indicate that voter turnout among all youth, ages eighteen to twenty-four, increased by 12 percent for women and 10 percent for men in 2004 (Lopez, Kirby, and Sagoff 2005). That same year, 11 percent more African American women and 9 percent more African American men voted. The turnout was somewhat less among Latinos, which can be partially explained by immigration status, with an 8 percent increase among Latinas and a 7 percent increase among Latinos. Although the voter turnout among minority youth appeared to mirror increases among white youth, black youth turnout (47 percent African American women and 42 percent African American men) was at a record high, surpassing any other election year since and including 1972. This was also true for Latino youth, with 32 percent voting. It was the second highest turnout among Latinas, with 34 percent voting as compared to 37 percent in 1992. Although we cannot attribute these findings directly to the efforts of HHMC, along with their self-reported increase in voter registrants in Philadelphia, they suggest that the larger mobilization effort to mobilize minority youth enjoyed a modicum of success. To this end, future research might ask event participants about their reasons for participating and their political engagement. Such responses will clarify our understanding of how successful HHMC has been in achieving political awareness and commitment among youth.

In sum, it appears that corporate social movements constitute a third type of social movement that combines professional and entrepreneur leaders, develops formal organizational structure with informal decision-making processes, possesses an inside leader donor base, and uses marketing strategies that connect cultural events with political ones to mobilize successfully for social change. The corporate SMO's characteristics facilitate a strategy of outreach that is both cadre and membership based and includes the dissemination of the movement's message through an entrepreneur leader's top-down corporate–artist network; a strategy of communication in which the professional leader largely controls the movement's message; and a financial strategy that does not depend on outside benefactors or inside donors (Ostrander 2005) but on inside philanthropic entrepreneur leaders who financially benefit from their altruism yet do not appear to co-opt the movement's goal.

Notes

1. The names of the organization and its leaders are fictitious to protect their confidentiality and to comply with internal review board requirements. The organization's leaders agreed to the study on the condition that the organization, its leaders, and its members remain anonymous when referenced in any published material.

2. Although not our subject here, HHMC's leaders appear to blend direct action and conventional political tactics to achieve their goals. Staggenborg (1988) has suggested that professional leaders support conventional tactics, while entrepreneur leaders prefer direct action. Our findings suggest that corporate social movements may engage in both types of tactics.

References

Alabi, Jessica Jeannine. 2007. "Rethinking the Political: Hip-Hop-Based Political Organizations, Urban Youth, Mobilization." Ph.D. diss., University of California, Irvine.

Allen, Robert. 1969. *Black Awakening in Capitalist America: An Analytic History.* New York: Doubleday.

Boyd, Todd. 2002. *The New H.N.I.C.: The Death of Civil Rights and the Reign of Hip-Hop.* New York: New York University Press.

Cable, Sherry. 1984. "Professionalization in Social Movement Organizations: A Case Study of Pennsylvanians for Biblical Morality." *Sociological Forces* 7:287–304.

Carson, E. D. 1999. "The Roles of Indigenous and Institutional Philanthropy." In *Philanthropy and the Nonprofit Sector in a Changing America,* edited by Charles Clotfelter and Thomas Ehrlich, 248–74. Bloomington: Indiana University Press.

Cloward, Richard A., and Frances Fox Piven. 1984. "Review: Disruption and Organization: A Rejoinder [to William A. Gamson and Emilie Schmeidler]." *Theory and Society* 13:587–99.

Cress, Daniel M., and David A. Snow. 2000. "The Outcomes of Homeless Mobilization: The Influence of Organization, Disruption, Political Mediation, and Framing." *American Journal of Sociology* 105:1063–104.

Gillham, Bill. 2000. *Case Study Research Methods.* New York: Wellington House.

Green, Andrew. 2004. "They've Got Rhythm, They've Got Politics." *Milwaukee Journal Sentinel,* July 19.

Kleidman, Robert. 1986. "Opposing 'The Good War': Mobilization and Professionalization in the Emergency Peace Campaign." *Research in Social Movements, Conflicts and Change* 9:177–200.

Lopez, Mark Hugo, Emily Kirby, and Jared Sagoff. 2005. "The Youth Vote 2004." Fact Sheet produced by the Center for Information and Research on Civil Learning and Engagement. http://www.civicyouth.org.

McAdam, Doug, John McCarthy, and Mayer Zald. 1988. "Social Movements." In *Handbook of Sociology,* edited by Neil J. Smelser, 695–737. Newbury Park, Calif.: Sage.

McCarthy, John D., and Mayer N. Zald. 1973. *The Trend of Social Movements in America: Professionalization and Resource Mobilization.* Morristown, N.J.: General Learning Press.

———. 1977. "Resource Mobilization and Social Movements: A Partial Theory." *American Journal of Sociology* 82:1212–41.

———. 1987. "The Trend of Social Movements in America: Professionalization and Resource Mobilization." In *Social Movements in an Organizational Society,* edited by Mayer N. Zald and John McCarthy, 37–391. New Brunswick, N.J.: Transaction.

McFarland, Andrew F. 1984. *Common Cause: Lobbying in the Public Interest.* Chatham, N.H.: Chatham House.

Negas, Keith. 1999. "The Music Business and Rap: Between the Street and the Executive Suite." *Cultural Studies* 13 no. 3:488–508.

Ostrander, Susan A. 2005. "Legacy and Promise for Social Justice Funding: Charitable Foundations and Progressive Social Movements, Past and Present." In *Foundations for Social Change: Critical Perspectives on Philanthropy and Popular Movements,* edited by Daniel Faber, Deborah McCarthy, Robert O. Bothwell, and Robert J. Brulle, 33–60. Lanham, Md.: Rowman & Littlefield.

Ostrander, Susan A., Ira Silver, and Deborah McCarthy. 2005. "Mobilizing Money Strategically: Opportunities for Grantees to Be Active Agents in Social Movement Philanthropy." In *Foundations for Social Change: Critical Perspectives on Philanthropy and Popular Movements,* edited by Daniel Faber, Deborah McCarthy, Robert O. Bothwell, and Robert J. Brulle, 271–90. Lanham, Md.: Rowman & Littlefield.

Robnett, Belinda. 1996. "African American Women in the Civil Rights Movement: Gender, Leadership and Micromobilization." *American Journal of Sociology* 101, no. 6:1661–93.

———. 1997. *How Long? How Long? Women in the Struggle for Civil Rights.* New York: Oxford University Press.

Rose, Tricia. 1994. *Black Noise: Rap Music and Black Culture in Contemporary America.* Hanover, N.H.: Wesleyan University Press.

Shea, Daniel M., and John C. Green. 2007. "Young Voter Mobilization Projects in 2004." In *Fountain of Youth: Strategies and Tactics for Mobilizing America's Young Voters,* edited by Daniel M. Shea, John C. Green, Melissa K. Comber, and Ivan Frishberg, 181–207. Lanham, Md.: Rowman & Littlefield.

Staggenborg, Suzanne. 1988. "The Consequences of Professionalization and Formalization in Pro-choice Movement." *American Sociological Review* 53:585–605.

Warren, Carol, and Tracy Karner. 2005. *Discovering Qualitative Research: Field Methods, Interviews and Analysis.* Los Angeles: Roxbury.

IV
Strategy and the
Consequences of Movements

10

Land Struggles in the Global South: Strategic Innovations in Brazil and India

Kurt Schock

Struggles over land are occurring throughout much of the less developed world. Although many of these struggles are rooted in centuries-old inequalities, conflicts have intensified in recent decades as a result of population pressure, environmental degradation, and the intensification of accumulation by dispossession. There is considerable sociological literature on why landless people and poor peasants rebel in order to attain land (e.g., Wolf 1969; Migdal 1974; Paige 1975; Popkin 1976; Scott 1976; Jenkins 1982; Skocpol 1982; McClintock 1984; Lichbach 1994; Wood 2003; Mason 2004). Yet the question of how peasants rebel has received relatively less attention. In much of the literature there is an implicit assumption that during normal times, when barriers to collective action are high, landless and poor peasants engage in everyday forms of resistance. When opportunities for protest arise or threats to survival escalate, violent rebellion breaks out. Many peasant rebellions, especially in the twentieth century, were in fact violent. Nevertheless, in the late twentieth century and into the twenty-first, a shift occurred in many places in the Global South with regard to how struggles over land were pursued. New peasant and landless movements emerged that eschewed violent methods of rebellion in favor of militant nonviolent resistance.

I examine two rural social movement organizations (SMOs) that have waged militant struggles for land reform through nonviolent resistance.[1] The first is the Landless Rural Workers Movement in Brazil (MST). The MST was founded in 1984 in southern Brazil and is currently active in twenty-two of Brazil's twenty-seven states.[2] The second is an Indian SMO called Ekta Parishad (Unity Forum). It was founded in 1990 in the state of Madhya

Pradesh and has spread its operations to neighboring states to the east and north as well as to states in the south. It is currently active in nine of India's twenty-eight states. Both SMOs have organized campaigns to mobilize people, to raise public awareness about land issues, to place land reform on the national agenda, to pressure the government to undertake land reform and rural development, and to create alternatives to exploitive political and economic relations. Both have implemented a wide variety of nonviolent actions, including land occupations, building occupations, occupations of public places, blockades, political rallies, protest demonstrations, and marches. Nevertheless, each SMO is characterized by a defining method. For the MST, it is the land occupation. For Ekta Parishad, it is the extended march, or *padyatra*.

I address three interrelated questions here. Why did social movements with radical goals, such as challenging private property relations and elite interests, opt for nonviolent resistance? Why were particular methods of nonviolent action implemented? Why have nonviolent resistance movements been successful in promoting land reform? In brief, I find that various methods of nonviolent resistance were selected as a result of their resonance with political, cultural, and geographic contexts. The effective matching of specific methods to the context also contributes to the successful promotion of land reform.

Literature Review

Figure 10.1 provides a simplified model specifying important factors influencing a social movement's adoption of strategies and methods. Figure 10.2 illustrates a simplified model specifying major factors influencing movement outcomes.[3] Social movement literature that addresses the concepts and relations identified in the figures is reviewed below.

The left half of figure 10.1 suggests that the strategy adopted by a challenger is influenced by the type of regime within which it operates and the movement's ideology. Strategy refers to the broad ways of prosecuting a challenge against an opponent—through institutional political and legal channels, outside institutional channels through violent or nonviolent actions, and various combinations and proportions of each. A regime refers to "repeated, strong interactions among major political actors including a government" (Tilly 2006, 19). Tilly makes a useful distinction between four regime types on the basis of two dimensions: government capacity and democracy. Government capacity refers to the "degree to which governmental actions affect distributions of populations, activities, and resources within the government's jurisdiction, relative to some standard of quality and efficiency" (Tilly 2006, 21). Democracy refers to the "extent to which persons subject to the government's

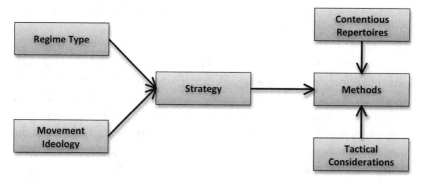

Figure 10.1. Simplified Model of Factors Influencing Social Movement Strategy and Methods

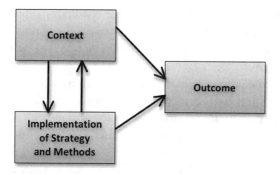

Figure 10.2. Simplified Model of Factors Influencing Social Movement Outcomes

authority have broad, equal rights to influence governmental affairs and to receive protection from arbitrary governmental action" (Tilly 2006, 21). A cross-classification of the two dimensions provides four crude regime types: high-capacity nondemocratic, low-capacity nondemocratic, high-capacity democratic, and low-capacity democratic.

Strategies of resistance and repertoires of contention vary across time and space, but there is a tendency for broadly similar strategies and repertoires to predominate in specific types of regimes (Tilly 2006). For example, institutional and nonviolent methods of contention predominate in high-capacity democracies, while violence is prevalent in low-capacity nondemocracies. Although democracies often work well for elites and their middle-class supporters, systematic biases and corruption tend to inhibit excluded groups from promoting meaningful change solely through institutional politics. Therefore, marginalized groups excluded from institutional access must engage in mass mobilization and implement noninstitutional methods of political action to promote change.

Challengers adopting a violent strategy in high-capacity democracies are typically extinguished by the superior repressive capacities of the state. In fact, no armed struggle in a high-capacity democracy has ever succeeded (Martin 2006). More specifically, with regard to landless and peasant-based social movements, communist-inspired movements adopting violent strategies may succeed in nondemocratic and low-capacity regimes like Nepal (under the monarchy) or Nicaragua (under Somoza), but are unlikely to succeed in democratic and high-capacity regimes such as India or Brazil.

Movement ideology also influences the strategy adopted by SMOs. Ideology is "a relatively stable and coherent set of values, beliefs, and goals associated with a movement . . . assumed to provide the rationale for defending or challenging various social arrangements and conditions" (Snow 2004, 396). At minimum, an ideology may imply a strategy or combination of strategies to be used to attain a movement's goals. More strongly, an ideology may proscribe or prescribe specific strategies.

When ideological concerns override the matching of an appropriate strategy to the political context, strategies may be adopted that are unlikely to promote change. Take, for example, late 1960s social movements in the high-capacity and democratic United States inspired by ideologies of third world national liberation movements such as the Weathermen and the Black Panthers. These movements, which adopted or promoted violence, were easily crushed by the superior violence of the state. Thus, when SMOs rigidly adopt an ideology that prescribes a strategy mismatched with the context, political traction is unlikely. Conversely, when SMOs adopt an ideology that prescribes a context-appropriate strategy, a challenge is more likely to generate leverage.

The right half of figure 10.1 suggests that the specific methods of action implemented by challengers are related to the broad strategy adopted by a movement, prevailing contentious repertoires, and tactical considerations.[4] Contentious repertoires are sets of methods embedded in existing history, culture, and social relations that are known and available to political actors to make collective claims (Tilly 2006; Tilly and Wood 2009). The development of new methods transpire on a small scale as changes occur within limits set by established repertoires in a given time and place (Tilly 2006). Tactical considerations concern strategic thinking about what actions are necessary and appropriate to attain a specific objective. For example, the objectives of building movement solidarity, raising public awareness, or undermining state power imply different methods. Tactical considerations also involve anticipating the effect of an action and the response of opponents and third parties. In some cases, challengers may select methods that are intended to avoid repression. In other cases, challengers may select methods intended to provoke repression if they believe it can be used to increase their leverage (see, e.g., chapter 8). Moreover, when the opponent effectively counters one method, challengers must shift to different methods (McAdam 1983). Other tactical considerations concern selecting the appropriate combination and sequencing of methods, shifting from methods of concentration to methods of dispersion, and engaging in offensive or defensive actions (Schock 2005). Generally, tactical considerations that shape the specific methods implemented by social movements are diverse yet underspecified in the social movement literature.[5]

Figure 10.2 suggests that the outcomes of social movements are a function of the strategies and methods implemented by challengers; the political, cultural, and geographic context; and their interrelation. By successful outcome, I mean favorable changes in policy or structure due, at least in part, to the actions of challengers. In his analysis of fifty-three challenging groups in the United States from 1800 to 1945, Gamson (1975) found that unruly groups—groups that adopted noninstitutional strategies and implemented violent or nonviolent action—were more likely to win new advantages or attain acceptance. In the second edition of *The Strategy of Social Protest*, Gamson (1990, 156) asserts that a common misinterpretation of the results of his study is that they show that violence is an effective strategy. He states, "It is more accurate to interpret the results as 'feistiness works' rather than 'violence works.' Feistiness includes the willingness to break rules and use noninsitutionalized means—to use disruption as a strategy of influence." Others have also emphasized the role of disruption in facilitating social movement success (e.g., Piven and Cloward 1977; McAdam 1983, 1999; Piven 2006). These findings suggest that for groups lacking institutional access in high-capacity democratic regimes, reliance on institutional methods is unlikely to promote a favorable outcome.

However, critics of Gamson suggest that the broader social or political context is more important than strategy in determining movement outcomes (e.g., Goldstone 1980). In an attempt to move beyond the strategy versus context debate, Amenta and colleagues have suggested a political mediation model in which challenger strategies must be matched to the political context to produce favorable results (Amenta, Halfmann, and Young 1999; Amenta, Caren, and Olasky 2005; Amenta 2006). In more favorable political contexts, less assertive methods, such as those that provide evidence of mobilization, may be sufficient to exert influence. In less favorable political contexts, evidence of mobilization is necessary, but more assertive methods, such as strong sanctions that have a direct bearing on elite interests, must also be implemented to exert influence. From a broader comparative perspective, the cultural and geographic context may come to the fore as well as the political context. Methods of resistance that resonate with cultural elements, that are appropriate to the geography (place and space) of an area, and that match the political context are more likely to exert influence.

This study is based on my reading of secondary sources on the two movements as well as on field research. I interviewed activists in both SMOs and was a participant observer in a statewide *padyatra* organized by Ekta Parishad in the Indian state of Orissa in February 2004, and in a local-level *padyatra* in the state of Madhya Pradesh in March 2005. I was also a participant observer in a land occupation organized by the MST in the Brazilian state of São Paulo in April 2004.

For historical context, I provide a brief background on land inequality in Brazil and India. Then I examine the two land struggles in light of the theoretical concepts and relationships discussed above.

Brazil

Land Inequality

The origins of land inequality in Brazil can be traced back to Portuguese colonization, when land was forcibly seized from indigenous peoples. Subsequently, a small handful of families, with the consent of the Portuguese monarchy, governed vast tracts of land in the territory that is now Brazil. To this day, much of the agricultural land in Brazil is owned by a small class of large landowners. An exception to the general pattern of large landholdings was in the southernmost states of Rio Grande do Sul, Santa Catarina, and Paraná, where a family farm tradition resulted from government policies in the nineteenth century that encouraged European immigrants to settle land to preempt claims by Uruguay, Argentina, and Paraguay. Nevertheless, by the 1970s, land inequality and conflict in the south intensified as well. One factor was population pressure, as over a few generations, family farms became too small to subdivide. Another factor was the government's policy of agricultural modernization, which favored large landowners, industrial agriculture, and export crops. The effect has been land alienation, concentration of land ownership, and environmental degradation. As a cumulative result of these factors and more, Brazil has one of the most unequal distributions of land in the world, with more than 50 percent of agricultural land owned by just 4 percent of the landowners (Wright and Wolford 2003).

Regime Type

Ruled by the military from 1964 to 1985, Brazil redemocratized and is now a high-capacity democracy, albeit one with extreme inequality. Brazil never implemented a serious land reform program despite the 1964 Land Statute, which reaffirmed the "effective use" principle whereby private land not being productively used could be legally attained by those who would work the land and make it productive, as well as the 1988 constitution, which provides the state with the responsibility to redistribute unused land. In practice, however, the powerful have been able to increase their concentration of landholdings through manipulating land laws and bureaucratic intransigence, as well as through fraud, intimidation, and violence (Holston 1991; Wright and Wolford 2003).

Given the inordinate power of the landed elite and the biases and corruption of institutional politics, activists realized that they could not depend on institutional means to promote change. A mass movement had to be mobilized that would generate pressure from outside the system in order to put the land issue on the agenda, to raise public awareness, and to pressure the government for land reform.

Ideology of the MST

The MST has developed an eclectic ideology that draws from various strands, most notably Marxism and liberation theology. A Marxist analysis of capitalist exploitation is utilized by the MST to explain the extreme land and income inequalities in Brazil. The MST views its struggle in terms of class conflict between exploited and dispossessed rural workers and large capitalist landowners, as well as, increasingly, international capital. A Marxist analysis explains the connections between capitalism and landlessness, and illustrates the need for political struggle to achieve structural transformation (Branford and Rocha 2002; Harnecker 2003; Wright and Wolford 2003). The term "rural workers" (*trabalhadores rurais*) in their name reflects their Marxist orientation, and the MST draws inspiration from Che Guevara, the Cuban revolution, and the Sandinistas. Nevertheless, while recognizing the heroic struggles of Marxist revolutionaries, the MST rejects the Marxist strategy of taking over the state through violence and becoming a ruling party, realizing that it would be counterproductive to land reform in the current context (Branford and Rocha 2002). That is, because the state is formally democratic and has the legal obligation to redistribute land, the more appropriate method of resistance is to generate pressure on the state rather than to take over the state apparatus.

Although the MST is a secular organization, it also draws from liberation theology to justify its activities and promote mass mobilization. Liberation theology emerged in Latin America in the 1960s in response to social inequalities and the perception that the Catholic Church was not doing enough to address social problems. Religious teachings traditionally focused on the individual and her or his effort to achieve salvation for an afterlife rather than to struggle for justice in the here and now, thus stifling the development of a critical consciousness. Informed by liberation theology, Catholicism was reinterpreted and people were educated to recognize injustice, question authority, and struggle for political rights. Progressive members of the church encouraged people to be agents of change by questioning the root causes of social problems and actively opposing the authority of the traditional oligarchy. As a result, the ideological hegemony of the trinity of priest, soldier, and landowner was challenged (Boff and Boff 1987; Löwy 1996).

While incorporating Marxist analysis to explain injustice, exploitation, and inequality, liberation theology does not imply the use of violent strategies of rebellion. Although liberation theology has motivated insurgents participating in violent rebellion in parts of Latin America (e.g., Lancaster 1989; Wood 2003), promoters of liberation theology in Brazil have largely renounced violence as a method for promoting change and have encouraged the use of nonviolent resistance to address violent repression and structural violence (e.g., Câmara 1971; Assmann 1991).

The networks of the Comissão Pastoral da Terra (Pastoral Commission on Land), of which liberation theology is a key inspiration, were crucial for the formation of the MST during the later stages of the military dictatorship. Members would not have lent their support for a violent land reform movement. Thus, the cultural context (which has a bearing on ideological resonance) and the political context contributed to the adoption of a nonviolent strategy by the MST.

Strategy and Methods of the MST

The strategy of the MST is that of a mass movement. It recognizes that substantial change cannot occur by relying on institutional political channels and therefore mobilizes large numbers of people to engage in protest and civil disobedience. Although not widely recognized as a nonviolent social movement, the MST has used an imaginative array of methods of nonviolent action to promote land reform.[6] The defining method of the MST is the occupation of unproductively used land by the landless. Although land occupations have a long history throughout Latin America (Hobsbawm 1974), the tactic reemerged in Brazil in the late 1970s during the later stages of the military dictatorship.

Independent of each other in different parts of the country, local activists planned and organized land occupations to take over land that was not in productive use. Recognizing the potential power of the method, and realizing that a national social movement would be in a much stronger position to resist repression and confront landowners and the state, activists affiliated with the Comissão Pastoral da Terra began organizing coordinated land occupations. Their efforts led to the founding of the MST in 1984.

In discussing the logic behind the land occupation, one of the MST leaders, João Pedro Stédile (2002, 82), states,

> You have a right to land. There are unused properties in the region. There is only one way to force the government to expropriate them. You think they'll do it if we write them a letter? Asking the mayor is a waste of time, especially if he's a landowner. You could talk to the priest, but if he's not interested, what's the point? We have to organize and take over the land ourselves.

Activists realized the pragmatic fit of the land occupation to the Brazilian context. First, there is a highly favorable ratio of unused agricultural land to people. Second, the Brazilian constitution provides legal justification for redistributing land that is not in productive use. Third, the government lacked the political will to implement land reform in the absence of mass pressure that exposed the contradictions of inequitable land distributions. Those who emerged as leaders of the landless movement realized that land occupations could be a potent method if implemented in an organized, disciplined, and strategic manner.

Before an occupation occurs, the MST identifies land that fulfills two characteristics: first, it is not in productive use and is thus eligible for redistribution under the law, and second, it is potentially productive and suitable for supporting an agricultural village, or *agrovila*. Once land is identified, MST activists locate communities with landless families interested in getting land. Ideally, the mobilization of families is facilitated by an important figure in the community sympathetic to the MST, such as a priest or a union leader. If no such person exists, MST activists go door to door recruiting people to participate in a land occupation.

Meetings are held in churches or schoolrooms where MST activists explain what the movement is about, why they struggle for land, and how land can be attained through occupation. Each person attending the meeting is requested to invite additional people to subsequent meetings, thus increasing participation. Multiple meetings are carried out in a parallel way in different communities. When there is a critical mass of people interested in participating, a regional meeting is held and a date is set for a land occupation.

The location of the land to be occupied is kept secret and is known only to the leaders so as to prevent the authorities or landowners from taking actions to prevent the occupation. Entire families participate and are transported to the site of the occupation in a manner that is not intended to attract the attention of authorities. Busloads of landless families leave in the middle of the night from different places and at staggered times, then converge at the site of the occupation. Basic necessities for living on the land are taken along, such as material for constructing shelter, agricultural tools, cooking equipment, and a supply of nonperishable food staples. Once on the land, they must not depend on outside help because police often set up roadblocks to prevent additional people or supplies from reaching the occupation site. When the sun rises, the MST flag is displayed in prominent places, a *mística* ceremony is held, and the encampment commences.[7]

After the land is occupied, the MST initiates legal proceedings to challenge eviction notices of local authorities and to have the land officially expropriated by the government. If the legal battle is won, then the encampment is transformed into a settlement and the occupiers begin constructing a more permanent community. If not, then planning and preparation for a new land occupation commences (Branford and Rocha 2002).

The MST realizes that its comparative advantage lies with nonviolent rather than armed resistance. Given that landowners and the state hold an enormous advantage with regard to the means of violence, it would be impractical for the movement to challenge or retaliate with violence. Thus, the MST engages in strategic actions to deter violence from being used against them and to prevent violence from escalating when it does occur. First, realizing that their strength is in numbers, the MST engages in land occupations with as many families as possible relative to the size of the land to be occupied. Land occupations that occur with a smaller number of families are more likely to be met with violence. Second, during direct confrontations, women and children often take up positions on the front lines to decrease the likelihood that violence will be used against them (Wright and Wolford 2003). Third, when evicted from land that they have occupied by the police, military, or *jagunços* (hired thugs), the movement's policy is to retreat and organize another land occupation rather than to retaliate with violence.[8] Fourth, because MST occupations are highly organized and led by experienced activists, there are fewer deaths due to landowner or police violence relative to land occupations and settlements undertaken by less organized movements (Wright and Wolford 2003). Fifth, the movement has a decentralized collective leadership structure that deters assassinations. By contrast, the heads of hierarchically structured farmers unions provide easy targets for landowners or the police (Stédile 2002). Sixth, from its local origins in the south, the movement developed into a national movement. Scale shift resulted as the MST sent activists throughout the country to organize the landless and carry out land occupations.[9] Localized and isolated movements are much less likely to remain resilient in the face of repression than are movements that operate on a national basis. The power discrepancy between landowners and the landless has diminished as the MST has territorialized (Fernandes 2005).

When violence is used against their members, the MST attempts to promote "backfire."[10] For example, in 1996, 1,500 MST activists were blocking a road while on a protest march near Eldorado dos Carajás in the state of Pará. On April 17, the police opened fire with automatic weapons, killing nineteen people and seriously injuring sixty-four. News reporters caught some of the massacre on videotape, and when it was broadcast on television, it generated public outrage against the police and large landowners; it also generated support for the MST.[11] The MST annually commemorates the massacre, and memorials have been constructed to remember those who lost their lives in the struggle. The international landless and peasant organization, Via Campesina, has designated April 17 as International Peasant Struggle Day, and people from around the world commemorate the nineteen unarmed MST activists who were killed.

Social movements are also more likely to remain resilient and therefore promote change when a range of diverse methods are implemented (McAdam 1983; Schock 2005). In this regard, the MST supplements land occupations with a variety of other nonviolent actions. For example, a number of long marches have been organized, such as the National March for Land Reform in May 2005, in which 13,000 landless people marched 230 kilometers from Goiânia to Brasilia to put pressure on the government for land reform.[12] It has also organized sit-ins inside or outside of the buildings of INCRA (Instituto Nacional de Colonização e Reforma Agrária), the government ministry responsible for determining whether the land occupied by the MST is eligible for redistribution. The MST also engages in symbolic occupations of land used by transnational corporations to grow genetically modified organisms to draw attention to the issue.

Outcome

Through the strategic use of land occupations, encampments, and the formation of *agrovilas* on occupied land, the MST has succeeded in putting the issue of land reform on the national agenda, redistributing land, and leading the struggle against corporate agriculture and for food sovereignty.[13] Since 1984, the MST has carried out over 230,000 land occupations (Wright and Wolford 2003) and forced the government to redistribute 20 million acres of agricultural land to 350,000 families (Wright and Wolford 2003). One hundred thousand more families are distributed in 500 temporary roadside encampments, waiting to participate in land occupations (Harnecker 2003).

India

Land Inequality

Current patterns of land inequality in India are related to the persistence of a historically feudal-style caste system of social stratification. When the British colonized India, they used the traditional Zamindari system to facilitate the collection of taxes from peasants.[14] After independence in 1947, the Indian government abolished the Zamindari system, and individual states passed land ceiling acts to limit the amount of land that individuals could own. Nevertheless, severe inequalities in the distribution of land remained as powerful landowners used the bureaucracy as well as cunning or force to maintain or increase their landholdings. Substantial portions of the rural population are landless Dalits.[15] Some Dalits have small plots of land that they have cultivated for years or even generations. Because many lack an official land title, however, they are subject to having their land confiscated at any time.

Adopting a developmentalist paradigm, the Indian government, with the support of the World Bank, built large dams to facilitate industrial agriculture. The result was environmental degradation and the displacement of people, often without adequate compensation. Moreover, since the early 1990s, India has adopted neoliberal economic policies that have opened the countryside to the penetration of transnational agribusinesses, pressuring states to eliminate land ceilings to facilitate the production of monoculture export commodities such as cotton or rice.

Landlessness has also intensified in India as a result of deforestation. Adivasis are increasingly alienated from forestland as a result of timber and mining operations and the encroachment of intensive agriculture.[16] Typically, people are not adequately compensated, if compensated at all, when displaced from forestland. As a cumulative result of these processes and more, the highest levels of poverty in India are in rural areas among landless Dalits and Adivasis (Sundaram and Tendulkar 2003).

Regime Type

India is a high-capacity democracy, although one with extreme poverty and sharp divisions between caste, class, religion, and linguistic region. The Indian constitution proclaims commitment to an egalitarian social order, and the government has in principle shown concern for land inequality. In practice, however, legal and administrative measures to promote land redistribution or prevent land alienation have not been effective. In the state of Madhya Pradesh, for example, Adivasis have been forced off their land despite the Madhya Pradesh Land Revenue Code of 1959 that banned the transfer of land from Adivasis to non-Adivasis without the permission of the government and despite a more stringent 1976 code that banned all such transfers. Moreover, the Madhya Pradesh Land Ceiling Act, which limits the amount of land an individual can hold, has not been adequately enforced (Ramagundam 2001). As in Brazil, systematic biases in institutional politics, along with corruption and violence, have been used to promote the interests of more powerful groups. In this context, Ekta Parishad emerged to struggle for the rights of small farmers and the landless.

Ideology of Ekta Parishad

Ekta Parishad draws explicitly from the ideas and philosophy of Mohandas K. Gandhi. Its name, "Unity Forum," reflects its Gandhian roots. Gandhi's conception of society rejected both state capitalism and state socialism, instead favoring a decentralized network of self-reliant and self-governing communities that used property held in trust.

Central to the work of Ekta Parishad are the Gandhian concepts of *swadeshi* and *sarvodaya*. Gandhi used the term *swadeshi* ("self-sufficiency") to refer to a way of life based on economic self-reliance, local production, and the meeting of basic human needs (Hardiman 2003). It captures Gandhi's critique that Western capitalist modernization was fundamentally flawed because it encouraged individual greed and led to extreme inequality. Gandhi used the term *sarvodaya* ("welfare of all") to refer to the uplifting of the poorest sectors of society and the leveling of extreme inequalities. The Gandhian idea of people-centered development rejects competition and private property, and embraces local production and self-sufficiency (Bondurant 1988; Das 1979; Vettickal 2002).

In the postindependence era, the Indian state distorted and co-opted Gandhism. The government claims to be the successor of the freedom struggle, holds up Gandhi as the father of the nation, and symbolically appropriates the prestige associated with Gandhi's name (Guha 2000). Nevertheless, inherent in Gandhism is a revolutionary content that, if properly framed, could address land inequality and contribute to the transformation of capitalist land use relations (Ramagundam 2001). Similar to how liberation theology has sought to revitalize the revolutionary ideas of early Christianity that promoted social justice, Ekta Parishad attempts to revitalize the original spirit of the revolutionary Gandhi. The founding convener of Ekta Parishad, Rajagopal Puthan Veetil, states,

> There is a need to redefine Gandhi or more correctly understand Gandhi and his philosophy with honesty. [In] post-independence India state appropriation of Gandhi has transformed the experimenter from a rebel to a meek seeker of spirituality. It has been fatal for his legacy. His thoughts have been mauled and reproduced to suit the state agenda. Any radical redefinition of Gandhi therefore is seen as un-Gandhian [by the state]. (quoted in Ramagundam 2001, 40)

The impetus driving the organization of Ekta Parishad was the realization that isolated rural struggles are more prone to repression, whereas a state- and national-level presence would empower and protect marginalized rural people. Ekta Parishad emerged in the early 1990s to broker connections between previously unconnected Gandhian organizations dealing with rural development issues.[17] By doing so, it forged a network through which their power could be magnified.

Strategy and Methods of Ekta Parishad

The strategy of Ekta Parishad is that of a mass movement. In other words, it recognizes that substantial change cannot occur by relying on institutional political channels. Therefore, it mobilizes large numbers of people to engage in militant protest and civil disobedience to pressure the government to address land-related problems.

The mechanism through which Gandhian ideology is translated into action is *satyagraha* ("the power of truth"). *Satyagraha* prescribes nonviolent action in which people refuse to cooperate with laws and social relations perceived to be unjust and willingly suffer the consequences of noncooperation. Along with noncooperation, *satyagraha* involves constructive programs such as building noncoercive, just, decentralized, and democratic social relations that are autonomous from oppressive state or economic forces. For example, to promote *swadeshi*, Gandhi organized boycotts of British manufactured cloth and the spinning of khadi. To promote *sarvodaya*, constructive programs were implemented by Gandhi to improve the lives of women, Dalits, and Adivasis, and to promote communal harmony.

A main method used by Ekta Parishad in its *satyagraha* campaigns for land reform is the *padyatra*. A *padyatra* is an extended foot march that may last from days to many months. It draws on the cultural tradition of Hindu spiritual pilgrimages and is used to mobilize the masses to generate pressure against the opponent. Perhaps the best-known *padyatra* was Gandhi's Salt March in 1930, a twenty-four-day march to the Arabian Sea where he stopped in villages to give talks, rally support, and encourage village officials to resign from their positions in the British administration. The Salt March was part of a broader campaign of civil disobedience that not only challenged the British salt laws, but also promoted the mobilization of people into the non-violent resistance movement against British imperialism (Weber 1997). Since its founding in 1990, Ekta Parishad has organized dozens of small-scale *padyatras*. Since 1999, Ekta Parishad has undertaken seven major statewide *padyatras*, and in 2007 it organized a major *padyatra* campaign referred to as Janadesh ("People's Verdict") that mobilized 25,000 landless people and supporters in a 350-kilometer march from Gwalior, Madhya Pradesh, to New Delhi, as I discuss below.

The *padyatra* is well suited to the Indian context. Culturally, it is a well-recognized repertoire rooted in Hinduism and the Gandhian tradition. Geographically, it is a useful method for providing a means for communicating among people in rural areas where the network of roads and electricity is sparse. The *padyatra* has been effective in mobilizing support in isolated rural villages and establishing connections between villages.

Similar to the use of the land occupation by the MST, Ekta Parishad has utilized the *padyatra* in a highly organized, disciplined, and strategic manner that requires substantial planning and preparation. Ekta Parishad activists based in the countryside make logistical arrangements concerning the route of the *padyatra*, and feed and accommodate the marchers. On the eve of the campaign, a "Declaration of a Satyagraha" is released that declares the intent and purpose of the *padyatra*. The declaration states the problems that exist concerning land issues such as land inequality, land alienation, violence against small farmers and the landless, and lack of rural development. The declaration states that repeated appeals concerning land rights to government officials have failed to bring any action, and there is therefore a need for large-scale mobilization and civil disobedience that the government cannot ignore.

Each statewide *padyatra* focuses on land-related problems in that particular state and begins with a mass rally in a major city that mobilizes thousands of people. At the rally, speeches are made by Ekta Parishad activists and movement sympathizers. After the rally, the *padyatra* commences with a core of activists and supporters traveling throughout the countryside from village to village by foot and jeep. A public hearing is held in each village where the activists stop. Ekta Parishad activists write up petitions based on the grievances aired by the villagers. The petitions are collected, and Ekta Parishad keeps records of the grievances expressed in each village. By the end of the *padyatra,* thousands of petitions are collected and submitted to the appropriate officials. Moreover, Ekta Parishad activists prepare a case study for each village visited during the course of the *padyatra,* documenting and summarizing the problems with regard to the distribution of land, land alienation, lack of infrastructure, corruption, and violence.

During the *padyatras,* press releases are written, and the media is encouraged to cover the events. Sometimes *padyatras* involve acts of civil disobedience, such as blocking highways with a march or holding sit-ins at government buildings. The *padyatra* ends in the same way that it begins: with a mass rally in a city. Depending on the length, the *padyatra* will pass through hundreds of villages. The first and longest statewide *padyatra,* the six-month-long Madhya Pradesh *padyatra* in 1999–2000, for example, passed through approximately 1,500 villages.

As a Gandhian organization, Ekta Parishad adopts the strategy of nonviolent resistance as a matter of principle. Nevertheless, it is strategic in its use of specific methods of nonviolent action. Ekta Parishad attempts to prevent the escalation of violence by avoiding violent confrontations with the police or *gundhas* (thugs) hired by landowners or corporations to facilitate the process of land alienation. Like the MST, Ekta Parishad realizes that its comparative advantage is with nonviolent resistance, and it prefers to deal with its opponents on its own terms, not the terms set by its opponents.

Moreover, when violence is used against activists, Ekta Parishad attempts to publicize the events to promote backfire. For example, in 2001, an Adivasi Ekta Parishad activist in Chhattisgarh was murdered by forest department officials engaged in evicting Adivasis from forestland. In an effort to educate the public, a booklet was produced documenting the violence. The booklet, *Truth Force: The Land Rights Movement in India,* was published in 2003 by the English NGO Action Village India in association with Ekta Parishad (Drakakis 2003). It has been translated and published in German and Portuguese and distributed in India, Europe, and Brazil. The booklet has served to educate people about Ekta Parishad and promote outrage against violence in rural India.

Ekta Parishad also implements a wide range of methods besides *padyatras* such as sit-in fasts (*dharnas*) at the offices of government officials. It has organized land occupations although the tactic has not been used nearly as systematically or extensively as in Brazil. The tactic is less suited to the Indian context for a variety of reasons, including the following: (1) more than in other cultures, in Indian culture, land provides a spiritual and cultural rooting and identity and is not perceived merely as a means of production; therefore, people find it difficult to occupy land in which they have no bond; (2)

as a result of population pressure and the way in which land has been divided, there are no large tracts of unused land in India, as there are in Brazil; (3) under the Indian law of eminent domain, the state claims ownership of all land not under private ownership, and hence the scope of unoccupied land is extremely limited; (4) to a greater degree than in rural Brazil, the landlord and the government official are often the same person in rural India; and (5) instances of successful land occupations in which occupiers become legal owners of the land are rare, dissuading others from taking the risky step (Pimple and Sethi 2005). Although effective in the Brazilian context, the land occupation has failed in other contexts where the strategy was not sufficiently matched with the context (Baletti, Johnson, and Wolford 2008).

The *padyatra*, on the other hand, is well suited to the Indian political, cultural, and geographic context. It draws on Hindu culture and the legacy of Gandhi. It is useful for mobilizing and connecting isolated rural villagers. It is effective in raising public awareness about land alienation and rural violence. In a context where land occupations are not feasible and direct confrontations with landowners are less productive, *padyatra* campaigns have succeeded in mobilizing large numbers of people, educating the public, and forcing the government to address the land problem.

Outcomes

Since 1999, Ekta Parishad has organized seven major statewide *padyatras*. In addition, in October 2007, Ekta Parishad organized the Janadesh campaign that involved a 350-kilometer march from Madhya Pradesh to New Delhi by 25,000 landless people and supporters. Each *padyatra* has had some level of success. The Madhya Pradesh *padyatra* in 1999–2000, for example, resulted in the distribution of over 150,000 land plots to landless people. Land titles were given to small farmers, and the eviction of tribal people from the forests was halted. Moreover, a statewide task force was organized to examine the problem of landlessness and to suggest mechanisms to redress the issue (Ramagundam 2001). Nevertheless, such task forces only represent a first stage in addressing land issues and the effectiveness of such entities is a function of continued vigilance and pressure by grassroots organizations.

The Janadesh *satyagraha* in 2007 was one of the largest Gandhian mass mobilizations since the struggle for national liberation against British imperialism. From October 2 to October 28, 2007, approximately 25,000 landless people—mostly Dalits and Adivasis, along with their supporters—marched 350 kilometers along the national highway from Gwalior, Madhya Pradesh, to New Delhi. Political rallies and press conferences were held along the way to publicize the event and the issues for which the landless were marching.

The campaign received national and international media attention. The purpose of the *padyatra* was to mobilize public awareness about land alienation and rural violence and to put pressure on the government to implement land reform.

Upon reaching New Delhi, the landless people set up an encampment at a fairground. Ekta Parishad then threatened to march to the parliament building and engage in a *dharna* for an indefinite period unless the government agreed to their demands for a new land reform policy. As a result of the pressure, the government accepted the demands of the Janadesh and agreed to organize a National Land Reform Committee headed by the Rural Development Minister, with 50 percent of its members selected by grassroots organizations. The committee is responsible for drawing up a new national land policy and is empowered to direct state governments to enact appropriate land reform legislation. It is too early to know what concrete reforms will be implemented. At a minimum, the Janadesh succeeded in raising the public's awareness about land-related problems and conflicts, forced the government to publicly acknowledge the legitimacy of the issues and concerns of the landless, and put land reform on the national agenda (Weedon et al. 2007).

Conclusions

Strategy is related to the political context and the ideology adopted by social movements. In high-capacity democracies like Brazil and India, violence is unlikely to promote change, given the state's overall legitimacy and capacity for repression. Movements embracing ideologies that promote violence are unlikely to succeed in these contexts. Although such challenges are able to operate in geographically remote and isolated areas (as do the Naxalites in India), they are unlikely to mobilize broad-based support in such contexts.

Nevertheless, while high-capacity democracies work reasonably well for elites and their middle-class supporters, groups excluded from political influence must turn to noninstitutional and disruptive methods to promote meaningful change in policy or structure (Gamson 1990; McAdam 1999; Piven and Cloward 1977). The MST and Ekta Parishad use institutional political and legal channels, but they realize that relying solely on these channels is futile for promoting substantive change. They understand that mass mobilization, disruption, and disciplined unarmed unruliness are necessary to make democracy work for marginalized people.

The selection of specific methods of protest is shaped by contentious repertoires (i.e., the set of methods known and available in a given context) and by tactical considerations (i.e., projections about the effects of implementing actions and the responses of opponents or third parties). Traction is more likely when the selection of specific methods of protest is appropriately matched to the political, cultural, and geographic context. The land occupation became a potent method for the MST because it was infused with *mística* (which adapted liberation theology to the struggle of the landless) and because it took advantage of the relatively high ratio of large tracts of unused agricultural land relative to the landless population. The *padyatra* as applied by Ekta Parishad has been effective because it draws from Gandhi's tradition, which is widely respected, and because it facilitates the mobilization and connection of small farmers and landless rural workers throughout the remote Indian countryside.

The MST and Ekta Parishad have been successful in promoting land rights because they have mobilized large numbers of people, remained resilient in the face of repression, and cultivated support beyond their constituencies. Mobilizing relatively large numbers of committed people is probably necessary to winning new collective benefits for those underrepresented in politics (Amenta et al. 2005). Land occupations and *padyatra* campaigns have provided the means for large numbers of people to actively pursue their interests while promoting solidarity and empowerment.

Moreover, both movements increased mobilization across geographic space through the process of territorialization (Fernandes 2005) or scale shift (Tarrow and McAdam 2005). From their local and regional origins, they overcame isolation thus increasing their capacity to remain resilient in the face of elite and government repression. Beyond merely surviving repression, both movements have, on occasion, been able to use it to their advantage while simultaneously undermining the power of opponents. In particular, through backfire, public support was mobilized for the challengers while government legitimacy was undermined.

Compared to violent movements, nonviolent resistance movements are more likely to mobilize broad-based support, gain influential allies, and limit social polarization (Martin 2006). Activists realize that given the contexts they face, their comparative advantage lies with the strategy of mass-based nonviolent, rather than violent, resistance. Both the MST and Ekta Parishad have cultivated the support of third parties and of the general public that they would not have been able to do if they engaged in violent resistance.

Conflict over the distribution of land is one of the most highly charged issues in the Global South. Historically, such conflicts have often been characterized by extreme violence and social polarization. Movements such at the MST and Ekta Parishad are significant because their strategic innovations have illustrated the possibilities of addressing an acute social problem through strategic nonviolent conflict. Through nonviolent resistance, the movements, although still a target of violence, have contributed to the attenuation of vicious cycles of violence and polarization in addition to promoting land reform. They have also illustrated the importance of appropriately matching strategy and methods to context—a lesson that activists in other places would do well to heed.

Notes

Earlier versions were presented at the biennial meetings of the International Peace Research Association in Sopron, Hungary on July 7, 2004, and the Collective Behavior and Social Movements workshop at Hofstra University, Hempstead, New York, on August 10, 2007. Thanks go to participants in those meetings who provided insightful comments and criticisms. In particular, I thank Greg Maney, Holly McCammon, David Meyer, and Deana Rohlinger. This research was partially funded by a grant from the United States Institute of Peace. The opinions, findings, and conclusions expressed in this publication are those of the author and do not necessarily reflect the views of the United States Institute of Peace.

1. By nonviolent resistance, I mean the implementation of political actions outside of institutional political and legal channels that may be unruly or disruptive, but that do not involve violence or the threat of violence against opponents.

2. The organization was officially founded in 1984 and adopted its current name, Movimento dos Trabalhadores Rurais sem Terra (MST), in 1985.

3. These models are simplified because they do not address identity or emotion and they assume that challengers are organized, have framed issues, and have mobilized resources.

4. Methods refer to specific actions such as a sit-in (nonviolent action), an armed attack (violent action), or a lawsuit (institutional action).

5. With some notable exceptions (e.g., McAdam 1983, 1999), the social movement literature has focused on the components of the model in figure 10.1 other than tactical considerations. Because tactical considerations are a central focus of the literature on strategic nonviolent conflict, a synthesis of the two would prove useful (Schock 2005).

6. For an exception, see Chabot and Vinthagen (2007).

7. *Mística* is the representation the struggle through words, art, symbolism, and music. It also refers to a more a more abstract emotional element of empowerment and solidarity. The origins of *mística* are found in liberation theology (Issa 2007).

8. Nevertheless, the defensive use of violence has occurred on some occasions.

9. Scale shift refers to a change in the number and level of coordinated contentious actions leading to broader contention involving a wider range of actors and bridging their claims and identities (Tarrow and McAdam 2005).

10. According to Hess and Martin (2006), *backfire* refers to a public reaction of outrage to an event that is publicized and perceived as unjust. See also Martin (2007).

11. See Chabot and Vinthagan (2007) for a discussion of the killings in Eldorado dos Carajás as a transformative event in the history of the MST.

12. Interestingly, MST activists cite Gandhi's Salt March along with Mao's Long March as inspirations for their extended protest marches (Stédile and Fernandes 1999).

13. According to Via Campesina, food sovereignty refers to the rejection of food and land as mere commodities to be bought and sold on the market; access to land and resources as a human right; the prioritizing of local agricultural production to feed the country's people rather than to supply products to the international market; and socially just, environmentally sound agricultural production.

14. In the Zamindari system, a Zamindar ruled over an area of land and was responsible for maintaining social order and collecting taxes for the state from those who worked the land.

15. Dalits, or Atishudras, are those at the bottom of the traditional Indian caste system. Formerly known as Untouchables, their official government classification is "Scheduled Castes." Dalits constitute the largest category of landless in India.

16. Adivasis are indigenous forest-dwelling people also referred to as "tribal people" or "tribals." The official government classification is "Scheduled Tribes."

17. According to Tarrow and McAdam (2005), brokerage refers to the transfer of information through movement actors that link two or more previously unconnected social sites.

References

Amenta, Edwin. 2006. *When Movements Matter: The Townsend Plan and the Rise of Social Security.* Princeton, N.J.: Princeton University Press.

Amenta, Edwin, Neal Caren, and Sheera Joy Olasky. 2005. "Age for Leisure? Political Mediation and the Impact of the Pension Movement on U.S. Old-Age Policy." *American Sociological Review* 70:516–38.

Amenta, Edwin, Drew Halfmann, and Michael P. Young. 1999. "The Strategies and Contexts of Social Protest: Political Mediation and the Impact of the Townsend Movement in California." *Mobilization* 4:1–24.

Assmann, Hugo. 1991. "The Strange Imputation of Violence to Liberation Theology." *Terrorism and Political Violence* 3:80–99.

Baletti, Brenda, Tamara M. Johnson, and Wendy Wolford. 2008. "'Late Mobilization': Transnational Peasant Networks and Grassroots Organizing in Brazil and South Africa." *Journal of Agrarian Change* 8:290–314.

Boff, Leonardo, and Clodovis Boff. 1987. *Introducing Liberation Theology.* Markynoll, N.Y.: Orbis Books.

Bondurant, Joan. 1988. *Conquest of Violence: The Gandhian Philosophy of Conflict.* Rev. ed. Princeton, N.J.: Princeton University Press.

Branford, Sue, and Jan Rocha. 2002. *Cutting the Wire: The Story of the Landless Movement in Brazil.* London: Latin American Bureau.

Câmara, Hélder. 1971. *Spiral of Violence.* London: Sheed and Ward.

Chabot, Sean, and Stellan Vinthagen. 2007. "Rethinking Nonviolent Action and Contentious Politics: Political Cultures of Nonviolent Opposition in the Indian Independence Movement and Brazil's Landless Workers Movement." *Research in Social Movements, Conflicts and Change* 27:91–121.

Das, Amritananda. 1979. *Foundations of Gandhian Economics.* New York: St. Martin's Press.

Drakakis, Helena. 2003. *Truth Force: The Land Rights Movement in India.* London: Action Village India.

Fernandes, Bernardo Mançano. 2005. "The Occupation as a Form of Access to Land in Brazil: A Theoretical and Methodological Contribution." In *Reclaiming the Land: The Resurgence of Rural Movements in Africa, Asia, and Latin America,* edited by Sam Moyo and Paris Yeros, 317–40. London: Zed Books.

Gamson, William A. 1975. *The Strategy of Social Protest.* Homewood, Ill.: Dorsey Press.

———. 1990. *The Strategy of Social Protest.* 2nd ed. Belmont, Calif.: Wadsworth.

Goldstone, Jack A. 1980. "The Weakness of Organization." *American Journal of Sociology* 85:1017–42.

Guha, Ramachandra. 2000. *The Unquiet Woods: Ecological Change and Peasant Resistance in the Himalaya.* Berkeley: University of California Press.

Hardiman, David. 2003. *Gandhi in His Time and Ours: The Global Legacy of His Ideas.* New York: Columbia University Press.

Harnecker, Marta. 2003. *Landless People: Building a Social Movement.* São Paulo: Editora Espressão Popular.

Hess, David, and Brian Martin. 2006. "Repression, Backfire, and the Theory of Transformative Events." *Mobilization* 11:249–67.

Hobsbawm, Eric J. 1974. "Peasant Land Occupations." *Past and Present* 62:120–52.

Holston, James. 1991. "The Misrule of Law: Land and Usurpation in Brazil." *Comparative Studies in Society and History* 4:695–725.

Issa, Daniela. 2007. "Praxis of Empowerment: *Mística* and Mobilization in Brazil's Landless Rural Workers' Movement." *Latin American Perspectives* 34:124–38.

Jenkins, J. Craig. 1982. "Why Do Peasants Rebel: Structural and Historical Theories of Peasant Rebellion." *American Journal of Sociology* 88:487–514.

Lancaster, Roger N. 1989. *Thanks to God and the Revolution: Popular Religion and Class Consciousness in the New Nicaragua.* New York: Columbia University Press.

Lichbach, Mark Irving. 1994. "What Makes Rational Peasants Revolutionary?" *World Politics* 46:383–418.

Löwy, Michel. 1996. *The War of the Gods: Religion and Politics in Latin America*. London: Verso.

Martin, Brian. 2006. "Paths to Social Change: Conventional Politics, Violence and Nonviolence." In *Nonviolent Alternatives for Social Change*, edited by Ralph V. Summy, 156–82. Oxford: Eolss Publishers.

———. 2007. *Justice Ignited: The Dynamics of Backfire*. Lanham, Md.: Rowman & Littlefield.

Mason, T. David. 2004. *Caught in the Crossfire: Revolutions, Repression, and the Rational Peasant*. Lanham, Md.: Rowman & Littlefield.

McAdam, Doug. 1983. "Tactical Innovation and the Pace of Insurgency." *American Sociological Review* 48:735–54.

———. 1999. *Political Process and the Development of Black Insurgency, 1930–1970*. 2nd ed. Chicago: University of Chicago Press.

McClintock, Cynthia. 1984. "Why Peasants Rebel: The Case of Peru's Sendero Luminoso." *World Politics* 37:48–84.

Migdal, Joel S. 1974. *Peasants, Politics and Revolution: Pressure toward Political and Social Change in the Third World*. Princeton, N.J.: Princeton University Press.

Paige, Jeffery M. 1975. *Agrarian Revolution: Social Movements and Export Agriculture in the Underdeveloped World*. New York: The Free Press.

Pimple, Minar, and Manpreet Sethi. 2005. "Occupation of Land in India: Experiences and Challenges." In *Reclaiming the Land: The Resurgence of Rural Movements in Africa, Asia, and Latin America*, edited by Sam Moyo and Paris Yeros, 235–56. London: Zed Books.

Piven, Frances Fox. 2006. *Challenging Authority: How Ordinary People Change America*. Lanham, Md.: Rowman & Littlefield.

Piven, Frances Fox, and Richard A. Cloward. 1977. *Poor People's Movements: Why They Succeed, How They Fail*. New York: Pantheon Books.

Popkin, Samuel. 1976. *The Rational Peasant: The Political Economy of Rural Society in Vietnam*. Berkeley: University of California Press.

Ramagundam, Rahul. 2001. *Defeated Innocence: Adivasi Assertion, Land Rights and the Ekta Parishad Movement*. New Delhi: Grassroots India Publishers.

Schock, Kurt. 2005. *Unarmed Insurrections: People Power Movements in Nondemocracies*. Minneapolis: University of Minnesota Press.

Scott, James C. 1976. *The Moral Economy of the Peasant: Rebellion and Subsistence in Southeast Asia*. New Haven, Conn.: Yale University Press.

Skocpol, Theda. 1982. "What Makes Peasants Revolutionary?" *Comparative Politics* 14:351–75.

Snow, David. 2004. "Framing Processes, Ideology, and Discursive Fields." In *The Blackwell Companion to Social Movements*, edited by David A. Snow, Sarah A. Soule, and Hanspeter Kriesi, 380–412. Oxford: Blackwell.

Stédile, João Pedro. 2002. "Landless Battalions: The Sem Terra Movement of Brazil." *New Left Review* 15:77–104.

Stédile, João Pedro, and Bernardo Mançano Fernandes. 1999. *Brava Gente: A Trajetória do MST e a Luta pela Terra no Brasil.* São Paulo: Fundação Perseu Abramo.

Sundaram, K., and Suresh D. Tendulkar. 2003. "Poverty among Social and Economic Groups in India in the Nineteen Nineties." Working Paper 118, Centre for Development Economics. New Delhi: Delhi School of Economics.

Tarrow, Sidney, and Doug McAdam. 2005. "Scale Shift in Transnational Contention." In *Transnational Protest and Global Activism,* edited by Donatella della Porta and Sidney Tarrow, 121–47. Lanham, Md.: Rowman & Littlefield.

Tilly, Charles. 2006. *Regimes and Repertoires.* Chicago: University of Chicago Press.

Tilly, Charles, and Lesley J. Wood. 2009. *Social Movements, 1768–2008.* 2nd ed. Boulder, Colo.: Paradigm.

Vettickal, Thomas. 2002. *Gandhian Sarvodaya: Realizing a Realistic Utopia.* New Delhi: Gyan Publishing House.

Weber, Thomas. 1997. *On the Salt March: A Historiography of Gandhi's March to Dandi.* New Delhi: Harper Collins.

Weedon, Jonathan, Ciaran M. Casey, Anaïs Hammel, Samuel L'Orphelin, Lisa Thacker, and Shannon Moran. 2007. *Janadesh Newsletter,* October 31.

Wolf, Eric R. 1969. *Peasant Wars of the Twentieth Century.* New York: Harper and Row.

Wood, Elisabeth Jean. 2003. *Insurgent Collective Action and Civil War in El Salvador.* Cambridge: Cambridge University Press.

Wright, Angus, and Wendy Wolford. 2003. *To Inherit the Earth: The Landless Movement and the Struggle for a New Brazil.* Oakland, Calif.: Food First Books.

11

Similar Strategies, Different Outcomes: Institutional Histories of the Christian Right of Canada and of the United States

Tina Fetner and Carrie Sanders

In the United States, the Christian right has been at the center of the national political scene since the 1990s. Having consolidated a massive voting bloc of socially conservative Christians and influenced the Republican Party at the state and federal levels, this movement has grown substantially since its roots in the 1980s Moral Majority movement (e.g., Oldfield 1996; Berlet and Lyons 2000; Fetner 2008). In terms of policy results, the U.S. Christian right has chipped away at access to legal abortions, limited adoption and foster care by same-sex couples or even uncoupled gay men and lesbians, and secured funding for abstinence-only sex education. The Christian right in the United States has also successfully entered party politics, forming strong ties with the Republican Party.

Canada and the United States are similar nations, socially and politically. They are strong allies with tightly linked economies. Canada also has a Christian right movement, but this movement has not been as successful in Canada as it has in the United States. In recent decades, and especially since the adoption of the Canadian Charter of Rights and Freedoms, both court decisions and laws implemented at the provincial and federal levels have more or less consistently moved in the direction of granting equal rights to lesbians and gay men, securing abortion rights, and guaranteeing equal rights for women (Bailey 2004; Miall and March 2005; Smith 2007). There is also a set of gay-inclusive immigration policies in place. In Canada, gay men and lesbians serve openly in the military, and criminal statutes against sodomy have been banned since 1969 (Dawson 1993; Smith 2005). Although Canadians recently elected a Conservative-led government, this nation's policies have not become significantly more socially conservative in recent years. Notably, Canada has moved in the opposite direction, passing legislature that is strongly opposed by the Christian right, such as in legally recognizing same-sex marriages—a policy that was implemented nationwide in 2005. Although access to abortion is often difficult for women who live in rural areas and especially in the Atlantic provinces, abortion is legal and in large part paid for by Canada's universal health care system. Further, United States and Canada differ in terms of political access: in Canada, Christian right political parties do not garner sufficient support to gain a foothold in the parliament. Although it claims to support many Christian right positions, the Conservative Party has avoided putting these socially conservative policies on the table.

Although the Christian right movements in the United States and Canada have used the same strategies, they have not produced the same results. U.S. and Canadian activists use the same rhetorical strategies and make similar claims (Smith 2007). They have similar collective identities, and the success of the U.S. movement has not been lost on its Canadian counterpart. The Christian right movements in the United States and Canada are closely tied both in terms of organizational connections and social movement goals. They also use similar strategies for social and political change. Both movements combine connections with political insiders and grassroots mobilization. Both movements deploy an evangelical Christian identity to encourage political participation by members of constituent churches. Each of these movements target sexualities issues and hold up an idealized traditional family form against which transgressors are negatively judged. In each country, these movements rely on the same frames to communicate their political claims. For example, Christian right activists in both countries are opposed to the legal recognition of same-sex marriages. In both cases, they frame their argument in terms of protecting the sanctity of traditional marriage. In addition, movements in both countries have built similar organizations, with many organizational connections bridging the U.S.–Canada border.

How is it that similar movements in two neighboring counties have used similar strategies in their activism and yet have seen quite different results? To explain this gap in movement outcomes, some scholars have argued that the higher religiosity of people living in the United States, relative to Canada, can explain the broader base of support for the U.S. Christian right (Bibby 2004). Others argue that it is not differences between the people living in Canada and the United States, but differences in political institutions that explain this divergence. For example, political scientist Miriam Smith (2005) argues that Canadian political institutions are more resistant to the sorts of policy change advocated by the Christian right than U.S. political institutions.

Although each of these arguments offers critical insights, they do not pay sufficient attention to institutional differences between the Christian right movements in the United States and Canada. Not only are audiences and political institutions less receptive to the Christian right in Canada, but the movement itself is weaker there, with fewer institutional supports than in the United States.

Miriam Smith (2005) offers an explanation centered on the political structures of Canada and the United States. She argues that U.S. and Canadian political institutions have proven more accessible to the Christian right in the United States than in Canada. She focuses on two institutions in particular, the courts and the party system, as well as the interactions between these two. Smith argues that the parliamentary system in Canada creates party alignments that are much stronger than in the United States and much more impervious to the sort of stronghold takeover of the Republican Party effected by Pat Robertson's organization, Freedom Council (a predecessor to the Christian Coalition), in the 1980s.[1] Documenting the court challenges both before and after the adoption of the Canadian Charter of Rights and Freedoms in 1982, Smith (2008) claims that the charter has been a better guarantor of LGBT rights than the U.S. Constitution.

Although we agree that religiosity and political systems differ between Canada and the United States, we argue that there is more to the story of why the Christian right has seen so much less success in Canada than in the United States. We focus on the different paths that evangelical Christian communities took in these two nations. U.S. evangelicals created a broad network of institutions apart from Protestant denominations as well as the secular sphere. Canadian evangelicals remained more closely tied to existing religious institutions. As a result, there are profound differences in the institutional infrastructures available to each of these social movements—that is, the organizations, constituents, networks, and communications channels that connect activists. We argue that although these disparities in institutional strength have not prevented the weaker Canadian Christian right movement from enacting the same strategies as its counterpart in the United States, it has mitigated the effectiveness of these strategies, making for much less political pressure on the Canadian system.

We consider the institutional bases of these movements as an important structural difference that affects the outcomes of activists' strategic actions. By going back to a period even before these movements emerged, it becomes clear that the institutional foundations upon which these movements stand are substantially different, with the U.S. movement resting on a vast network of churches, parachurch organizations, rich media empires, and large-scale movement organizations, all of which have large numbers of supporters and deep financial pockets. In Canada, we would expect the Christian right movement to be smaller, given the smaller population and the lesser proportion of the population that adheres to evangelical Christianity. However, even accounting for these size differences, the institutions upon which the Christian right stands are smaller, of modest means, and more loosely connected with each other than their neighbors to the south. These institutional differences affect not only which strategies and tactics are possible for activists to use, but also how effective their strategic choices will be in the political sphere.

We argue that the reasons for these differences lie in the divergent paths of evangelical Christian communities in the United States and Canada over the nineteenth and twentieth centuries, and especially in their institution-building work between 1920 and 1950. We consider the institution-building projects of the historical predecessors of the Christian right: evangelical Christian communities. It was in this historic period that U.S. evangelical communities embarked on a massive project of institution building that substantially outpaced Canadian efforts. Although the intent of these communities was not to affect politics or to create a social movement, the differences in institution building by conservative evangelical Christians in the mid-twentieth century led to a far different set of institutions available when, later in the century, the Christian right emerged as a social movement.

As historical institutionalist scholars make clear, the trajectories established by predecessors are a major influence on the direction of political—or in this case, social—movement organizations (e.g., Skocpol 1979; Tilly 1989). To explain this divergence in outcomes, we examine differences in the institutional infrastructures, or the set of organizations, constituents, networks and communication tools of the two movements. Not only do these infrastructures determine what kinds of strategies are available to movement actors, but they also determine whether a set of strategies will succeed or fail. We argue that the much weaker institutional infrastructure of the Christian right in Canada limits its effectiveness, even when using the same set of strategies as the U.S. movement.

Strategies and Infrastructures

Scholarship on social movements often examines the organizations in which activists build movement strength to levy strategic actions against a target (Clemens and Minkoff 2004). People are mobilized, elite ties are established, communications networks are created, and plans are made about when, where, and how protest actions will be done. These organizations can be formal or informal, as captured by McCarthy's (1996) concept of mobilizing structures.

The institutional foundations of social movement activity have been well established in any number of social movements, including the civil rights movement (Morris 1981), the women's movement (Staggenborg and Taylor 2005), the New Left (Evans 1980), and the lesbian and gay movement (Armstrong 2002). Recent work on networks in social movements also demonstrates the importance of institutional infrastructures in social movements. In this case, establishing nodes of communication between activists and organizations is understood to be central to supporting strategic action by movements (Diani and McAdam 2003). Networks have always been understood to be at the root of collective action, and social movement scholars have recently focused attention on the process of network building as a mechanism for supporting activism (e.g., Smith 2005).

In thinking about the relationship between social movement organizations and the strategies chosen by activists, this established body of work in social movements makes it clear that resources and networks support strategies. Some strategies are simply not available to social movements that do not have sufficient resources such as volunteers, constituents, or communications networks. Whether these institutional supports come in the form of informal friendship ties (Evans 1980) or formal organizations (McAdam 1982), they provide an infrastructure for strategic action. However, although it has been shown that institutional supports are diverse in form (Marwell and Oliver 1993; Staggenborg and Taylor 2005), this literature is less clear about the relationship between the institutional infrastructures of movements and the strategies they support. Is the size and strength of a movement's infrastructure related not only to whether activists can enact a strategy, but also to that strategy's outcome?

We know that institutional infrastructures can vary widely, but we do not understand much about how these variations can affect the outcomes of social movement actions. To learn more about the relationship between institutional infrastructure, strategy, and outcome, we examine two movements that have different infrastructures (weak in Canada, strong in the United States) but used similar strategies. The historical record is clear that one movement was more successful than the other, and we argue that the lack of infrastructural support offered by the movement with weaker institutions was a factor in this difference in outcomes.

Case, Data, and Methods

The U.S. and Canadian Christian right both have roots in conservative evangelical Christian communities. By this claim, we do not mean to imply that the Christian right movement and the evangelical Christian community are the same thing. Indeed, the evangelical Christian community has been shown to be politically and socially diverse (Smith 2002). However, the Christian right movement draws its constituents primarily from this community (Fetner 2008). As we discuss below, the community-building activities of evangelical Christians produced many of the institutions upon which the Christian right movements rely to conduct their activism. These include churches and parachurch organization, missionary groups, youth groups, and media institutions that include print, television, film, music, and Internet communications.

To understand the key differences in institution building by U.S. and Canadian evangelical Christians, we perform a historical comparative analysis of these communities, focusing in particular on community development and institution building by evangelical Christians in Canada and the United States in the middle of the twentieth century, especially 1920–50, which was a point of growth in evangelicalism in both countries. We also examine accounts of the patterns of coalition building and connections both among conservative evangelicals and between conservative evangelicals and more moderate and liberal Protestant denominations.

To lay out the historical record of institution building among evangelical Christians in the United States and Canada, we rely on a large body of secondary sources, including case studies written by historians, sociologists, and religious studies experts from both Canada and the United States. Fortunately, the historical record on the development and spread of evangelical Christianity in Canada and the United States has been well documented and preserved by these scholars.

Evangelical Christian Institution Building

The twentieth century was a time of rapid growth of evangelical Christianity in both Canada and the United States. In the United States, this growth was marked by a unique combination of factionalism and disintegration of denominational ties on the one hand, and fear of modernity and science on the other. This combination led to a period of evangelical Christian withdrawal from the modern world. In Canada, although evangelicalism was in a similar growth spurt, the overall character of evangelicalism was different from that of the United States. Canadians had markedly less antimodern ideology in their evangelical churches. For this and other reasons, Canadian evangelicals experienced less factionalism and less movement away from existing denominations. As we discuss below, the 1925 establishment of the United Church of Canada alleviated much of the internal conflict that the United States underwent over this time.

In the United States, attempts to reconnect dispersed factions of conservative evangelicals led to an intense project of institution building that started in the 1930s and continued throughout the century. Below, we briefly outline the history of the U.S. case of institution building. Canada's growth in evangelical Christianity, we argue, was not accompanied by a similarly large project of institution building. As a result, in the 1980s, when the U.S. Christian right began its activism, it had a vast network of resource-rich Christian evangelical institutions to foster and support its activism, while the Canadian movement had a smaller and weaker infrastructure to support its work.

The United States

Evangelicals in the United States are suspicious of modernity, more so than evangelicals in other parts of the world (Smith 1998). As scientific discoveries and social change challenged traditional biblical teachings, many Protestant denominations began to bend their emphasis on literal interpretations of the Bible, instead seeing it as a historical document that did not need to be scientifically accurate. In the United States, many conservatives criticized Protestant denominations for taking this conciliatory stance on science and politics. These critics feared that the sins of the modern world were affecting the church itself, causing it to stray from what they considered to be the proper path. Unable to reconcile their differences with what would come to be known as mainline Protestant denominations, U.S. evangelicals, or fundamentalists, as they called themselves in the 1920s, broke away from many of the major denominations within the Protestant church, including Presbyterian, Episcopal, and Methodist. As fundamentalists formed their own churches, they fell into further theological disputes with each other. Thus, the fundamentalist break with Protestantism was not characterized by a single schism between antimodernist fundamentalists and mainline denominations. Rather, fundamentalist churches fractured and segmented into many disparate groups, some of which retained denominational affiliations such as the Southern Baptist Convention, but many others of which broke all ties with other churches. In fact, theological schisms among fundamentalists were so common in the United States that conservative evangelical Christianity in this period has been characterized by religious historians as a series of neighborhood churches, each run independently, with a theological doctrine determined by its pastor (Carpenter 1984; Wilcox 1992).

With such a wide variety of churches captured under the term *fundamentalist*, it is difficult to say with great clarity what the characteristics and actions of fundamentalist, and later, evangelical, Christianity have been. Nonetheless, historians and sociologists generally agree that U.S. fundamentalist

Christians in the late nineteenth and early twentieth centuries have a few common characteristics, including a drive to eschew the cultural influences of modern life, a theology that includes a belief in a literal interpretation of the Bible, and a belief in premillennial dispensationalism or rapture (Smith 1998). One of the clashes with modernity that garnered much attention for fundamentalist Christianity was its rejection of the scientific theory of evolution (Scott 1997). In 1925, the Scopes trial overturned a Tennessee law that prohibited evolution from being taught in public schools (*Scopes v. State*, 152 Tenn. 424, 278 S.W. 57). This case reinforced many fundamentalist Christians' commitment to creating Christian schools for their children, not only to promote a creationist vision of the origins of the earth and humans, but also to avoid what they saw as the government's invasion into their lives. The next several decades were characterized by a withdrawal from the secular sphere.

In the 1940s, a group of reformers who called themselves neoevangelicals—later known simply as evangelicals—sought to establish deeper connections among the highly fragmented fundamentalist community. Seeking to address the factionalism among their peers, they mobilized like-minded conservative Christians and created a national network of independent churches. These neoevangelicals were similarly committed to withdrawing from the modern world, but they also created cohesion among a wide group of conservative Christians that previously had not existed (Carpenter 1984). In order to facilitate evangelical communities' cohesion and their retreat from the modern world, neoevangelicals over the next several decades built a wide variety of parachurch organizations. Parachurch organizations are religious institutions not tied to any denomination, but that provide religious materials or services. In the United States, the scope of these evangelical Christian parachurch organizations became vast, providing services and information to far more people than denominational organizations do on a for-profit basis (Marsden 1980; Carpenter 1984; Ostling 1984; Apostolidis 2000). These organizations include educational institutions, such as Bible institutes, liberal arts colleges, and summer Bible camps for children and young adults (Carpenter 2000). They also include youth ministries that provide after-school evangelical education, summer activities, and Sunday school events. There are a large number of parachurch missionary agencies that organize international travel. They also include a large number of Christian media outlets that have been particularly useful means of communication for activism for the U.S. Christian right.

Precise estimates of the number, size, and scope of parachurch organizations in the United States are difficult to come by (Miller 1999). However, evidence of the longevity, size, and largesse of these institutions can be found easily in U.S. culture, as many of these institutions remain active and strong today. For example, the National Association of Evangelicals, founded in 1947, still exists, claiming memberships of churches that house 4.5 million evangelicals (National Association of Evangelicals n.d.). The primary goal of this organization continues to be the development of networks among evangelicals and advocacy and lobbying for evangelical churches.

Media institutions have been particularly important in developing a collective identity, creating and enriching community ties, and mobilizing grassroots activism within the U.S. Christian right. In the United States, conservative evangelical Christian media are large in scale, rich in resources, and extremely easy to access. This is largely the result of the efforts of evangelical Christians in the early days of radio and television. For example, one of the early actions of the National Association of Evangelicals was to establish an official radio arm in 1944, the National Religious Broadcasters. As of 1983, the National Religious Broadcasters had over 900 radio station members. Richard Ostling (1984, 48) claims that daily and weekly radio shows are "probably still the backbone of evangelical broadcasting, complemented by largely or wholly religious radio stations." Christian radio stations are still broadcast widely throughout the United States. Later, this organization expanded to include television as well, and the success of U.S. televangelists is unparalleled in Canada or elsewhere around the globe. In the early 1980s, viewership of religious television broadcasts was estimated to range from 13 to 61 million (Diamond 1989). In addition, the fund-raising capacity of Christian radio and television has been vast. For example, Pat Robertson's media organization, the Christian Broadcasting Network, earned $230 million in 1986 (Oldfield 1996). To put that in context, the entire U.S. Democratic Party raised $98 million for its 1984 presidential campaign.

Another successful example of a parachurch organization established in this period is the Campus Crusade for Christ. Established in 1951 by Bill Bright on the University of California, Los Angeles, campus, this organization has attracted millions of young adults, expanding into a national, then international, organization. With annual revenues in the United States exceeding $500 million and a staff of over 25,000, this organization has reached out to millions of young adults (Campus Crusade for Christ 2008). Campus Crusade for Christ not only provides social supports for young adults, but also connects with activism through its missionary work, leadership training, and direct activism on various social issues. Similar evangelical Christian youth organizations such as the Intervarsity Christian Fellowship and Youth for Christ were also founded in this era.

Parachurch organizations provide services to a wide array of evangelical Christians regardless of the doctrinal theology of their particular congregation. By emphasizing the commonalities among evangelical Christians in general, these parachurch institutions have been vital in creating and sustaining a broadly defined Christian identity that is distinct from mainline Protestantism. These organizations supported and connected U.S. evangelicals and fostered the growth of this community, which outpaced that of Canadian evangelicals (Reimer 2003). More important to our argument, these institutions grew throughout the twentieth century and became an important infrastructure for U.S. Christian right activists.

Canada

Contemporary understandings of who counts as an evangelical differ greatly in Canada and the United States. In describing conservative evangelical Christians in the United States, we have adopted the terminology used within that community—first fundamentalist, then evangelical. However, we cannot simply review the history of evangelical Christians in Canada because most self-identified evangelicals in Canada are theologically and politically liberal (Bibby 2004). As we discuss below, what would be the equivalent of mainline Protestant denominations in the United States such as Presbyterians and Methodists use the term *evangelical* to describe themselves. Thus, it is important to emphasize the distinction between the conservative evangelical Christians in Canada—a group that largely shares the socially conservative agenda of the Christian right in the United States—from other evangelical Christians who tend to oppose this agenda. As we discuss below, conservative evangelical Christians in Canada do exist, but they have always been a much smaller group than in the United States.

Similar to the United States, changes in the modern world also affected denominations within the Canadian Protestant church. Biblical criticism and liberal theologies began to challenge orthodoxies, and people began to question and challenge literal interpretations of the Bible (Stackhouse 1999). Economic challenges caused by the great wars and the Depression created disparate religious views in Canadian life (Airhart 1990; Wright 1990). Like their neighbors to the south, most Protestant denominations began to move away from biblical literalism and embrace scientific discovery. In addition, mainline denominations began to embrace a staunchly liberal political agenda in Canada, supporting universal health care, woman's suffrage, minimum wage, welfare, and social security. Theologically, this focus on social welfare was accompanied by a deemphasis of individual sin and repentance and an emphasis on community service and redemption (Christie and Gauvreau 1996).

As in the United States, a group of resisting fundamentalists broke off from mainline Protestantism and formed their own churches (Wright 1990). However, this group would not become as large or as influential as in the United States. Still, Protestant churches were concerned with declining memberships and sought to stave off further schisms. Leaders in the Presbyterian church, the largest Protestant denomination in Canada, worked for years with Methodists leaders as well as the Congregational Union of Ontario and Quebec, and the Association of Local Union Churches (an amalgamation of these denominations that served the sparsely populated prairies in the West) to form the United Church of Canada (UCC) in 1925. This move established the largest Protestant denomination in Canada by far, and according to some historians, the establishment of the UCC may have alleviated some of the criticisms of Protestantism that caused major schisms among U.S. evangelicals (Wright 1990). Rather than be seen as drifting aimlessly toward the modern world without a clear mission, by reorganizing itself in this way, the UCC staked out a positive vision of the role of the church in modern society. This vision included commitments to social service, poverty relief, and woman's aid, but particularly relevant to this analysis is the church's embrace of science, which is evidenced in its bankrolling of several academic schools of social work throughout Canada (Christie and Gauvreau 1996). The UCC was liberal both politically and theologically, and its establishment demonstrated a uniquely Canadian spirit of moderation, rejecting what was considered the extremely conservative evangelicalism of the United States. The UCC's ecumenical makeup can be interpreted as a demonstration of the tolerance for diversity and the distaste for extremes present in Canadian Protestantism during this era (Reimer 2003). Although the UCC was firmly liberal, it also considered itself evangelical, seeing its social service role as central to its evangelical mission.

It is against this backdrop of ecumenicalism, mergers, and social activism within mainline denominations that several small sets of conservative evangelicals in Canada split off from the church. These conservatives had similar motivations to their U.S. counterparts. For example, one key leader, Thomas Todhunter (T.T.) Shields, was a strong advocate of withdrawal from modernism. He made it clear that his followers should avoid "worldly amusements," and he was highly critical of more liberal evangelical denominations. Shields's model of evangelicalism was much like U.S. evangelicalism at the time. Shields established the Baptist Bible Union with U.S. fundamentalists and even made a failed attempt to run a Bible institute in Des Moines, Iowa. But Shields's biggest impact was in Ontario, where he stood strongly against the forces of modernism, especially in higher education. On the board of McMaster University, then a Christian university, Shields fought to turn the curriculum toward a literal reading of the Bible and to establish a Bible institute there, seeking to "evangelize the rationalist university and teach the rationalist scholar" (quoted in Rawlyk 1988, 60). However, this move was resisted by others at McMaster, and Shields decided eventually to form an alternative institution, the Toronto Baptist Seminary, which became one of the leading voices for conservative evangelical Christians in Canada.

Although T. T. Shields is an excellent example of conservative evangelicalism in Canada, his stance was not the norm for Canadian evangelicals. Shields's legacy is rife with conflict, as moderate evangelical leaders refused to go along with his antimodern vision for transforming Canadian evangelical institutions. Although he attracted a number of followers and successfully preached for forty-five years, he was considered an extremist among Canadian evangelicals (Stackhouse 1999). In Canada, although there were a number of Canadian evangelicals who feared modernism, there was not a systemic fundamentalist–modernist divide, "and evangelicals did not polarize or encapsulate to such an extent" as in the United States (Reimer 2003, 27).

In addition, there were regional differences in Canadians' embrace of conservative evangelicalism (Rawlyk 1990). Although Ontario and Alberta had conservative evangelical movements, evangelicalism in the remaining provinces was much more moderate, leading to important progressive social developments in the prairies and in eastern Canada. In Canada, what has counted as evangelical has had a much broader definition throughout the twentieth century. This more moderate character of Canadian evangelicals affected their institution-building project throughout the twentieth century. The much smaller faction of conservative evangelicals did establish a number of Bible institutes, radio programs, publishing houses, and youth ministries. However, the size and scope of these institutions were dwarfed by their American neighbors. For example, as of 2007, the Campus Crusade for Christ in the United States had ministries on over 1,000 university campuses,[2] compared to fifteen chapters in Canada.[3] Similarly, Youth for Christ, an organization created to minister to teenagers founded by the Reverend Billy Graham in the 1940s, reports annual revenues of $64 million in the United States with organizations in over 1,300 schools and another 200 in urban centers. In Canada, the group reports less than $1 million in total income supporting twenty-seven chapters across the country.[4] These examples can be repeated many times over. What appears on the surface to be two countries with similar conservative evangelical Christian organizations turn out to be similar in name only, with vast differences in resources, especially membership and income. Other organizations that originated in Canada, such as T. T. Shields's Toronto Baptist Seminary and the Baptist Missionary Council in British Columbia, have done well enough to carry on as organizations through the decades, but they do not attract the mass support of U.S. organizations. Overall, the institution-building efforts of conservative evangelical Christians in Canada were fewer in number, smaller in scope, and less coordinated and networked than those in the United States.

Institutional Foundations of Social Movements

The differences in the patterns of development of evangelical Christian communities in the United States and Canada over the middle of the twentieth century has made a lasting impact on the abilities of social movement organizations in the Christian right to implement a set of strategies. In particular, the parachurch organizations that evangelicals built in each country during this period laid out an institutional infrastructure upon which each movement was built, although decades had passed between these historical events. The parachurch organizations that conservative evangelicals built in the United States were more numerous, more densely networked, and had more fluid paths of communication than Canadian evangelicals. Because Canadian evangelicals did not separate so distinctly from Protestant denominations, they did not build separate structures.

This difference in the character of institution-building projects by evangelicals affected the abilities of activists in recent days in several ways. First, the audience for socially conservative Christian messages is smaller in Canada than the United States (Bibby 2004), and yet the larger proportion of evangelical Christians in the U.S. population is insufficient to explain the differences between the movements. Rather, the organizational development in the United States led to larger, more lasting institutions that supported the Christian right movement later in the century. Because many of these institutions have generated substantial revenues, one important result is a huge discrepancy in the financial capacities of U.S. and Canadian conservative evangelical Christian organizations. In the United States, a massive stream of revenue has supported organizational growth and attendant recruitment and outreach projects to further solidify its institutional infrastructure, both within social movement organizations and in wider evangelical Christian communities. Finances and a volunteer pool are necessary to enact a wide variety of social movement strategies; as the resource pool, expands so does the pool of available strategies.

In addition, one of the important consequences of evangelical institution building in the United States was the development of a Christian identity that was tightly linked to both social conservatism and antimodernist ideology. This Christian identity was supported by the network of institutions that transcended denominational and geographic divisions among evangelical Christians and focused instead on the common grounds of biblical literalism and evangelism as a practice of everyday life. Although there is abundant evidence that evangelical Christians in the United States are much more ideologically diverse than this socially conservative Christian identity implies, this identity has been useful for activists in the U.S. Christian right. For example, this conservative Christian identity was deployed successfully in support of policies that limited access to abortion or granted rights to lesbians and gay men.[5] By contrast, in Canada, an evangelical Christian identity has not been linked as tightly with social conservatism (Reimer 2003). The lack of a tight link between a Christian identity and conservative policy positions undermines the Canadian Christian right's claims to speak for Christian Canadians in general, putting them in a much less powerful position politically. In this case, institution building has determined whether a particular identity deployment can be used effectively by a social movement.

Finally, the institutional infrastructure for the Canadian Christian right was dwarfed by its counterpart in the United States. Thus, not only do Canadian activists have far fewer revenue-generating organizations that can fund their activism, but they also lack the dense networks in which these organizations are embedded. In particular, evangelical Christian media institutions such as radio and television stations and the programs that run on them provide easy access to millions of potential constituents for U.S. Christian right activists. In the United States, Christian right activists routinely use these media to reach potential supporters that number in the tens of millions. They also distribute political information such as voter guides through church networks and other membership-based parachurch organizations, such as youth ministries and Bible study groups. In Canada, there are relatively few conservative evangelical Christian media, church networks are looser and more sparse, and there is much less overlap between conservatives and evangelicals. In Canada, communication among leaders and constituents willing to engage in political action—be it voting, writing a letter, or participating in a protest—is much more difficult.

Combined with the differences in the political institutions in Canada and the United States, especially those identified by Miriam Smith (2005), the similar strategies enacted by Christian right movements in these two countries met with different results. These strategies rest on different institutional infrastructures, leading to different outcomes. It is not that the Canadian Christian right did not have the capacity in terms of volunteers, constituents, or other resources to enact the same strategies as the U.S. movement. Rather, the Canadian movement engaged in similar strategic action, but the institutional supports of organizations, in dense networks, with fluid channels of communication, were much stronger for activists in the United States than in Canada, and this infrastructural support has led to greater policy success for the U.S. Christian right.

Scholars of social movements would be wise to pay attention to this comparative case because it reveals some of the hidden framework upon which strategic action rests. In the United States, the Christian right relies on an institutional infrastructure that supports its strategic actions, such as deploying a unifying Christian identity, mobilizing grassroots actions such as e-mail campaigns to legislators, and bloc voting. By generating resources, facilitating communication, and contributing to a cohesive collective identity, this infrastructure makes a wide array of strategic actions possible. However, because of significant differences in the paths of the evangelical Christian community in Canada, there is a much smaller and less densely connected set of institutions supporting the Christian right movement there. To some extent, this has limited the pool of strategic choices available to activists there. In addition, it may have limited the effectiveness of the strategies that have been used. Where these strategies are the same as those used by the U.S. movement, they have resulted in much less policy change. In fact, policies have been recently moving in a liberal direction despite activism from the Christian right.

From the perspective of activists, this case may well highlight the value of institution building. Although in this case the institution builders in the mid-twentieth century did not have political activism on their minds, the work they did paid off for U.S. Christian right activists down the road. It supported their strategic action, making them effective at changing policy at federal, state, and local levels. Although in the short run there are significant costs to institution building, in the long run, doing the work of building lasting institutions and establishing ties to others with similar interests has important payoffs. Strategies may not work without the institutional infrastructure of community, identity, and communication.

Notes

1. For a historical account of this takeover, see Fetner (2008).
2. See Campus Crusade for Christ (http://www.campuscrusadeforchrist.com).
3. See Power to Change (http://powertochange.com).

4. Data from annual reports produced by each group for 2006 are available at Youth for Christ USA (http://www.yfc.net) for the United States and Youth for Christ Canada (http://www.yfccanada.com) for Canada.

5. See Bernstein (1997) for a discussion of identity deployment in social movements.

References

Airhart, Phyllis. 1990. "Ordering a New Nation and Reordering a Protestantism." In *The Canadian Protestant Experience, 1760–1990,* edited by George A. Rawlyk, 98–138. Burlington, Vt.: Welch.

Apostolidis, Paul. 2000. *Stations of the Cross: Adorno and Christian Right Radio.* Durham, N.C.: Duke University Press.

Armstrong, Elizabeth A. 2002. *Forging Gay Identities: Organizing Sexuality in San Francisco, 1950–1994.* Chicago: University of Chicago Press.

Bailey, Mary. 2004. "Regulation of Cohabitation and Marriage in Canada." *Law and Policy* 26:153–75.

Berlet, Chip, and Matthew N. Lyons. 2000. *Right-Wing Populism in America.* New York: Guilford Press.

Bernstein, Mary. 1997. "Celebration and Suppression: The Strategic Uses of Identity by the Lesbian and Gay Movement." *American Journal of Sociology* 103:531–65.

Bibby, Reginald. 2004. "Ethos Versus Ethics: Canada, the U.S., and Homosexuality." Paper presented at the annual meeting of the Pacific Sociological Association, April, San Francisco, Calif.

Campus Crusade for Christ. 2008. "Annual Report, 2007." http://www.ccci.org.

Carpenter, Joel A. 1984. "From Fundamentalism to the New Evangelical Coalition." In *Evangelicalism and Modern America,* edited by George Marsden, 3–16. Grand Rapids, Mich.: William B. Eerdmans.

———. 2000. "Fundamentalist Institutions and the Rise of Evangelical Protestantism, 1929–1942." In *More Money, More Ministry: Money and Evangelicals in Recent North American History,* edited by Larry Eskridge and Mark A. Noll, 259–73. Grand Rapids, Mich.: William B. Eerdmans.

Christie, Nancy, and Michael Gauvreau. 1996. *A Full-Orbed Christianity: The Protestant Churches and Social Welfare in Canada.* Montreal–Kingston: McGill–Queen's University Press.

Clemens, Elisabeth S., and Debra C. Minkoff. 2004. "Beyond the Iron Law: Rethinking the Place of Organizations in Social Movement Research." In *The Blackwell Companion to Social Movements,* edited by David A. Snow, Sarah A. Soule, and Hanspeter Kriesi, 155–70. Malden, Mass.: Blackwell.

Dawson, T. Brettel. 1993. "Sexual Orientation and Human Rights Law in Canada:

An Overview." In *Women, Law and Social Change: Core Readings and Current Issues*, edited by T. Brettel Dawson, 401–9. North York: Captus Press.

Diamond, Sara. 1989. *Spiritual Warfare: The Politics of the Christian Right.* Boston: South End Press.

Diani, Mario, and Doug McAdam, eds. 2003. *Social Movements and Networks: Relational Approaches to Collective Action.* New York: Oxford University Press.

Evans, Sara. 1980. *Personal Politics: The Roots of Women's Liberation in the Civil Rights Movement and the New Left.* New York: Vintage Books.

Fetner, Tina. 2008. *How the Religious Right Shaped Lesbian and Gay Activism.* Minneapolis: University of Minnesota Press.

Marsden, George. 1980. *Fundamentalism and American Culture: The Shaping of Twentieth-Century Evangelicalism, 1870–1925.* New York: Oxford University Press.

Marwell, Gerald, and Pamela Oliver. 1993. *The Critical Mass in Collective Action: A Micro-social Theory.* Cambridge: Cambridge University Press.

McAdam, Doug. 1982. *Political Process and the Development of Black Insurgency, 1930–1970.* Chicago: University of Chicago Press.

McCarthy, John D. 1996. "Constraints and Opportunities in Adopting, Adapting and Inventing." In *Comparative Perspectives on Social Movements: Political Opportunities, Mobilizing Structures, and Cultural Framings*, edited by Doug McAdam, John D. McCarthy, and Mayer N. Zald, 141–50. New York: Cambridge University Press.

Miall, Charlene, and Karen March. 2005. "Social Support for Changes in Adoption Practice: Gay Adoption, Open Adoption, Birth Reunions, and the Release of Confidential Identifying Information." *Families in Society* 86:83–92.

Miller, Sharon L. 1999. "Financing Parachurch Organizations." In *Financing American Religion*, edited by Mark Chaves and Sharon L. Miller, 119–30. Walnut Creek, Calif.: AltaMira Press.

Morris, Aldon. 1981. "Black Southern Sit-in Movement: An Analysis of Internal Organization." *American Sociological Review* 46:744–67.

Oldfield, Duane M. 1996. *The Right and the Righteous: The Christian Right Confronts the Republican Party.* Lanham, Md.: Rowman & Littlefield.

Ostling, Richard N. 1984. "Evangelical Publishing and Broadcasting." In *Evangelicalism and Modern America*, edited by George Marsden, 46–55. Grand Rapids, Mich.: William B. Eerdmans.

National Association of Evangelicals. n.d. "History of the NAE." http://www.nae.net.

Rawlyk, George A. 1988. "A. L. McCrimmon, H. P. Whidden, T. T. Shields, Christian Higher Education, and McMaster University." In *Canadian Baptists and Christian Higher Education*, edited by George A. Rawlyk, 31–62. Montreal–Kingston: McGill–Queen's University Press.

————. 1990. *Champions of the Truth: Fundamentalism, Modernism, and the Maritime Baptists.* Montreal–Kingston: McGill–Queen's University Press.

Reimer, Sam. 2003. *Evangelicals and the Continental Divide: The Conservative Protestant Subculture in Canada and the United States.* Montreal–Kingston: McGill–Queen's University Press.

Scott, Eugenie C. 1997. "Antievolution and Creationism in the United States." *Annual Review of Anthropology* 26:263–89.

Skocpol, Theda. 1979. *States and Social Revolutions: A Comparative Analysis of France, Russia, and China.* New York: Cambridge University Press.

Smith, Christian. 2002. *Christian America? What Evangelicals Really Want.* Berkeley: University of California Press.

Smith, Christian, with Michael Emerson, Sally Gallagher, Paul Kennedy, and David Sikkink. 1998. *American Evangelicalism: Embattled and Thriving.* Chicago: University of Chicago Press.

Smith, Miriam. 2005. "Social Movements and Judicial Empowerment: Courts, Public Policy, and Lesbian and Gay Organizing in Canada." *Politics and Society* 33:327–53.

————. 2007. "Framing Same-Sex Marriage in Canada and the United States: Goodridge, Halpem and the National Boundaries of Political Discourse." *Social and Legal Studies* 16:5–26.

————. 2008. *Political Institutions and Lesbian and Gay Rights in the United States and Canada.* London: Routledge.

Stackhouse, John G., Jr. 1999. *Canadian Evangelicalism in the Twentieth Century: An Introduction to Its Character.* Vancouver: Regent College Publishing.

Staggenborg, Suzanne, and Verta Taylor. 2005. "Whatever Happened to the Women's Movement?" *Mobilization* 10:37–52.

Tilly, Charles. 1989. *Big Structures, Large Processes, and Huge Comparisons.* New York: Russell Sage Foundation.

Wilcox, Clyde. 1992. *God's Warriors: The Christian Right in Twentieth-Century America.* Baltimore: Johns Hopkins University Press.

Wright, Robert A. 1990. "The Canadian Protestant Tradition, 1914–1945." In *The Canadian Protestant Experience, 1760–1990*, edited by George A. Rawlyk, 139–97. Burlington, Vt.: Welch.

12

Strategic Choices in Cross-National Movements: A Comparison of the Swedish and British Plowshares Movements

Sharon Erickson Nepstad and Stellan Vinthagen

Cross-national movements are increasing as new information technologies permit activists in one region to learn about and experiment with the ideas, tactics, and strategies of movements in other parts of the world.[1] However, organizers who appropriate external movement repertoires must make alterations in order for the imported movement to take root in a new country. Such alterations often entail choice points—that is, decisions about how to resolve strategic dilemmas (see chapter 2). Yet we know little about the consequences of such strategic decisions, especially for cross-national activists who are trying to implement a foreign-born movement in a new context.

We examine the strategic choices of Swedish and British activists who imported the controversial tactics of the U.S. Plowshares movement. The Plowshares movement began in 1980 when radical American Catholics broke into military facilities and weapons manufacturing sites, armed with household hammers and bottles of their blood. They used the hammers to damage nuclear weapons, symbolically enacting the prophet Isaiah's vision of "beating swords into plowshares," and they poured blood to represent death, sacrifice, and redemption. International media coverage of U.S. Plowshares actions piqued the interest of activists abroad, who began experimenting with this radical approach. Soon movement branches emerged in Germany, the Netherlands, Sweden, Great Britain, and Australia (Nepstad 2008).

Establishing these branches was not simple, as organizers soon realized that they could not wholly adopt the U.S. movement's infrastructure, symbolism, tactics, and leadership system. European and Australian activists were operating in different cultures and political systems that constrained their ability to import certain U.S.-style Plowshares techniques yet also provided new opportunities. Hence, Swedish and British activists faced numerous choice points that led them to implement strategic changes. However, those changes yielded divergent consequences: the British Plowshares movement prospered, while the Swedish Plowshares movement struggled and collapsed. By examining the choice points that each group faced and tracing the effects of their choices, we offer insights into the factors that shaped the British and Swedish Plowshares movements' ability to survive in a new context.

Data Sources

Our analysis of the international Plowshares movement draws on numerous sources. The first author, Nepstad, conducted exploratory interviews and engaged in participant observation at Jonah House, an intentional community that organizes many Plowshares actions, and at the Atlantic Life Community, a network of Catholic left antiwar activists. From these data, she designed a survey that addressed demographic information activist experiences, as well as religious beliefs and practices. At the end of the survey, activists were asked if they were willing to participate in a follow-up interview. Subsequently, a total of thirty-five in-depth interviews were conducted in the United States and Europe. Each interview was tape-recorded and transcribed. Finally, archival documents, including trial transcripts, movement newsletters, and correspondence among activists, were used to verify and expand on the survey and interview findings. The second author, Vinthagen, draws on information collected during the nearly fifteen years that he was a Plowshares activist. He is a cofounder of the Swedish Plowshares movement, and his data consist of Swedish movement newsletters, meeting minutes, and other documents, as well as his own interviews and field notes that focus on the problems with Plowshares groups' preparation processes (see Vinthagen 1998).

Cross-National Movement Choice Points

Cross-national movements such as the Plowshares movement begin in one country and spread to others, in contrast to transnational movements that reflect groups of collaborating activists in various regions that share the same goals and targets. Studies of cross-national movements have therefore typically focused on the conditions needed for diffusion. On a basic level, every cross-national movement includes the following: the transmitter (the original movement), the adopter (those abroad seeking to implement the movement), and the item of diffusion (tactics, strategies, or ideologies). According to several scholars, three conditions are necessary for a movement to spread. First, the item of diffusion must be of interest to both the transmitting and adopting groups. Second, the groups must be linked through direct ties such as personal contact, indirect ties through the mass media, or both. Third, there must be a shared identity and a degree of structural and cultural similarity between transmitters and adopters (McAdam and Rucht 1993; Strang and Meyer 1993; Soule 1997).

If all these conditions are met, some scholars argue that movement diffusion can occur, following a five-stage process. The first step is the *knowledge stage,* where potential adopters learn of the movement for the first time, typically through media coverage of a protest event. The second step, known as the *persuasion stage,* occurs when would-be adopters deliberate the merits of the movement. This leads to the *decision stage,* when activists choose to embrace or reject the new ideas and practices. If they decide to adopt them, then they transition to the *implementation stage,* where they organize a parallel movement in their own country. The culminating step is when activists assess whether their adopted movement is working and if they wish to continue it. This is called the *confirmation stage* (Rogers 1995).

This cross-national diffusion model has been criticized for two reasons. First, Snow and Benford (1999) argue that the emphasis on diffusion channels and structural similarities between transmitters and adopters overshadows human agency. Organizers' decisions and activities can determine whether an imported movement will take root, and thus human actions merit greater attention. Second, diffusion rarely proceeds in a tidy sequence of linear steps, as the diffusion model posits. As Chabot (2000) argues, implementation of external ideas and tactics is likely to occur only after significant debate, experimentation, and adaptation. To this list of criticisms, we add yet another: the diffusion literature fails to explain why some cross-national movements flourish while others struggle and fail. The literature is so narrowly focused on movement origins and diffusion that issues of implementation, adaptation, and outcome have largely been overlooked.

We anticipate that an imported movement's potential to survive is largely shaped by organizers' ability to adapt it to new cultural and structural conditions. This adaptation process will inevitably generate choice points whereby activists must decide which elements of the originating movement to retain, modify, or reject. Common decisions include whether or not to adopt the originating movement's decision-making process and infrastructure. Because political systems vary across societies, movement leaders will also need to assess whether they can reach their goals with a small cadre of activists or whether a mass movement with multiple coalitions is required. Even tactics may be modified because the adopting movement's opponent may be more or less amenable to negotiation that the originating movement's opponent. Finally, cross-national organizers will need to determine if they can keep the originating movement's frames and symbols, or if they must be altered to resonate with a new audience (Benford and Snow 1988).

To examine the consequences of such strategic choices for cross-national movements, we compare the experiences of the Swedish and British branches of the international Plowshares movement. We find that organizers in each branch faced similar choice points regarding how to modify the U.S. Plowshares movement's symbols, tactics, organizational infrastructure, and leadership. Building on Meyer and Staggenborg (chapter 1), we highlight how each branch's choices were shaped by the cultural and structural constraints and opportunities in their respective nations.

Background on the Plowshares Movement

The U.S. Plowshares movement emerged from a tradition of radical, pacifist Catholicism. Plowshares organizers were strongly influenced by Dorothy Day, the founder of the Catholic Worker movement. Starting in the 1930s, Day established "houses of hospitality" that offered shelter and food to the destitute. Yet she never considered these works of mercy to be enough. She forcefully argued that the causes of poverty and homelessness need to be addressed through nonviolent action (Klejment and Roberts 1996). During the Vietnam War, Day's commitment to social justice activism inspired many Catholics to resist the war and a number refused military service. But priests Philip and Daniel Berrigan introduced an even more controversial form of resistance: draft board raids. During these raids, Catholic activists would forcibly remove conscription files, douse them with blood, or burn them with homemade napalm. Although participants faced long prison sentences for these campaigns, dozens of raids occurred throughout the country (Meconis 1979; Forest 1997).

Because the draft board raids were hotly debated within the Catholic Church and the broader peace movement, the Berrigans turned to scripture to justify their tactics. They argued that Christ offered a model of provocative, confrontational action in situations of injustice. In particular, they cite the story of Christ cleansing the temple that had been transformed from "a house of prayer into a den of thieves" (Mark 11:17). Outraged that bankers were making loans (at exorbitant rates) to poor worshippers who needed to purchase a sacrificial animal, Christ drove them out and shut the temple down. U.S. Catholic resisters note that he did not merely appeal for lower interest loans; he challenged the entire system and disrupted business as usual (Nepstad 2004, 2008).

Not everyone was persuaded by this justification, but the Berrigans continued to work against war even as they served prison terms for the draft raids. When they were released, they planned to use these controversial tactics again, but they knew that such high-risk tactics required strong support. Thus, they began building intentional resistance communities. In the early 1970s they formed Jonah House, modeled after the Catholic Worker communities, and organized retreats for faith-based activist communities on the East Coast. These retreats evolved into a loosely coordinated network known as the Atlantic Life Community.

During this time, the Berrigans looked for a new opportunity to use disruptive tactics to impede the escalating arms race. They found it when someone suggested entering the General Electric plant outside Philadelphia that was producing the nuclear warheads. The Berrigans and six others decided to enact the biblical prophesy of "beating swords into plowshares" by damaging the warheads with household hammers. Since the G.E. action in 1980, roughly fifty Plowshares actions have occurred across the United States (Laffin 2003).

One of these actions took place in 1983 at the Griffiss air force base near Syracuse, New York, where several Plowshares activists damaged B-52 bombers. When the activists went to trial, a Swede named Per Herngren followed the trial closely. Herngren was living in Syracuse on an international peace organization exchange program. Although he knew little about the Plowshares movement at that point, he quickly learned more as he attended support rallies and met other activists. It did not take long before Herngren joined the movement. In 1984, he destroyed parts of a Patriot missile launcher at a Martin Marietta plant in Florida (Herngren 1993; Laffin 2003). The Swedish media covered Herngren's trial extensively. When he was deported a year later, he received considerable support. Encouraged by this, Herngren and other activists began planning a Swedish Plowshares movement (Nepstad 2008).

The Swedish Plowshares Movement

Using the five-stage diffusion model as a starting point, we can see how Plowshares activism spread from the United States to Sweden. The first stage, the *knowledge step,* entailed the initial transmission of information about the Plowshares movement. This occurred through the indirect ties of media coverage, including a documentary film on the movement that Herngren saw before moving to the United States. Then, after Herngren took part in a Plowshares action, the news reports of his case disseminated information even farther. Upon returning to Sweden, Herngren served as a direct link to the U.S. movement because he had personal contact with Jonah House, the Atlantic Life Community, and other Plowshares activists. However, the mere presence of diffusion channels does not explain the emergence of the Swedish movement.

Human agency is crucial here: activists attempted in the *persuasion stage* to convince others to adopt this foreign-born movement. Herngren started conversations within the Swedish Fellowship of Reconciliation while activist Gunn-Marie Carlsson spoke with members of a national woman's peace organization and Stellan Vinthagen traveled to various peace camps. Although large numbers of Swedes were not convinced, eventually a core group chose to adopt Plowshares ideas and practices in their struggle against Swedish weapons sales. Yet the *implementation stage* was challenging as Swedish organizers realized that they could not model themselves completely after the U.S. movement because they were operating in a far more secular culture and were challenging a different type of government. They had to decide which elements of the original movement they wished to retain, change, or eliminate.

The first choice point they faced was whether to keep the Catholic symbolism of U.S. Plowshares practices. Initially, Swedish activists tried using many of the U.S. movement's symbols, including the pouring of blood that reflects the Catholic emphasis on sacrifice, suffering, and redemption. However, they quickly encountered cultural constraints when these religious symbols did not resonate in this historically Protestant but largely secular nation. One activist described an unsuccessful attempt to use this symbol:

> In the U.S., blood is used as a symbol in connection with the disarmament of weapons. The blood comes from the activists themselves and is poured from babies' bottles over the weapons and other equipment. . . . In Sweden, blood has been very scarcely used in civil disobedience actions. One group used pig's blood in an action. . . . When the guard dogs arrived it became quite nasty. The dogs became tense and aggressive from the smell of pig's blood. The action didn't work very well. . . . It is difficult to say how people understand the symbols in an action. However, I think blood can actually be dangerous from a contamination point of view and [here] it gives also associations to religious fanaticism, which creates an unnecessary polarization to the opponent. (Leander 1997, 12)

Eventually, the Swedish activists stopped using blood and agreed to retain only the symbolic use of household tools to disarm weaponry.[2]
The Swedish activists also downplayed the religious justification for these tactics. Organizers did not perceive their task as prophetic enactment or replication of Christ's action in the temple, but rather a challenge to the culture of obedience that enables militarism to continue. They hoped to convince their fellow citizens that they do, in fact, have the power to change these policies and practices if they are willing to take responsibility and pay the price for disarmament. Herngren (1993, 13–14) explained,

It is considered self-evident that only governments in disarmament negotiations can decide which weapons should be destroyed. When workers at
a weapons factory or other people suddenly start disarming weapons on
their own, our view of what is possible and who can act changes. . . . In
Plowshares actions, we use hammers to disarm weapons. My hammer
symbolized for me the paradox of militarism. A Pershing II missile can
annihilate my home town of Gothenburg, Sweden. There are no weapons
that could stop such an attack. But my small, ridiculous hammer made it
impossible to fire that particular missile. And similarly, it isn't raw strength
that can stop the arms race. . . . The arms race could not continue without the obedience of citizens, which is caused mainly by people's fear of
the consequences of disobedience.

The message of civilian responsibility for disarmament, therefore, led Swedish
organizers away from scriptural justifications of these tactics. Instead, they
made stronger reference to the ideas of Thoreau, Gandhi, and international
law. In short, a shift in the movement's message necessitated a shift in their
ideological justifications.

While the secular culture of Sweden constrained activists' capacity to
effectively use Catholic symbolism, some structural conditions—namely the
Swedish government's tolerance of radical groups—provided new opportunities for Plowshares activists. This led to a second choice point: should Swedish activists adopt the U.S. Plowshares practice of operating in secret? They
decided to depart from the U.S. tradition, informing the police and weapons
producers in advance about their campaigns, leaving only the time and the
date a secret. They also integrated interested family members into the preparation process, giving them an opportunity to voice their concerns before the
actions. One Swedish activist explained:

Part of the explanation is that the differences in the Plowshares movements
mirror the differences between the American and Swedish societies. Sentences are much longer in the U.S. and conspiracy charges are common,
and it presents itself immediately to let as few people as possible know
anything about actions beforehand. Conspiracy charges mean that people
are charged . . . for having the knowledge that an action is being planned
but not going to the police with that information. Many people in the
American Plowshares movement think it is irresponsible to let people, who
themselves have not chosen to take the risk, know about an action beforehand. One way of coping with this [here] is to let the action be public in
advance (except the date). When I told my father I was planning to do a

Plowshares action, his response was to call the police to stop it. "Go ahead," I said. "We have already contacted them." (Leander 1997, 11)

Despite the fact that authorities did press conspiracy charges in a few cases, Swedish activists continued this policy of openness.

The third choice point dealt with the organization dilemma (Jasper 2004). In the beginning, Swedish organizers adopted a movement infrastructure that closely mimicked the decentralized U.S. model that combines local resistance communes and an activist retreat network. In 1989, Swedish organizers created an intentional community called Omega. Although communes are rare in Sweden, the idea was directly inspired by Jonah House in the United States. In a 2003 interview with the first author, Vinthagen explained.

> The major influence [on community building] definitely came from the U.S. Plowshares movement. It grows from our commitment to creating a movement that is able to sustain itself for decades. . . . The only thing that makes that possible is if you are able to sustain a life of resistance and . . . I can't really imagine how that is ever possible on an individual basis when you live a normal, bourgeois life and you need to sustain yourself in this capitalist society. So you need to create your own society . . . [with] an alternative economy, child rearing, other kinds of schools, all that stuff in order to be able to challenge these powerful forces that sustain the power structures of today.

Complementing the Omega community was a group of activists who lived in the surrounding area. Because not everyone wanted to reside in an intentional community or engage in civil disobedience, this affiliated group provided support to the movement without full involvement in Omega or a Plowshares action. In the early 1990s, roughly fifty to sixty people moved to the area to be involved with one of these two communities.

Swedish organizers also sponsored retreats that paralleled the Atlantic Life Community gatherings, but they made some changes. Because many participants were not religious, they changed the name of the retreats from "Faith and Resistance" to "Hope and Resistance." They kept certain elements of U.S. retreat practices, such as studying and discussing texts, but often the texts were not scriptural. Moreover, they included workshops on topics ranging from parenting and activism to juggling and salsa dancing. Basically, these retreats blended the U.S. Plowshares movement's Bible study/action tradition with the Scandinavian informal education system that stems from the nineteenth-century folk high schools and study circles.

They also changed their leadership form. The U.S. Plowshares movement coalesced around Philip and Daniel Berrigan, but the Swedes had no comparable charismatic leaders. Nor did they want one, because they wished to create a nonhierarchical, highly egalitarian movement. To that end, they borrowed democratic techniques that other progressive movements use, including the appointment of sexism watchers and time facilitators, while adding democratic methods of their own (Herngren and Vinthagen 1992; Polletta 2002).

The fourth choice point centered on whether to shift the strategy from acts of moral witness toward the formation of a broad-based, politically oriented movement. In other words, Swedish activists debated whether they wanted to put more emphasis on witnessing or winning. In contrast to U.S. Plowshares participants who consider these acts an important form of prophetic testament regardless of the outcome, many Swedes wanted to be politically effective. One Swede described these differences:

> There is a widespread idea amongst Plowshares activists in the U.S. about not worrying about what is effective or about attaining results. They mean that it is not possible to judge what is effective, but that the results lie in the hands of God. The only thing they can do is to witness about the truth. In Sweden, most people think that Plowshares actions and other civil disobedience are important just because it makes the nonviolence work more effectively. . . . I think that if activists in Sweden noticed that the actions didn't lead to change, most of them would think about doing it differently. . . . In Sweden and Europe I have taken part in many discussions about how the movement can grow. Plowshares activists in the U.S. don't seem to view it like this. As far as I have understood it, there is not much interest in how their actions are received by the rest of the society, if they really work as a challenge. The important thing is to enflesh the Gospels. (Leander 1997, 12)

After numerous discussions, many Swedish activists decided to move away from the normative and expressive strategy of the U.S. movement toward a more instrumental and communicative approach that would have greater influence on the Swedish weapons trade. However, building a politically effective movement required that they expand their ranks, recruit a broader membership base, and build ties to other progressive groups. To that end, they sponsored disarmament camps modeled after the British Greenham Common peace camp. Organizers distributed flyers inviting "environmental activists, feminists, Plowshares members, syndicalists, anarchists, socialists, liberals, atheists, new agers, and Christians" to participate.[3] In the summer of 1992, 200 people attended. Some attended for just a day or two, and only a small

minority engaged in civil disobedience. The next summer, Plowshares organizers required that campers stay for a minimum of one week. As a result,
the camp drew only sixty participants. The third peace camp was held in 1995.
The numbers dropped to twenty-five because organizers clearly stated that
the purpose was to engage in direct action, and thus campers were expected
to stay for the entire three weeks.

The peace camps' declining numbers indicated that the costs associated
with the Plowshares movement were prohibitive because many potential
supporters were not willing to commit civil disobedience or to go to prison.
On the basis of this concern, some activists made a proposal to redesign the
movement in two ways: emphasize more low-risk forms of participation and
change the infrastructure from decentralized resistance communities to a formalized membership organization. The suggested shift was also prompted
by the fact that the Omega experiment was collapsing as a result of personal
conflicts and disagreements about the community's purpose and policies.
Additionally, some thought that the intentional community structure was
ineffective because of Swedish cultural constraints. One activist reflected,

> The intentional community movement is much bigger in the U.S. . . .
> There is a difference in context also. Sweden is a country where the . . .
> average person here is a member of five or six organizations, maybe more.
> You're a member of the union, a sports organization, some nature group,
> a solidarity thing. Once a year you pay your membership and you get mail-
> ings. You're not so active; sometimes you go to a meeting, perhaps, but
> that kind of activism is very common here. . . . Most of the day-to-day
> work is done by people employed by the organization. So there are a lot
> of formal organizations but not these kinds of grassroots communities of
> resistance. (interview with Nepstad)

Intentional communities also had little religious resonance in Sweden, whose
Protestant tradition has no comparable form of communal monastic life.
This is a sharp contrast to the U.S. movement, where, according to the first
author's survey, nearly 60 percent of Plowshares activists have lived in a Catholic worker community for one or more years and roughly one-third are or
were at one time members of a Catholic religious order. Thus, the notion of
giving up personal possessions and living communally was not as foreign to
them as it was to many Swedes, who were less likely to join a movement that
required such living arrangements.

After lengthy deliberations, the Swedish Plowshares activists decided in
1995 to reject the commune-based U.S. Plowshares infrastructure and replace
it with a formal membership organization called Svärd till Plogbillar (Swords

into Plowshares). One activist recalled, "We created the organization . . . to open it up for people to get involved without moving into community or being part of a Plowshares group in which they risked jail. So that was an important aspect since many people wanted to widen the possibilities for people to get involved" (interview with Nepstad).

However, this change in strategy and infrastructure did not solve the nascent movement's problems. In fact, it created new ones because some Swedish activists disagreed with the changes, refusing to join the new organization and continuing to plan witness-oriented, high-risk actions. Others maintained that intentional communities were critical, and thus they (unsuccessfully) attempted to reestablish them. Within the newly created (and more heterogenous) Svärd till Plogbillar organization, conflicts quickly arose over various issues. For instance, activists fiercely debated which types of political influence were acceptable. This topic became particularly contentious from 1997 to 2000, when the movement initiated a dialogue with the manufacturing company Bofors, which sold weapons to the Indonesian military. Some activists considered this to be co-optation, but others thought that dialogue was an essential feature of nonviolent resistance and a viable way to achieve real results (Engell-Nielsen 2001). Another tension was over the new organization's decision-making process. Although all agreed to a consensus format, many thought that their actual practice was not completely democratic because a few powerful personalities seemed to have the greatest influence. Activists also fought over how much time and energy to spend dealing with internal group dynamics versus executing actions.

Although the new organization was designed to help the Swedish Plowshares movement grow by offering more low-risk forms of participation and creating a larger, more diverse membership, it soon began to unravel. The group's internal conflicts became so heated that some members resigned while others moved on to other causes. Eventually, the group splintered, and by 2000, they faced the question of whether they wanted to continue. In this fifth step of the diffusion model, the *confirmation stage,* they decided that this movement was no longer workable. They suspended the organization and the Swedish Plowshares movement came to an end. Some activists subsequently attempted to recreate the movement, but in the last ten years, only one Plowshares action has occurred in Sweden.

The British Plowshares Movement

The diffusion of Plowshares activism to Great Britain began when Stephen Hancock, an Oxford University student, became intrigued by the radical commitment of the U.S. Plowshares movement and traveled to Jonah House in

Baltimore to learn more. Upon returning to the United Kingdom, Hancock tried to recruit participants for a British Plowshares campaign. Eventually, a Quaker named Mike Hutchinson joined him, and in 1990, the two men entered the Upper Heyford U.S. air base. When they located an F-111 fighter plane, they used hammers to smash the cockpit and poured blood on the nuclear weapons control panel. They were arrested and convicted of criminal damage, resulting in a fifteen-month prison sentence (Laffin 2003). Three years later, Chris Cole launched the second Plowshares action when he spilled blood and hammered on the European fighter aircraft and the Hawk strike attack aircraft at a British Aerospace factory. He was convicted of criminal damage and ordered to serve eight months in prison (Nepstad's interview with Chris Cole).

These first two campaigns closely replicated the U.S. Plowshares model in terms of tactics, religious symbolism, and an emphasis on moral witness. However, the third British action, known as the Seeds of Hope action, revealed that experimentation was underway. This campaign occurred in 1996 when three women—Andrea Needham, Joanna Wilson, and Lotta Kronlid (a Swede)—broke into a British Aerospace facility to smash an attack plane that was being sent to the Indonesian military that was responsible for the deaths of 200,000 people in East Timor—roughly one-third of the total population (Aditjondro 2000). When the three women were brought up on criminal charges, along with Angie Zelter, who was charged with conspiracy, they decided to fight for an acquittal, arguing that their action was warranted by the necessity defense. This defense holds that someone is allowed to break a law when imminent danger is present, when the normal channels of dealing with a threat are ineffective, and when that person is acting to prevent a greater harm. For example, a person who enters a burning house to rescue those inside is not guilty of trespassing because this action was done to save lives.

Although U.S. Plowshares activists use similar legal arguments in court, they are almost always convicted. However, because they emphasize fidelity to the prophetic tradition, they are not deeply concerned with the outcome of their trials; they view prison as merely an extension of their witness (Nepstad 2008). In contrast, the Seeds of Hope women wanted to win. Departing from the U.S. Plowshares custom of defending themselves, the Seeds of Hope activists secured an attorney who had an impressive record with political cases, including some notable victories with Irish Republican Army–related trials. The women also had the foresight to provide video documentation of their previous efforts to stop weapons shipments to East Timor. Strategically, they brought this video along when they conducted their action at the British Aerospace factory, leaving it at the scene when they were arrested. When the police confiscated it, the video became part of the evidence that the jury was allowed to see. This video was critical in demonstrating a key element of the necessity defense, namely that drastic measures were justified because the normal channels for addressing this concern had proven ineffective. The activists also presented evidence that linked the use of British Aerospace weaponry to human rights abuses in East Timor, thereby supporting their claim that they were using reasonable force to prevent a greater crime. On the stand, Joanna Wilson stated that their situation paralleled a recent shooting spree at a Scottish school. She argued that if someone had tried to take away the gunman's weapon, that individual would have been honored, not prosecuted. Wilson said that she and her codefendants were trying to stop a similar slaughter of children in East Timor. After deliberations, the jury found the women not guilty on all accounts, marking the first full acquittal in the history of the Plowshares movement.

The success of this campaign led British activists to their first choice point: should they continue the U.S. movement's emphasis on prophetic witness or shift to a more politically efficacious approach? The acquittal convinced some activists that they could win cases, setting a legal precedent that could force the British government to change its military practices. As activists debated whether to change their strategy, a political opportunity arose in 1996 that influenced their decision. The International Court of Justice released a document known as the "Advisory Opinion on the Legality of the Threat or Use of Nuclear Weapons." In this document, World Court advisors stated that humanitarian law prohibits preparation for genocide and forbids any military practice that causes unnecessary suffering. Because nuclear missiles are weapons of mass destruction, court advisors argued that all nations should move toward disarmament (Boisson de Chazournes and Sands 1999). They also confirmed the Nuremberg Charter, emphasizing that citizens must uphold international law even when their governments violate it (Zelter 2001).

Convinced that the "Advisory Opinion" would enable activists to effectively challenge British military policies, Angie Zelter made the decision to build an instrumentally oriented Plowshares movement. She recognized that this would require a critical mass, yet at the time, there were only a handful of Plowshares activists in Great Britain. Believing that the long prison sentences associated with the movement deterred prospective participants, Zelter redesigned the movement to incorporate lower-cost forms of protest. Then, using a technique from the 1960s group known as the Committee of 100, she planned to recruit 100 people for a direct action campaign. She hoped that thousands would eventually mobilize against the United Kingdom's nuclear weapons, especially the Trident nuclear submarines located at the Faslane Royal Naval base in Scotland.

Zelter discussed her proposal with experienced peace activists, and eventually six people became the architects of the Trident Plowshares movement. They drafted a handbook that spelled out the movement structure and participation rules. They also established a time line to recruit and train activists. By August 1998, several hundred people gathered at the Faslane Royal Navy base. More than 100 were arrested for civil disobedience, mainly for blockading and trespassing onto the base. Over the next years, the actions expanded so that campaigns at Faslane and other British military bases were routinely held four times a year, resulting in thousands of arrests (Berrigan-McAlister Archive Collection 2000).

One reason why the British Trident Plowshares movement succeeded in mobilizing many campaigns is that organizers decided to reject much of the U.S. Plowshares movement's Catholic symbolism, addressing a second choice point. For example, Trident Plowshares organizers decided not to use blood in their actions, arguing that the theological significance would not resonate with the largely secular British population. Similarly, Trident organizers emphasize that while their campaign is inspired by the U.S. Catholic Left, it is not explicitly faith based. The Trident Plowshares handbook states:

> The Plowshares movement originated in the North American faith-based peace movement. Many priests and nuns in the 1970s began to resist the Vietnam War, thereby connecting with the radical political secular movements. When the war ended, the arms race and nuclear weapons became the focus of resistance. . . . *Although the name comes from the Hebrew scripture, the [British] Plowshares movement is not a Christian or Jewish movement.* It includes people of different faiths and philosophies. Actually, in most Plowshares groups the members adhere to a range of different faiths or philosophies. Some people have seen their action arising out of the Biblical prophecy of Isaiah and as witnessing to the kingdom of God. Others, coming from a secular perspective, have viewed their action as being primarily motivated by a humanist or deeply held conscience commitment to nonviolence and solidarity with poor. Then again there have been other people with a range of religious, moral or political convictions. What they all have in common is a striving to abolish war, an engagement in constructive conversion of arms and military related industry into life affirming production, and the development of nonviolent methods for resolving conflicts. (Berrigan-McAlister Collection 2000, emphasis added)

By adapting the movement to the secular culture of the United Kingdom, Trident Plowshares organizers appealed to a wider segment of British citizens.

The third choice point that Trident Plowshares organizers faced was whether to focus on high-risk actions, as the U.S. movement does, or to place greater emphasis on low-risk tactics. Although a small number of British activists were willing to engage in the U.S. tradition of hammering and property destruction, leaders thought that this was an obstacle to mass recruitment. Therefore, they experimented with alternatives that had more cultural resonance, such as blockades and trespassing actions that are a familiar, long-standing part of the British peace movement's tactical repertoire. For example, as early as 1961, 5,000 British citizens conducted a sit-in at the Ministry of Defense to express their opposition to their government's nuclear policies. In the 1980s, dozens of blockades and trespassing actions occurred at the Greenham base (Berrigan-McAlister Collection 2000). Moreover, these tactics did not require participants to make costly personal sacrifices. In most cases, activists are quickly released from jail and receive modest sanctions— typically a fine of fifty British pounds, which is roughly equivalent to a speeding ticket in the United Kingdom.

The fourth choice point that Trident Plowshares activists faced was whether or not to adopt the U.S. Plowshares movement's organizational form. Like their Swedish counterparts, British organizers decided to reject the commune-based model. Yet unlike those in the Swedish movement, Trident Plowshares organizers did not spend a lot of time or energy developing and sustaining an organizational infrastructure. Because organizers anticipated that thousands would eventually join their campaign, they set forth the following operating system. First, all recruits are asked to join or form an affinity group—a small organizing cell of three to fifteen people who serve as a support system. Each affinity group registers with the core group that serves as the coordinating force of the movement, handling the administrative and logistical tasks. However, Trident Plowshares organizers did not want a centralized, hierarchical form of leadership, so new activists join the core group as others cycle out. In addition, every six months, a meeting is held where each affinity group sends one or two representatives to discuss movement policies and strategies. Since the initial organizers put this system into place and declared that it was not open to debate, recruits have not challenged it. Consequently, this infrastructure provided a stable foundation for movement expansion without consuming a lot of its members' time and energy.

How did these changes shape the British movement? After significant experimentation and changes, Trident Plowshares organizers created a movement that barely reflects the original U.S. Plowshares movement. Yet these changes enabled them to accomplish some notable gains. First, the movement has mobilized thousands of people in opposition to Great Britain's nuclear policies. To date, the Trident Plowshares movement claims that it has generated 2,504 arrests for civil disobedience.[4] Second, in a number of trials, activists have won full acquittals—something that is virtually never achieved in the U.S. movement—thereby attaining some legal recognition that weapons of mass destruction violate international law. Third, the Trident Plowshares movement has succeeded in sustaining these actions over time, providing more than a decade of resistance to British militarism. This capacity to maintain opposition was particularly apparent in a 2007 movement campaign called Faslane 365, which provided a near-continuous blockade of the Faslane Trident base for an entire year. Fourth, there is evidence that the movement has had a tangible influence on public opinion. A 2001 poll indicated that 51 percent of Scottish people (who live closest to the nuclear naval bases) held favorable attitudes toward Trident Plowshares actions, while only 24 percent opposed them (Laffin 2003). By 2007, polls placed Scottish opposition to Trident nuclear weapons between 58 to 70 percent of the overall population (Johns 2007; Johnson 2007; "Trident in Scotland" 2007). Finally, the movement's activities have helped to keep the issue of nuclear weapons alive in national discourse, which may have contributed to renewed opposition from government leaders and other public figures. In June 2007, the Scottish parliament rejected the British government's plan to replace the Trident nuclear system by a vote of 71 to 16 ("Trident in Scotland" 2007). Additionally, numerous religious leaders, including the Catholic bishops and the leaders of the Church of Scotland, released statements calling on the British government to disarm.

Theoretical Implications

As Swedish and British organizers imported the U.S. Plowshares movement's style of war resistance, they resolved strategic dilemmas and addressed choice points in similar ways. Each group chose to: (1) establish a more formalized movement infrastructure; (2) broaden the movement by recruiting a more diverse group of participants; (3) include more low-risk forms of resistance, thereby minimizing the level of sacrifice required for participation; and (4) become a more politically influential force. If both movement branches enacted comparable changes, why were their outcomes so different? A closer comparison of these two Plowshares groups can shed light on this question.

Organizational Form

Both the Swedish and British Plowshares movements altered the originating movement's organizational form. Because the U.S. Plowshares movement is rooted in a network of resistance communities, Swedish organizers initially attempted to emulate this. However, it quickly became evident that this was not working, largely because communes are foreign to Swedish culture. When their commune experiment failed, in part because of this cultural constraint, a sizable number of Swedish activists decided to create a new infrastructure that resembled a traditional social movement organization. They collectively established an organization that emphasized dialogue, transparent decision making, and empowering group processes. Despite this commitment to radical democracy, the task of forming a Swedish Plowshares movement organization turned out to be highly contentious for two reasons. First, by recruiting diverse participants, Swedish organizers created a high degree of heterogeneity within the movement. This led to differing views regarding movement policies and priorities. Second, the renewed recruitment effort generated numerous clashes between veteran Plowshares organizers (who had initiated the movement and had developed strong leadership skills) and the young, relatively inexperienced recruits who claimed that the veteran organizers exercised undue influence. Soon, Swedish activists spent more time arguing than organizing, and as their conflicts became more personal and destructive, the movement collapsed.

In contrast, British Trident Plowshares organizers were able to establish an organization that effectively guided the movement with relatively little conflict. However, the process of establishing a movement infrastructure varied notably in these two cases. Before they recruited participants, Trident Plowshares organizers set up their system and declared that it was not open for debate. In all likelihood, those who had serious problems with it did not join the movement, thereby minimizing any confrontations. Swedish organizers did the reverse; they recruited participants first, then attempted to collaboratively build a movement infrastructure. Given their emphasis on equal input, every decision and aspect of the movement was discussed, creating space for internal differences to surface.

We must also emphasize that the purpose of these movement organizations were distinct. British organizers viewed their infrastructure as nothing more than a coordinating mechanism. Swedish activists, however, saw their organization as a way to prefigure a radically democratic, nonviolent society. Thus organizational processes and group dynamics had greater significance and thus became a greater focal point for conflict because they were viewed as a direct reflection of the movement's utopian goals and vision.[5]

This leads us to revisit standard arguments about organizational form that have been put forth by William Gamson (1975) and Frances Fox Piven and Richard Cloward (1977). From his analysis of dozens of movements, Gamson posits that a centralized organizational infrastructure increases a movement's chance of success and survival. Yet Piven and Cloward claim that as movements become centralized, they lose their radical edge because energy is diverted from protest to sustaining the organization and appeasing donors. In contrast to these arguments, we maintain that the *process* of establishing the infrastructure and its perceived *purpose* may be more important than its particular *form*. Collectively forming an organization with activist cadres is likely to entail endless hours of debate, discussion, and experimentation. In the long run, this may mean that members are more invested in an organization that they helped to create, but the risk for internal conflict (and subsequent movement collapse) is greater than those cases where leaders present a completely formed and functional system and pronounce it nonnegotiable. Moreover, when infrastructure is handled not only as a means but also as a goal in itself, principled conflicts are more likely to occur because organizational work has greater significance: it is no longer seen merely as an administrative necessity, but rather a reflection of the movement's moral vision.

Political Efficacy, Broader Recruitment, and Increased Movement Heterogeneity

Another similarity between the Swedish and British Trident Plowshares movements is that both groups changed the overarching strategy from moral witness to political efficacy. This new instrumentalist approach led to two further changes: broader recruitment efforts, and the introduction of lower-risk tactics that required less sacrifice. As organizers recruited widely to expand activist ranks, the level of heterogeneity within both movements increased. Although Swedish activists experienced significant internal conflicts that were exacerbated by the divergent views of its heterogeneous membership, the British movement did not. This is partly because Trident Plowshares activists had less contact with others in the movement because they primarily operated in small affinity groups. Twice a year, affinity groups send a member to a meeting of representatives, where activists discuss policies and other matters of concern. This loose affiliation meant that there were fewer opportunities for members to disagree with one another over the movement's direction and form. In contrast, Swedish participants had ongoing contact at movement retreats and monthly organizational meetings. Thus, the frequency of contact among activists, combined with the number of key decisions that participants must collectively make, affects whether heterogeneity will be an obstacle.

Conclusions

Our study reveals that existing cross-national diffusion theories do not give enough emphasis to human agency. We have demonstrated that movements cannot be successfully adopted into a new national context unless organizers make adaptations. This adaptation process will yield numerous choice points as activists decide which elements of the originating movement to retain, modify, or reject. Yet while activists contemplate these changes, their decisions will be heavily shaped by the constraints and opportunities that exist in their national context. For Swedish Plowshares activists, cultural constraints were evident in the secular orientation of their population and the absence of communes. These constraints made it difficult to adopt the Catholic symbolism and the commune-based infrastructure of the U.S. Plowshares movement. Yet Swedish activists also had opportunities to create open operational policies because their government was less repressive than the U.S. government, and they had the potential to gain political influence because their parliamentary system was more open to radical groups. The secular British culture posed similar constraints for Trident Plowshares organizers. Their decision to shift toward an instrumental strategy was largely driven by two opportunities: the acquittal of the British Seeds of Hope activists, which established a legal precedent for their actions, and the 1996 "Advisory Opinion" of the World Court, which ruled that nuclear weapons are incompatible with international law.

Our study also indicates that not all adaptations and changes have the same degree of impact. Decisions to alter movement strategies are more likely to instigate comprehensive transformation than changes in tactics, symbols, or operational policies because a shift in strategy—from expressive to instrumental, in our case—may necessitate new recruitment approaches or infrastructural forms. Moreover, the question of recruitment appears critical to understanding successful versus problematic diffusion. When movement organizers choose to enlist a heterogeneous group of activists, the likelihood of conflict may increase. In this situation, leaders may find that they can limit internal tensions if they make key decisions beforehand, such as the type of movement organization and decision-making process that will be used. Also, our investigation raises the question of how much a diffused movement repertoire can be altered before it actually becomes a new movement. In our case, we argue that although many of the movement's definitional criteria were altered (e.g., use of blood, biblical references, sabotage of weapons, and witness orientation), it is still an example of cross-national diffusion because the Trident Plowshares movement historically grew out of the U.S. movement and it continues to use the Plowshares name to reflect its shared heritage.

More comparative research is needed to shed light on the types of choice points and strategic dilemmas that cross-national actors face. As we systematically trace the decisions that movement leaders make, we must also examine the cultural and structural constraints that shape their choices. In so doing, we will develop an understanding of how specific strategic changes increase or decrease the likelihood that an imported movement will take root and prosper in a new environment.

Notes

Some of the ideas within this chapter were developed in "Strategic Changes and Cultural Adaptations: Explaining Differential Outcomes in the International Plowshares Movement," *International Journal of Peace Studies* 13, no. 1 (2008): 15–42. We thank Greg Maney, Jeff Goodwin, and an anonymous reviewer for their comments.

1. In a Clausewitz-inspired understanding, we define *tactics* as the means and plan to win a single campaign (one battle) and *strategy* as the plan of how to win the struggle (the war). Thus, tactics involve the small-scale repertoire and subgoals of the movement, while strategy is about how a movement reaches its goals.

2. Vinthagen's personal collection.

3. Vinthagen's personal collection.

4. See Trident Ploughshares (http://www.tridentploughshares.org/).

5. Vinthagen's personal collection.

References

Aditjondro, George. 2000. "Ninjas, Nanggalas, Monuments, and Massad Manuals: An Anthropology of Indonesian State Terror in East Timor." In *Death Squad: The Anthropology of State Terror,* edited by Jeffrey A. Sluka, 158–88. Philadelphia: University of Pennsylvania Press.

Benford, Robert, and David Snow. 1988. "Ideology, Frame Resonance, and Participant Mobilization." *International Social Movement Research* 1:197–217.

Berrigan-McAlister Collection. 2000. *Tri-denting It Handbook: An Open Guide to Trident Ploughshares.* DePaul University Archives, Box 15, Chicago, Ill.

Boisson de Chazournes, Laurence, and Philippe Sands, eds. 1999. *International Law, the International Court of Justice, and Nuclear Weapons.* Cambridge: Cambridge University Press.

Chabot, Sean. 2000. "Transnational Diffusion and the African American Reinvention of Gandhian Repertoire." *Mobilization* 5:201–16.

Engell-Nielsen, Klaus. 2001. *Samtal med ett Vapenföretag* [Dialogue with a weapons corporation]. Göteborg: Stiftelsen för Fredsarbete.

Forest, Jim. 1997. *Love Is the Measure: A Biography of Dorothy Day.* Maryknoll, N.Y.: Orbis Books.

Gamson, William A. 1975. *The Strategy of Social Protest.* Homewood, Ill.: Dorsey.

Herngren, Per. 1993. *Path of Resistance: The Practice of Civil Disobedience.* Philadelphia: New Society Publishers.

Herngren, Per, and Stellan Vinthagen. 1992. *Handbok: Avrustningslägret i Linköping* (Handbook: The Disarmament Camp in Linköping). Göteborg: Omega and Avrustningslägret.

Jasper, James. 2004. "A Strategic Approach to Collective Action: Looking for Agency in Social Movement Choices." *Mobilization* 9:1–16.

Johns, Rob. 2007. "Trident and Public Opinion: Evidence from the 2007 Scottish Election Study." Paper presented at the Academic Blockade Conference, June, Faslane, Scotland.

Johnson, Rebecca. 2007. "The Trident Dispatches No. 1: An Overview of the Debate." *Bulletin of Atomic Scientists Online,* February 5. http://www.thebulletin.org.

Klejment, Anne, and Nancy Roberts, eds. 1996. *American Catholic Pacificism: The Influence of Dorothy Day and the Catholic Worker Movement.* Westport, Conn.: Praeger.

Laffin, Arthur. 2003. *Swords into Plowshares: A Chronology of Plowshares Disarmament Actions, 1980–2003.* Marion, S.D.: Rose Hill Books.

Leander, Hasse. 1997. "The Ploughshares Movement in Sweden and the U.S.: A Comparison." *Daily Hammer: Newsletter of the Ploughshares Support Network* 14:10–12.

McAdam, Doug, and Dieter Rucht. 1993. "The Cross-National Diffusion of Movement Ideas." *Annals of the American Academy of Political and Social Science* 528:56–74.

Meconis, Charles A. 1979. *With Clumsy Grace: The American Catholic Left, 1961– 1975.* New York: Seabury Press.

Nepstad, Sharon Erickson. 2004. "Disciples and Dissenters: Tactical Choice and Consequences in the Plowshares Movement." *Research in Social Movements, Conflict, and Change* 25:139–60.

———. 2008. *Religion and War Resistance in the Plowshares Movement.* New York: Cambridge University Press.

Piven, Frances Fox, and Richard Cloward. 1977. *Poor People's Movements: Why They Succeed, How They Fail.* New York: Pantheon.

Polletta, Francesca. 2002. *Freedom Is an Endless Meeting: Democracy in American Social Movements.* Chicago: University of Chicago Press.

Rogers, Everett. 1995. *Diffusion of Innovations.* 4th ed. New York: Free Press.

Snow, David A., and Robert D. Benford. 1999. "Alternative Types of Cross-National Diffusion in the Social Movement Arena." In *Social Movements in a Globalizing World,* edited by Donatella della Porta, Hanspeter Kriesi, and Dieter Rucht, 23–39. London: Macmillan.

Soule, Sarah. 1997. "The Student Divestment Movement in the United States and Tactical Diffusion: The Shantytown Protest." *Social Forces* 75:855–82.

Strang, David, and John W. Meyer. 1993. "Institutional Conditions for Diffusion." *Theory and Society* 22:487–511.

"Trident in Scotland." 2007. Scottish government news release, October 22. http://www.scotland.gov.uk.

Vinthagen, Stellan. 1998. *Förberedelse för motstånd* [Preparation for resistance: A critique of the preparation methods and internal conflict management of the Plowshares movement]. Göteborg: Omega Förlag.

Zelter, Angie. 2001. *Trident on Trial: The Case for People's Disarmament.* Edinburgh: Luath Press.

Conclusion: Conceptualizing Strategy in an Interactive Processional Model

Rachel V. Kutz-Flamenbaum

In this chapter, I integrate insights and findings from the volume to create a model that reflects the processual and reiterative nature of strategy as a series of interactions between actors, targets, and opponents within specific cultural and structural frameworks. I begin with some reflections on different ways of defining strategy and the implications of those definitions for scholarship on strategy. Those reflections are then brought together to develop a model of strategy that integrates and interrogates the volume as a whole. The chapter concludes with some overarching lessons and implications for future research.

A strategy is a plan of collective action intended to accomplish goals within a particular context. A good strategy accounts for multiple players, anticipates likely scenarios, can be adapted, and negotiates multiple (and sometimes contradictory) objectives. In some cases, strategies are detailed and explicit plans. In other cases, they may be only partially articulated, shifting, contested, or poorly developed. Regardless of whether or not a strategy is effective or well developed, social movement actions frequently are the products of strategy. Movement actors seek to make change; they develop strategic plans that they hope will help to make this change. Sometimes these plans are small and limited and barely scrape the surface of the problem. Holding a protest on campus to object to a speaker, for example, may draw only a few dozen people to the protest and serve only to confirm a known disagreement between two groups. In other cases, strategic plans are extensive, elaborate, complicated, and detailed—so complicated and detailed, in fact, that it is hard for all of the actors (as well as researchers) to appreciate the full scope of planning and intention behind the movement actions. For example, a coalition of movement groups may decide to implement a boycott of a well-known corporation in an effort to persuade that corporation to change its production process. That boycott may be announced and sustained through periodic rallies, promoted through a public education media campaign, and dramatized through street theater performed in busy locations during rush hour. Such a campaign, sustained over months or years, would require regular analysis of the tactics' effectiveness and adaptability as well as a commitment from multiple actors of both time and resources. If successful, the campaign could result in changes in public opinion, corporate policy, or the law. That coalition's strategy could, in turn, be deployed again and again by the same actors, a subset of those actors, or other groups that learned of the campaign through shared networks or media visibility.

The choices to hold protests, organize boycotts, and engage in street theater are strategic ones. However, these strategic decisions are made, like all human decisions, within webs of possibilities and limitations—possibilities and limits of time, experience, knowledge, ideology, resources, and the broader political–economic environment. The model of strategy that this volume seeks to develop is one that acknowledges and records the intense thoughtfulness and intentionality of much, if not most, social movement action by drawing attention to the agency of social movement actors while simultaneously acknowledging contexts that influence actors' decisions. Approaching all social movement action, including that which appears primarily expressive as well as that which is quite formally political as strategic, legitimates those actions and actors as being concerned about short- and long-term goals and trying to act in ways consistent with those concerns.

Taking an inclusive view of social movement action has analytical risks for scholars. One significant risk is that social movement scholars may ascribe meaning to action that is not necessarily strategic. We may observe actions and campaigns and conclude that the outcomes were the result of intentional strategies, thereby missing important elements of the process, overlooking failures, and flattening the interactional and dynamic elements of campaigns and movements. As scholars observing and analyzing movements, our models of strategy can simultaneously be enhanced and endangered by categorizing social movement action as strategic when the strategies were only partially articulated or not at all. In this worst-case scenario, social movement scholars risk reifying movements and misattributing meanings and intentions of movement actors. In the best case, we help to articulate and analyze the full potential of strategies habitually reproduced and only semiconsciously constructed. As Jasper argues in chapter 2 and Ryan, Jeffreys, and Blozie illustrate in chapter 4, a useful model of social movement strategy should simultaneously incorporate movements' accounts of actions and plans as well as apply the critical and reflexive analytical lens of social movement scholarship.

Strategy is an important theme in social movement scholarship because it centers on the core of sociology: the interplay of structure and agency. Strategy is a response to the recursive structuring of structures and acting of agents in an interactive process that reshapes those structures and changes those agents. Social movement scholarship has increasingly embraced the idea that understanding movements requires analysis of culture as well as structure. Too often, though, structure and culture are then represented in oppositional ways, flattening culture to either mean some set of symbolic structures or a proxy for human agency and simplifying structure to mean institutions. The work presented in this volume suggests that the study of strategy may provide a path between these extremes.

Many scholars have worked to challenge the structural and organizational biases that emerged in response to the paradigms of resource mobilization and political process theories of social action that dominated the field of social movement scholarship (Polletta 1997, 2004; Goodwin and Jasper 2004; Staggenborg and Taylor 2005; Armstrong and Bernstein 2008). This volume offers several visions that thoughtfully deal with the relationship between culture and social movement strategy. In chapter 3, Polletta focuses on collective action repertoires, institutional norms of cultural expression, and metonymy. These three elements each show how culture influences the range of potential options that social movement actors perceive. As illustrated by Maney in chapter 8, activists plan actions that fit their ways of articulating and thinking about social problems and social change. Collectively, the chapters in this volume show that models of strategy must account for culture not as a discrete variable in an analysis but in nuanced and complicated ways. In doing so, this volume challenges models of movement action that dichotomize the instrumental and expressive. Social movement culture is not only the symbolic content of movements; it is also the habitus of activists, a context that influences movement organizations, the fabric of ideology and collective identity, and a target of movement action. This way of thinking about culture undermines clear divisions between cultural and political, and instead emphasizes the ways that culture shapes structures and structures shape culture. Therefore, movement actors seek to simultaneously navigate and re-form existing cultural dynamics, movement organizations, and the political–economic environment. Understanding structure, culture, and agency as mutually constitutive elements within a recursive relationship is central to understanding strategy as a process—a series of interactions and relational decisions. The chapters in this volume show that although our research efforts may only capture a moment in time, we need to be mindful that strategy is an outcome as much as a starting point, and that the outcome is influenced not only by broad social forces, but also by interactions within, among, and between groups. Strategy is the aggregate of a series of strategic choices and decisions. Even a clearly planned strategy is challenged as it is tested in the real world of social movement action. The interactions between groups are often complicated by different assumptions, experiences, values, and tastes for distinct strategic options. Understanding the process of strategy is about studying broad groups of actors and paying as much attention to the range of topics and options discussed (and not discussed) as to the options selected.

The chapters in this volume examine the production and implementation of strategy at both microlevels and mesolevels through a focus on individual movement actors as well as movement organizations. Each chapter spotlights specific forces that shape and influence movement strategy, including internal organizational and movement dynamics, the actions of targets and opponents, audience perception, ideology and collective identity, and the broader political, economic, and cultural environment. These findings and insights combine to generate a model that identifies strategy as the outcome of a cyclical process that depends on the interaction of movement actors within mobilization organizations and is influenced by cultural forms, opponents, and targets all within a broader social environment. The model is a recursive one that plays out over time.

The following pages focus in detail on *movement actors, movement organizations, external forces, political–economic systems,* and *culture* to define and develop each element's role in the development of strategy.

Movement Actors

Movement actors are the individual people who participate in movements. The relationships between movement actors may be formally organized and tightly bound to one another or loosely connected in a temporary or transitory relationship. Movement actors have a multiplicity of organizational, movement, and political identities that vary in locational, temporal, and contextual ways. Their individual biographies and activist experience result in broad variation in skills, knowledge, and experience; that variation affects the range of strategic choices considered and selected within a movement campaign.

Actors Skills, Knowledge, and Experience

Movement actors, both individuals and groups, have varying amounts of experience, knowledge, and skills. Skills may be finely honed within a particular movement, and knowledge may include painstaking detail of a stable set of opponents and targets. Some or none of those skills may be transferable to another arena. Skills may also be developed through transitory participation in a broad number of distinct campaigns or finely honed within one cohesive enduring movement. For example, in chapter 7, Whittier describes a group of activists against childhood sexual abuse that emerge from the woman's rights movement and violence against women's movement. Activists were deeply immersed in their community, creating a committed and insular movement. In contrast, in chapter 9, Robnett and Alabi describe movement newcomers working with civil rights movement activists to create a social movement organization that recruited broadly to develop a loosely knit social movement group. Participation in either of these movements would result in very different types of skills, knowledge, and experience. Participation in movements facilitates the opportunity to develop concrete skills such as web design, grant writing, and media literacy. Participants may learn how to build barricades or handle firearms. They may also obtain specific knowledge, including how to obtain permits, who to talk to in specific offices, how police are likely to respond, how to counter the effects of police weapons, where to park buses, and on what days reporters are more eager for news pieces. Movement experiences include getting a sense of what the possible outcomes may be of specific strategies, learning new ideas for getting messages out, obtaining information about other activist groups, and building large numbers of contacts and broader networks. These concrete skills, specific knowledge, and movement experiences matter because they vary from one movement actor to another and because they shape the activist repertoire.

Repertoires

Experience matters not only because it provides the opportunity to practice, but also because it can expose actors to a broader range of possibilities. In chapter 12, Nepstad and Vinthagen, for example, show the precise path of diffusion for the Plowshares repertoire. In both the British and Swedish cases, an individual activist learned of the repertoires through movement participation and then told others of what he had learned. In turn, he and those others formed an organization that adapted the repertoire to fit the local context—an important example of movement actors' agency. In chapter 2, Jasper points out that "protest groups may borrow repertoires, but they do so one decision at a time." Activists' repertoires are always theoretically broader than the smaller set of possibilities the group will consider. Some tactics are dismissed as too confrontational and others as ineffective; some are never considered because they don't fit into the frameworks of meaning. In reading several chapters in this volume, in particular Nepstad and Vinthagen's work on the Plowshares movement in chapter 12, Maney's work on the civil rights movement in Northern Ireland in chapter 8, and Schock's research on land struggles in Brazil and India in chapter 10, we see examples of how protest groups can only borrow what they have learned about, how they will only want to borrow it if it is meaningful to them, and how they believe it will be effective in influencing audiences and targets.

Collective Identity

Collective identity provides a shared sense of purpose and unifies a group of individuals in ways that make mass action possible (Gamson 1991). Collective identities are not abstract concepts. Rather, they are historically specific and culturally bounded phenomena that emerge from movement experience (Bernstein 2008; Rupp and Taylor 1999). Collective identities also form parts of the processes, products, and outcomes of movement strategizing. In chapter 7, Whittier shows how the development and promotion of collective identities can be a strategy in itself. Whittier examines how victims of child abuse developed and used individual coming-out stories to claim and recover from their own individual experiences, while groups also use coming-out strategies to build a collective identity that pushes for social change. The development of strong and transformative collective identities through the process of coming out and claiming one's relational position within a collective redefines individual's lives and helps to build movements. Collective identity, activist repertoires, skills, experience, and knowledge influence movement actors' range of strategic choices and decisions about movement strategy. They do so within movement organizations.

Movement Organizations

Movement organizations can be both formal and informal and include nongovernmental organizations (NGOs), social movement organizations (SMOs), transnational social movement organizations (TSMOs), emerging social movement groups, informal networks, and both informal and formal coalitions. Although movement organizations are variable in their degree of organizational formality, they share in common the fact that they are groups of individuals who are acting through and on behalf of the organization. As such, movement organizations are, at least in part, independent of individual movement actors. Concurrently, they are also a countenance of the movement actors that form, support, run, staff, and represent them. These interdependent and fluid relationships between individual movement actors and movement organizations have important implications for strategizing. Organizations are limited internally in their range of possible strategic choices by their formal status, organizational ideology, leadership, resources, decision-making structures, and organizational diversity. In the following pages, I discuss some of the findings from this volume as they relate to organizational diversity, decision making and leadership, resources, and organizational ideology.

Diversity

It is clear from movement research that one way activists learn to innovate repertoires and improve on strategies is through integrating diversity—campaigns that bring together people and groups with a wide range of movement experiences and from different ideological viewpoints (Ganz 2000). In chapter 5, Aunio describes how diversity in age and experience allowed for a multiplicity of tactics within the 2005 Climate Action Network at the United Nations Climate Change Conference in Montreal. She found a deliberate bifurcation between strategies and level of age/movement experience, with older and more experienced activists focusing on policy change and younger activists engaging in direct action. She argues that this bifurcation allowed the Climate Action Network to maximize their impact and increase participant engagement. In chapter 6, Smith also highlights the benefits of heterogeneity. Smith finds that social forums provide an opportunity to bring together a wide range of groups that do not normally interact. Drawing on her research and participation in social forums, Smith applied her observations in her own efforts to create diversity through her work with the Michiana social forum and a local currency project.

Diversity comes at the cost of taking time to debate and deliberate, explain, and argue. Many scholars have found that successful movement strategies may best be developed through cohesive networks, which have shared ideologies, high levels of trust, and tightly knit communities. These findings suggest that homogeneous networks also have powerful advantages for developing successful campaigns. Nepstad and Vinthagen (chapter 12) directly compare two cases that had different levels of heterogeneity and find that concentration of decision-making powers within a homogenous group at the beginning of a movement or campaign had distinct advantages in promoting movement growth and longevity. They argue that one of the reasons that the Plowshares model was able to be more successfully adapted in Great Britain but not in Sweden was that the founding group in Great Britain remained small and homogenous while the Swedish group opened up deliberation on organizational structure from the start, creating opportunities for participation from a broad number of actors, but also creating increased opportunities for discord.

Decision Making

Many of the chapters in the volume highlight the importance of decision-making structures and the way that they shape actors' range of opportunities. Maney (chapter 8) and Nepstad and Vinthagen (chapter 10) argue that it was the structure of the decision-making process that determined whether diversity among participants was an advantage or disadvantage. Similarly, Aunio's (chapter 5) findings about heterogeneity are within the context of an established social movement organization, with much of the decision-making power centered in the more homogenous old guard. Smith's (chapter 6) observations about the social forum process are, in large part, about movement building and the short-term goals of organizing a local social forum and the specific local currency campaign.

Leadership and leaders are an important component of decision making at the individual level. Several chapters in this volume draw attention to individual leaders in addition to the decision-making structures. In chapter 12, Nepstad and Vinthagen reference the importance of the charismatic leadership of the Berrigan brothers in the U.S. Plowshares movement. Robnett and Alabi, in chapter 9, draw our attention to leadership as the critical source of organizational structure, arguing that their case represents a unique form of SMO, the corporate SMO, that relies on business actors to shape the organization. In chapter 5, Aunio also shows how important central leadership is for shaping movement strategy. Her chapter suggests that the 'youth' at the Climate Action Network conference were a carefully courted and supported group (by the old guard) that was able to use riskier and more confrontational strategies. Aunio's chapter includes several references by more established leaders of the movement that they wished they could be engaging in the more innovative tactics, but that they thought they would lose some of the legitimacy that they had accrued and ultimately undermine the goals of the movement. The creation of the insider/outsider dynamic in this case allowed for the leadership to distance themselves from riskier tactics but still indirectly allow the implementation of the full range of tactics.

Resources

Material resources are an important part of what builds movement organizations. Material resources include money for staff, office space, legal support for filing applications and protecting members, meeting spaces, and communication technologies. Fund-raising concerns and requirements tie many organizations into narrow ranges of possibilities through both tax law requirements and fear of alienating donors. Yet access to resources can provide decisive advantages. In chapter 11, Fetner and Sanders, for example, explain much of the success of the Christian right in the United States by its strong institutional structures and access to resources. In chapter 9, Robnett and Alabi similarly identify internal monetary resources as critically important for the formation of the Hip-Hop Movement Connections, and its resulting ability to mobilize large numbers of otherwise disenfranchised youth. As Smith also illustrates in chapter 6, access to material resources are shaped by the constituency and membership of a group as well as ties with institutions (consider churches in supporting the religious right, but also Smith's example of universities supporting many progressive movements indirectly through participation by faculty and students).

Social movement actors and movement organizations think up, develop, adapt, and implement strategies within a field of movement action and alongside other movement actors. Their actions and reactions are shaped by those of allies, opponents, bystanders, and targets. They engage in those actions within a broader political, economic, and cultural environment. Cultural norms, public discourses, and hegemonic processes shape the range of possibilities available to movements and filter interpretations of the range of possible interpretations for targets, bystanders, and the public. Chapters in this volume have drawn our attention to the importance of external influences, including both media and culture, as mediators of movement messages and actions and as filters of movement strategy.

External Influences

In addition to the elements of movements that are highlighted above and that are largely internal to movements, movement actors and organizations are also shaped by external forces, including three categories: movement audiences and political targets; media; and culture and ideology. Just as these external forces shape movement actors and influence movement strategizing, they are each often the focus of movement strategies and important measures of movement outcomes.

Movement Audiences and Political Targets

Movement audiences are composed of supporters, targets, opponents, and bystanders. Targets are the individual people, like legislators, or the groups of people, like the public, that movement action is intended to persuade and influence. Opponents may be targets, but they also include organized countermovements and less organized groups of opponents. Bystanders are those not yet committed to a position but may still be influenced and leveraged, depending on the strategy. In chapter 1, Meyer and Staggenborg draw our attention to the fact that opposition and bystanders influence strategy through interaction with movement actors. As they state, "Choices are shaped by expectations about the responses of targets and bystanders as well as by their actual responses." More abstractly, choices are also shaped by perceptions of the broader political context—the permeability and transparency of governmental decision-making bodies; the degree of threat, violence, and repression; the degree of citizen participation in the political system; the political ideology of the party in power; and the religious and civic beliefs and values of the populace.

The final chapters of this volume deal explicitly with the process of understanding how strategies can be transferred successfully from one political or cultural environment to another. Fetner and Sanders (chapter 11) find that institutional differences mediate the meaning of cultural frames and strategies developed by the religious right. Nepstad and Vinthagen (chapter 12) find that repertoires transferred from one country to another require adaptation to different cultures if they are to resonate and succeed. Similarly, Schock (chapter 10) found that resonating with a broader set of religious and cultural values facilitated diffusion. Movement audiences and political targets are often difficult to reach, and it is even more difficult to be sure that the message is interpreted properly. This is why the media is such a powerful external influence.

Media

One of the external targets that has a profound and well-documented effect on movement actors and structures is the media. For both internally and externally oriented strategies and for both short- and long-term campaigns, publicity and visibility can serve to strengthen the movement, facilitate recruitment, and influence opponents and targets. As a result, media coverage is often a central component of movement strategy. It shapes the options available to movement actors and influences opponents' actions, public opinion, the targets' responses. Aunio (chapter 5) describes the media attention that the youth generated with their bed-in. This media attention was in direct contrast with the type of serious and policy oriented comments made by the old guard in the Climate Action Network. The integration of the two strategies of performative street theater combined with policy-oriented conferencing allowed the Climate Action Network to transmit their messages simultaneously to the broader public and political targets. In chapter 4, Ryan, Jeffreys, and Blozie detail their experience in developing a media strategy for the Rhode Island Coalition Against Domestic Violence (RICADV) and their resulting model of movement–media interaction. They describe a model that requires the difficult feat of maintaining relationships with mainstream media out-lets with the result of successfully distributing advocacy and policy messages that increased visibility of domestic violence issues using frames that resonated for both movement participants and members of the public. RICADV suc-ceeded in using media as an integral part of their strategy, but they did so by devoting considerable time and resources. All movement actors negotiate how much of their time and resources they want to dedicate to dealing with media and attempting to get their messages transmitted in the press. Both when well prepared and ill, media attention can be a powerful influencing force. While the media records the action and translates the message, culture and ideology shape both the transmission and the reception.

Culture and Ideology

Ideology and collective identity are forces that facilitate and inhibit actors' ability to engage in campaigns and also to shape organizational decision-making structures. Evidenced in terms like "feminist process" or "anarchist process" to represent participatory decision making and non-hierarchical col-lectives, ideology is manifest in the types of organizations that activists form and the ways that they agree to make decisions about the organization's activ-ities. In chapter 10, Schock shows how religious beliefs and ideology may provide the shared cultural frameworks that allow repertoires to succeed by tapping into cultural norms. Differences in ideology create struggles as well. In chapter 8, Maney finds that ideological differences were at the root of struggle within the coalitions of the Northern Ireland civil rights movement.

In chapter 9, Robnett and Alabi provide an example of how ideology shapes the organizational form, creating, in their case, a corporate SMO. They identify a hybrid organization that blended hip-hop music and consumerism with social action and civil rights, reflecting an ideology that emphasizes mar-keting in a consumerist environment while also promoting a social justice message. Hip-Hop Movement Connections represents a model of action that blends cultural expression with political action. This organization was limited in its potential tactics and targets by its donors and its structures, but it was also able to organize large-scale and expensive events that reached out to a large number of politically disenfranchised youth.

While the Hip-Hop Movement Connections is distinct in its leader-ship, resources, and organizational structure, many movement organizations develop strategies that seek to integrate music, art, and performance within a political message. Furthermore, many cultural events are prefigurative in that their purpose is to transform the culture by living the world activists seek to create.

To summarize, strategy is the outcome of a cyclical process that depends on the interaction of movement actors within movement organizations and is shaped by broader forces of culture and the political–economic environment. The chapters in this volume provide elaborate examples of how these processes interact to shape strategy.

Lessons and Applications

This volume, *Strategies for Social Change,* has sought to encourage students of social movements, new and more experienced, to take social movement strategy seriously. We argue that not only has it been under-theorized and therefore is worthy of analytical attention, but also that it is a particularly important element of social movement scholarship because it is a fulcrum that may enable the theoretical, empirical, and practical balance that many social movement scholars are looking to find. Strategy provides a balance between structure and agency and politics and culture as well as a path for scholars to engage in research that is useful to activists.

In chapter 1, Meyer and Staggenborg argue that research on strategy requires analysis at the micro-, meso-, and macrolevels. The chapters in this volume support Meyer and Staggenborg's point that strategy is developed, implemented, and shaped at all levels of analysis as individual movement actors within and outside movement organizations work within the broader structures they seek to change. The breadth of these case studies shows not only that social movement strategy is developed at multiple levels, but also that strategy is developed in interaction between individuals, organizations, coalitions, targets, opponents, and bystanders. By researching the interactions between individuals and groups within political and cultural contexts, this volume points toward research methods that value activist participation in defining research questions, collecting data, and interpreting and presenting findings, immersion in movements, and studies conducted over time.

Similarly, Jasper in chapter 2 argues that the study of strategy requires research that is grounded in the real, emphasizing the importance of taking seriously the experiential knowledge of activists and the participatory experience of scholars. Grounded research relies upon inductive reasoning; basing a theory on immersion in the field or the archives, on conversations with activists, review of first hand reports, on observations and on research, rather than deductive reasoning. Keeping social movement research on strategy grounded in the real challenges social movement scholars to be fully engaged in the movements that they study. This is not to say that scholars must only study contemporary movements or those with which they are aligned. Instead, the challenge is for scholars to immerse themselves in movements in ways that allow us to be challenged and questioned by the voices of activists within the movement, either virtually through archives and personal accounts or through direct conversation. This approach rejects models that assume things about activists (e.g., that they are purely rational actors; that they are taking the only opportunities open to them given structural constraints; that the outcomes are the same as the strategies; that different groups with ideological differences don't work well together). Instead, it puts human agency at the center of our theoretical models and it suggests that the study of social movement strategy should be grounded in empirical studies that take seriously the ways that activists account for their own actions.

The recognition of strategy as an interactive process has methodological and theoretical implications for scholars. It also has important implications for activists. For some activists, the fact that strategy is developed by individuals, groups, and coalitions and through interaction and negotiation is an obvious one. They are the activists who have been on the inside of strategic planning sessions and have worked as organizers of campaigns. For less experienced activists or the rank and file, illuminating the relational elements of decisions and putting strategic decisions in their historical, political, and cultural contexts may make strategic decisions and strategic planning more transparent to newcomers and outsiders and therefore may facilitate innovation and movement expansion. In taking the time to explain the history and process, assumptions may often be uncovered, and new possibilities may emerge. Engaging in grounded social movement research is likely to facilitate activist–scholar collaboration. It may also serve to make social movement scholarship more accessible to activists.

Through our focus on thinking about strategy as a multilevel interactional process, several key findings have come into focus. One is that leadership matters. With the widespread adoption of nonhierarchical and consensual decision making, frequent preference for decentralized action, increased professionalization of some segments of SMOs, and the dramatic increase in the number of new social movement organizations, analysis of decision making in movements has perhaps shifted away from leader-based models and moved toward more collective frameworks. Several of the chapters in this volume suggest the importance of continued attention to the role of leaders in creating and implementing strategy. Leaders are the decision makers, and it is their role to develop, adapt, and assess strategies. In collective groups, informal leaders may guide strategy discussions. In hierarchical forums, leaders may develop strategy and pass it down to be implemented. Although strategy may be developed and implemented at all levels of action, the bulk of its development lies in the hands of the decision makers.

Increasing attention to leadership in social movement scholarship may be essential for understanding aspects of strategy. Yet it should be approached with methodological caution. Generating relationships with leadership, particularly in large and professional organizations, is most likely to reward the researcher and the movement leader; academic elites speaking to movement elites. These sorts of interactions and relationships are certainly valuable for developing social movement scholarship and for providing support to movement goals. Yet they also make strategy scholarship less accessible for non-elites on both sides. Furthermore, this model is likely to prioritize organizations with formal leadership, external legitimacy, and professional structures. Thus, the call to pay more attention to leadership in research on strategy must be met with the qualifications that we must also think of leadership in fluid and nonpredetermined ways. Our models of leadership must emphasize interactions and be grounded in the real.

It is also clear in reading this volume that strategy, in both its formation and implementation, is about both instrumental calculations and expressive manifestations—both purpose and passion. Strategy both shapes and is shaped by people's emotions and social relationships. Research on movement strategies that focuses on the role of actors while they are engaging in strategic planning should pay careful attention to the interrelated instrumental and expressive aspects of strategy construction. Similarly, focusing on the emotional expressions that are successful in influencing strategy formation would provide some valuable empirical grounding for theories and analyses on the role of emotions in social movement strategy.

Another important theme with potential for future research is the finding that "strategy" is almost always plural. Multiple strategies exist for multiple goals that are intended to target multiple audiences with implications for different time frames. Several chapters in this volume suggest that analysts should look for the possibility of multiple strategies within the same movement, coalition, and even organization (see chapters by Jasper; Maney; and Nepstad and Vinthagen). The existence of multiple strategies, targets, and time frames is due not only to the interactive, processual nature of strategy, but also the fact that there is no ideal target for all purposes. As Maney argues in chapter 8, this is due to multiple goals and conflicting ontological assumptions. The chapters in this volume suggest that there are some clear patterns. Research that systematically evaluated tactics using the frameworks developed in this book could provide important lessons for both activists and scholars.

To understand strategy, social movement scholars must look for the interpretive, interactive, and processual relationships among decision making, planning, acting, and reacting. Taking an interactional approach that considers multiple levels of analysis among multiple players takes us quite a bit closer to understanding social movement action, social change, and social life.

References

Armstrong, Elizabeth A., and Mary Bernstein. 2008. "Culture, Power, and Institutions: A Multi-institutional Politics Approach to Social Movements." *Sociological Theory* 26:74–99.

Bernstein, Mary. 2008. "The Analytic Dimensions of Identity: A Political Identity Framework." In *Identity Work in Social Movements,* edited by Jo Reger, Daniel J. Myers, and Rachel L. Einwholer, 277–302. Minneapolis: University of Minnesota Press.

Gamson, William A. 1991. "Commitment and Agency in Social Movements." *Sociological Forum* 6:27–50.

Ganz, Marshall. 2000. "Resources and Resourcefulness: Strategic Capacity in the Unionization of California Agriculture, 1959–1966." *American Journal of Sociology* 105:1003–62.

Goodwin, Jeff, and James M. Jasper, eds. 2004. *Rethinking Social Movements: Structure, Meaning and Emotion.* New York: Rowman & Littlefield.

Polletta, Francesca. 1997. "Culture and Its Discontents: Recent Theorizing on the Cultural Dimensions of Protest." *Sociological Inquiry* 67:431–50.

———. 2004. "Culture Is Not Just in Your Head." In *Rethinking Social Movements,* edited by Jeff Goodwin and James M. Jasper, 97–109. New York: Rowman & Littlefield.

Rupp, Leila J., and Verta Taylor. 1999. "Forging Feminist Identity in an International Movement: A Collective Identity Approach to Twentieth-Century Feminism." *Signs* 24:363–86.

Staggenborg, Suzanne, and Verta Taylor. 2005. "Whatever Happened to the Women's Movement?" *Mobilization* 10:37–52.

Contributors

JESSICA AYO ALABI is assistant professor of sociology and gender studies at Orange Coast College.

KENNETH T. ANDREWS is associate professor of sociology at the University of North Carolina at Chapel Hill. He is the author of *Freedom Is a Constant Struggle: The Mississippi Civil Rights Movement and Its Legacy.*

ANNA-LIISA AUNIO is a postdoctoral fellow at the Center for Research in Ethics at the University of Montreal.

LINDA BLOZIE is director of public affairs for the Connecticut Coalition Against Domestic Violence (CCADV).

TINA FETNER is associate professor of sociology at McMaster University. She is the author of *How the Religious Right Shaped Lesbian and Gay Activism* (Minnesota, 2008).

JEFF GOODWIN is professor of sociology at New York University. He is author of *No Other Way Out: States and Revolutionary Movements, 1945–1991* and coeditor of *The Social Movements Reader, Social Movements: Critical Concepts in Sociology* (four volumes), *Rethinking Social Movements: Structure, Culture, and Emotion,* and *Passionate Politics: Emotions and Social Movements.*

JAMES M. JASPER teaches in the sociology Ph.D. program at the Graduate Center of the City University of New York. He is the author of *Nuclear Politics, The Animal Rights Crusade, The Art of Moral Protest, Restless Nation,* and

Getting Your Way, and coeditor of *The Social Movements Reader, Rethinking Social Movements, Social Movements,* and *Passionate Politics.*

KAREN JEFFREYS is associate director of the Rhode Island Coalition for the Homeless.

RACHEL V. KUTZ-FLAMENBAUM is assistant professor of sociology at the University of Pittsburgh.

GREGORY M. MANEY is professor of sociology at Hofstra University. He is the coauthor of *Contesting Patriotism: Culture, Power, and Strategy in the Peace Movement.*

DAVID S. MEYER is professor of sociology and political science at the University of California, Irvine. He is author of *The Politics of Protest: Social Movements in America* and *A Winter of Discontent: The Nuclear Freeze and American Politics,* as well as coeditor of *The Politics of Protest: Social Movements in America, Routing the Opposition: Social Movements, Public Policy, and Democracy* (Minnesota, 2005), *Social Movements: Identity, Culture, and the State, The Social Movement Society: Contentious Politics for a New Century,* and *Coalitions and Political Movements: The Lessons of the Nuclear Freeze.*

SHARON ERICKSON NEPSTAD is professor of sociology at the University of New Mexico. She is the author of *Convictions of the Soul: Religion, Culture, and Agency in the Central America Solidarity Movement, Religion and War Resistance in the Plowshares Movement,* and *Nonviolent Revolutions: Civil Resistance in the Late Twentieth Century.*

FRANCESCA POLLETTA is professor of sociology at the University of California, Irvine. She is author of *It Was Like a Fever: Storytelling in Protest and Politics* and *Freedom Is an Endless Meeting: Democracy in American Social Movements* and coeditor of *Passionate Politics.*

BELINDA ROBNETT is associate professor of sociology at the University of California, Irvine. She is author of *How Long? How Long? African-American Women in the Struggle for Civil Rights* and coeditor of *Social Movements: Identity, Culture, and the State.*

DEANA A. ROHLINGER is associate professor of sociology at Florida State University.

CHARLOTTE RYAN is associate professor of sociology at the University of Massachusetts–Lowell and codirector of the Movement and Media Research and Action Project. She is author of *Prime Time Activism* and coeditor of *Rhyming Hope and History: Activists, Academics, and Social Movement Scholarship* (Minnesota, 2005).

CARRIE SANDERS is assistant professor of criminology at Wilfrid Laurier University.

KURT SCHOCK is associate professor of sociology and global affairs at Rutgers University, Newark. He is the author of *Unarmed Insurrections: People Power Movements in Nondemocracies* (Minnesota, 2005).

JACKIE SMITH is professor of sociology at the University of Pittsburgh. She is the author of *Social Movements for Global Democracy*, coauthor of *Global Democracy and the World Social Forums*, and coeditor of *The World Social Forums and the Challenge of Global Democracy, Coalitions across Borders: Transnational Protest and the Neoliberal, Globalizing Resistance: Transnational Dimensions of Social Movements*, and *Transnational Social Movements and Global Politics: Solidarity beyond the State*.

SUZANNE STAGGENBORG is professor of sociology at the University of Pittsburgh. She is the author of *The Pro-choice Movement: Organization and Activism in the Abortion Conflict* and coeditor of *Methods of Social Movement Research* (Minnesota, 2002).

STELLAN VINTHAGEN is associate professor of sociology at University West, Sweden. He is the author of (in Swedish) *The Disarmament Camp in Linköping, A Critique of the Preparation Methods and Internal Conflict Management of the Plowshares Movement*, and *Prison Letters* and coeditor of *Resistance*.

NANCY WHITTIER is professor of sociology at Smith College. She is the author of *Feminist Generations* and *The Politics of Child Sexual Abuse: Emotion, Social Movements, and the State*.

Index

Canadian Youth Climate Coalition, 113
capacity building, 107
capitalism, 134, 202, 227, 233
Carlsson, Gunn-Marie, 267
Carmin, Joann, 16
Caron, Zoë, 106, 108–9, 112
Carson, E. D., 203
Carter, Morag, 106, 109, 113
Case for Animal Rights, The, 32
Castells, Manuel, 62
Catholic Church/Catholicism, 170,
    176–79, 183, 188, 192, 228, 263–64,
    266–68, 273, 276, 278
Center for Disease Control and Prevention
    (CDC), 160, 163
Charter of Rights and Freedoms, 13
Chicago, Illinois, 205, 210–11
Chicano movement, 146
children, xii
child sexual abuse, 145–66; and anti-
    homophobia, 150; and antiracism,
    150, 154; and antisexism, 150
choice points, xxi, 31–35, 38
Chomsky, Noam, 122
Christian Broadcasting Network, 253
Christian Coalition, 247
Christianity, 145
Christian Right, xxv, xxxiii, 17, 245–59,
    293
Chrysler, 213
civil rights movement (Northern Ireland).
    See Northern Ireland civil rights
    movement
civil rights movement (U.S.), xxv, 11, 52,
    63, 84, 110, 114, 146, 157, 202, 208,
    249, 289
claims, 7, 8, 9, 11, 14; moderate claims,
    7; radical claims, 7
claims-making strategies, 7, 10–11, 46
Clamshell Alliance, 44
Clear Channel Communications, 213
clergy, xi, xii
Climate Action Network (CAN), xxxii,

94–95, 97, 99, 99–103, 105, 107–9, 111,
    113–16
climate change, 7, 93, 97, 101, 108–9,
    111–12, 114
climate justice, 97, 113
Clothesline Project, 159
Cloward, Richard, xiv, xxvi, xxvii, 23, 34,
    171, 279
coalition, xii–xiii, xxviii, xxx, 34, 47, 82,
    95, 100, 103, 105, 107, 111, 114; of
    activists, xxxi, 150; building, 123;
    dynamics of, xxxii; grassroots, 106;
    insider–outsider, 94, 97, 98, 115;
    institutionalization of, 104; multi-
    movement, 14; of organizations, 171,
    174–77, 182–83, 187–88, 191–92;
    strategizing, xiii; tactics of, xxxii;
    transnational, 98, 105
Cold War politics, 136
collective action, 5–6, 8, 10, 13, 18, 101,
    124, 136, 148, 157–58, 171, 175,
    190, 221, 249, 285; frames, 44, 121;
    repertoires of, 10
collective action repertoires, 43, 46–48, 55
collective identity, xviii, xxvi, xxxii, 9, 13,
    27, 30, 145–49, 152, 155, 164–66,
    246, 259, 288, 290, 295; development,
    9; processes, 70
Combs, Sean "Puffy," 200
Comeau, Louise, 101, 104, 106
coming-out, 145, 146, 149, 152,
    155–59, 163–64; collective, 147;
    individual, 147; strategies, 164
Comintern, 182
Comissão Pastoral da Terra (Pastoral
    Commission on Land), 228–29
Committee of 100, 275
communication, 79, 86; networks, 83;
    platform, 64; strategic communications
    organizing, 77; strategies, 71; studies,
    67, 84; systems, 70
Communist Party, 178–82, 184–86, 189
Congregational Union of Ontario, 255

(continued from page ii)